ORDNANCE SURVEY MEMOIRS OF IRELAND

Volume Twenty

PARISHES OF COUNTY TYRONE II
1825, 1833–5, 1840

Published 1993.
The Institute of Irish Studies,
The Queen's University of Belfast,
Belfast.
In association with
The Royal Irish Academy,
Dawson Street,
Dublin.

Reprinted 2013 by Ulster Historical Foundation

Grateful acknowledgement is made to the Economic and Social Research Council and the Department of Education for Northern Ireland for their financial assistance at different stages of this publication programme.

Copyright 1993.

All rights reserved. No part of this publication may be reproduced, stored in a retrieval system or transmitted, in any form or by any means, electronic, mechanical, photocopying, recording or otherwise, without the prior permission of the publisher.

British Library Cataloguing-in-Publication Data.
A catalogue record for this book is available from the British Library.
ISBN: 978-0-85389-460-5

Printed in Ireland by SPRINT-print Ltd.

Ordnance Survey Memoirs of Ireland
VOLUME TWENTY

Parishes of County Tyrone II
1825, 1833–5, 1840

Mid and East Tyrone

Edited by Angélique Day and Patrick McWilliams.

The Institute of Irish Studies
in association with
The Royal Irish Academy

EDITORIAL BOARD

Angélique Day (General Editor)
Patrick S. McWilliams (Executive Editor)
Nóirín Dobson (Assistant Editor)
Dr B.M. Walker (Publishing Director)
Professor R.H. Buchanan (Chairman)

CONTENTS

	Page
Introduction	ix
Brief history of the Irish Ordnance Survey and Memoirs	ix
Definition of terms used	x
Note on Memoirs of County Tyrone	x
Note on Memoir for Tamlaght	xi
General Notes	xiv

Parishes in County Tyrone

Aghaloo	1
Artrea	6
Ballinderry	11
Ballyclog	15
Bodoney	20
Carnteel	21
Clogherny	25
Clonoe	29
Desertcreat	32
Donaghenry	37
Drumglass	40
Errigal Keerogue	46
Kildress	58
Killeeshil	62
Killyman	66
Lissan	69
Pomeroy	70
Tamlaght	73
Tullyniskan	138

List of selected maps and illustrations

County Tyrone, with parish boundaries	vi
County Tyrone, 1837, by Samuel Lewis	viii
Statistical table for Coagh	101
Statistical table for Mullaghtironey	123

List of O.S. maps, 1830s

Aughnacloy	22
Ballygawley	47
Coalisland	139
Cookstown	65
Dungannon	41
Stewartstown	38

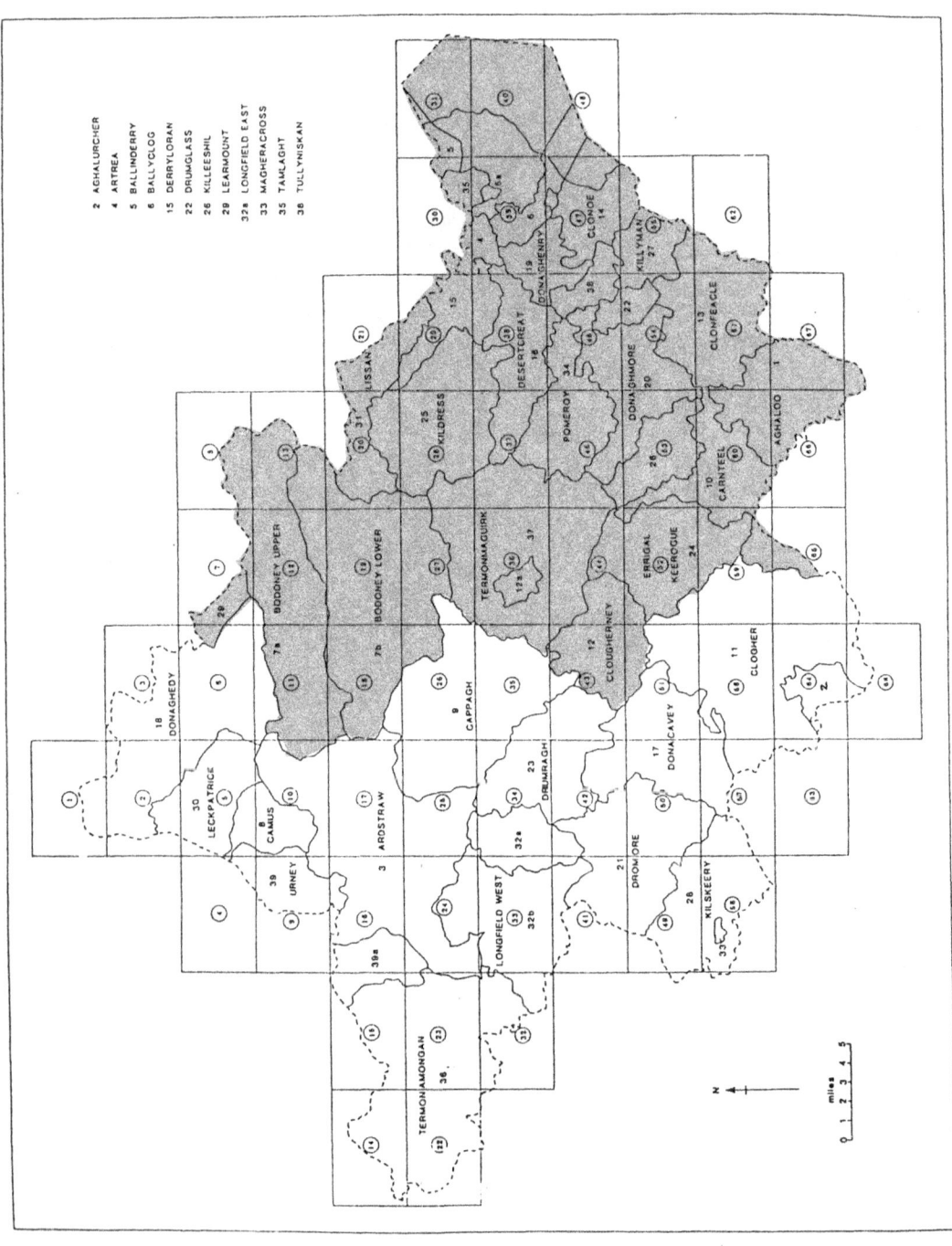

ACKNOWLEDGEMENTS

During the course of the transcription and publication project many have advised and encouraged us in this gigantic task. Thanks must first be given to the Royal Irish Academy, particularly former librarian Mrs Brigid Dolan and her staff, for making the original manuscripts available to us. We are also indebted to Siobhán O'Rafferty for her continuing help in deciphering indistinct passages of manuscript.

We should like to acknowledge the following individuals for their special contributions. Dr Brian Trainor led the way with his edition of the Antrim Memoir and provided vital help on the steering committee. Dr Ann Hamlin also provided valuable support, especially during the most trying stages of the project. Professor R.H. Buchanan's unfailing encouragment has been instrumental in the development of the project to the present. Without Dr Kieran Devine the initial stages of the transcription and the computerising work would never have been completed successfully: the project owes a great deal to his constant help and advice. Dr Kay Muhr's continuing contribution to the work of the transcription project is deeply appreciated. Mr W.C. Kerr's interest and expertise have been invaluable. Professor Anne Crookshank and Dr Edward McParland were most generous with practical help and advice concerning the drawings amongst the Memoir manuscripts. We would like to thank the Director of the Ordnance Survey, Dublin and the keepers of the fire-proof store, among them Leonard Hines. Finally, all students of the nineteenth century Ordnance Survey of Ireland owe a great deal to the pioneering work of Professor J.H. Andrews, and his kind help in the first days of the project is gratefully recorded.

For their invaluable assistance with this particular volume, we are indebted to Brenda Collins, Dr W.H. Crawford and Dr E.M. Crawford. Mr John McAtasney of the Lisburn Museum also offered practical advice.

The essential task of inputting the texts from audio tapes was done by Miss Eileen Kingan, Mrs Christine Robertson, Miss Eilis Smyth, Miss Lynn Murray, and, most importantly, Miss Maureen Carr.

We are grateful to the Linen Hall Library for lending us their copies of the first edition 6" Ordnance Survey Maps: also to Ms Maura Pringle of QUB Cartography Department for the index maps showing the parish boundaries. For providing financial assistance at crucial times for the maintenance of the project, we would like to take this opportunity of thanking the trustees of the Esme Mitchell trust and The Public Record Office of Northern Ireland.

Left:

Map of parishes of County Tyrone. The area described in this volume, the parishes of Mid and East Tyrone, has been shaded to highlight its location. The square grids represent the 1830s 6" Ordnance Survey maps. The encircled numbers relate to the map numbers as presented in the bound volumes of maps for the county. The parishes have been numbered in all cases and named in full where possible, except those in the following list: Aghalurcher 2, Longfield East 32a, Magheracross (no Memoir) 33, Skirts of Urney and Ardstraw 39a.

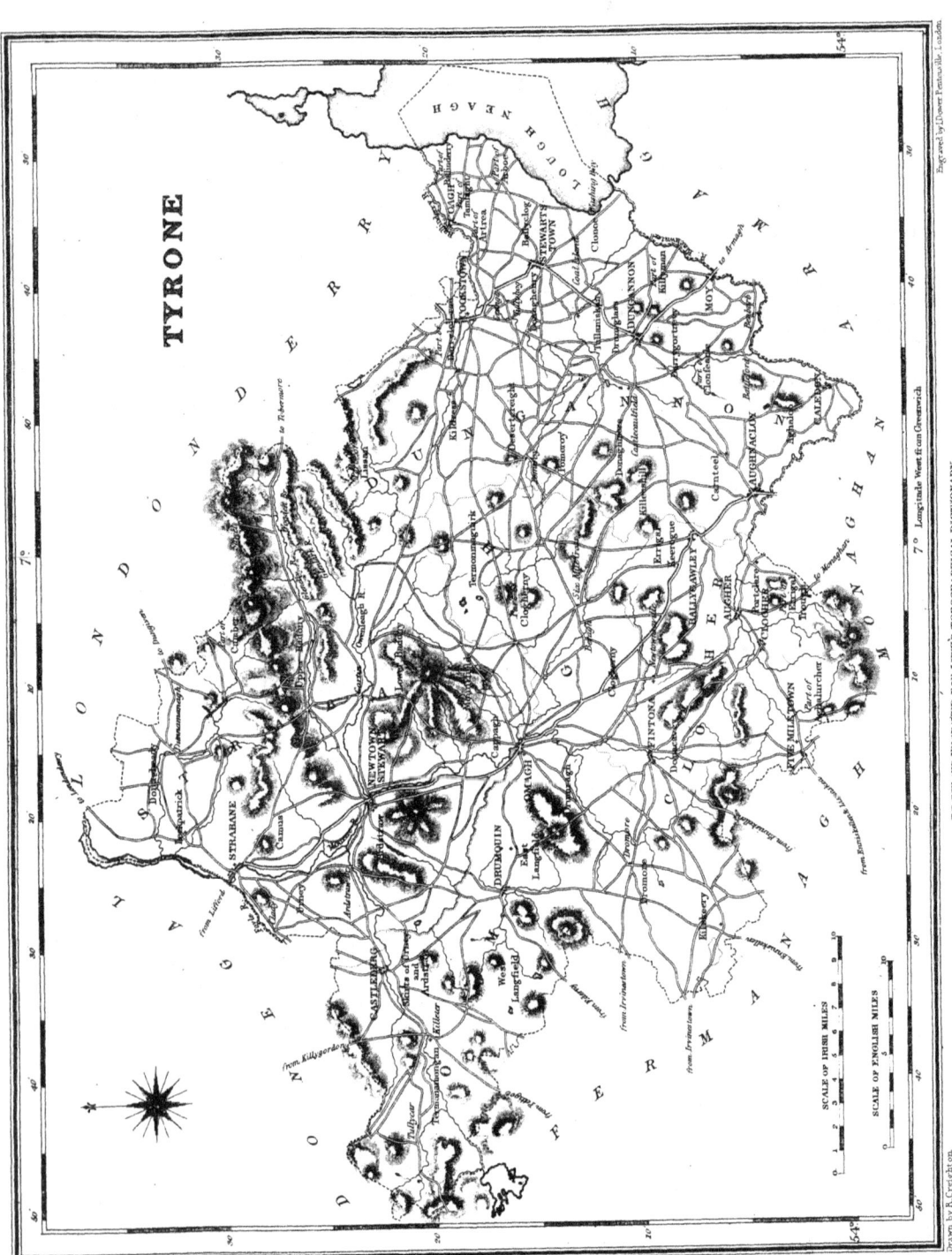

INTRODUCTION AND GUIDE TO THE PUBLICATION OF THE ORDNANCE SURVEY MEMOIRS

The following text of the Ordnance Survey Memoirs was first transcribed by a team working in the Institute of Irish Studies at The Queen's University of Belfast, on a computerised index of the material. For this publication programme the text has been further edited: spellings have been modernised in most cases, although where the original spelling was thought to be of any interest it has been retained and is indicated by angle brackets in the text. Variant spellings for townland and lesser place-names have been preserved, although parish and major place-names have been standardised and the original spelling given in angle brackets. Names of prominent people, for instance landlords, have been standardised where possible, but original spellings of names in lists of informants, emigration tables and on tombstones have been retained. We have not altered the Memoir writers' anglicisation of names and words in Irish.

Punctuation has been modernised and is the responsibility of the editors. Editorial additions are indicated by square brackets: a question mark before and after a word indicates a queried reading and tentatively inserted information respectively. Original drawings are referred to in the text, and some have been reproduced. Manuscript page references have been omitted from this series. Because of the huge variation in size of Memoirs for different counties, the following editorial policy has been adopted: where there are numerous duplicating and overlapping accounts, the most complete and finished account, normally the Memoir proper, has been presented, with additional unique information from other accounts like the Fair Sheets entered into a separate section, clearly titled and identified; where the Memoir material is less, nothing has been omitted. To achieve standard volume size, parishes have been associated on the basis of propinquity.

There are considerable differences in the volume of information recorded for different areas: counties Antrim and Londonderry are exceptionally well covered, while the other counties do not have quite the same detail. This series is the first systematic publication of the parish Memoirs, although individual parishes have been published by pioneering local history societies. The entire transcriptions of the Memoirs made in the course of the indexing project can be consulted in the Public Record Office of Northern Ireland and the library at the Queen's University of Belfast. The manuscripts of the Ordnance Survey Memoirs are in the Royal Irish Academy, Dublin.

Brief history of the Irish Ordnance Survey in the nineteenth century and the writing of the Ordnance Survey Memoirs

In 1824 a House of Commons committee recommended a townland survey of Ireland with maps at the scale of 6", to facilitate a uniform valuation for local taxation. The Duke of Wellington, then prime minister, authorised this, the first Ordnance Survey of Ireland. The survey was directed by Colonel Thomas Colby, who had under his command officers of the Royal Engineers and three companies of sappers and miners. In addition to this, civil assistants were recruited to help with sketching, drawing and engraving of maps, and eventually, in the 1830s, the writing of the Memoirs.

The Memoirs were written descriptions intended to accompany the maps, containing information which could not be fitted on to them. Colonel Colby always considered additional information to be necessary to clarify place-names and other distinctive features of each parish; this was to be written up in reports by the officers. Much information about parishes resulted from research into place-names and was used in the writing of the Memoirs. The term "Memoir" comes from the abbreviation of the word "Aide-Memoire". It was also used in the 18th century to describe topographical descriptions accompanying maps.

In 1833 Colby's assistant, Lieutenant Thomas Larcom, developed the scope of the officers' reports by stipulating the headings or "Heads of Inquiry" under which information was to be reported, and including topics of social as well as economic interest. By this time civil assistants were writing some of the Memoirs under the supervision of the officers, as well as collecting information in the Fair Sheets.

The first "Memoirs" are officers' reports covering Antrim in 1830, and work continued on the Antrim parishes right through the decade, with special activity in 1838 and 1839. Counties Down and Tyrone were written up from 1833 to 1837, with both officers and civil assistants working on Memoirs. In Londonderry and Fermanagh research and writing started in 1834. Armagh was worked on in 1835, 1837 and 1838. Much labour was expended in the Londonderry parishes. The plans to publish the Memoirs commenced with the parish of Templemore, containing the city and liberties of Derry, which came out in 1837 after a great deal of expense and effort.

Between 1839 and 1840 the Memoir scheme collapsed. Sir Robert Peel's government could not countenance the expenditure of money and time on such an exercise; despite a parliamentary commission favouring the continuation of the writing of the Memoirs, the scheme was halted before the southern half of the country was covered. The manuscripts remained unpublished and most were removed to the Royal Irish Academy, Dublin from the Ordnance Survey, Phoenix Park. Other records of the Ordnance Survey, including some residual material from the Memoir scheme, have recently been transferred to the National Archives, Bishop Street, Dublin.

The Memoirs are a uniquely detailed source for the history of the northern half of Ireland immediately before the Great Famine. They document the landscape and situation, buildings and antiquities, land-holdings and population, employment and livelihood of the parishes. They act as a nineteenth century Domesday book and are essential to the understanding of the cultural heritage of our communities. It is planned to produce a volume of evaluative essays to put the material in its full context, with information on other sources and on the writers of the Memoirs.

Definition of descriptive terms

Memoir (sometimes Statistical Memoir): an account of a parish written according to the prescribed form outlined in the instructions known as "Heads of Inquiry", and normally divided into three sections: Natural Features and History, Modern and Ancient Topography, Social and Productive Economy.

Fair Sheets: "information gathered for the Memoirs", an original title describing paragraphs of information following no particular order, often with marginal headings, signed and dated by the civil assistant responsible.

Statistical Remarks/Accounts: both titles are employed by the Engineer officers in their descriptions of the parish with marginal headings, often similar in layout to the Memoir.

Office Copies: these are copies of early drafts, generally officers' accounts and must have been made for office purposes.

Ordnance Survey Memoirs for County Tyrone

This volume contains the Memoirs for eighteen parishes in mid and east Tyrone and covers an area bordering on the western shores of Lough Neagh. The material includes replies to the queries of the North-West of Ireland Society, the results of a questionnaire circ...ated by the society whose aim was to promote improvement in farming techniques and practices in the 1820s. Although this material predates the Memoirs proper, it does provide an interesting comparative backdrop to the later accounts.

The main material consists of Memoirs and draft Memoirs mostly by officers, although there are some early contributions from George Scott. A note from Thomas Colby survives which is unique among the Memoir material; this and other references to him reflect the early days of the scheme before T.A. Larcom took charge and introduced the Heads of Inquiry. There are also some notes on townlands penned by a sapper and miner, one Trimble, which probably arose in connection with the work of the topographical and place-name side of the Ordnance Survey rather than with that of Memoir writing. There is no Memoir for the parish of Derryloran but there are many references to that area in the accounts of the adjacent parishes. The material for Tamlaght parish contains very detailed statistical tables which are fully explained below.

The accounts provide valuable information about the productive economy of this area and the useful descriptions of the linen industry serve to augment the tabulated statistics in Tamlaght. There are many notes on bleaching greens and mills, including a reference to a mill at Wellbrook, now Wellbrook beetling mill, property of the National Trust. There are descriptions of the collieries at Drumglass, the clayworks at Meenagh in Clonoe parish and an account of the Tyrone Canal with its unusual engineering. Glimpses of social life are revealed in brief but illuminating notes about a small local community of Quakers, the musical instruments played in different localities and the traditions and lore associated with Lough Patrick.

Notes on Memoir of Tamlaght Parish

Much of the information for Tamlaght is presented in the form of detailed statistical tables which, because they are rendered into prose, require more interpretation and amplification than is usual with the Memoirs. The editors have, in some cases, had to make interpretations of the information on the basis of their experience with similar Memoir material, but their aim has been, above all, to present the information in its totality and allow the readers to form their own judgment. Any additional editorial remarks which are interpolated, other than summaries of tables and their contents, are indicated by italics within square brackets. However, the editors would urge the interested reader to consult the originals through the microfilm or in the manuscript form for confirmation of some details, as for instance the diagrams of drainage systems, rotation of crops, family occupations.

The parish of Tamlaght contains some of the most interesting and unique information about the linen industry and its part in individual household economies to be found in the Ordnance Survey Memoir manuscripts. There are 2 main sections of tabulated information. First, there are tables enumerating weavers and their manufacturing of linen in 8 townlands around and including the town of Coagh; and second, tables classifying the families farming and working in 6 townlands (overlapping with those describing the weavers). These tables are different from, but undoubtedly related to, the Productive Economy tables in county Londonderry which were designed by Captain J.E. Portlock. The Tamlaght tables contain significantly more demographic information, analysing labour of family members and hired servants, also farming goods and stock as well as domestic furniture.

These tables were compiled in the last year of the Memoir Scheme (June 1840), even later than the Memoir for Carrickfergus (dated December 1839 and February 1840). The individual format of the tables suggests that Tamlaght was chosen as a last pilot scheme for collecting statistical information relating to Productive

Economy, probably to illustrate the state of the domestic handloom linen industry. The material was collected under supervision of John Hanna, who does not contribute to the Ordnance Survey in any other parish but must have been involved with the linen trade. An excellent introduction to the domestic linen industry in the 19th century with many good illustrations will be found in *They Wrought Among the Tow, Flax and Linen in County Tyrone* by Pat McDonnell, Ulster Historical Foundation Publications, 1990.

First section: Weavers' Tables

To introduce the weavers' tables there are notes on Coagh and the local economy which are more like the usual Memoir material and which put into context much of the statistical material. There are also lists of householders and occupations in Coagh, given street by street, which identify the chief householder and other residents; these give details about family composition and include lodgers or hired help lodging with the family. Here, as in other tables, the editors have interpreted the fractional representation of numbers thus: upper figure equals older, lower equals younger members of the family. The subdivision by sex is always given. The editors have adopted the convention of supplying the full fraction, even in cases where there was only an upper or lower figure, by introducing the figure "0" to draw attention to the figure conveying the age group. 0 does not presume a negative value and is included purely for formal reasons. Throughout the whole Memoir the editors have consistently followed this fractional representation of the family.

In the weavers' tables the denomination is given, 9/28 or 10/32, which describes the quality of linen woven; the top figure expresses hundreds on the reed, the setting which determined the fineness of the cloth; the bottom figure gives the breadth of the web, which was either 28 inch (three-quarters wide) or 32 inch (seven-eighths wide) webs. The cloth woven was coarse, and this is described in the text as well as in the dimensions given for both warp and weft yarns. These were probably handspun here, although it is significant that in nearby areas millspun yarn was being introduced.

John Hanna remarks at the end of the weavers' table for Drumard, "The above denominations were generally woven in this neighbourhood.. the farmers are anxious to have a great crop of flax .. and sow it on potato ground. The flax is coarse in consequence and the yarn cannot be spun fine." The weavers used yarn bought from the local markets or spun in their own households. The tables give information about the price and therefore the quality of the yarn by giving the amount used. Thus measurements for yarn in warp and weft are given.

Yarn was measured in cuts and hanks and quarters: a cut was about 300 yards, the full of a reel; and a hank was 12 cuts. A quarter was a quarter cut, hence a hank was 48 quarters. 3 hanks generally weighed a lb, although this depended on the quality of the yarn. In Coagh market, "it is chiefly 2 hanks and 6 cuts to the lb, selling from 4d to 4d ha'penny per hank; and 3 hanks to the lb, generally at 4d ha'penny per hank." The tables give the grist of the yarn, both warp and weft, in the form of fractions which relate to hanks, cuts and quarters. As each individual's output is given, plus the above details, it is possible to analyse in minute detail the earnings of any named handloom weaver in the 8 townlands recorded.

The tables also give the status of the weaver, whether independent, weaving for himself or family, or dependent, weaving for a farmer for wages or in lieu of rent, as some cottiers did. They give the grade of weaver, master or apprentice, indicating proficiency and experience, and also whether weaving is a sole or part-time occupation. It was most commonly associated with farming, although other occupations, like waterkeeper, are recorded. The weavers' tables give the townlands where the weaver resides, and there are cross-references to the appropriate farm number in the second set of tables if the weaver combined this occupation with farming. This second set of tables gives a detailed analysis of land use, labour, stock and material belongings of farmers and cottiers in each townland.

Second section: Townland Statistics

In this section, where the same tables or forms are reproduced for each townland, the table headings are reproduced for the first townland only (Aghaveagh), and subsequent tables are presented without headings. There are, for instance, considerable variations in the value of stock and implements between the different townlands. The 6 townlands are analysed through 9 forms, in which each farmer and householder is given a sequential number.

Form 1 gives farmer's name, for the only time unless he has a secondary occupation or farm. There are also details of drainage systems which show a variety of types. It has been impossible to identify the types, so the reader may check the originals. The dimensions have been given as near to their original form as possible. In Form 1 crop rotation sequences are given, and we have interpreted the fractional representations of crops as alternative rotations, and have used commonsense to interpret crop abbreviations written underneath or alongside the main crops as a series of undersowings and combined sowings. Nothing has been omitted and the editors conclude that these crop rotations indicate a general pattern or model for each farmer given the appropriate circumstances, rather than actual crop sowings each year.

Form 2 lists stock and implements with values and uses fractional representations to describe stock and implements: this has been generally interpreted (as with members of family) as upper figure identifying older stock and lower figure younger stock; also implements and machinery, on a scale of values which are given at the head of the columns; we would like to stress that this is a suggested reading of the statistics and close examination of the context of all these figures and abbreviations in the townland tables do reveal variations from place to place. In the case of inanimate objects like spades, we know from the text that fractional representation indicates different types: agricultural spades over turf spades. There are variations in the value of stock and implements between all the townlands.

Form 3 lists cottier, occupation and farm on which resident. Form 8 gives the description of cottier's dwelling, and furniture is recorded by abbreviations for which there is no key. From internal evidence the editors have deduced what these abbreviations represent, e.g. s.l. referring to a building material as stone and lime because later on brick is referred to. Advice from specialists in vernacular furniture has been taken on the equivalents for furniture abbreviations; and again these equivalents are suggested and not definitive.

Forms 4 and 4a analyse the farmer's family and labour, with occupations in abbreviated form: c = carter, n = non-working, s = spinner, w = weaver, t = thatcher. Younger members of the family are frequently described as "n", which the editors suggest as non-working (either because of going to school, see townland of Drumard which gives a note on a small girl's labour and notes her going to school other days, or because they are not at home). Table 4 give details of hired labour, resident and non-resident with family, under the heading occasional labour. Table 4a shows where the farmer's own family work outside the home farm, under the heading family labour, together with remarks on domestic occupations which help build up a picture of men and women's work in the household, as well as the importance of the domestic linen industry in the income of that household.

Form 5 gives details of manures and applications from selected farms and, often in a fractional form i.e. number of men over number of days, records the number of men and time taken to fertilise land. Form 6 gives seed and produce for different crops taken from the same few farms selected from Form 5. This form relates back to Form 1 and crop rotations. Form 7 gives list of trades in the townland and sometimes, details of wages or earnings. Form 9 provides a synopsis of the productive economy in the townland and gives overall areas of drainage, numbers of pumps, types of implements, types of mills, breeds of livestock and individual kinds of crops cultivated, and in general provides information which sets in context the tabulated statistics of the preceding 8 forms.

General Notes

There are no drawings extant in these Memoirs but there are ground plans of churches which are referred to in the text but not reproduced here. The manuscript material is to be found in Boxes 51 and 52 of the Royal Irish Academy's collection of Ordnance Survey Memoirs, and section references are given beside each parish below in their printed order.

Box 51			Box 52		
Aghaloo	II	2, 1.	Desertcreat	VII	2, 3, 1.
Artrea	V	2, 1.	Donaghenry	III	2 and 1, 1.
Ballinderry	V	1, 2.	Drumglass	V	2, 1.
Ballyclog	VI	2 and 3, 1.	Errigal Keerogue	VIII	2, 1, 3, 4, 5; also Box 51 X 5.
Bodoney	VII	1.			
Carnteel	IX	1, 2.	Kildress	X	1, 2.
Clogherny	XI	1.	Killeeshil	XI	1, 2.
Clonoe	XII	2, 1.	Killyman	XIII	1, 1a.
			Lissan	XV	1.
			Pomeroy	XX	1, 2.
			Tullyniskan	XXIII	1 and 2.

Parish of Aghaloo, County Tyrone

Office Copy of Draft Memoir [by Lieutenant C. Bailey], with Note by Thomas Colby

NATURAL FEATURES

Hills

The surface of this parish is very undulating. It consists principally of small hills separated by valleys or plains. The hills are generally of the greatest altitude at the north west and become gradually of less elevation towards the south east. The following are the names of the townlands containing the principal elevations, with their altitudes in feet above the level of the sea: Rahaghy, 635 feet, Carricklongfield, 608 feet, Bohard, 479 feet, Glendarragh, 412 feet. The forgoing are in the north western portion and in the south eastern are Knockaginy, 251 feet, Drumess, 298 feet and Mullynaveagh, 258 feet.

Lakes

There are several lakes, within and bordering on this parish, the total area of which amounts to 140 acres 26 perches. Creeve lough is about 1,000 yards long and 330 feet broad and extends over 60 acres, 9 acres of which are in Aghaloo parish. Mullycarnan lake is 440 yards by 286, area 48 acres. Rahaghy lake contains 22 acres 2 roods.

Rivers

The Blackwater forms the boundary of the parish for 18 miles. For 12 miles its course is to the south east, to the southern extremity of the parish. At this point its direction changes to the south west towards Lough Neagh. There are various nameless watercourses which serve as feeders to the lakes and are useful to small mills.

[Crossed out: There is a fine spa well in Cavan Oneil townland which is much resorted to. It is strongly impregnated with sulphur and [? iron].

Bogs

The bog is principally confined to small patches in the valleys or low grounds. The largest tract is on the north western boundary in Carricklongfield, Rahaghy and Cronghill townlands.

MODERN TOPOGRAPHY

Towns: Caledon

Caledon is situated in the south eastern portion of the parish, on the high road from Monaghan to Dungannon. It is 89 miles from Dublin, [blank] from Monaghan and [blank] from Dungannon. The ancient name of the town was Kinnard. It was the site of a castle belonging to Sir Phelim O'Neill. The town consists of 1 street which presents a remarkably neat appearance. The public buildings are a church, a Presbyterian meeting house, a schoolhouse and an inn. There is a general market every Saturday, a grain market every Tuesday and a fair on the second Saturday in each month. A day coach from Belfast to Enniskillen passes through it every Sunday, Tuesday and Thursday and returns every Monday, Wednesday and Friday.

Public buildings: Roman Catholic chapel in Derrygooly.

Gentlemen's Seats

Lord Caledon's magnificent demesne is situated on the southern side of the town. The house is a fine building with a handsome front supported on pillars of the Ionic order. The terrace is spacious and the demesne is tastefully planted.

Crilly House, Annaghoe, Annagh, Limepark Lodge.

Bleach Greens, Manufactories and Mills

The flour mills at Caledon rank among the most extensive of the class in the kingdom. The water power is [supplied] by a weir across the Blackwater at right angles with the river. The height of the weir is [blank] feet and the length of the mill-race [blank] yards, giving a fall of [blank] feet. There is also a subsidiary low pressure steam engine of 25 horsepower. The average consumption of coal is 4 cwt per hour. It is procured at [blank] for [blank] per ton and the cost of carriage is [blank].

The seeds or refuse of the grain is also used as fuel and it is found that 1 ton of seeds is equal to 4 cwt of coal.

Corn mill in Dyan, corn mill in Drummond.

Communications

The principal road is that from Monaghan to Dungannon through Caledon. It traverses the parish on the eastern side from north to south for 6 and a half miles.

Another main road traverses the parish from the south east to north west, leading from Armagh to Omagh through Aughnacloy. Its length within Aghaloo parish is 9 miles.

Productive Economy

Influence of Lord Caledon

[Insert note: Lord Caledon is sparing no expense in improvements here, and the flour mills which he has erected supply the country from Belfast to Lough Erne <Earne> and nearly equal distances north and south. They sell about 250 pounds worth of flour per diem. Bailey is to get the dimensions of the water wheels. The subsidiary steam engine is 25 horsepower, low pressure. The agent told me they burned the seeds (refuse) to save coal for the engine and that 1 ton of seeds or 4 cwt of coal supplied the engine with fuel for an hour. Yours very truly, Thomas Colby].

Memoir, 1835

Memoir Writing

Memoir Writing

Only moderate, refer to Mr Boyle, 24 September 1835. The heights of some of the principal points should be given [initialled] R.K. Dawson.

Natural Features

Hills

The surface of the the parish is extremely broken and irregular, consisting of a number of small hills but slightly connected with one another. It has a general fall on the east, south and south west to the banks of the Blackwater.

Lakes

Lough Enagh or Anagh, situated about half a mile to the north of the village of Caledon and partly in the town of Enagh, is a small lake about 16 acres in extent. The peasantry suppose it to be 20 fathom in depth. They say that on a late occasion when it was frozen over, an opening was made in the centre of the ice through which they endeavoured in vain to sound it. This was most probably owing to their not having a rope sufficiently long, as it is not likely from the nature of the surrounding ground that the lake has any extraordinary depth. It is 104 feet above the level of the sea. It contains perch, roach, pike and eels.

Creve lough, situated near the centre of the parish, comprises about 45 acres. It is said to be very deep on the north eastern side. It has no islands on it. It is about 200 feet above the sea. It contains pike and eels in considerable quantities.

Rivers

The Blackwater, running in a south easterly direction, forms the south western boundary of the parish for about 7 miles and then, changing its direction and running nearly north, it forms the eastern or south eastern boundary for 5 and a half miles. Its average breadth is 80 feet and its average depth 8 [feet]. It rises in the parish of Clogher. It cannot be well applied to machinery as its average fall is not more than 4 or 5 feet in a mile. It is more usefully situated for drainage. There are no falls or rapids on it. It used to overflow considerably in wet weather and do great damage by washing away the soil and crops. This, however, is now prevented in all ordinary cases by a dike which has been constructed by the Earl of Caledon along its banks. It impedes communication. Its bed is soft and earthy and its banks fertile and hilly.

The parish is very well supplied with water from rivulets and springs. There are no mineral or hot springs in it.

Bogs

There is no bog of any great size in the parish but a number of patches varying in extent from 8 to 30 acres whose average depth may be stated as 6 feet. Their height above the sea varies from 100 to 200 feet. Their most remarkable feature is a total absence of timber, with the exception of a few small fragments of fir scattered through some of them.

Woods

There are no natural woods in the parish. The planting in Caledon demesne is extensive and varied. There are no evidence of natural woods having existed.

Climate

Wheat is generally sown in October and barley, oats and potatoes in April or May. The harvest is mostly <moastly> in September. Potatoes are dug in the end of October.

Modern Topography

Towns: Caledon

The village of Caledon is situated near the southern extremity of the parish and on the western bank of the Blackwater, within 67 miles (Irish) of Dublin. It is about 1,300 feet in length. Its general appearance is peculiarly neat, owing to the style of its houses. The predominance of slated roofs and the regularity of its masonry gives it, from some points, the appearance rather of a portion of a large town than the entire of a village.

Buildings and Streets

The church, situated close to the village, is a neat building. The date of its erection and its cost are unknown. The congregation is about 600 and the average attendance 200. It is about 102 feet in length. Its sides are irregular but the breadth of the principal part is 33 feet. It is capable of accommodating 500 or 600. Some additions and improvements were made to it about the year 1828. It is only a chapel of ease, the parish church being at Aughnacloy.

The Seceding Presbyterian meeting house is situated close to the village. It is 48 feet in length and 25 feet in breadth. It is capable of accommodating about 300. It was built in the year 1824 at a cost of 300 pounds, which was defrayed by its congregation.

[Insert note by Dawson: "about 600", "about 102", "500 or 600", "about the year 1828": we should endeavour to give precise information in every case].

The Wesleyan Methodist chapel is a small neat building measuring 40 feet by 22 and capable of accommodating about 200 persons. It was built in 1834 at a cost of 108 pounds, 50 pounds of which was defrayed by its congregation, the remainder by the Earl of Caledon.

The court house is a neat and substantial building. It was erected for the purpose for which it is used, together with the dispensary and inn which may be said to constitute 1 building, by the Earl of Caledon at a cost of 3,000 pounds, about the year 1822.

There is a neat barrack in the village which measures 135 feet in front. A sergeant-major, 16 sergeants and 8 men of the militia are stationed at it.

There is an excellent inn and post house in the village.

Schools: see table.

General Appearance of Caledon

The village consists principally of 1 street about 1,300 feet in length and 55 in breadth, which has a pleasing and regular appearance owing to its cleanliness and the peculiar neatness of its houses, some of which are built in a very ornamental style, having projecting roofs with hanging fringes of wood at the eaves. There are 120 houses in the village, of which 100 are slated and the remainder thatched. 2 are 3-storeys high, about 100 2[-storeys] and the remainder 1[-storey]. The houses are all built of stone and very few of them whitewashed. The village is in a state of improvement.

SOCIAL ECONOMY

Local Government

There are 8 magistrates in the parish. Petty sessions are held in the court house once a week. There is a court leet held once a year and a manor court once a month.

General Economy

Such of the people as are not engaged in the trifling traffic of the town or as mechanics employ themselves in agricultural pursuits. There is a news room in the town where Belfast and Dublin papers are taken. Markets are held every Saturday and fairs on the second Saturday of every month. No houses are insured from fire.

Dispensary

The dispensary is supported half by subscription from the people and half by the grand jury. Its beneficial effects on the comforts and health of the poorer classes are evident.

For schools, see those mentioned in the table as in the townland of Caledon.

Poor and Amusements

There is no public provision for the poor, but the Earl of Caledon has the sum of 3 pounds 16s 3d distributed among them every Saturday and at Christmas 80 pounds worth of clothes <cloathes> is given to them by him besides a quantity of money.

The people do not appear to be very fond of amusements of any kind or remarkably hospitable. The village is, and has been, improving for some time through the highly praiseworthy exertions of the Earl of Caledon, who derives his title from it.

Dyan Village

Dyan is a collection of about 30 houses on the road from Caledon to Dungannon, 9 miles from the latter. They are almost all thatched and with the exception of 4 or 5 have but 1-storey. There is a public house and a grocer's in it. It has a scattered and insignificant appearance and scarcely deserves the name of a hamlet.

Public Buildings

There is a Roman Catholic chapel in the townland of Derrygooley. Its shape and dimensions are: [ground plan, main dimensions 66 by 47 feet, "T" shape]. It is partly thatched and partly slated. It is surrounded with hawthorn and has a rustic appearance. It accommodates about 600 persons. It was built about the year 1805 and considerably enlarged about 1823. It stands upon a fort, upon which the congregation used to assemble previous to its erection.

There is a Presbyterian meeting house in the townland of Lismulladown. Its shape and dimensions are: [ground plan, main dimensions 66 by 52 feet, "T" shape]. It is capable of accommodating about 400. The building of it was commenced in the year 1831 but it is still in an unfinished state for want of funds. The expenses of erection are defrayed by subscriptions from the congregation. The Earl of Caledon contributed 50 pounds, [insert addition: James Collins 50 pounds 7s 5d]. It is a very neat, regular and substantial building.

[Insert addition: Presbyterian, Wesleyan, hospital].

Gentlemen's Seats

Caledon House, the residence of the Earl of Caledon, is situated near the southern extremity of the parish, on an elevated position close to the Blackwater and about a mile from the village of Caledon. The date of its erection is unknown. Considerable improvements are at present being made to it. It is a large and splendid house. The demesne occupies 700 or 800 acres. There is a very fine garden in it and an extensive library in the house.

Table of Mills

[Table gives townland, diameter and breadth of wheel, type of wheel, type of mill].

Dyan, 16 feet by 14 feet, breast wheel, corn mill.

Drummond, 14 feet by 2 feet 2 inches, undershot wheel, corn mill.

Caledon, 18 feet by 18 feet, breast wheel, flour mill; 18 feet by 18 feet, undershot wheel, flour mill.

Communications

The main road from Caledon to Dungannon passes through the parish for about 4 miles. Its average breadth is 35 feet. It was made and is kept in very good repair by the barony. *It is tolerably well laid out, considering the irregularities of the ground.*

The road from Caledon to Aughnacloy runs through the parish for about 7 miles. Its average breadth is 35 feet. It was made and is repaired by the barony. It is tolerably well laid out and kept in very good order.

The road from Caledon to Glaslough and Monaghan passes through the parish for about 2 miles. Its average breadth is 30 feet. It was made by the barony with the exception of about half a mile close to Caledon, which was made at the expense of the Earl of Caledon. It is kept in very good repair but not judiciously laid out.

The road from Caledon to Carnteel passes through the parish for about 6 and a half miles. Its average breadth is 28 feet. It was made and is kept in good repair by the barony. It is tolerably well laid out.

Cross and by-roads are not at all numerous. They are kept in very good repair.

General Appearance

The character of the grounds (which consist of an endless succession of small hills), while it gives us a number of individual spots which may be termed picturesque, makes a general appearance of the parish tiresome and monotonous. The want of wood is striking. The ground, however, is well cultivated and the cottages have generally a tolerably neat exterior.

SOCIAL ECONOMY

Early Improvements

The exertions of the Earl of Caledon appear to form the most striking cause of improvement in the parish, which has recently been very considerable.

Obstructions to improvement: none.

Local Government

There are 8 magistrates in the parish, not stipendiary. Their residences are within convenient distances and they are firm and respected by the people. The usual force of police is a sergeant and 3 men. Manor courts, courts leet and petty sessions are held in Caledon, see Caledon. The number of magistrates in attendance varies from 2 to 5. The number of outrages committed in the parish has decreased greatly recently and the people are now extremely peaceable and honest. Illicit distillation is not carried on. Property is not insured.

Dispensaries: see town of Caledon.

Schools

[Table contains the following headings: townland, number of pupils subdivided by religion and sex, how supported, date established].

Mullaghmore East, 101 Protestants, 6 Catholics, 72 males, 35 females, total 107; the Earl of Caledon contributes 5 pounds and the Reverend Mr McCreight 1 pound 1s per year, parents subscribe from 1d to 3d per week; not known when established.

Corlough, 42 Catholics, 74 males, 35 females, total 109; established 17 June 1816.

Ramaket, 78 Protestants, 142 Catholics, 131 males, 89 females, total 220; Earl of Caledon contributes 5 pounds and Mr McCreight 2 pounds 2s per year, parents pay from 1s to 5s per quarter; established 1815.

Mulnahorn, 30 Protestants, 18 males, 12 females, total 30; Earl of Caledon contributes 5 pounds and Mr McCreight 1 pound 1s per year, parents contribute from 1s 1d to 10s 6d per quarter, established 1833.

Mullycarnon, 115 Protestants, 48 Catholics, total 163; Earl of Caledon contributes 5 pounds and Mr McCreight 1 pound per year, parents subscribe 1d per week.

Caledon Demesne, 20 Protestants, 20 Catholics, 40 females; supported entirely by Lady Caledon, established 1829.

Habits of the People

The cottages are almost all built of mud and thatched. Glass windows are universally used. Very few of the houses are more than 1-storey high and the number of rooms varies from 2 to 5. The cottages are generally whitewashed and have a tolerable exterior. The insides are in many cases unclean and uncomfortable. Some which are near Lord Caledon's demesne are extremely neat and ornamental. The food of people for the greater part of the year is principally potatoes; oatmeal is also much used. Their dress is extremely irregular and exhibits a remarkable contempt for appearances. The most striking peculiarity in it is that old regimental coats are frequently worn.

Persons of 93, 94 and 97 years of age have recently died in the parish and the people in general live to a good age. There are no instances of marriages before 18. Amusement does not appear to be much sought after in the parish. As usual, dancing forms the principal.

Emigration

Emigration to America used formerly to prevail to a great extent. It has decreased considerably of late.

Remarkable events: none.

Parish of Artrea, County Tyrone

Statistical Report by Lieutenant C. Bailey, June 1833

NATURAL STATE

Situation and Boundaries

It is partly in the barony of Loughinsholin <Loughinshollin>, county Londonderry and partly in the barony of Dungannon, county Tyrone. The portion which is in the county Londonderry is bounded on the north by the parish of Ballyscullion and Lough Beg, on the north east by the River Bann, which divides it from the county Antrim, and on the east by Lough Neagh, south east by the parish of Ballinderry which also forms, in conjunction with the parishes of Tamlaght and Arboe, its southern boundary, south west by a small portion of the parish of Derryloran and a part of the parish of Lissan, and on the west by the parishes of Desertlyn and Magherafelt. The county Tyrone portion is quite detached from the body of the parish and is bounded on the north by the parishes of Derryloran and Arboe, on the east by the parish of Arboe, on the south by the parishes of Ballyclug and Donaghenry, south west by the parish of Desertcreat and on the west and north west by the parish of Derryloran.

Divisions and Content

The county Derry portion is divided into 30 townlands, of which 19 are held by the Marquis of Londonderry and Sir Robert Bateson by terminable lease under the Salters' Company, 2 native freeholds in the manor of Salters, 2 belong to the Drapers' Company, 3 to the manor of Castledawson <Castle Dawson> and 1 glebe of Magherafelt parish. The part in the county Tyrone contains 18 townlands, including the glebe, 13 of which belong to the primate and 4 to John Lindsay of Loughry, Esquire. The area of the whole parish amounts to 18,437 statute acres.

NATURAL FEATURES

Surface

The greater part of the parish is composed of small basaltic hills varying in height from 200 to 460 feet. A district of country called the Creagh and the land along the lough shore are very flat. A great part of the Creagh is under water during winter, consequently can only be kept for pasture.

Soil

In the northern extremity of the parish the soil is clay and light loam with a great deal of bog. The Creagh is a stiff clay and sand. The southern portion is clay and rich loam, and in the immediate neighbourhood of Moneymore, a very rich loam; the whole very stony. The county Tyrone portion is a stiff clay with very little bog.

PRODUCTIVE ECONOMY

Agriculture

The parish may be considered under tolerably good cultivation. The Irish or the Scotch Cunningham measure is generally employed. The average rent of the greater part is 1 pound 1s per acre. Some of the land in the vicinity of the white limestone lets at 1 pound 10s per acre, the town parks of Moneymore at 2 pounds. The *statute* measure is made use of in the county Tyrone portion. The average rent is about 16s per acre.

The usual crops are wheat, oats, potatoes and flax. About 14 cwt of wheat, 30 bushels of oats or 150 bushels of potatoes are considered average crops per statute acre. Flax is for the most part grown only in small quantities, just sufficient for home consumption. The land is manured with stable dung or a composition of bog and soil mixed with lime brought from Ballymoghan [insert addition: Beg], Carmean, Moneymore or Coagh. The lime is not often used alone. It is procured at the kilns for 10d or 1s per barrel of 4 bushels but is situated at too great a distance from most of the farmers to enable them to use it in large quantities. The county Tyrone portion is supplied with lime from the Cookstown quarries.

Manufacture: Spinning

The only manufacture carried on is that of spinning and weaving which is at present in a very depressed state, as will appear by the following observations. A stone of flax of 16 lbs weight costs 5s. The flax dresser gets 6d and his food for dressing it. Thus it stands the spinner in altogether about 6s. The dresser divides it into about 7 lbs of good flax and 5 pounds of tow. It loses 4 lbs in the dressing. A spinner will get 3 hanks out of 1 lb of flax and can spin a hank in a day. So, allowing the stone of flax to produce 36 hanks and each hank to be worth 6d on an average (the tow yarn sells just now at rather a higher rate than the fine yarn), it will amount to 15s. The flax costs 6s, which leaves 9s for 36 days employed spinning it, or 3d a day.

Weaving

A weaver receives 5s for weaving a narrow web and from 8s to 10s for a broad one (a web is 52 yards long). A good workman will finish a narrow web in a week or a broad one in a fortnight but *will require a second person constantly to attend him.* This duty is generally performed by a boy or girl. A journeyman weaver or one who goes out to work is fed and attended by his employer and receives half the above prices. Another system is sometimes followed viz. weaving "web-about", which is done in the following manner. The weaver is fed and attended during the time he is weaving a web for his employer. As soon as he has finished it, he purchases yarn and receives his food and attendance while he is weaving one for himself and so on alternately. The only remuneration he gets is diet and attendance but no money. This, however, is not a very common practice. It is much more profitable for the weaver to buy yarn and to work on his own account but this requires a small capital, which few possess.

Pieces of calico are given out from the Castledawson factory. Each piece contains 150 yards but is divided into three when given out. The weaver receives the warp ready for the loom, with sufficient quantity of weft weighed out to him. He can finish the whole in about a fortnight and receives from 8s to 12s for it. The warp is of much superior cotton to the weft. Boys and girls are generally employed weaving the cotton webs as they are much easier done than the linen.

Bleaching

There are 2 bleaching establishments, one in the townland of Derrygonigan, belonging to Mr Hull and another in the townland of Tullyveagh, belonging to Mr Atkinson.

MODERN TOPOGRAPHY

Towns and Villages: Moneymore

Moneymore, the principal town on the Drapers' Company estate, is situated partly in the parish of Artrea and partly in Desertlyn parish. It contains about 130 houses and 700 inhabitants. The company have erected 2 very good schools, one for boys, the other for girls. They are both well attended. The master receives 50 pounds Irish per annum with house and turf, the mistress 35 pounds Irish per annum with house and turf. Their salaries are paid by the company.

There is an excellent dispensary for the relief of the sick poor on the Drapers' estate. The surgeon receives 100 guineas a year with a good house and garden, also an allowance of 25 pounds for a horse.

A market house with a town hall over it and a large inn are in the same range of buildings with the dispensary. The inn is kept unusually clean and comfortable. A very handsome church has just been completed. The Drapers' Company subscribed 5,000 pounds towards it.

PRODUCTIVE ECONOMY

Fairs and Markets

A fair is held on the 21st of every month. About 1,500 webs is the average quantity of linen sold on each fair day, which amounts to about 2,500 pounds. It is also celebrated as a cattle fair. There are sometimes 700 or 800 horses and as many horned cattle, besides pigs, but very few sheep. A corn market is held every Friday.

MODERN TOPOGRAPHY

Buildings

Several very nice houses are about being built, to be let at 20 pounds or 25 pounds a year, which will be the means of introducing respectable families and will much improve the town. The cottages are very clean and comfortable and indeed, Moneymore is proverbial for its cleanliness.

Villages: Artrea and Ballyronan

The village of Artrea is situated in the county Tyrone portion of the parish. It is a very small place of no importance.

Ballyronan is a small village situated on the shore of Lough Neagh. Messrs Gaussen, brewers and general merchants, ship a great quantity of corn and other agricultural produce for Belfast and in return import timber, iron, coals.

Places of Worship

The parish church is in Artrea village. There is a chapel of ease (called the Woods chapel) in the townland of Lisnamorrow. A large Presbyterian meeting house capable of accommodating 800 persons and a Seceding meeting house are situated in the town of Moneymore. There are 3

Roman Catholic chapels in the parish: one in the townland of [crossed out: Derrygerriff], another in Ballynenagh and a third in Moneymore.

[Insert note: In the county Tyrone portion of the parish there is also a very handsome new church in Moneymore].

Rectory

The rectory of Artrea is in the diocese of Armagh, the right of presentation being vested in Trinity College, Dublin. Dr Kennedy is the incumbent. It is under composition for 800 pounds Irish per annum.

NATURAL FEATURES

Loughs

Lough Neagh and Lough Beg form the north eastern boundary of the parish. Lough Lug, a small isolated lough, is situated to the left of the road leading from Moneymore to Ballyronan. It is supplied by internal springs. The only outlet is at its southern extremity, passing under the road and along the mearing between the townlands of Doluskey and Ballygruby. It could be drained with very little trouble or expense.

It is probable that the town of Moneymore was at some distant time supplied with water from Lough Lug. Pieces of pipe have frequently been dug up lying in that direction.

Rivers

The Moyola river, after leaving the parishes of Magherafelt and Ballyscullion, flows through the north east part of Artrea parish and empties itself into Lough Neagh about 2 miles above Toome Bridge.

The only other river is the Artrea river, which is formed by the junction of the Loughry and Kildress rivers in Killymoon demesne. It flows east and becomes for some distance the boundary between the counties of Londonderry and Tyrone.

PRODUCTIVE ECONOMY

Fishery

Pike, eels, trout, pullen and perch are taken in great abundance in Lough Neagh and Lough Beg. Trout weighing 18 lbs and sometimes a few salmon are caught in Lough Neagh. An eel fishery has been established in Toome Bridge for some years. It is carried on with great success. The proper season for fishing is from the 1st June to 1st March. The eels vary from 1 lb to 5 lbs in weight. 100 pounds worth have been taken in a night. They are generally sold at 2d per lb, which would amount to the enormous quantity of 5 tons 7 cwt 16 lbs. I have even heard of 150 pounds worth being taken in one night but I should rather trust the former account. Lord O'Neill rents the fishery and liberties of[f] Lord Donegall <Donegal>.

Quarries

The whole of the parish abounds in whinstone. There are no limestone quarries except along the ridge extending from Moneymore brae to Coagh. There are several freestone quarries in the county Tyrone portion but none in the county Derry, with the exception of a small one in Springhill wood which has never been regularly worked. The lime is burnt with coals procured at Coalisland for 4d per cwt. The carriage to Moneymore is 2d ha'penny per cwt. Lime is sold at 10d a barrel of 4 bushels, limestone at 8d per ton.

MODERN TOPOGRAPHY

Roads and Communications

The principal roads are those leading through Moneymore and along the direct communication over Toome Bridge to county Antrim. They are repaired with broken stone but are not kept in very good order.

SOCIAL ECONOMY

Fuel

Most of the county Derry portion is well supplied with turbary but not so the county Tyrone part. It is customary with the landlords to give their tenants as much as they require for fuel, merely making a nominal charge of 1s per year to pay a person the trouble for allotting it. A great deal of coal is now brought from Coalisland and Drumglass.

Population

The country is thickly populated and the cottages are tolerably clean and comfortable.

Moravians

In the townland of Ballymaguigan there is a small Moravian settlement called Gracefield, a branch of the Gracehill Society in county Antrim. It consists of about 200 members. There are 100 English [insert addition: statute] acres of land belonging to the establishment taken at the yearly rent of 5s per acre. It is relet to the Moravian brethren at 15s per acre and a small rent for the house, which altogether amounts to about 1 pound per acre. There is a neat little chapel. The clergyman has a small salary with house and 9 acres of land and stipends from his congregation. There is also belonging to the establishment a female boarding school, generally from 25 to 30 scholars, divided into 2 classes. The higher class are not obliged to belong to the society and pay 20 pounds a year; the second class belong to the society and are educated free but are charged 12s per month for diet.

MODERN TOPOGRAPHY

Mills

There are 3 corn mills: one in the town of Moneymore, another in the townland of Ballygurk and a third in the townland of Edernagh called Kings mills. [Signed] Charles Bailey, Lieutenant Royal Engineers, 22 June 1833.

Queries and Answers by Lieutenants Larcom and Bailey, June 1833

MEMOIR WRITING

Queries and Answers

To C. Bailey.
  Many a good quantity of coal is now brought into Artrea. Have you any notion of the quantity? [Answer] My dear Larcom, it would be impossible to answer this satisfactorily. Coal is burned in all gentlemen's houses, in such quantities as they may require.
  Goods embarked at Ballyronan for Belfast go by the coast I suppose, after crossing the lough? [Answer] No, by the Belfast Canal.
  I see you have no heading Antiquities? Perhaps there are none in the parish? [Answer] There are none.
  The colonel has now resolved to draw the whole up by counties not parishes, therefore it would be desirable to give the portions of divided parishes separate. [Answer] Very well, it shall be done.
  I suppose neither the Moyola nor the Artrea river have any pretension to be considered navigable? [Answer] They are not navigable.
  Are any of the people supported by fishing alone? [Answer] A few during the season.
  Are the boats their own? [Answer] Yes.

Ever truly yours, Thomas Larcom, 24th June 1833. Yours truly, C. Bailey, 25th June 1833.

Draft Memoir by 2 Authors

NATURAL FEATURES

Hills

The surface is for the most part formed into small basaltic hills. The principal are Tullyconnell, 262 feet and Knockanroe, 209 feet above the level of the sea.

Lakes and Rivers

Lakes none.
  The Ballinderry river is connected with this parish for 2 and a half miles of its course, 1 and a half of which lies within the parish and the remainder forms its northern boundary. A stream which has its source in Ardpatrick lough in Donaghenry parish traverses the parish of Artrea for 1 and a half miles from north to south.

Bogs

There are 5 small detached pieces of bog, 3 on the western boundary, 1 on the eastern and 1 on the southern boundary.

Woods

In the southern portion adjoining the county Londonderry is a small oak wood which appears to be the remains of an oak wood a long time cut down. The trees are small and scraggy.

MODERN TOPOGRAPHY

Towns

Artrea village, on the direct road from Grange to Coagh.

Trades or Callings

Watch and clockmaker 1, publicans 2, blacksmith 1.

Public Buildings

The church in Tullyraw, adjoining the village of Artrea, contains 28 pews in the aisle and would accommodate 348 persons. There is no gallery. It was erected in the years 1828 and 1829 at the cost of 1,200 pounds.

Gentlemen's Seats

The rectory, situated a very short distance from the church and village of Ardstraw: it looks a pretty house and has a good view of Killymoon demesne. The Reverend J. Kennedy D.D. is the incumbent.

Bleach Greens, Manufactories and Mills

A bleach mill in Tullyreagh repaired in 1825: an undershot wheel 13 feet diameter, 3 feet 6 inches breadth.

Bleach mills in Tullyweeny and Tullyraw.

King's (corn) mills in Edernagh, well supplied with water: a breast wheel 13 feet 8 inches diameter by 3 feet breadth.

Communications

The principal [road] is that which leads from Stewartstown to Moneymore. It traverses the parish from north to south for 1 and a half miles. The second line of road crosses the parish from east to west, leading from Coagh village to Cookstown through Artrea. These roads are in better order than some in the adjoining parish, with the exception of some hills near Cookstown. Their average breadth is 40 feet.

General Appearance and Scenery

Nothing by any means remarkable, which may be accounted for from the want of gentlemen's seats and also the scarcity of timber; and, in fact, to sum up all it is a parish which would never be remarked for its beauty or wildness.

ANCIENT TOPOGRAPHY

Antiquities

Nothing worthy of notice in the parish.

SOCIAL ECONOMY

Schools

[Table contains the following headings: townland, number of pupils subdivided by religion and sex, remarks as to how supported, when established].

Tullyreagh, 50 Protestants, 20 Catholics, 66 males, 4 females, total 7[0]; supported by the parents, established 1795.

Ballymagluire, 81 Protestants, 62 Catholics, 128 males, 15 females, total 143; the London Hibernian Society pays 6 pounds per annum and the children pay 1s per quarter, established 1820.

Religion

The Protestant religion is the prevailing one here. There are but very few Catholics. I have heard but one lives in the parish.

Habits of the People

The appearance of their cottages are in some places neat but indeed for the most part very dirty. They are built of stone and whitewashed and generally contain 2 rooms. The average may be considered at about 6 in a family. Food and fuel are much the same as in other parts of the country. Fuel is plentiful from the number of detached portions of bog surrounding.

PRODUCTIVE ECONOMY

Wages

Daily labour in their own or neighbours' farms is the general occupation. They weave and spin a little and sell the produce in Cookstown market.

Fairs and Markets

Neither are held in this parish. Cookstown is the market to which people bring their produce, as is the case for miles around.

ANCIENT TOPOGRAPHY

Antiquities

None except some few forts.

Parish of Ballinderry, County Tyrone

Statistical Report by Lieutenant C. Bailey, July 1834

NATURAL STATE

Locality

This part of the parish of Ballinderry is situated in the north east corner of the county of Tyrone and barony of Dungannon, bounded on the north and north west by the Ballinderry river, north east by a small portion of Lough Neagh, east by the parish of Arboe <Ardboe>, and on the south and south west by Tamlaght parish; mean length 1 and a quarter miles, mean breadth 1 and three-quarter miles. It is divided into 6 townlands containing 1,947 statute acres, of which 1,500 are under cultivation. The remainder consists of bog and unreclaimed ground.

NATURAL FEATURES

River

The Ballinderry river, which divides the counties of Tyrone and Londonderry, is the only river in the parish. It is formed by the junction of the Kildress and Desertcreat rivers (which take their rise in the mountains of Kildress and Pomeroy parishes) and empties itself into Lough Neagh at Mullan Point. It is from 80 feet to 100 feet broad and about 5 feet deep above the bridge, but below the bridge it is 10 feet and in some places over 20 feet deep. It is not navigable and the mouth is obstructed by a deposit of sand and gravel. This river is subject to rapid floods which soon subside and do not much overflow its banks. The parish is well supplied with springs.

Bogs

The bogs are from 60 feet to 100 feet above the level of the sea. The substratum is of bluish clay or more generally of sand. Patches of hard ground, or small insulated hills of gravel, rise through the bogs, but there are no islands artificially made. Many roots and stumps of fir trees are embedded in the bogs, generally broken at the same height, but very few logs of timber are found.

NATURAL HISTORY

Zoology

The Ballinderry river abounds with trout. In the harvest time a great many large bull trout called dologan are taken, frequently from 10 lbs to 15 lbs in weight. They are sold in the neighbouring towns at 3d per lb. They are generally soft and bad eating at that time of year. A few salmon run up the river during the spawning season and are sometimes killed.

MODERN TOPOGRAPHY

Mills

In the townland of Derrycrin-Eglish there is a corn mill and kiln, and some years ago a mill was erected in the townland of Lanaghy close to the river, but it was abandoned for want of a good supply of water.

Communications

The principal roads intersecting this part of the parish are those leading from Ballinderry bridge to Coagh and Arboe; they are made and repaired with gravel at the expense of the county and are kept in tolerably good order.

ANCIENT TOPOGRAPHY

Old Burial Ground

There is a very old burial ground in the townland of Gort, but it does not appear ever to have been the site of a place of worship. The Gort, which is sometimes called Eglish, belongs to the Glebe, and the burial ground is still made use of.

MODERN TOPOGRAPHY

General Appearance and Scenery

The ground lies low and is particularly flat. A great portion of it consists of bog which, however useful it may be, does not much improve the scenery. There are besides very few trees or hedges to enliven the prospect, the cottages are bad and dirty and upon the whole it can only be considered a poor and uninteresting tract of country.

SOCIAL ECONOMY

Poor

There is no provision whatever for the poor, aged or infirm, nor any endowments of a charitable nature.

Religion

The inhabitants are principally Roman Catholics. There is no permanent place of public worship. An altar has been raised in the townland of Derrycrin-Cunningham at which service is performed every Sunday.

Habits of the People

The cottages are built with rough stone, or more generally of mud, with small glass windows, thatched, 1-storey high and divided into 2 and sometimes 3 rooms. There is a great want of cleanliness and comfort about them. The ordinary food of the people consists chiefly of potatoes with a little milk and butter, or of oatmeal prepared in various ways. Turf is used for fuel and is easily obtained. St Patrick's Day is observed in the usual way, and Easter Monday is spent in cock-fighting and other amusements of a more innocent nature.

PRODUCTIVE ECONOMY

Manufacturing

Hand-spinning and weaving prevails in the cottages to a considerable extent, both in linen and cotton. Country commissioners connected with houses in Belfast employ a great many hands in weaving cotton. The weaver receives the necessary quantity of spun cotton and gets a certain sum for weaving the web. It is much easier to do than linen and is chiefly performed by boys and girls at a cheap rate.

Fairs and Markets

There are no fairs or markets within the parish. Those usually attended for the sale of cloth, yarn, cattle and all agricultural produce are Magherafelt, Moneymore, Cookstown, Coagh and Stewartstown, all within a convenient distance.

Rural Economy

The farms are very small indeed, containing only from 3 to 10 Irish acres. The soil is for the most part light and sandy but in some places it is a stiff blue clay difficult to work. Average rent of arable land 1 pound 2s per Irish acre, which will produce about 12 cwt of wheat, 30 bushels of oats and 130 bushels of potatoes. Flax is grown only in small quantities, just sufficient for home consumption. The cut-out bog is generally let at 10s per acre for the first 2 or 3 years, being a low rent to counterbalance the trouble and expense of reclaiming. The fields are small and badly shaped, and enclosed with banks of earth. There are very few quickset hedges. The land is manured with stable dung or a composition of soil and bog mixed with lime, but indeed very little lime is employed, the people being too poor to purchase it.

Labourers' wages are in the winter 10d and in the summer 1s per day. The common wheel and slide cars are made use of. In the present state of husbandry they are found to answer the purpose much better than carts of a larger description, particularly in the low boggy ground so prevalent in this part of the country.

Uses made of the Bogs

The bogs are used as fuel or drawn away for manure. The logs of timber found in them are employed in building and the stumps and roots are cut up for firing.

NATURAL FEATURES

General Remarks

The general height of the country above the level of the sea is 100 feet. The aspect is cold and much exposed. The prevailing winds are from the south west and north west. The soil upon the rising ground is sand and gravel; in the low ground it is bog. The manure best suited to it is lime, which is purchased at the Springbank quarry near Coagh about 2 miles distant, at from 10d to 1s per barrel of 4 bushels. The land is best adapted for tillage. The bog affords an abundant supply of fuel to the surrounding country and is becoming more valuable every year. [Signed] Charles Bailey, Lieutenant Royal Engineers, 4th July 1834.

Answers to Queries of North West of Ireland Society, 1825

MEMOIR WRITING

Memoir Writing

Copy of a letter from Thomas Paul to William Marshall Esquire, Secretary to the North West of Ireland Society.

Letter

Sir,

I herewith send you a report of the parish of Ballinderry, as far as I find my judgment and local knowledge enable me to form an opinion. Indeed I have much reason to regret that my short residence in this parish must render me incompetent to give so full and satisfactory an account of its various circumstances as the nature of the subject might require. I am Sir, your most obedient humble servant, (signed) Thomas Paul, Ballinderry Glebe, 21st June 1825.

SITUATION AND LOCALITY

Townland Divisions

Answer to 1st query. Townlands in the county of Derry part of the parish: viz. Ardagh, Ballylifford, Ballydonal, Ballymultrea, Ballagharty, part of Ballyronan, Ballinderry and lastly Killymuck, being the glebe of the parish.

Townlands in the county of Tyrone: Derrychrin <Derrychir>, Lanaghey and Mullan.

Rivers, Lakes and Plantations

Answer to 2nd query. Soil partly gravelly and partly a heavy loam, no mountains. River of Ballinderry rising in the mountains above Cookstown, forming a confluence with the Loughry river in the demesne of Killymoon and discharging itself with a beautiful serpentine winding into Lough Neagh. This lake, which is of great extent, bounds the parish from north by east from one extremity to another. Plantations are confined to a few made by James Gaussen Esquire, and around the Glebe House which are all young and not numerous.

Quarries

Answer to 3rd query. Gravel quarries pretty numerous but no others.

MODERN TOPOGRAPHY

Gentlemen's Seats

Answer to 4th query. Glebe House, built 20 years ago by the late Reverend Mr Bourne and commanding a beautiful view of Lough Neagh and the county of Antrim on the opposite shore. Mr James Gaussen's, the only gentleman's seat, no town, no inn. The public road running in a direct line from north by south east and so on to the village of Coagh.

Church

Answer to 5th query. Parish church, standing on the summit of Ballinderry hill and commanding an extensive prospect of all the surrounding country and of the lake.

Castle

The walls of the old castle of Salterstown are still standing on the edge of the shore, and I think was built as a defence to any incursions that might have been made into the interior of the country from the lake.

SOCIAL ECONOMY

Food and Health

Answer to 6th query. The food of the peasantry is that of potatoes and meal with herrings, eels and pullen; turf fuel. Diseases: occasionally fever; no remarkable instance of longevity as I know of.

Habits of the People

Answer to 7th query. Genius and dispositions of the inhabitants sharp and intelligent. Language purely English, without anything remarkable in its pronunciation or dialect. Manners generally correct. Christenings many in number and registered, marriages very few, wakes and funerals frequent and also registered. Traditions: none that I know of.

Education and Child Labour

Answer to 8th query. Education such as prevails in country schools. Children employed chiefly in preparing yarn for the loom and, at certain seasons of the year, picking up potatoes and drawing home turf. Schools: 3 in number; books procured from the different institutions in Dublin and from the London Hibernian Society; no manuscripts.

PRODUCTIVE ECONOMY

Tithes

Answer to 9th query. Tithes set for incumbency; 1 church, 1 Methodist place of worship and 1 Roman Catholic chapel.

Agriculture, Fairs and Wages

Answer to 10th query. No mode of agriculture but what has been practised for a century past. No rotation [of] crops judiciously applied. Stock of horses and black cattle wretched and of the common kind, sheep few and of a bad kind. No fairs nor markets. Price of labour 10d in winter and 1s in summer.

Trades and Manufactures

Answer to 11th query. Trades: chiefly weaving; manufactures: linen and cotton weaving almost exclusively; commerce: little or none; navigation from Belfast to Ballyronan by Lough Neagh.

Improvements

As there are no resident gentry in this parish, so I know of no means for ameliorating the condition of the poor. Sir Robert Bateson, one of the proprietors of the Salterstown proportion, lives in the neighbourhood of Belfast and is always ready to redress the grievances of the tenantry and to contribute to their necessities.

Letter addressed to William Marshall Esquire, Secretary to the North West of Ireland Society.

Parish of Ballyclog, County Tyrone

Statistical Report by Lieutenant C. Bailey, July 1834, with insertions from Draft Memoir

NATURAL STATE

Name and Locality

The usual way of spelling the name is Ballyclog sometimes Balliclug. It is situated in the north east corner of the county of Tyrone and barony of Dungannon, and bounded on the north by the parish of Artrea, east by the parish of Arboe, south east by Lough Neagh, south by the parish of Clonoe and a detached part of Arboe, and on the west by the parish of Donaghenry; extreme length 5 miles, extreme breadth 2 miles. Divided into 23 townlands (including Kilsally which is removed from the body of the parish) containing 4,704 statute acres, all of which are under cultivation with the exception of about 50 acres of bog, 60 acres of wood and plantation and 30 acres of rough ground.

NATURAL FEATURES

Hills

The only hill of any consequence is Legmurn on the southern side of the parish, which is 438 feet above the level of the sea and about 200 feet above the adjacent country.

Lakes

Lough Neagh forms the south east boundary of the parish for 2 miles. Its altitude above the sea is 46 feet. There are no insulated lakes.

Bogs

There are only 2 small bogs: one, called Drumbulgan bog, containing about 25 acres and situated 140 feet above the sea; the other, called Ochill bog, about the same size and 190 feet above the sea. Blocks of fir and oak timber are found embedded in them, generally broken at the same height, the roots and stumps remaining upright. The substratum is of clay or sand.

Woods

There is a natural wood in the townland of Ochill containing about 40 acres.

Coast

The land along the shore of Lough Neagh is from 10 feet to 20 feet above the water, forming a bank or barrier to the lough. There is no wharf or pier for loading or unloading barges. The adjacent country is very flat.

Climate

The parish of Ballyclog is not distinguished by any peculiar metereological character. The season at which the various crops ripen are: wheat at the latter end of August or beginning of September, oats in September. A few early potatoes are dug in the middle of July but the principal crop not before November. Grass is cut for hay in July.

NATURAL HISTORY

Zoology

Lough Neagh abounds in pike, eels, trout, perch, pullen (a freshwater herring) and a few salmon. Wild ducks, widgeon, teal, divers, cormorants, gulls and sandpipers are found along the shore. Hares, pheasants and woodcocks are common in Ochill wood. Partridges and quail are rare, snipes and landrails common.

MODERN TOPOGRAPHY

Gentlemen's Seats

There are no gentlemen's seats of any great size and beauty. The principal residences are those of Captain Bell of Bellmount, Mr Bryan of Gortnaskea and Mr Magaw of Eary, and the Glebe House.

Public Buildings

The parish church is a very small building with a low spire, which is a pretty object in the country. [Insert addition: There is no gallery. There are 14 pews in the aisle which would accommodate 120 persons].

There is a large Presbyterian meeting house at Brigh [insert addition: established in the year 1781, repaired in the year 1834. It contains 43 pews which would accommodate 774 persons. The cost of erection cannot be ascertained. There is no gallery].

A small Roman Catholic chapel in Drumbanaway. [Insert addition: No person at the place when called to who could get the key].

Bleach Greens and Mills

A few years ago there was an extensive bleaching establishment in Lower Back and close to Lough Neagh. It was given up at the commencement of the depression of the linen trade and the buildings have been allowed to go to ruin.

There is a corn mill in the townland of Leck with a good supply of water but much out of repair.

Communications

The main road from Moneymore to Stewartstown passes through the parish for a distance of 2 miles. Average breadth of roads 15 feet, made and repaired with broken stone or gravel and are kept in tolerably good order at the expense of the county.

ANCIENT TOPOGRAPHY

Antiquities

There are several mounds or forts within the parish and many years ago in the townland of Ballywhoolan (and a little on the left of the road from Stewartstown to Moneymore) stood a large monastery. There is none of the building remaining. The last of the foundation stones were removed a few years ago and are now lying at the foot of the field.

The townland of Ballywhoolan is abbey land and exempt from tithe.

MODERN TOPOGRAPHY

General Appearance and Scenery

The formation of the ground is pretty, varied by hill and dale which, being well clothed by trees and hedges, has a lively and picturesque appearance, particularly in the neighbourhood of Bellmount.

SOCIAL ECONOMY

Schools

There is an excellent parish school in the glebe, assisted by the Erasmus Smith charity. There are at present 120 children on the school books. From 60 to 70 are in constant attendance. There are 3 other schools under the Hibernian Society, one in Eary, another in Upper Back and a third in Ochill, all of which are well attended, so that in every part of the parish the children are within a convenient distance of some school or other. The people are anxious to obtain information and I may safely say that the general introduction of schools through the country has decidedly led to a perceptible improvement in their habits.

Poor

There is no provision whatever for the poor, aged or infirm. Begging is permitted. Indeed the inhabitants are very liberal as far as their means go and but seldom refuse alms or a night's lodging to their poorer neighbours.

Religion

The greater part of the inhabitants are Protestants, and those chiefly Presbyterians. There are but few Roman Catholics.

Habits of the People

The cottages are generally built with stone except in the town of Upper Back (where they are mostly of mud), 1-storey high, divided into 2 or 3 rooms and are in many instances very clean and comfortable. Turf is burnt in all the cottages and coals in many of the principal houses. This immediate neighbourhood contains so little bog that it is difficult to obtain and it must be baked for firing. A great deal of turf is purchased in the district of Montrevlin or near Donaghey, a distance of from 3 to 5 miles.

Schools

[Insert addition: Table contains the following headings: townland, number of pupils subdivided by sex and religion, remarks as to how supported, when established].

Eary Lower <Lowery>, 100 males, 30 females, 65 Protestants, 65 Catholics, total 130; from London Hibernian Society 10 pounds per annum, from children 6d per quarter; established 1815.

Killoon, 68 males, 36 females, 88 Protestants, 16 Catholics, total 104; from Erasmus Smith Esquire 30 pounds per annum, from children 5 pounds per annum; established 1811.

Teagh, 66 males, 56 females, 116 Protestants, 6 Catholics, total 122; from London Hibernian Society 5 pounds per annum, from children 1s per quarter; established 1825].

PRODUCTIVE ECONOMY

Manufacturing

The principal and indeed the only staple manufacture of the parish is hand-spinning and weaving linen. A weaver can earn 5s 6d to 6s per week and

Parish of Ballyclog

a spinner 2d or 3d per day. Most of the families engaged in this work have small farms which they cultivate at their leisure hours. Linen and yarn are disposed of at the markets of Stewartstown, Cookstown and Moneymore.

Proprietors and Farms

The principal proprietors are Sir Thomas Staples Baronet and E.H. Caulfield <Caulfeild> Esquire. A great part of the parish is churchland held under the see of Armagh. The farms contain from 3 to 20 Cunningham acres, which measure is generally made use of. Average rent per acre: of the best land from 1 pound 5s to 1 pound 10s; middling from 1 pound to 1 pound 5s; and the worst from 17s to 1 pound. The farmers are at present farming for subsistence only. The fields are small, tolerably well shaped and often enclosed by good hedges. The farm buildings are kept in repair by the tenants. The soil is in general strong and capable of producing good crops. In the south east corner of the parish soil is a stiffish cold clay and not so good as the rest. Stable dung or earth and bog mixed with a little lime is used for manure. Lime can be put on the land at 1s per barrel for 4 bushels and it takes about 40 or 50 barrels per acre to give the land a tolerably good dressing.

Carts and Cars

Carts and wheel cars are used in husbandry. 2 horses are employed when ploughing and if they both belong to the same person or have been often worked together, the ploughman manages them with reins without the assistance of the driver, but if (as is often the case) the second horse is hired or borrowed, it is then necessary to have a driver. Only 1 horse is used in a cart or car.

Crops

About 16 cwt of wheat, from 60 to 70 bushels of oats, or 200 bushels of potatoes are considered fair average crops per Cunningham acre. All agricultural produce is disposed of in the neighbouring market towns. The price of wheat this season has been from 8s to 10s per cwt, oats from 6d to 1s per stone and potatoes from 10d to 1s per bushel. A great quantity of grain is bought up and taken to Coalisland for exportation.

Wages

Farm servants' wages are 10d a day in winter and 1s a day in the summer without board and lodging, but if hired by the year they are paid something less. Women, boys and girls receive about half the wages of a labouring man.

Cattle

There are very few sheep kept in the parish. The common Irish cow prevails generally. A few of the Ayrshire breed have been lately introduced but as they require better pasture than this part of the country usually affords, they can only be kept by the principal farmers and consequently are not likely to answer so well as the others. The horses are small. The average value might be about 12 pounds. Green feeding is not much practised, although it is becoming much more general. Nearly every small farmer deals more or less in cattle.

Uses made of Bogs

The small quantity of bog which the parish affords is used wholly as fuel which is consumed in the neighbourhood. The imbedded timber is employed in building, the roots and stumps are cut up for firing.

Fishing

A few individuals are employed fishing during certain seasons of the year in Lough Neagh, but it is not carried to any considerable extent nor is it considered a very profitable employment. The fish are taken by nets or ground lines.

General Remarks on Agriculture

The greater part of the parish is under *good* cultivation. There is very little bog or unreclaimed ground. The soil is strong and considered good wheat land. Lime is much used for manure. It is purchased at the kilns near Stewartstown or at Dromore, both within a convenient distance, at 10d or 1s per barrel unslacked [?]. There are limestone quarries in the parish. The stone is drawn away and burnt at home, but from the scarcity of fuel it is considered quite as cheap to purchase the lime at the public kilns. The land is best adapted for tillage. Grazing is not much attended to although there are some good dry hills about Legmurn and Gortnaskea, well calculated for feeding sheep. The fences are pretty good but the holdings are too small to admit of extensive grazing. [Signed] C. Bailey, Lieutenant Royal Engineers, 7th July 1834.

Answers to Queries from the North West of Ireland Society by Dr W. Smith, July 1825

NATURAL STATE AND NATURAL HISTORY

Name and Extent

Ballyclog, <Bollyclog>, July 4 1825. Sir,

In reply to a letter from the corresponding committee of the North West Society of Ireland, which letter I did not receive until a few days ago, I hasten to give you all the information in my power respecting this parish. Its name in English, I believe, is "the town of the bell <belle>", clogher signifying in Irish "bell." It consists of 18 townlands and contains by computation about 4,000 acres English measure, lying in the heart of a fine country but not having within its limits mountains or river. The eastern extremity borders Lough Neagh between the parishes of Clonoe, Ardboe and it is well entrenched with roads.

Geology

There are quarries of limestone and freestone in the parish, but the limestone seldom used on account of our contiguity to public lime-kilns in the parish of Donaghenry <Donaghendry> and Desertcreat <Desarterack>, where lime is purchased at a very moderate price. The freestone has in some instance been used for building, but it lies so deep that it is exceedingly troublesome and expensive to raise. Its colour is red, which is also the colour of the soil in places where the stone is to be had. I consider it a bad stone for building. It casts the rough cast and, if laid on its edge in a wall, throws off a coat of considerable depth every year. We have also a quarry containing stones of a dark brown colour somewhat resembling whinstone, which we consider a better building stone than the other. We never have searched for coals but there is a townland called Balliswhillen which is very near Annahon collieries and within it, in the opinion of scientific men, are coals.

Generally speaking, the soil is good but it varies <various> much.

MODERN TOPOGRAPHY

Gentlemen's Seats

We have no town in the parish.

There are 2 gentlemen's seats established, another just commenced by Mr Bryan, a gentlemen of property residing at present in the neighbourhood of Slievegallion <Slievegallon>. The former seats are in the possession of the Earl of Castlestuart <Castlehart> and Andrew Thomas Rile Esquire. They are finely planted. With the exception of my glebe, [they] are the only places containing any trees.

Church

One very small church serves a very small congregation; no ancient buildings.

SOCIAL AND PRODUCTIVE ECONOMY

Food and Health

The potato is the food of the inhabitants from September until May, you may say for 9 months. In summer those who are able to afford it have oatmeal, but he must be a substantial full farmer that has at any time flesh meat. In this respect I observe a great change (in my time). I remember when every cabin <caban> with the exception of the very poor had its chimney hung round with bacon <beacon>, a thing you never see now.

The people are healthy and I am seldom called on for a dispensary ticket. Scrofulous complaints are the most prevalent. The instances of remarkable longevity are rare.

Occupations and Customs

The genius <genious> of the inhabitants seems to lie very much towards dealing at fairs and markets. Cock-fighting as an amusement has not yet expired but I think it is giving way. They are very fond of reading and particularly newspapers, which is incurred very much by the present unfortunate state of the country. Were I to give an opinion of the manners, I would say that they are addicted to pleasure or amusement, too fond of dress and not sufficiently impressed with respect for their superiors. This, however, arises from Presbyterian habits and education and is perhaps better than its opposite extreme, crouching adulation which deceives the object of it and is used as a mask to cover bad designs.

Schools

Education is attended to. We have 5 schools in the parish: Erasmus Smith's, Kildare Place and London Hibernian, and 2 independent, besides the school that Lady Castlestuart has at home for her own tenants' children.

Religion

One church, one meeting house of regular Presbyterians are the only houses of worship we have.

Parish of Ballyclog

The Roman Catholics are very few and have no chapel here. My tithe is set at 1s an acre (English measure).

Farms

We have no large farms. The general practice through the country is to labour the ground year after year until it gives up and then to restore it either by rest or setting it in potatoes. A worse mode you can hardly imagine.

Livestock

As to stock, they care not a farthing if their cow is bulled, by what sort of beast it is. When I came here (in the year 1818) I brought a fine Devon bull with me, thinking he would improve the stock of the country and I found the commonest sort answered them just as well. The only way in which I can account for this is in the perpetual barter and sale of cows that prevails, of the different kinds of stock. I certainly think the swine are the best in the country. I see some fine pigs. We abound in fairs and markets in our immediate neighbourhood.

Wages

A farmer gives a man resident in his house from 3 to 5 guineas a year. When he hires him by the day 1s 1d without meat, 5d with it. 10d a day the year round is the wages the gentry give.

Linen and Employment

The linen trade is almost exclusively the occupation of the inhabitants. There are a few farmers who may be said to confine themselves to agriculture and who make money by the sale of their crops, but their wives, within doors, always contrive to have some branch of the linen business going on.

Breeding

This year there seems to be a universal desire to rear the calves, which proceeds from the high price of black cattle. They seem also to have turned their thoughts to breeding horses. There are no less than 3 stallions within 2 miles of this house.

There is neither natural curiosity, remarkable occurrences nor eminent persons that I know of or have heard of.

Poor and Improvements

To ameliorate the condition of the poor is a work, in my opinion, that must be begun in themselves, or to express the idea better, you must create in them a disposition towards comfort and cleanliness and regularity which they do not seem at present to possess. How easy is it for a man, be he ever so poor, to have an enclosed garden, a patch of clover or turnips for his cow, some little increase of implements beyond the mere spade and shovel, and if they could be induced to leave the fair or market when their business is done!

There is at present, and there has been for some time, great exertions made by different societies and individuals for the benefit of the poor, and I have no doubt that time will bring about a great reformation; but even here, where there is an ambition or thirst for improvement compared with other parts of Ireland, the progress is but slow. We will take, for instance, one considerable branch of improvement: the learning to read and write. Now from the efforts above alluded to, I am not far from the truth when I say that every child in my parish might be taught at this moment to read and write, pay or no pay. And yet, how few there are that profit by this facility: I think I may safely say, not a tenth part. In every other branch of improvement we may conclude it is the same, so that we must alter their disposition to effect any good.

Markets for Wheat

Our ground gives wheat and barley and oats but we have to complain of the want of a good wheat market. There is a flour mill at Coalisland about 5 miles from here where they bring only some part of the year, and when they do they are considerably below the Portadown and Armagh prices. To send our produce so far is a great inconvenience and a great objection to the cultivation of wheat crops.

Shebeens

I almost forgot to mention a great nuisance that prevails here: the number of what is called shebeen <shibeen> houses, a great incitement to drink to which the people of this country are terribly devoted. The legislature should contrive something stronger than the present law for putting an end to them.

If there is anything further the society would wish to be informed of, I should feel great pleasure in furnishing it and remain, Sir, your very humble servant, William Smith.

Parish of Bodoney, County Tyrone

Draft Memoir for Bodoney Upper

NATURAL FEATURES

Hills

The ground on the northern extremity is of a very mountainous character. The greatest elevation is 2,234 feet above the sea. From this point there is a gradual fall eastward, occasionally broken by mountains varying little in height from the above-mentioned point. There is also a considerable fall westward, occasionally broken by large mountains. The ground on the southern side is also mountainous. The greatest elevation is 1,841 feet above the sea. From this point there is a gradual fall westward.

Lakes and Rivers

Lough Ouske, situated on the eastern boundary of the county Tyrone: its extent is [blank].

Rivers and Woods

A stream rises in the eastern extremity of the parish and pursues a winding course in a westerly direction for 11 miles.
Woods: there are none.

MODERN TOPOGRAPHY

Towns

There is no town within the parish but there are 2 hamlets viz. Sperrin and [blank].

Public Buildings

Parish church has 22 pews which contain 180 persons. There are no galleries.
Roman Catholic chapel in Cranagh, established in 1815, has 2 galleries which contain 200 each, the body 600. There are no seats either in the body or gallery.
Gentlemen's seats: none.

Bleach Greens, Manufactories and Mills

Corn mill in Sperrin, breast wheel 12 feet diameter by 2 feet broad.
Glenroan corn mill, breast wheel 13 feet diameter by 2 feet broad.
Oughdourish corn mill, out of repair in July 1835, breast wheel 17 feet diameter by 1 foot 7 inches broad.
Corn kilns: 15.

Communications

The main road from Strabane to Tobermore traverses the parish from west to east for [blank] miles; also the main road from Strabane to Gortin extends from west to east for [crossed out: 1] mile and then turns from north to south for half a mile.

General Appearance and Scenery

Wild and uncultivated, especially in the east, but as you draw near the west the country begins to open and is more cultivated.

SOCIAL ECONOMY

Schoolhouses

[Table contains the following headings: townland, number of pupils subdivided by religion and sex, how supported, when established].
Glenchiel, no master attending in July; from National Board 8 pounds per annum, established 1835.
Clogkerny, 28 males, 14 females, 3 Protestants, 39 Catholics, total 42; from children 1s 1d per quarter; established 1821.
Glenroan, 15 males, 12 females, 1 Protestant, 26 Catholics, total 27; from Major Unphrey [Humphrey] 5 pounds per annum, from children 1s per quarter; established 1835.
[Insert note: more in the parish].

Parish of Carnteel, County Tyrone

Memoir by George Scott

NATURAL FEATURES

Lakes

In this parish there are 2 small lakes, of no consequence whatever. They are situated at the east end of the parish, about 5 miles from Aughnacloy and 6 miles from Dungannon; their depth is about 9 feet.

Rivers

There are not any rivers in this parish. The leading streams fall to the south of the parish into the Blackwater, for information of which vide Memoir of the parish of Killyman.

Bogs

The portion of bog in this parish is extremely small, only occurring at the base of some of the sandhills. The depth is not more than 10 or 12 feet. The bog in this neighbourhood does not last long, for whenever it is possible it is cultivated. Many portions of ground which the farmer cut turf from 2 years ago now supply them with a good crop of potatoes.

Woods

There are not any natural woods in this parish, or are there evidences of any having existed in former times. The young plantations in this parish are very numerous and the whole parish presents a very fair supply of wood.

Climate: vide Memoir of Killyman.

MODERN TOPOGRAPHY

Public Buildings

Church, Presbyterian meeting house, Wesleyan Methodist preaching house, Primitive Wesleyan Methodist preaching house.

Church

The church was erected in the year 1736; the cost cannot be ascertained. It would accommodate 355 persons, average number in attendance from 150 to 200. Dimensions 100 feet by 36 feet. The style of architecture is very plain. There is a good steeple of cut stone.

Presbyterian Meeting House

The Presbyterian meeting house is an old building at the back of the town, erected in the year 1774, dimensions 65 feet by 24 feet; the cost cannot be ascertained. It would accommodate about 300 persons, average number in attendance 130.

Methodist Preaching Houses

The Wesleyan Methodist preaching house was formerly a dwelling house, but was altered in the year 1805 or 1806. The alterations cost 150 pounds, paid by public subscription. It would accommodate about 350 persons, average number in attendance during service 150. It is kept in repair by voluntary subscriptions from the congregation, dimensions 36 feet by 18 feet.

The clergymen belonging to this sect cannot marry for 4 years after they first officiate as ministers, during which time they are obliged to travel about the country, for which they receive 16 pounds a year. After 4 years they can marry and receive 16 pounds a year for their wife, a house and coal. For each child they receive 4 pounds a year until it arrives at the age of 6, from which time it is placed on the education list. Shortly after, there is an allowance of 8 pounds a year extra allowed for the education of the child, until it arrives at the age of 14, at which period all allowances are stopped, it being presumed that at that age either the boy or girl is able to earn its own living.

The Primitive Wesleyan Methodist preaching house is a very small building kept in repair by the congregation. There is service performed here every Sunday evening.

Gentlemen's Seats

Bellmont, the residence of Dean Stackford; Captain Richardson.

Communications

The following main roads pass through this parish: from Ballygawley to Aughnacloy for 4 miles; from Aughnacloy to Monaghan for 1 mile; from Aughnacloy to Dungannon for 3 and a quarter miles; from Aughnacloy to Caledon for a quarter of a mile. The main road from Ballygawley to Aughnacloy is in very good repair, judiciously laid out, average breadth 36 feet. The other roads are in bad order, their breadth being about 30 feet. The cross roads are not unnecessarily numerous. There does not appear to be the slightest attention paid to the manner in which they are kept. The expense of making and repairing roads is paid by the county cess. There are not any railroads or canals in this parish.

General Appearance and Scenery

The soil throughout this parish is extremely fertile. It is well studded with wood, and the neat farmhouses appearing through the trees gives it a picturesque <picturesk> appearance. There is scarcely a cottage without a cluster of trees surrounding it.

SOCIAL ECONOMY

Habits of the People

The cottages throughout the country are small, generally speaking only 1-storey, mostly clean with small glass windows; their only fuel turf. There is not any remarkable instance of longevity; usual number in a family 6. The chief amusement appears to be handball. Patrons days are quite forgotten. It is a very common thing in this parish for 2 or 3 persons to go out after dark, or late in the evening, and on the top of some hill to play the drum and fife; the chief air is the "Boyne Water." In the town of Aughnacloy the houses principally are small and dirty.

MODERN TOPOGRAPHY

Towns: Aughnacloy

Aughnacloy, situated almost in the boundary of the counties Monaghan and Tyrone, it is a small dirty town. There are not more than 4 good houses in it, the remainder are either slated or thatched. The latter are generally small with broken windows, and no attention at all paid to the cleanliness of the place. Almost every house in the town is [? licensed] to sell ale and spirits, vide trades and occupations for this town.

The public buildings in the town are exceedingly few, viz. the church and Methodist preaching house, the other houses of worship being at the back or a little out of the town. The church is the only ornament to this town. The hotel appears particularly uncomfortable. I do not think there is much inducement for any person to remain in the town. The post arrives here from Dublin at 10 minutes past 5 a.m. and leaves here for Dublin at 20 minutes past 10 p.m. There is also a stagecoach which passes through this town on alternate

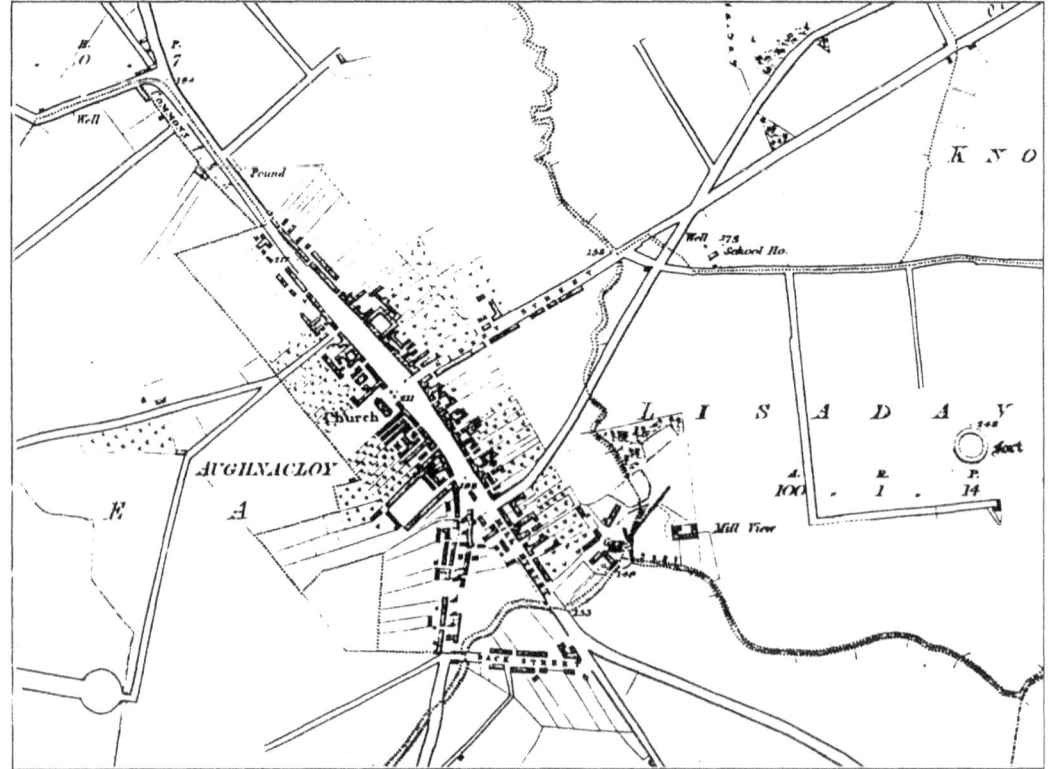

Map of Aughnacloy from the first 6" O.S. maps, 1830s

Parish of Carnteel

days between Derry and Dublin. The town is not paved or lighted.

SOCIAL ECONOMY

Local Government

There are 2 magistrates, neither of which are stipendiary. The one, E. Moore Esquire, resides in the town; the other, Captain Richardson, a short distance from the town. The usual force of police is 4, but not any revenue [police]. The petty sessions are held here, but there are no other particular jurisdictions such as manor courts, court[s] leet. The number of outrages committed in the town is comparatively small. There is not any illicit distilling carried on in the parish. The houses are not generally insured.

Poor

There does not appear to be any provision made for the poor.

Religion

The majority of persons in this parish appear to be Protestants.

Schools

[Table contains the following headings: townland, number of pupils subdivided by religion and sex, religion of master, how supported, when established]. [Name blank] Protestants 59, boys 32, girls 27, total 59; master a Protestant. This school is supported at present by the parents of the children. It is under the Hibernian Society, the master receives 1d per week. It cost 81 pounds, paid by Sir Hugh Steward [sic]; established 1835.

[Name blank] Protestants 42, Catholics 8, boys 30, girls 20, total 50; master a Protestant. This school is not under any board. The master receives 1d per week from each child. The schoolhouse was formerly a cabin. The alterations cost 20 pounds, paid by general subscription; established 1834.

Poor

There is not any provision for the poor.

Trades and Occupations

[Table gives trade or calling and number] Surgeon 1, apothecary 1, grocer 1, whiskey shops 33, cloth merchants 3, bakers 3, inns 2, milliner 1, smiths 3, reed maker 1, houses of entertainment for the poorer classes 7, shoemaker 1, tailors 2, nailers 3, saddler 1, confectioner 1, leather shops 2.

Draft Memoir

NATURAL FEATURES

Hills

The strip of land which extends northwards between the parishes of Errigal and Killeeshil obtains at one point an elevation of 823 feet above the level of the sea, being one of the minor features of Shantavney mountain. With the exception of this strip there is no portion of the parish which partakes of a mountainous character, the surface being for the most part formed of low hill with alternate valleys or plains [insert addition: declining in height as they approach the south and east end of the parish: Culnaver 623, Moutray Fort 459, Solan 568, Cravenny Irish 513, Killyneary 521].

Lakes

Crans lough is situated in the north western portion of the parish. It extends over 22 acres 3 roods 24 perches. To the westward of Crans lough is Craigs lough, of which 8 acres 3 roods 21 perches belong to Carnteel parish. Southward of the above is a third lake of about 10 acres in extent, the portion within the boundary of Carnteel being 2 acres 2 roods 31 perches.

Rivers

The Ballyreagh alias the Ballygawley water crosses the southern portion of the parish and afterwards becomes the parish boundary on the west till it empties itself into the Blackwater river.

Bogs

There is very little bog in the lower part of the parish. The northern extremity contains a large extent of mountain bog.

MODERN TOPOGRAPHY

Public Buildings

Roman Catholic chapel in Dunabane.
Gentlemen's seats: Bellmont, Stormhill.

Bleach Greens, Manufactories and Mills

There are 2 mills in Aughnacloy; the Ballyreagh mill in Inishrush townland.

Communications

The main road from Monaghan to Omagh traverses the south western part of the parish for 3 and a half miles; also the main road from Monaghan to Dungannon in a north easterly direction for 5 miles, including its length through the detached portion of Killeeshil.

Towns

Aughnacloy is situated in the southern part of the parish, on the main road from Dublin to Londonderry and within a quarter mile of the county boundary. It is [blank] miles from Dublin, 4 from Ballygawley and 15 from Dungannon. It consists of 1 main street with 3 smaller ones branching from it. The public buildings are a church, a Presbyterian meeting house, 2 Methodist meeting houses, 1 inn and a [insert addition: good schoolhouse].

There is a [insert addition: large] general market every Wednesday and a good grain market on Saturdays. Fairs are held on the first Wednesday in every month.

Carnteel village is situated nearly 2 and a half miles north east of Aughnacloy. There are 8 fairs held here during the year, viz. 15th January, 1st Monday after the 12th February, 6th April, 26th May, 1st Monday after the 12th July, 25th August, 14th September and 26th November.

Parish of Clogherny, County Tyrone

Statistical Report by Lieutenant W. Lancey, March 1834

NATURAL STATE AND NATURAL FEATURES

Situation

This parish is situated in the county Tyrone, barony of Omagh and diocese of Armagh, and lies from 3 to 7 miles east of Omagh. It is surrounded by the parishes of Drumragh, Cappagh, Termonmaguirk <Tarmonmaguirk>, Errigal Keerogue, Clogher, Donacavey and contains 17,800 acres, having Mullaghslina townland, one of its glebes, isolated in the parish of Termonmaguirk.

General Appearance

Its general appearance is good. It possesses fine valleys and large sweeps of accessible ground drained by small rivers. The land is not usually so well cultivated as the adjacent parishes but the soil is good and, if properly managed, might be rendered as productive as the parish of Drumragh. The landscape is enlivened by gentlemen's seats, plantations and groups of trees, and the parish considered as a whole is equal if not superior to most of those adjacent.

Mountains

The slopes of the hills of which Shantavney forms the summit are the only high ground in Clogherny.

Rivers

It is drained by the Cloghfin river, a small stream dividing it from Termonmaguirk, which at the parish of Cappagh falls into the Camowen <Cammon>. The last river divides it from Cappagh till it meets Drumragh; one dividing it from Clogher and Donacavey and running through Seskinore into the Drumragh river. But the 2 first-named streams are the only ones of consequence through the parish.

Lakes

The only lake is that of Lough Patrick, situated in the townland of Donaghanie near the ruins of the old church.

MODERN TOPOGRAPHY

Principal Buildings

The largest building is Somerset, the residence of the Reverend James Lowry. The main body of this house was erected by the Reverend John Lowry, the late rector, and 2 wings were added by the present incumbent in 1829. It is situated in the lower glebe, surrounded with young plantations, and is a very conspicuous object for many miles round the country.

Seskinore Lodge, the country residence of Mrs Perry of Dublin, is a small house in a demesne kept in the best order with good gardens and conservatories producing peaches, nectarines, grapes.

Mullaghmore House is a large building a mile from Seskinore, the property of Mrs Perry, let to Robert Burgess Esquire. The lands are not laid out in a demesne but there is a lawn, garden, paddocks etc. about the house, which is surrounded with good trees and has an air of respectability and wealth.

Greenmount, the seat of John Galbraith Esquire, is a modern building of moderate dimensions with new plantations around it and appears a snug residence.

Roscavey, the family seat of the Galbraiths and now the residence of James Galbraith Esquire, is surrounded with trees and is well situated but the house is fast falling into ruin and the whole place is very much neglected.

Places of Worship

The parish church is a modern building situated in the glebe not far from the rector's house. It is generally well attended, has no gallery and could hold 280 persons.

A Presbyterian meeting house at Dervaghcroy in middling repair is well attended and is considered large enough. It can accommodate 300 persons. It is fully pewed and has 2 galleries.

The Secession Church have a meeting house in Seskinore, where there is a middling congregation every alternate Lord's day. This house will hold 200 worshippers.

There are some Methodists in Clogherny but they have no chapel.

The Roman Catholic chapel at the village of Beragh, built by private contributions under the superintendence of the present priest, MacGuirk, is much crowded and can contain about 1,000 persons.

Villages

The village of Beragh, the property of Lord Belmore, is 1 long wide street of very mean houses whose tenants for the most part appear to be poor; but Seskinore, though small, contains some good houses, the property of Mrs Perry whose agent resides in the village.

SOCIAL ECONOMY

Inhabitants

The inhabitants are generally in good circumstances. There is nothing peculiar in their mode of living, which is equal to or superior to the adjacent parishes. Potatoes, meal, milk and a little meat for the more wealthy farmers form their usual diet. They regularly attend their different places of worship. Few speak Irish. They seldom migrate for harvest and are generally contented and quiet. No parish near Omagh has so many resident landlords. The principal proprietors are Lord Belmore, Colonel Verner, Mr James Lowry, Mrs Perry, Messrs James and John Galbraith.

The dress of the peasantry is similar to the adjacent country, composed of home-made cloth, flannels, stockings and linen, with cheap cottons and English goods purchased in Ballygawley or in Omagh. Those who can afford to wear better materials can be supplied with them in Omagh, where competition in the cloth trade is carried to a great extent.

Schools

There are 6 schools in the parish but I have not been able to ascertain all the particulars respecting them. They are situated thus: 1 in Lower Clogherny glebe, to which the rector subscribes 2 pounds annually and the scholars pay the rest; they amount to 30; 1 school in Beragh under the London Hibernian Society; 1 in Aughnagar under the Kildare Street Society, on Colonel Verner's property, who gives the master of this school and all others on his estate an acre of land and 7 guineas a year; a school in Seskinore; a hedge-school in Dervaghcrog supported by the scholars, who average 20; a school in Ballyhallaghan supported by voluntary subscription, in which from 40 to 70 children are taught reading writing and arithmetic, and the girls sewing.

The curate of the parish states the usual average of the scholars varies from 30 to 60 in all the schools except Lower Clogherny glebe and that they are pretty well attended in winter and summer but the children are a good deal employed in agriculture in spring and autumn. The 2 sexes sit together. The schoolhouses in Clogherny and Aughnagar are in good repair and the others tolerably so. A school is much wanted in Roscavey and another in Greenmount.

Dispensary

The parish is usually very free from disease. The dispensary patients apply to Omagh as there is no establishment of this nature in Clogherny.

PRODUCTIVE ECONOMY

Farms

The farms are larger in Clogherny than in Drumragh, the general average being about 30 acres of land. Some graze but not to any great extent.

Rents

The usual rents vary from 15s to 30s an acre, most of the parish being held under old leases.

Crops

The usual crops are potatoes, barley, flax, and oats; a few sow wheat. Wooden ploughs are still very generally in use.

Manure

Farmyard compost mixed with lime is the chief manure. The lime is obtained from Ballygawley, 7 miles distant, at the rate of 18d a cart-load and 15d a car-load.

There are no farming societies in Clogherny.

Wages

Wages are from 10d to 1s for men in summer and 6d to 8d for women, but in winter something less for day labourers. Men hired for the half-year receive from 35s to 55s and diet.

Livestock

There is plenty of cattle but of no particular breeds. Their prices are regulated by the adjacent markets of Omagh and Ballygawley and they vary from 3 pounds 10s to 7 pounds, according to the demand and quality.

Common farm horses are to be purchased in Clogherny but none of a superior kind. Their prices vary from 5 pounds to 15 pounds. Good sheep are reared in Seskinore Lodge and sell from 30s to 50s a head. Country sheep are to be had at

Parish of Clogherny

most of the farms and sell for 10s 6d to 30s. Common pigs here as elsewhere about Omagh abound, at prices from a few shillings to 4 or 5 guineas.

Fish and Game

A few salmon and trout are taken in the rivers. Grouse, hares and partridge are not uncommon.

Fruit

The gentlemen's seats already mentioned have fruit trees and the farmhouses the usual proportion of small fruit. No scarcity need prevail as the parish is within a reasonable distance of Aughnacloy, the great fruit market of this part of the county.

Mills

There are 8 mills in this parish, of which 6 are for corn and 2 for flax. The former are situated in the townlands of Coolesker (with kiln attached); 1 in Rathnelly, which originally had 16 towns for succour <sucker>; Mr Perry hired the leap mill and gave it to the same families to assist their wheels; 1 in Roscavey; 1 in Seskinore; 1 in Beagh, on the parish mearing; and 1 in Moylagh. The flax mills are in Upper Clogherny Glebe and Gorteclar.

Many of the parish go to Mr Gervais' <Jervis> mill near Clogher, where they get their flax dried, beetled and scutched at once. The wheels of most of the mills in this neighbourhood do not exceed 10 or 12 feet. The flax mills are turned with less powerful machinery and they are generally over-shot wheels.

Manufactures

Linen cloth is made in most of the houses in Clogherny, as it is celebrated for good flax which is grown in great abundance.

Bricks are made and sell from 13s to 15s a thousand at the kiln, and 3s 6d a day for cart hire would bring them into Omagh.

MODERN TOPOGRAPHY

Roads

There are plenty of roads kept in good repair. The principal is the mail road from Dublin to Derry and cross branches to Beragh, Sixmilecross, Mountfield, Fintona and Dromore.

There are 7 principal bridges, built of stone: 1 in Cur, called the Barony bridge, on the mail road, 2 in Seskinore, 1 in Letfern, 1 in Beagh, 1 in Beragh and 1 in Coolesker.

NATURAL FEATURES

Woods and Plantations

There are no natural woods and only a few plantations about the residences of the gentry and principal farmers.

Fuel

Turf and bog fir are the only fuel used in Clogherny, unless it may be in the houses of the landlords who can afford to send their carts to Dungannon for coal. There is a good deal of bog yet unconsumed. Lord Belmore's tenants do not pay extra for it, other tenants do. The bog wood may be raised with the permission of the agent.

Rocks

The lower part of the parish lies on clay sandstone, the upper on beds of talc slate and coarse rolled sandstone conglomerate, which latter is a very common rock in the adjacent parish of Clogher. Eskers are met with here and at Fintona. They are low ridges of gravel at the feet of the mountains presenting a section of an isosceles triangle, the apex of which is about 40 or 50 feet above the base. Eskermore derives its name from this gravel formation. There is no limestone in the parish.

ANCIENT TOPOGRAPHY

Old Church

The principal antiquity, and that which makes Clogherny celebrated through this part of Tyrone, is the ruins of an old church in Donaghanie said to have been founded by St Patrick in the 5th century. It is strikingly situated on a small hill at the foot of which is St Patrick's lough. The eastern window and the foundations yet remain, and the graveyard which is still used by the Roman Catholics.

Pattern

On the first Sunday in August crowds of persons of all denominations assembled at Lough Patrick, either to take part in or to witness the superstitions practised at the pattern <paton>. The first part of the penance which these benighted people perform is to go round the lough on their bare knees and add a handful of earth to the hillocks of clay which surround it. This, with the water of the lough (in which the principal charm consists), is supposed to cleanse them from sin and cure their diseases. A stone at the church bearing on it the supposed mark of St Patrick's knee is circumambulated by the penitents on their bare knees.

This pattern has not been so numerously attended lately in consequence of party riots which took place at it and, by the influence of the magistrates on one hand and the priest on the other, is not so publicly sought after now as 8 years ago. People, however, come from all parts of Ireland to it. Tents and booths are erected and, after the superstitions are completed, the usual amusements of dancing, deeply mingled with whiskey, conclude this desecration of the Lord's holy day. Whether those who do penance join in these festivals, it is not easy to say, as there are persons of all denominations present.

Legends

St Patrick's power over reptiles was exhibited in Donaghanie in the destruction of an amphibious animal that lived in the lough and was the terror of the country; but St Patrick's horse, whom the animal was going to destroy, kicked with his hind foot and killed him!!

There are no holy wells or any other antiquities in Clogherny except the Danish forts.

Forts

They have nothing particular about them. 3 of them are situated in the townland of Redergan, 1 in Ballykeel, 2 in Coolesker, 1 in Beragh, 1 in Laragh, 1 in Anney, 1 in Rathnelly, 4 in Donaghanie, 1 in Killydroy, 1 in Cur, 2 in Roscavey, 1 in Upper Clogherny, 3 in Mullaghmore, 3 in Seskinore, 1 in Letfern, 1 in Beagh, 2 in Moylagh, 2 in Raw, 1 in Tullyharm and 1 large one in Mullaslinna, making 33 in all.

Abbey

The leap mill on the mearing of Cappagh and Clogherny is said to be built on the site of an old abbey.

SOCIAL ECONOMY

General Remarks

Donaghanie is antiparochial. It pays neither tithe nor church cess and takes no part in vestries. Clogherny parish taken in the aggregate is not inferior to any in my portion of Tyrone. The land is good and of easy access and if the proprietors would shelter it by plantations and assist in draining it, it might take a decided lead in agricultural produce. [Signed] William Lancey, Lieutenant Royal Engineers, 7 March 1834.

Parish of Clonoe

Parish of Clonoe, County Tyrone

Statistical Report by Lieutenant G. Dalton, July 1833

NATURAL STATE AND NATURAL FEATURES

Situation, Extent and Proprietors

This parish is in the county Tyrone and barony of Dungannon, and is a rectory in the province and diocese of Armagh, the right of presentation being in Trinity College, Dublin, as lately decided by law against the primate. The present incumbent is the Reverend Dr Buck and the living is worth about 400 pounds per annum, arising from glebe land and tithes, the latter being compounded for under the Tithe Composition Act for the sum of 350 pounds late Irish currency.

It is bounded on the north by the parishes Arboe <Ardboe>, Ballyclog and Donaghenry, on the east by Lough Neagh, on the west by Donaghenry and on the south by Killyman and Tartaraghan parishes. It is a square tract of land gradually narrowing from north to south and is divided into 30 townlands, and contains 9,126 acres. The principal proprietors are Lord Annesley, A. Annesley Esquire, Charles G. Gardiner Esquire and 7 townlands belonging to the Royal College of Dungannon.

Surface and Soil

There are no very high hills. The highest are on the west and north side. The eastern and southern parts of the parish are very flat, the land sloping gradually down to the shores of Lough Neagh.

Soil

There is some rich and good land with a large proportion of heavy clay and also of a light sandy and gravelly soil; and in the southern portion of the parish are some very extensive bogs, too soft and wet to be of any use except on their edges, which are cut for fuel.

PRODUCTIVE ECONOMY

Agriculture

With the above exception, the whole parish is under cultivation, which has increased and improved in proportion as the linen trade has decreased. The general course of crops are potatoes, wheat, oats and flax. Hardly any barley is grown and of late years very little flax, whilst the cultivation of wheat is much more attended to and several very fine crops of it are now grown in this parish.

Farms

The farms are too small to admit of a very regular plan as to the succession of crops according to any good and approved system. Their average size is 6 acres and the largest in the parish is but 20 acres.

Manures

Lime mixed with bog earth is extensively used and is of great use on the heavy clay lands; and bog earth mixed with horse and cow manure is also in very general use. A great improvement in agriculture is gradually taking place in the increased assiduity of the farmer in the collection of manure, and also in the increased use of lime.

Turbary

The south and west of the parish are well supplied from the edges of the extensive bogs which lie there, and the inhabitants also procure good and cheap coal from the neighbouring coalfield of Tullyniskan <Tullaniskin> parish. The northern and eastern portions are not well supplied and the people have to get, and in many cases purchase, their fuel from the south.

Quarries and Minerals

Limestone of an excellent quality is found in the townlands of Shanliss and Tumpher, and is sold, burnt as low as 8d per barrel of 4 bushels. Coal of a middling quality is found in Lisnastrane and Annagher townlands. In the former, three-fourths of the coalfield, which does not exceed 20 acres, is worked out, and in the latter it is not at present worked, perhaps owing to the roof being soft and difficult to support, and consequently requiring a great quantity of timber for the purpose. No trial has ever been made under this seam. In Dirnagh townland, which adjoins Annagher, a trial by boring to the depth of 340 feet was made some years ago, but without finding coal.

Clay

In Meenagh townland, which is probably a corruption of the Irish word mineah or "mine", potter's clay of the best description and in great abundance is found at the depth of 20 yards from the surface. It is in some places 49 feet in thickness and is suitable for all the purposes of fine pottery ware, being thought by some not to be inferior to the Staffordshire clays. The bed extends over a great portion of the townland, in some places cropping out to the surface.

Modern Topography

Towns

There is no town or even village in this parish, but Coalisland and Stewartstown are both on its borders and have excellent markets for yarn, linen, grain and the produce of a farm.

Productive Economy

Manufactures

The manufacture of coarse linen cloth was formerly very general in this parish, but has of late years much decreased. The weaving of cotton has succeeded it and is generally done by commission, the yarn being given out to the weaver and 4s 6d paid for weaving a web of 80 yards, which will employ an active man 4 days. Pottery ware of a coarse description and bricks of an inferior quality are manufactured in the southern parts of the parish, but only to a trifling extent.

Modern Topography

Roads

The high coach road from Dungannon to Stewartstown and the north passes through the townlands of Tumpher and Mousetown; another high road from Armagh to Stewartstown, avoiding Dungannon, traverses the parish; and a third from the county Armagh to Stewartstown at the north enters the parish at Maghery ferry. There are also several by or crossroads. The whole of these roads are in moderately good order and the country abounds in excellent materials for their repair.

Natural Features

Rivers

The Rivers Blackwater and Torrent bound this parish on the south and south east. The latter falls into the former 3 and a quarter miles short of its mouth and where it enters Lough Neagh. The Blackwater is navigable for vessels and barges as far up its course as Blackwatertown.

Modern Topography and Productive Economy

Canals

The Tyrone Canal, partly in this and partly in Tullyniskan parish, runs parallel and close to the Torrent river, by a portion of whose waters it is fed. It is under the direction of the Board of Public Works and was made between the years 1746 and 1752 at an expense of 20,000 pounds, granted by the Irish Parliament with a view to the encouragement of the Tyrone collieries, which had been but a short time previously discovered and which were then confidently calculated upon for supplying Dublin from Drumglass for a period of at least half a century. Its length from the head of the basin at Coalisland to the point where it enters the Blackwater river is 4 and a quarter miles, with a fall of 42 feet, having in this distance 6 single and 1 double lock, constructed with cut stone to admit lighters of 70 tons burthen upon 6 feet of water. The outward trade consists of coal, grain of all kinds, cut stone, firebrick tiles, pottery ware, fireclay and common brick; inwards of timber, iron, slates, flax seed, lead ore for the potteries and all the heavy description of goods, tallow and groceries.

The cargoes inward last year were 389, averaging 50 tons each lighter. Each one pays a toll of 2s 4d out and 18s 5d for the cargo inward, except flax seed which only pays 2s 4d, the sum charged upon empty boats. Some alteration in these charges is intended at the end of the present year. As many articles of home produce are exempt from toll, the annual amount received does not exceed 160 pounds, but were the rates upon the ordinary scale it would pay about 400 pounds.

It was originally intended to extend this canal to Drumglass colliery, but the project failed from an insufficient supply of water. A civil engineer named Ducart attempted several years afterwards to carry this plan into execution, for an account of which see statistical report of Drumglass and Tullyniskan parishes.

Natural Features

Lakes

The shore of Lough Neagh, bounding the east of this parish, is very shallow and flat and formed of light sand. Several of the inhabitants who live near it keep boats and nets and earn their livelihood by the sale of trout, pike, eel and pullens, a sort of freshwater herring, all which are brought in great quantities during the season to the markets of Dungannon and Stewartstown.

Parish of Clonoe

Modern Topography

Churches and Chapels

There is only 1 church, which is old and small and the churchyard very confined and crowded. There is 1 chapel, a large new building, and also a mass yard where the Roman Catholic service is performed. There is no other place of worship in the parish.

Social Economy

Schools

There are 7 schools, 2 of which are under the care and patronage of the Commissioners of National Education.

Ancient Topography

Antiquities

In the townland of Magherlamfield stand the remains of an old castellated mansion called Mountjoy Castle, which appears to have been formerly a place of some strength. It was built by Charles Blount, afterwards Lord Mountjoy, in the reign of Elizabeth.

Social Economy

Population

The country is thickly inhabited, principally by Roman Catholics, the proportion being 900 Catholic families and 120 Protestant. [Signed] George Dalton, Lieutenant Royal Engineers, 20th July 1833.

Office Copy of Draft Memoir

Natural Features

Hills

The hills are not high, the extreme elevation, which is on the northern boundary, being only 330 feet above the sea. The high ground extends along the western boundary.

Lakes

There are 4 miles of the shore of Lough Neagh which belong to this parish, and 2,940 acres 2 roods 38 perches of the lake included within the parish boundary.

Rivers

The Blackwater flows for 3 and a quarter miles on the south eastern side of the parish and the Torrent river for 3 miles on the south western side.

Bogs and Woods

In the south of the parish there is a very large tract of bog.
  Woods: Bellville wood.

Modern Topography

Public Buildings

The only public buildings are a church and a Roman Catholic chapel. The church is situated towards the centre of the parish in Killary glebe. The Roman Catholic chapel in Magheramulkenny is a large new building.

Manufactories and Mills

The spade forge in Aughdrimony, mill in Meenagh, mill in Annagher, mill in Cluntybacker.

Communications

The high road from Dungannon northwards through Stewartstown passes through the townlands Tumpher and Mousetown. Another high road from Armagh to Stewartstown avoiding Dungannon traverses the parish, and a third from the county of Armagh to Stewartstown enters the parish at Maghery ferry. There are also several by-roads. The roads are in general kept in good order and the country abounds in excellent material for their repair.

Tyrone Navigation

The Tyrone Navigation consists of 4 and a quarter miles of a canal extending from the Blackwater river to Coalisland. It was originally intended to extend this canal to the Drumglass collieries, but the supply of water was found insufficient. To overcome this difficulty an Italian engineer named Ducart projected a canal from Coalisland to the collieries, having slides or inclined planes with rollers instead of locks, by means of which the empty vessel proceeding to the pit was by some slight mechanical assistance drawn up by the laden vessel coming down. He obtained a considerable grant from the House of Commons to enable him to put his plan into execution, and the unfinished remains of the work are still to be seen in Tullyniskan parish.

Parish of Desertcreat <Dysertcreaght>, County Tyrone

Statistical Report by Lieutenant C. Bailey, February 1834

NATURAL STATE

Situation, Boundaries and Content

The parish of Desertcreat is situated in the barony of Dungannon, in the county of Tyrone and bounded on the north by the parishes of Kildress and Derryloran, on the east by the parishes of Artrea <Ardtrea> and Donaghenry, south east by the parish of Tullyniskan <Tullaniskin>, south by the parish of Pomeroy and on the west by a small portion of Termonmaguirk parish.

It is divided into 69 townlands containing 14,400 statute acres.

NATURAL FEATURES

Surface

The ground on the western side lies high and falls gradually eastward, the surface being broken by small round hills.

Soil

The soil in the upper part or mountain part of the parish is of a cold wet nature and very poor, but in the lower part it is of a much richer quality, consisting of a strong clay resting upon a limestone bed, and is considered good wheat land.

PRODUCTIVE ECONOMY

Farming

The farms are small, containing from 3 to 20 Irish acres, and are generally held under leases of 3 lives or 31 years at a yearly rent of about 1 pound per acre. The system of farming has been much improved within the last 5 or 6 years, owing in some degree to the decline of the linen trade, which obliges people to depend more upon their land than their loom for support. Still, however, there remains much to be done in the way of draining, collecting manure and having a succession of crops.

Agriculture

The average crops upon an Irish acre of moderately good land would be about 1 ton of wheat, 50 bushels of oats, or from 250 to 300 bushels of potatoes. Flax sown only in small quantities: a peck of seed will yield from 3 to 4 stones of flax. The wages of labourers if hired by the year are from 8d to 10d per diem; if hired by the day from 10d to 1s. There are very few old leases and in reletting the land, the English or statute measure is now generally made use of.

Manufactures

The principal manufacture carried on is that of linen. There are 2 bleach greens in the townland of Tullyleggan ¹ in the townland of Desertcreat and 2 others (not now at work) in Donaghrisk and Edendoit. There is also in the townland of Gortindarragh a small tuck mill for dressing coarse flannel and frieze cloth.

Markets

The markets usually attended are Cookstown and Dungannon. The average prices at the present time are: of fine linen from 2 pounds to 2 pounds 15s and of coarse linen from 1 pound 4s to 1 pound 10s per web of 52 yards; flax from 5s to 8s per stone of 16 lbs; wheat 8s per cwt; oats 8d per stone; and potatoes from 10d to 1s per bushel.

MODERN TOPOGRAPHY AND SOCIAL ECONOMY

Villages and Fairs

There are 4 small villages within the parish viz. Grange, Tullaghoge, Sandholes and The Rock. A yearly fair is held at Tullaghoge on the 17th December and at The Rock on the last Monday of every month, principally for the sale of cattle and pigs. They are both free from custom.

Schools

A national school under the new Board of Education has lately been erected at the slate quarry. From 60 to 70 scholars attend, who pay from 1d to 3d each per week according to their means. There are several other private schools supported by the landlords for the use of their tenantry.

Places of Worship

The parish church is situated in the townland of Desertcreat. There is a meeting house at Grange, another at Sandholes and a small one belonging to

Parish of Desertcreat

a society of Anabaptists in townland of Moree. A Roman Catholic chapel is situated near The Rock village in Tullyodonnell and a Roman Catholic altar at the slate quarry, where service is performed every second Sunday.

NATURAL HISTORY

Rocks and Quarries

The lower part of the parish abounds with limestone. Freestone is also found under the limestone in the Donaghrisk quarries and again near the Sandholes in townland of Skenarget. A freestone quarry was opened close to the river at Tullyleggan bridge, from which the stones were taken to build Tullyleggan House. The limestone does not appear to extend more westward than in the neighbourhood of The Rock.

There is a slate quarry in the townland of Bordahessia. The slates are raised in very large slabs from 1 to 1 and a half inches thick and are used principally for flooring. Slate is found all along the bed of the river as far as the tuck mill in Gortindarragh, where it appears to be of a nature better adapted for roofing. These quarries are not regularly worked.

PRODUCTIVE ECONOMY

Fuel

The lower part of the parish is not very well supplied with turbary. Where a townland contains a *great quantity* of bog, it is usually given free to the tenants; if only a small quantity, it is often let at the same rate as the arable land; and when none at all, the tenants are allowed to get it in some other part of the estate or must purchase it in the neighbourhood, at the rate of about 10s per rood for cutting and drying. Coals are burnt in most of the respectable homes, purchased at Drumglass in Coalisland at 5d per cwt as they are raised.

Manure

Lime is much used for manure. In the lower part of the parish it is burnt with coals and sold at 10d per barrel of 4 bushels, but in the upper part where turf is plentiful the limestone is usually bought at the pit at from 2d ha'penny to 5d a load and burnt at home.

NATURAL FEATURES

Rivers

A considerable stream rises near Craignaguiroe mountain, flows east through the centre of the parish and, uniting with another stream at Finvey, forms the Desertcreat river, which abounds with trout of a small kind seldom exceeding a quarter of a lb in weight. In this, as well as the Kildress river, mussels <muscles> are found containing very nice pearls. Some are really very handsome.

MODERN TOPOGRAPHY

Roads

The principal roads intersecting the parish are kept in tolerably good order, but the by-roads (or lonings as they are more generally called) are very bad indeed. Limestone broken small is used to repair the roads. It is easily procured.

Communications

The mail coach from Dungannon to Coleraine passes through Tullaghoge every morning at about 9 o'clock and returns in the afternoon between 3 and 4 o'clock.

SOCIAL ECONOMY

Inhabitants

The country is rather thickly populated. The inhabitants in the lower part keep their houses tolerably clean and appear to live comfortably. Towards the mountains they are very much the reverse but still are not so poor as their manner of living would lead one to suppose. [Signed] C. Bailey, Lieutenant Royal Engineers, 24 February 1834.

Office Copy of Draft Memoir

NATURAL FEATURES

Hills

The ground in the western extremity is of a mountainous character. The greatest elevation is 811 feet above the sea.

Lakes

Lough Bracken is situated on the north western boundary. Its extent is 27 acres 26 perches, of which 13 acres 3 roods 17 perches belongs to this parish.

Rivers

A stream rises in the western extremity of the parish and pursues a winding course in a south easterly direction of 7 miles. It is then joined by a larger stream from the south, with which it forms the Desertcreat river. The course is then changed to the north east till it meets the Ballinderry river in Killymoon demesne.

MODERN TOPOGRAPHY

Towns

There is no town within the parish but there are 5 hamlets viz. Milltown, Grange, Tullaghoge <Tullyhog>, The Rock and the Sandholes.

Gentlemen's Seats

Pomeroy demesne, Lime Park, Rockvale, Tirnaskea, Rock Lodge.

Bleach Greens, Manufactories and Mills

Bleach mill in Tullyleggan, bleach mill in Desertcreat, bleach mill in Edendoit, tuck mill in Gortindarragh.

Communications

The main road from Cookstown to Dungannon traverses this parish from north to south for 3 miles; also the main road from Stewartstown to Omagh which extends through the southern part for 9 miles.

Replies to Queries of the North West of Ireland Society by the Reverend Dr Buck, [1820s]

MEMOIR WRITING

Memoir Writing

Answer to statistical queries of the North West Society of Ireland by the Reverend Doctor Buck of Ballymully near Stewartstown.

NATURAL STATE

Locality, Incumbent and Proprietors

(1) Tyrone.

(2) Barony of Dungannon.

(3) Desertcreat <Dysertcreaght>, Reverend John Buck D.D., rector.

(4) William Stewart Esquire, resident at Killymoon <Killymoun>; Robert Lowry <Lower>y Esquire, resident at Pomeroy; James Lowry Esquire, resident at Rochdale; Robert Lindsay Esquire, resident at Lochry; Thomas Grier Esquire, resident at New Hamburg. There are several non-resident landlords but their properties in this parish are so small that they need not be specified in this report. 70 townlands in the parish, comprising at an average 80 acres each.

PRODUCTIVE ECONOMY

Agriculture

(5) From 30 acres down to 5. Mostly thorn hedges but in mountainy land, stone. Many of the occupiers are inattentive to the state of their fences. The spade husbandry mostly used in the planting of potatoes. The crops mostly in use are potatoes, oats, barley, fine wheat, a little rye, flax. The proper succession of crops is scarcely attended to, but in general after potatoes comes flax, barley or wheat and then oats or rye. The land capable of much improvement were a judicious system of management adopted.

(6) But little land appropriated exclusively to pasture, especially for fattening cattle which is mostly confined to the larger landed properties. Capable of much improvement.

NATURAL FEATURES

Mountains

(7) The mountainy townlands are Baradahissia, Edendoita and Limehill; mostly barren, some parts pasturable, a little arable.

Bogs and Woods

(8) No bog of considerable extent but several small ones. Some timber is found in them, mostly fir, at various depths but in general not very low.

(9) A few plantations of forest trees about landlords' houses, an oak coppice in Tirllarcevy. Orchards, nurseries are not enough encouraged by landlords.

(10) Larch, ash and Scotch fir.

PRODUCTIVE ECONOMY

Rent and Agricultural Improvements

(11) [Rents] Highest 2 pounds and 2 guineas.

(12) Value from 2 guineas to 1 per acre, annual rent. The majority of the tenants pay no rent for turf bog but have a certain quantity assigned to them rent free. But in many instances where this is not in the power of the landlord, the tenant is obliged to payment to some other landlord for occupation of turf bogs.

(13) Very little, however, though little some

Parish of Desertcreat

improvement (in all these particulars) has generally but slowly taken place for 40 years past.

(14) Sunk quickset <quickest> hedges seem best adapted as they furnish drains in wet ground and screens in high and exposed situations.

Employment

(15) At spring and harvest labourers grow scarce. Many are employed in the linen manufacture.

(16) Labourers engaged by the year can be had at 10d per day (without diet). Those not so engaged obtain highest wages.

Crops

(17) [Green crops] Only by a few gentlemen.

(18) [Grasses] Red clover and rye grass among the better order of farmers.

Draining, Manure and Agriculture

(19) Some surface draining, not considerable, still less underdraining; indeed, hardly any except by gentlemen.

(20) The better class of farmers and gentlemen make composts of clay, bog and with lime. The lower order of farmers burn clay and soil to a considerable extent, making large kilns (as they call them) of sods to which they set fire. This practice is considered disadvantageous as exhausting the ground for the future and not being so productive (for the present) as compost manure <manner>.

(21) [Irrigation] None in this parish, few in neighbouring parishes but not with much application.

(22) [Dairies] None, nor is it supposed they would succeed.

(23) [Oxen] Very little and those among the wealthy.

(24) [Spade tillage] Practised much in potato planting but even there plough tillage is beginning to gain ground.

(25) [Grain] Oats, barley, wheat, rye.

Land Units

(26) Various measures in different parts of this parish; the Irish are most prevalent.

Livestock

(27) [Cattle] The old Irish breed.

(28) Every sort usual in other <uther> parts of Ireland.

(29) [Sheep] Some few of different descriptions reared by the gentry, tolerably well adapted.

(30) [Horses] Various kinds: in general rather of a good sturdy kind.

(31) [Pigs] Varies, mostly of the Irish, long bodies and rather long legs.

(32) [Livestock] Pretty well stocked in every description, more so now than 4 years ago.

(33) [Improvements in breeding] Some little in all.

NATURAL FEATURES

Rivers

(34) One small river rises in the west end of this parish near Pomeroy and runs eastward, passes into Derryloran <Derrylorn> then into Artrea <Ardtrea> parish, then Ballinderry parish and falls into Lough Neagh. No loughs.

Mines, Quarries and Minerals

(35) [Mines] None in this parish.

(36) [Quarries] One, situated in the townland of Bardahessia. It was wrought between 30 and 40 years ago but did not prove successful, owing probably to want of skill in those who wrought. Many people think it would succeed if well sunk.

(37) [Limestone] Abundant, chiefly grey, some blue. NB The grey has been wrought as marble for house uses and with some success burned with both coal and peat. Sold at the kiln at from 12d to 1s 6d per barrel.

(38-40) [Coal, chalybeate springs, marl] None.

SOCIAL ECONOMY

Habits of People

(41) Not in general comfortable, rather industriously disposed, especially where encouraged by landlords. Money earned chiefly by the linen manufactures.

(42) In general, rather mean and shabby, especially the houses of mere cottiers <cotters> (who hold no land).

(43) Fuel in general not scarce. For the price of turf bog, [see] no.12. Pit coal in the neighbouring parish of Stewartstown is sold at 20s per ton at the pit. NB Coal is but little used among the farmers.

Food or Diet

(44-6) The hired labourers or weavers live almost entirely on potatoes and salt, perhaps in the summer season enriched with milk or butter. The middling farmers, besides potatoes, have stirabout and oaten bread for about one quarter of the year. The better class have it all the year round and now and then a treat of flesh meat, mostly poultry and bacon with cabbage and in the season, peas and beans. NB With us, the farmers are manufacturers and vice versa. The farmer carries on the manufacture by his children or by hired weavers.

Education

(47) There is a general wish for it not confined to any class. Poverty is the chief, perhaps sole, hindrance.

(48) It varies according to the matter taught. On an average, it amounts to about 20s per annum, rather under; 4 schools in this parish in which the rates are so low that the teachers can hardly make 15 pounds each per annum.

(49) [Improvement] As yet hardly discernible.

Health

(50) The people are rather healthy in general. Various diseases, however, take place among them here and there, the most prevalent (though still rare) *scrofula* <skrofula>, *cancer* and *itch*. Not being cleanly, they are very subject to catch infection of any kind, particularly fever.

MODERN TOPOGRAPHY

Villages and Improvements

(51) [Banks] None.

(52) 3 small villages or hamlets viz. Tullaghoge <Tullahog>, Grange and Sandholes. NB Sandholes so called as being built adjoining to certain gravel pits which the peasantry called "holes."

(53) The better sort of farmers who are at their ease as to pecuniary circumstances show a turn for improvement which would probably spread among the rest in proportion to the amendment of their circumstances.

Farmers

(54) Robert Lowry Esquire, Pomeroy near Dungannon; James Lowry Esquire, Rochdale near Cookstown; Thomas Grier Esquire, New Hamburgh near Dungannon; William Grier Esquire, Milton near Dungannon; Reverend M. Heron, Shivey near Cookstown <Corkstown>.

PRODUCTIVE ECONOMY

Linen Manufacture

(55) Rather increasing for the last 2 years but so little that it is hardly worth mentioning.

(56) 4 bleach greens are now at work in this parish and 1 idle. Bleaching in this country seems to be discouraged viz. the increasing export of brown linens.

(57) [Flax] It is generally (in this parish) sown after potatoes but our best judges prefer preparing the ground for fallow after an oat crop in a clay soil. The rough flax (stripping and dying) is partly manufactured at home and partly sold for other countries. Some little seed is saved but the best judges consider the saving it not to be beneficial.

Preparation of Flax

(58) By both; invariably dried by fire.

(59) [Quality of yarn and spinners' earnings] From 1 hank and half to 3 hanks per lb, from 3d to 4d per day.

(60) [Price of yarn] 2 hanks of yarn from 1s 11d to 2s 1d; 2 and a half hanks from 2s 2d to 2s 1d; 3 hanks 2s 6d. NB Very little of this, principally in home manufacture.

(61) Some grow it but more purchase it, i.e. all the farmers occupying 8 acres of land or more grow it and some of them even sell it; the rest purchase.

(62) [Double wheel] No.

Preparation of Yarn and Bleaching

(63) Most of them purchase it but not prepared for the loom. This they do themselves, boiling it in alkaline lye and bleaching it before it can be fit for use. Expense about 10d or 12d for the yarn of each web.

(64) [Yarn greens] None, but the establishing of them would considerably facilitate and improve the manufacture.

(65) [Quality of webs] A considerable quantity, from 4 hundred to 7 hundred wrought for half bleaching, the rest from 7 hundred to 11 hundred. Present price of 10 hundred from 9d ha'penny to 11d ha'penny per yard; 11 hundred from 12d to 14d; sold at the markets of Stewartstown, Cookstown and Dungannon.

Woollen and Cotton Manufacture

(66-7) [Woollen manufacture] None.

(68) Some wool spun merely for private use, small wheel.

(69) Some knit stockings but not for sale.

(70) [Shearing] No.

(71) Some inconsiderable instances of cotton weaving.

(72) [Cotton manufacturing] Not any.

Parish of Donaghenry, County Tyrone

Statistical Report by Lieutenant C. Bailey, January 1834, with additions from Draft Memoir

NATURAL STATE

Situation, Boundaries and Divisions

The parish of Donaghenry is situated in the county of Tyrone and barony of Dungannon, bounded on the north by the parish of Artrea and part of Desertcreat parish, on the east by the parish of Ballyclog and Clonoe parish, on the south by the parishes of Clonoe and Tullyniskan, and on the west by the parish of Desertcreat. It is divided into 52 townlands, altogether containing 7,154 statute acres.

PRODUCTIVE ECONOMY

Agriculture

The greater part of the parish is well cultivated and not much unreclaimed ground. The farms are small, containing from 6 to 30 acres Irish, which measure is made use of over the whole parish with the exception of a few new leases, and the land is let at from 15s to 1 pound 10s per acre; but in the immediate neighbourhood of Stewartstown it lets as high as 2 pounds 10s per acre. The soil is strong and good, resting upon a limestone rock. One ton of wheat, 50 bushels of oats, or 250 bushels of potatoes are considered fair average crops per acre; very little barley sown. Flax generally sown only in small quantities: a peck of seed will produce about 40 stone of flax. The markets attended for the sale of agricultural produce are Stewartstown, Coalisland, Cookstown and Dungannon. Lime is much used for manure and is easily procured in almost any part of the parish.

There are not more than 6 or 8 old leases. In any new leases the land is taken by the English measure.

Manufactures

The principal manufacture carried on is that of linen, which is disposed of at Stewartstown or the neighbouring market towns. There is a small tape manufactory in the townland of Sherrigrin which keeps 5 or 6 looms at work; each loom contains from 25 to 40 pieces of tape. A man may weave 50 yards a day (on each piece) and can earn from 12s to 15s per week and a woman from 8s 6d to 10s.

There is a bleaching establishment in the townland of Roaghan.

A large flour mill, a spade mill and a pottery are situated close to the town of Coalisland.

MODERN TOPOGRAPHY AND PRODUCTIVE ECONOMY

Stewartstown

The town of Stewartstown is situated on the eastern side of the parish of Donaghenry, about 6 miles from Dungannon and 3 from Cookstown [insert addition: on the mail coach road from Dungannon to Coleraine, about 24 miles from the former and 5 and a half from Cookstown]. It consists of 1 principal street (and a cross street called West Street) with a market place in the centre of the town. It contains about 1,060 inhabitants. A neat church, 2 meeting houses and a Roman Catholic chapel are situated within the town. 12 fairs are held during the year, viz. on the first Wednesday after the 12th of every month, principally for the sale of cows and pigs. A market is held every Wednesday, which is tolerably well supplied with all agricultural produce, provisions, cloth and yarn. The cloth market is very much fallen off of late years. It used to be very good indeed and now not more than a 150 or 200 pounds worth of linen is sold on a market day, which is considered very little. The Dublin mail arrives at about 8 o'clock a.m. and returns at 4 o'clock p.m. every day.

Table of Trades

[Insert addition: The different trades or callings in Stewartstown: grocers 5, publicans 13, bakers 4, haberdashers 2, apothecary and surgeon 1, tailors 5, boot and shoemakers 2, saddler 1, bible repository 1, painter and glaziers 2, wheelwright 1, delph shop 1, watch and clockmaker 1, hatters 3, reed maker 1, smith 1].

Public Buildings: Mills

[Insert marginal note: Parish of Aghenry] Shankay corn mill, 1 breast wheel which is 12 feet 8 inches diameter by 2 feet 2 inches in breadth.

Templereagh corn mill, 1 breast wheel 12 feet in diameter by 3 feet 2 inches in breadth.

Post

[Insert marginal note: Parish of Aghenry]

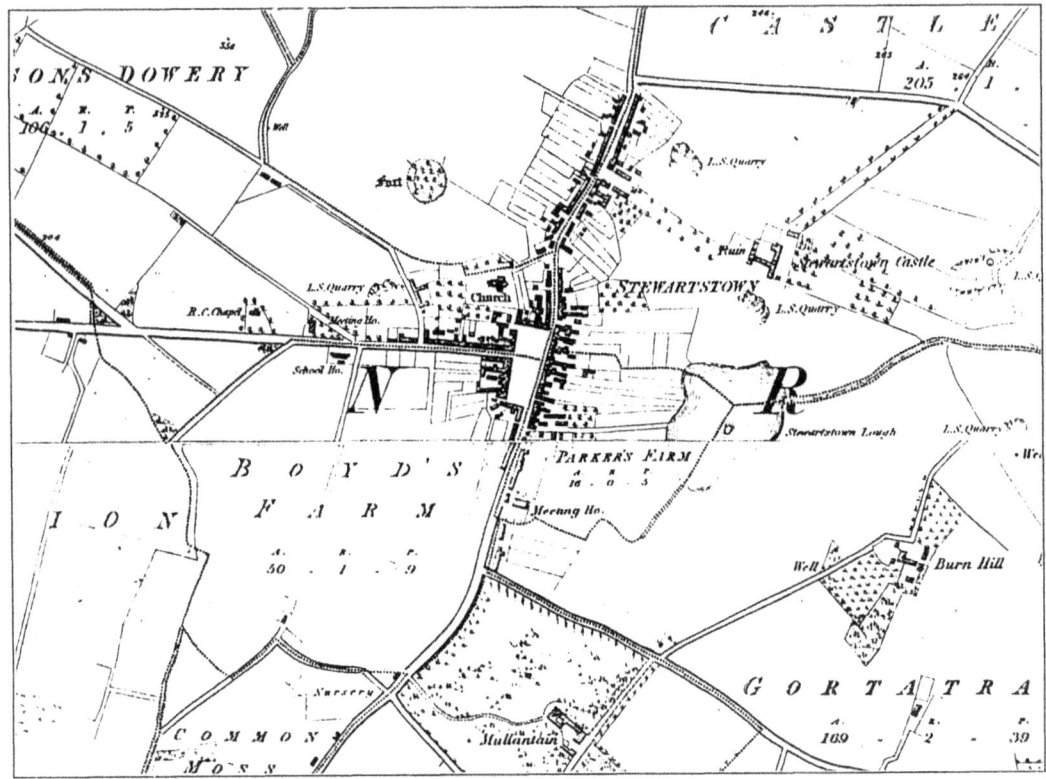

Map of Stewartstown from the first 6" O.S. maps, 1830s

Stewartstown post arrives off Dublin mail half past 8 a.m.; Coleraine mail delivered half past 4 p.m.

Public Buildings: Ecclesiastical

Stewartstown Roman Catholic chapel, established 1797, repaired in 1807, has no seats; contains 450 persons; parish of Aghenry.

Stewartstown church contains 240 persons in the body. There are 3 galleries: 2 of them hold 22 persons each, in the third, 50 persons; parish of Aghenry.

Coalisland

Coalisland is a small town situated partly in the parish of Donaghenry and partly in the parish of Tullyniskan <Tullaniskan>, and is connected with Lough Neagh by a canal which admits barges of 70 tons burden. It trades with Belfast, Newry and Portadown in grain, iron, timber and coals. A market is held on Tuesday and Friday of each week, for the sale of wheat, oats, barley and other agricultural produce. A cattle fair is held on the first of every month but it is not well attended.

Quarries and Coals

There are a great many limestone and several freestone quarries in the parish, with plenty of gravel and sand. Coal used to be dug in the townlands of Brackaville and Annaghone but the pits have been closed for the last few years. There is every appearance of coal in the valley between the townlands of High Cross and Sessia; indeed, some *carts full* have actually been procured there.

Communications

The mail coach road from Dungannon to Coleraine passes through the parish of Donaghenry.

A new line of road from Dungannon to Stewartstown, passing by Roaghan lough and thus avoiding several bad hills which occur on the old road, has been for some time formed but is left in a very unfinished state.

The roads are repaired with limestone broken small, which forms the most excellent material and is easily procured.

NATURAL FEATURES

Loughs

There are several small loughs. The principal one

Parish of Donaghenry

is called Roaghan lough, from its being partly situated in the townland of that name. They contain pike, eels, perch and some tench but no trout.

SOCIAL ECONOMY

Rectory

It is a rectory in the diocese of Armagh. The presentation to it belongs to Sir Thomas Staples and E. Caulfield Esquire, who appoint alternately. The Reverend Francis Gore is the present incumbent. The parish is under composition for 315 pounds per annum, exclusive of glebe land.

Inhabitants

The country is rather thickly populated and the inhabitants appear to be tolerably comfortable but not by any means rich. The greater number are Dissenters and very few Roman Catholics.

Fuel

The parish is not well supplied with turbary except the townlands of Donaghey and Sherrigrim. The tenants of other townlands procure turf here or at the Washing bay. Coal is much used, brought from Coalisland in Drumglass.

ANCIENT TOPOGRAPHY

Roaghan Castle

In the townland of Roaghan, and near the lough, are the ruins of an old castle (sometimes called Phelimy Roe's Castle), said to be a place of defence of the O'Neills <O'Neals>. There is nothing standing but a square tower with its corner rounded. It does not appear to have been a place of residence.

MODERN TOPOGRAPHY

Village of Donaghey

On the western side of the parish is situated the small village of Donaghey. 2 fairs are held in it during the year, principally for the sale of cattle, but they are not well attended. They take place in May and November. [Signed] Charles Bailey, Lieutenant Royal Engineers, 15th January 1834.

Office Copy of Draft Memoir

NATURAL FEATURES

Hills

This parish presents but little variety of feature, the highest point, Crew hill, being only 398 feet above the level of the sea and the lowest level, which is in the southern extremity, about 100 feet.

LAKES AND RIVERS

There are 3 lakes within the parish. Those at Stewartstown and Ardpatrick are inconsiderable. Roaghan lake, situated 2 miles south west of Stewartstown, extends over 50 acres 3 roods 13 perches.

Rivers none.

Bogs

There only remains about 300 acres of unreclaimed bog. This for the greater [part] is situated on the western side adjoining the parish of Desertcreat.

MODERN TOPOGRAPHY

Bleach Greens, Manufactories and Mills

The bleaching establishment in Roaghan, tape manufactory in Sherrigrin, pottery, flour mill.

Parish of Drumglass, County Tyrone

Statistical Report by Lieutenant G. Dalton, July 1834, with additions from Office Copy

NATURAL STATE AND NATURAL FEATURES

Name and Locality

The name of this parish is pronounced as it is written and I am not aware of any other modes of spelling it. It is in the county Tyrone and in the eastern portion of the barony of Dungannon; is bounded north and west by Donaghmore parish, south by Clonfeacle, east by Tullyniskan <Tullaniskin> and Killyman parishes. Its mean length is 4 miles and breadth 2, and it contains 3,506 acres, of which 3,459 are cultivated, 30 uncultivated and water 17; is valued at 431 pounds per annum to the county cess.

Hills

The hills are abrupt but not of great height, the principal ones being in Mullaghadun and Rossmore townlands. The height of the former above the level of the sea is 426 feet and of the latter 407 feet. A high point immediately adjoining the town is called the Gallows hill, probably from having formerly been used as a place of execution.

Lakes

There are 3 small lakes on the confines of this parish, none of which are of great depth. In one named Loughcullien, the townlands Killybrockey in this parish and Cullean in Tullyniskan parish divide. In the second, named Loughnacrilly, the townlands Kingarve, Cornamuckla in this parish and Gortshalgan, Killyman parish, divide. In the third, which is in the demesne of Lord Ranfurly, the 3 parishes Drumglass, Donaghmore and Clonfeckle divide. This last is an artificial piece of water formed by damming up the foot of a valley into which a strong stream from the north runs.

Rivers

A small river commonly called the Carland river divides for a distance of 1 and a half miles this parish from Donaghmore. It is seldom more than 40 or 50 feet broad, is not deep and there are not on this portion of it any mills. The parish is well supplied with water.

Bogs and Woods

A small patch of bog in Killybrockey townland is the only one in the parish.

Woods: there are none.

MODERN TOPOGRAPHY

Towns: Dungannon

At the southern extremity of the parish, and in the townland of Drumcoe, is the post and market town of Dungannon, considered the largest in the county. It stands on very high ground and on the south and west sides of a steep hill, having a square or diamond with 4 streets leading from it. In one of these stands the church, a modern building, the ruins of the old one with its graveyard being still visible about 1 mile north west of the town, in Rossmore townland. This graveyard is still used by the Roman Catholics and is the only place in the parish where they bury their dead.

In different streets of the town are a Presbyterian and 3 Methodist meeting houses, and in the eastern suburb a Roman Catholic chapel, a large and handsome building having a schoolhouse attached to it. A new and handsome court house and corn market have been lately erected and several improvements made in the approaches to the town, which, particularly from the south, are very steep and difficult.

The corn market is held on each Monday and is generally a full one, great quantities of corn being bought up for the distillery. The general market is on each Thursday. The quantity of linen sold at it formerly exceeded 5,000 pounds per week and does not now average more than 1,000 pounds. The first Thursday in each month is held as a fair, and there were formerly 4 registered ones which are not now attended. This change is deeply regretted by the inhabitants, the registered fairs having been very superior to the present monthly ones.

The town is governed by a provost and 12 burgesses, the former being annually elected, and returns 1 member to parliament. The post arrives from Dublin at 7 a.m. and starts for it at 5.30 p.m. It is conveyed by a mail which travels beteen Newry and Coleraine, being a branch of the Belfast and Dublin Mail.

Parish of Drumglass

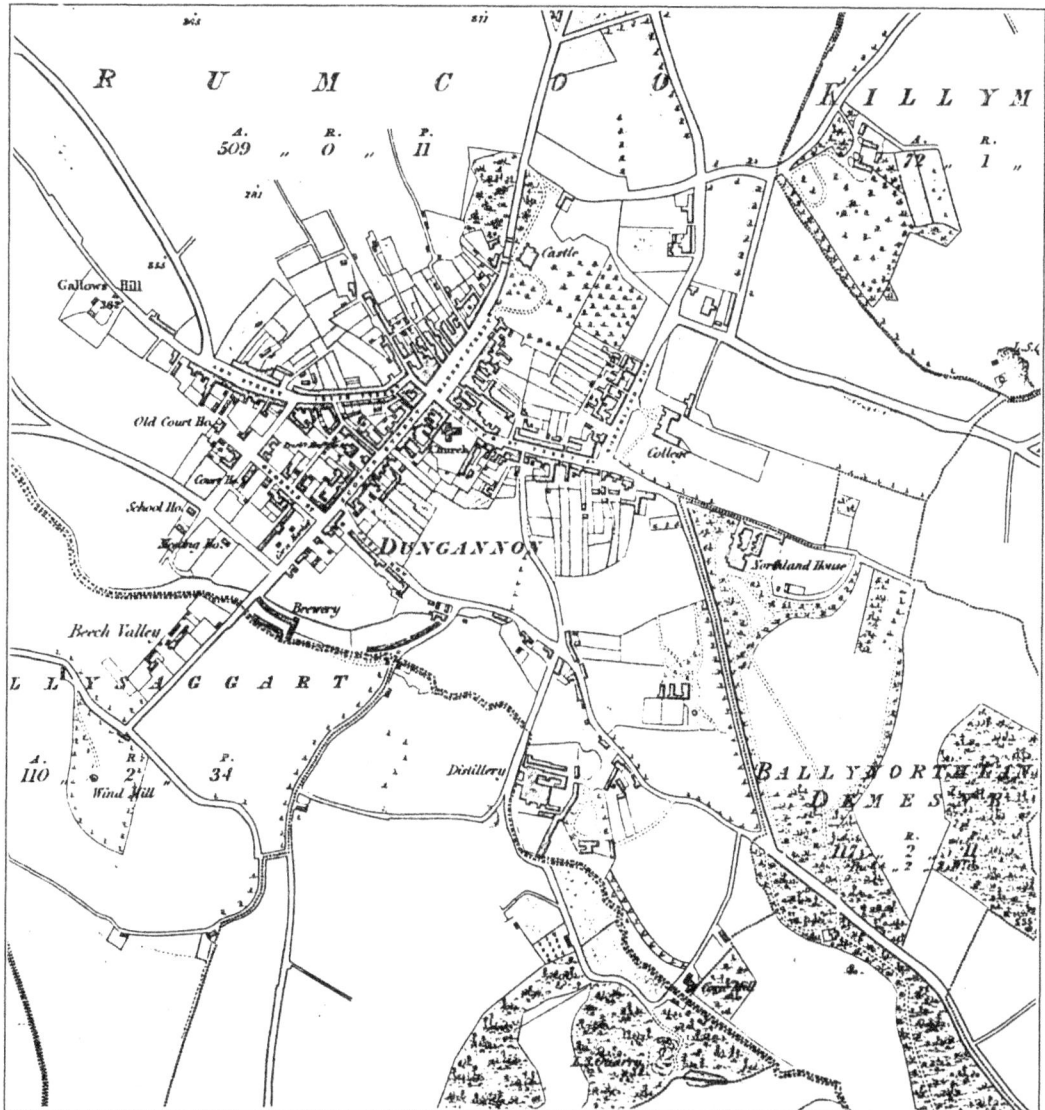

Map of Dungannon from the first 6" O.S. maps, 1830s

From the immediate vicinity of limestone quarries there are great facilities for building. There is a very extensive distillery at the southern extremity of the town, and at the eastern stands the college, one of the royal endowed schools of which there are several in the province of Ulster.

Dungannon Royal College

It is a large and fine building occupying, with its offices, gardens and grounds, about 9 acres. Several large townlands in Clonoe parish belong to and form its revenues. The lease of them has lately expired and they are now held by the Board of Education, who are making great improvements in them. The principal regulations of the establishment, the salaries of the professors and masters are subject to the control of this board; see House of Commons Report 1809.

History of Dungannon

On high ground overlooking the town, and near where Mr Hannyngton's house stands, there was formerly a large mansion house belonging to the O'Neill family and which had round it (probably erected at a later period) a large fort. It is likely that the town owes its origin to the protection afforded by this once powerful family. It was, even in the remembrance of persons now living, a very small and insignificant place, formed (with one or two exceptions) of poor thatched houses.

Gentlemen's Seats

Close to the south east [insert addition: north east] end of Dungannon stands [insert addition: Northland House] the mansion of the Earl of Ranfurly, a large, square but not handsome building. It has attached to it a fine garden and some ornamental grounds. It has also a beautiful demesne divided into 2 parts by the high road from Dungannon to Armagh, under which it is joined by a tunnel lately constructed. Near the offices is the dwelling house of R. Evans Esquire, and at short distances to the north of the town are the handsome and beautifully situated residences of the Reverend R.N. Horner and James Shiel Esquire.

Communications

The main road from Newry to Coleraine passes through the parish and also high roads leading from Portadown to Omagh. The cross and by-roads are not unnecessarily numerous. They are not kept in good order though the former are better attended to than the latter. All are in bad repair though there is abundance of cheap and excellent materials at hand. Collieries are situated on the first-named main road and it is injured by the quantity of narrow-wheeled carts constantly employed in drawing coal. The roads are repaired at the expense of the county.

SOCIAL ECONOMY

Local Government

There are 4 magistrates residing in the town of Dungannon and 1 residing in Coalisland, John Richardson Esquire, who is also seneschal of the town. There is a police officer, D. Duff Esquire, with a party of from 8 to 12 men, and the inspector of police for the Ulster district (Sir Frederick Stoven K.C.B.) makes it his headquarters. A manor court is held in the court house every 3 weeks. Quarter sessions are held twice a year and petty sessions every fortnight. There is a dispensary under the care of Dr Hamilton, the salary being 75 pounds per annum. It is raised by subscription in the place, subscribers being entitled to tickets for patients in proportion to the amount they give, the average number of which is 2,000 a year. The parish is not subject to any particular disease.

Schools

One Erasmus Smith's school; an infant school on the Wilderspin system; a school to which several tradesmen have subscribed to send their children; a Catholic school; a private school; also some very small ones; 2 Sunday schools, all of which are in the town of Dungannon.

Poor

There is in Dungannon a mendicity association kept up by subscription of the townspeople and from which several poor people have an allowance of from 4d to 10d weekly. The small sums collected at church are divided among the most deserving Protestant poor at Easter and Christmas.

Religion

The people are Catholics, Protestants and Presbyterians, the former being the most numerous, and in the town are several Methodists.

Habits of the People

The cottages are generally of stone or brick and are comparatively comfortable and good. The people are industrious and numbers applying for work assemble at an early hour in the morning in the diamond of Dungannon, and are called throughout the place "corner men." The common rate of wages is 1s for men and 4d for women, mowers getting 2s 6d. The custom of Beal Tine prevails through the country.

Emigration

Emigration to America prevails, but not to any considerable extent. Several families and also single men go annually to England to assist in the harvest, as also to Scotland.

PRODUCTIVE ECONOMY

Spinning and Weaving

Hand-spinning and weaving is carried on by the cottagers and though for some years back it has much declined, it has of late improved again. This probably arises from the duty with America being taken off.

Parish of Drumglass

Fairs and Markets

The only ones are those before-mentioned as being held in the town.

Rural Economy

The principal proprietors are the Earl of Ranfurly, James Irwin Esquire and the Reverend James Davis. The first and last of these are non-resident, having agents residing in Dungannon who are paid a percentage on the receipts. [?] Calumb Stronge Esquire, also a magistrate, holds this situation for the Earl of Ranfurly and Andrew Morton Esquire for the Reverend James Davis.

There is much clay, particularly in the southern parts of the parish, the northern parts containing much of a light gravelly and sandy nature with some portions of good land. The principal crops are oats, potatoes, barley, wheat and very little flax, both some years ago cultivated more extensively. The clay lands produce good wheat which as well as barley is more sown than formerly. For both there is a ready sale in the neighbouring markets and the latter has proved the most beneficial crop to the farmer during the past year. There are some fine meadows in the southern part of the parish and in the vicinity of Dungannon. The farms are generally small, the common size being from 6 to 12 acres, though a few richer farmers hold from 20 to 30 acres. The land lets at a high rate, the general average being 25s per English acre. This does not include the land in the immediate vicinity of Dungannon, which is let by the Earl Ranfurly as townparks, at from 2 pounds to 3 pounds per acre.

Large quarries close to and on each side of Dungannon produce a quantity of excellent lime, which is sold at from 8d to 10d for the 4-bushel barrel and is of great use on the clay lands and in reclaiming bog; the consumption has of late years increased. The town of Dungannon furnishes a quantity of manure for the neighbouring farms, a proportion of which land is annually set [let] to the poorer classes for the cultivation of potatoes and also sometimes for flax.

Cattle

The common Irish breed prevails, and some of the better sort of people have Ayrshire and Devon cows, though the pastures are not reckoned sufficiently rich for the latter. Few, if any, good horses are bred in this parish, in which are great numbers of asses and goats. The breed of pigs has much improved of late years, the people beginning to find the advantage of getting the Cavan sort, as introduced there by Lord Farnham, and which are in fact the Berkshire breed. They are much more easily fed and fattened than the old Irish pig.

Turbary and Coals

The parish is plentifully supplied with bogs in the adjoining parishes of Killyman, Donaghmore and Pomeroy, and coals from the pits in Killybrockey townland are both cheap and abundant.

Quarries

There are large limestone quarries in the western and southern parts of the parish, and freestone more to the northward.

Coal Mines

There is an extensive coalfield in this parish, the principal mine being in Killybrockey townland. It is worked with activity and supplies a large tract of country with good coal at a low rate, being sold at the pit mouth at 9s 2d a ton. The principal pit is worked with 2 steam engines, the largest being employed in clearing it of water and the smaller one in raising coal. The first is 70 and the latter 30 horsepower. The depth from the surface to the top of the coal is 128 yards, the seam is 4 feet high, with a parting in it of slate or clearing 12 inches thick, leaving in it about 3 feet of pure coal.

About the year 1760 a civil engineer named Greatorix stated to a committee of the Irish House of Commons that this coalfield was of sufficient extent to supply Dublin for 60 years, and on this report they subsequently granted the sum of 200,000 pounds to form a ship canal from the colliery to Dublin, taking advantage of Lough Neagh and the coast. The plan and estimates for this canal by Mr Omer may be seen on the journals of the House. It was commenced but was never completed. At a later period Ducart, an Italian engineer, projected a canal from the colliery to Coalisland, having instead of locks, sleds or inclined plains with rollers, by means of which the empty vessel proceeding to the pit was with some slight mechanical assistance drawn up by the full one leaving it. He obtained a considerable grant from the House to enable him to put his plan into execution and the unfinished remains of it, principally in Tullyniskan parish, are still to be seen.

General Remarks

This small parish, generally speaking, is in a high state of cultivation. There is hardly any moor or waste land in it and there is, year by year, an improvement taking place in the management of farms, particularly in the course and system of crops, in draining, fencing and above all in the increased value now set on manure. Plenty of lime may be had at a very cheap rate and the farmers are daily becoming more convinced of its use. Green crops are more attended to than they formerly were and instances occur of farmers reading and following several of the instructions given in pamphlets on agriculture and farming. There is much clay land, but where lime is judiciously used it produces excellent wheat; and this crop is more in request than formerly. The abundance of coal affords facility for manufacturing industry.

SOCIAL ECONOMY

Ecclesiastical Summary

[Table] name Drumglass, diocese Armagh, province Armagh, a rectory, is not a union; patron the Archbishop of Armagh, incumbent the Reverend R.N. Horner; extent of glebe: in Drumglass 55 acres, in Donaghmore 352 acres; the tithes belong to the rector: they are compounded for under the Tithe Composition Act for 200 pounds sterling per annum. [Signed] George Dalton, Lieutenant Royal Engineers, 21 July 1834.

Office Copy of Draft Memoir

NATURAL FEATURES

Hills

The hills are in general steep but not high. The principal points are Mullaghdrin, 426 feet, Rossmore, 407 feet, Congo, 352 feet and Gallows hill on the north west side of Dungannon, 382 feet above the level of the sea.

Lakes

There are 2 lakes on the confines of the parish, viz. Loughnacrilly, extending over 21 acres 1 rood 34 perches, of which 6 acres 3 roods 18 perches belong to Drumglass parish. There is also an artificial pond on Lord Ranfurly's <Ranfarly's> demesne, the extent of which exceeds 9 acres.

Loughcullien, situate on the north east boundary, extends over 8 acres 3 roods 15 perches, 5 acres 31 perches of which is in this parish.

Rivers

A stream running from west to east, the breadth of which varies from 40 to 50 feet, bounds the parish on the north west for 1 and a half miles. It is known in different parts of its course as the Carland, the Farlough and the Torrent river.

MODERN TOPOGRAPHY

Towns: Dungannon

The town of Dungannon is situated on the southern and western sides of a steep hill on the south western boundary of the parish. It is 96 miles from Dublin, 14 from Armagh, 11 from Cookstown and 28 from Omagh. On the high ground to the north of the town there was formerly a large mansion house surrounded by a fort, belonging to the O'Neills. The origin of the town is attributed to the protection afforded by this ancient and once powerful family. The fortress was demolished by the parliamentary forces in 1641.

Buildings

Its public buildings are a church, 1 Presbyterian and 3 Methodist meeting houses, a Roman Catholic chapel, a college, a port house, a barrack and a market house.

Dungannon College

The college is a large fine building occupying, with offices and gardens, 9 acres 16 perches. It is endowed with land situated about 5 miles from the town, containing above 1,600 English acres, the leases of which have lately expired, and they are now held by the Board of Education.

PRODUCTIVE ECONOMY

Markets

There is a general market held on Thursdays. The average value of the linen sold on each market day is about 1,000 pounds. A corn market is held on every Monday, which is in general largely supplied. The distillers are the principal purchasers.

NATURAL FEATURES

Bogs

There are 5 small fields of bog in the northern part of the parish, the total area amounting to about 30 acres.

MODERN TOPOGRAPHY

Manufactories and Mills

The distillery, the brewery, coal mines.

Parish of Drumglass

Communications

The mail coach road from Newry to Coleraine traverses the parish for 3 miles, and the main road from Portadown to Omagh for 2 and a quarter miles. The by-roads are not too numerous but all are in bad order, although the materials necessary for repairing them are abundant and cheap. The number of narrow-wheeled cars which ply from and to the collieries cause the roads in this neighbourhood to wear out very rapidly.

Parish of Errigal Keerogue, County Tyrone

Draft Memoir by G. Scott

NATURAL FEATURES

Hills

Shantavny mountain is the highest point in this parish. It is 1,035 feet above the level of the sea. The principal point on this mountain is almost in the centre [crossed out: of the parish], from which, to the south of the parish, there is a long steep fall for the distance of 1 mile or 1 mile and a half; after which, to the more southern point, the ground is low, consisting of those small round sandhills so characteristic of the south east of this county. The more northern portion is a large top, covered with broken hills of various lengths.

Lakes

In this parish there is half of a small lake and a few others of very little importance on the higher ground, formed in hollows at the base of the hills that cover the large top.

Rivers and Springs

The mountain streams are few and none of any consequence. For information respecting the sulphuric spring, vide Statistical Account of this parish.

Bogs

There is a considerable portion of bog at the northern part of the parish, at [blank] height above the level of the sea, the nearest river the Blackwater. There is not very much timber found in this bog. There are not any artificial mounds but numerous small hills, frequently cultivated or partly so. This bog supplies most of the adjoining county.

Woods and Coast

There are not any natural woods in this parish, but young plantations are rather numerous.
   Coast none.

Zoology

Eels are sometimes taken in the small lakes about this country.

MODERN TOPOGRAPHY

Public Buildings

The church, meeting house, Catholic chapel.

Church

The church is situated a short distance from the town. It is exceedingly small: would accommodate 458 persons. About one-third of that number are generally in attendance. It was erected in 1830. It is a plain building with 6 spiral pillars in the front and not any in the rear, which gives it an unfinished appearance. The interior is neatly fitted up. The communion table faces the north. It cost 950 pounds, being a grant from Board of First Fruits.

Presbyterian Meeting House

A square plain building and not the slightest ornament. It could contain [blank], average number in attendance [blank].

Chapel

A long narrow building situated 2 miles from the town. It is a little off of a country road in the townland of [blank]. It is surrounded with trees and could scarcely be recognised as a place of worship.

Gentlemen's Seats

Ballygawley House, the residence of Sir H. Stewart.

Communications

The main road to Omagh passes through this parish for the distance of 6 miles; the main road to Augher for 2 and a half miles; the main road to Aughnacloy for a quarter of a mile. The main road to Omagh and Aughnacloy is kept in very good repair at the expense of the county. The road to Augher is not near so good. The crossroads are not unnecessarily numerous; they are kept in pretty good repair.
   Ancient: for information, vide Statistical Memoir of this parish.

General Appearance and Scenery

The general character of the country is fertile. The mountain slope is cultivated to the top and the large plantation in the rear of Sir H. Stewart's, winding up the top of the mountain, affords a strong relieve to the low ground. To view this country from the upper ground the sandhills are reduced nearly to a flat, slightly undulated, weaving to and fro with the richest crops.

Social Economy and Modern Topography

Habits of the People

The cottages are small throughout the parish, generally consisting of 2 rooms, not very clean. There are mostly a few trees round each, thatched, 1-storey, windows broken, their only fuel turf. Their only amusement appears to be playing musical instruments. In the evening it is very common throughout the parish to hear some person playing the clarinet <clarionet>, flute, pipe or drum. The persons living in the country seem to think that when the crops are down they have performed all the requisite services for the season and few, if any, endeavour to improve the external appearance of their cottages. Gaps in hedges, instead of having gates, are most commonly filled with a few bushes.

Towns: Ballygawley

Ballygawley, a small village on the main road between Dublin and Derry. It is on a small hill sufficient to drain off the water. It is rather clean. There is not any public building in the town, or any ornament whatever. The houses are mostly slated, 2-storeys high. The only commerce is within itself. There is 1 very good hotel, chiefly supported by the posting. This town is a very great thoroughfare <throughfare> to Omagh and Derry. The post leaves this for Dublin at a quarter past 8 p.m. and arrives here at 6 a.m. The northern letters leaves here at 6 a.m. and arrives here at a quarter past 8 p.m. This town is not paved or lighted.

Local Government

There are 2 magistrates, both residing a short distance from the town. They are not stipendiary; the usual force of police [?] 6. Petty sessions are held here the first Monday in every fortnight. There are not any other courts held here. The number of outrages are very few. There was illicit distilling carried on in this parish some time ago. Lately it has not been carried on, in consequence of the revenue having seized the casks. The houses are not insured.

Dispensaries

Information could not be obtained, the doctor not being in the country.

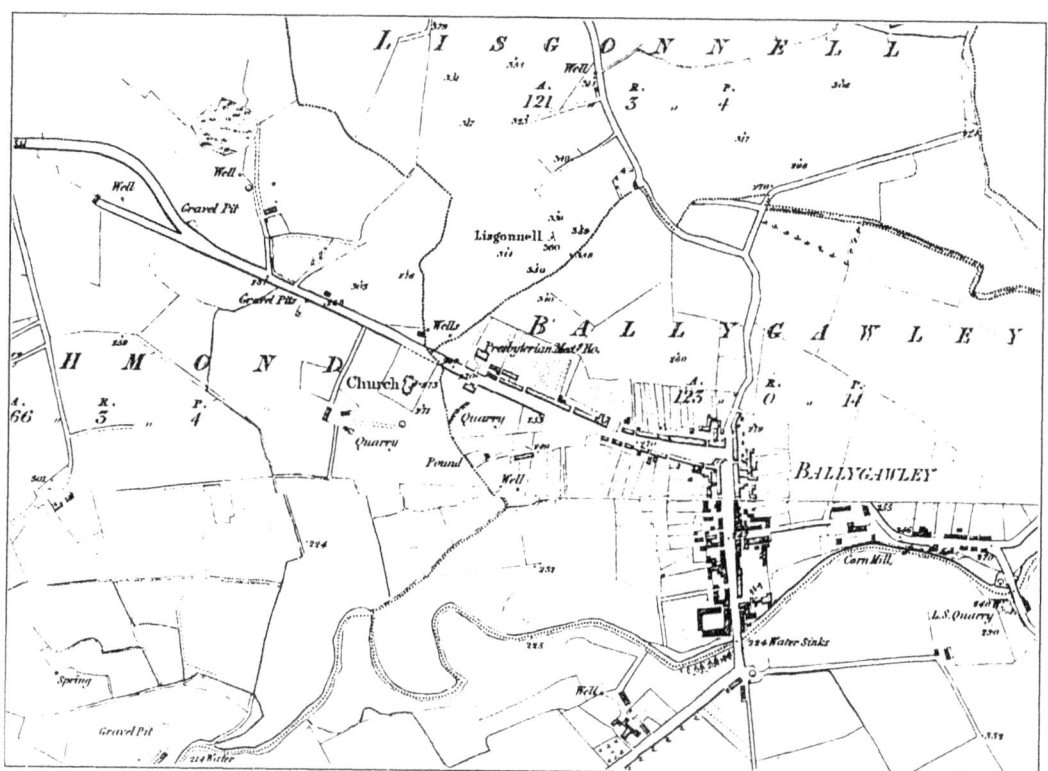

Map of Ballygawley from the first 6" O.S. maps, 1830s

Poor

There does not appear to be any permanent provision for the poor, but a number of beggars come into the town every Saturday and are relieved by the shopkeepers.

Religion

The principal religion appears to be Catholic <Chatholic>.

Schools

[Table contains the following headings: townland, number of pupils subdivided by religion and sex, religion of master, how supported].

[Name blank] Protestants 8, Presbyterians 5, Catholics 44, boys 26, girls 31, total 57; master a Catholic. The master receives 4 pounds from Board of Education and from 1s to 2s 6d per quarter from children, [established] 1833.

[Name blank] Protestants 11, Catholics 69, boys 42, girls 38, total 80; master a Catholic. This school is supported the same as above, [established] 1833.

Trades and Occupations

Grocers 6, whiskey shops 12, cloth merchant 1, bakers 3, butcher 1, innkeeper 1, milliners 2, smith 1, reedmakers 2, houses of entertainment for the poorer classes 6, bonnetmaker 1, shoemakers 2, tailors 2, leather-cutters 3, carpenters 2, wheelwrights <rights> 2, saddler 1.

Notebook by Lance-Corporal H. Trimble, March and April 1834

TOWNLAND DIVISIONS

Altnagore

Townland of Altnagore: landlord Sir Hugh Stewart M.P., agent Marbel Mann. On the north side of the townland is mountain, a few patches of cultivated ground. The south and centre of townland is arable and well cultivated. Average rent per acre is from 25s to 35s, soil very good. The ground is chiefly manured by lime. Turbary very scarce. March 20th 1834.

Ballylagan, Rougan and Keady

Townlands of Ballylagan and Rougan: landlady Widow Leslie <Lasley> of Glaslough <Glasslough>, agent William Murdock of Glaslough. The above townland is remarkable good ground in general, turbary plenty. Average rent per acre 32s, rent is chiefly made by oats and butter.

Townland of Keady: landlord Edward Moore of the Bann <Ban>, no agent. The above townland is of the same description as that of Ballylagan and Rougan.

Ballynasaggart

Townland of Ballynasaggart: landlord John Moutray Esquire, agent John Dale of Augher. The above townland is good ground, average rent 28s per acre. There is a church and schoolhouse in the above townland, average number of scholars 70, both male and female. Rent is chiefly made by oats and butter.

Crew

Townland of Crew: landlord John Moutray Esquire, agent John Dale of Augher. The above townland is chiefly cultivated, soil good. Inhabitants pretty wealthy. Average rent 32s per acre. Rent is chiefly made by butter, pigs and corn.

The townlands of Tullybryan, Carran, Crossbuy, Drumcork, Ballnana, Rough Hill, Less and Lisnabunny: same description as the above townland of Crew; also same landlord and agent. [Signed] Henry Trimble, Lance-Corporal Royal Sappers and Miners, 1st April 1834.

Foremas

Townland of Lower Foremas: landlord Colonel Verner, agent Captain Crossley. The above townland is chiefly arable, farmers pretty wealthy. They in general consider the landlord very considerate, particularly in reducing the rent so that the farmer can live comfortable and pay his rent. Average rent per acre from 21s to 28s; soil very good. Rent is chiefly made by butter and oats. April 2nd 1834.

Townland of Upper Foremas: same landlord and agent as [above], also same description.

Garveghey

Townland of Garveghey: landlord John Moore, attorney, Aughnacloy <Augoracloy>, no agent. The above townland is chiefly mountain, two-thirds reclaiming. In this townland is the Star bog, Star well and Star bridge. The reason of it being so called the Star bog is at the rebellion of Ireland the above townland was chiefly inhabited by robbers, and under the Star bridge was 2 of the

Parish of Errigal Keerogue

principal robbers' habitation, named O'Neill <O'Neil> and McDonnell <McDonnoll>. In robbing 2 cloth merchants by night McDonnell hid part of the money, unaware to O'Neill, in a well convenient to this bridge. When in the act of robbing the cloth merchant the night was very dark. A star appeared, which gave light so that McDonnell and O'Neill made off to this bog, adjacent to the old road leading to Omagh. That is the reason why the bog is so called the Star bog. Inhabitants very poor, soil poor. Average rent for what is cultivated 25s per acre. Rent is chiefly made by turf and potatoes.

Grange

Townland of Grange: landlord Mr Moore, Aughnacloy, agent Mr Montgomery. The above townland is chiefly cultivated. Farmers wealthy, in general yearly tenants. Average rent per acre 30s. Rent is made by oats, butter and pigs.

Letterry

Townland of Letterry: landlord John Moutray Esquire, agent John Dale of Augher. The above townland is entirely cultivated, ground very good, soil bare. Average rent per acre from 30s to 36s. The farmers buy their turf, no bog being in townland. Children is instructed in the national school of Ballygawley. The rent is chiefly made by corn and butter.

Lisnaweery and Cullenbrone

Townland of Lisnaweery: landlord John Moutray <Moutrey> Esquire, parish of Errigal Trough, agent John Dale of Augher, parish of Clogher. The above townland is chiefly cultivated, soil remarkable good, farmers wealthy. A new schoolhouse building on the west side of townland. Average rent 30s per acre. Rent is made by butter, pigs and oats.

Townland of Cullenbrone: same description, landlord and agent as above described. April 1834.

Lower Shantaveny

Townland of Lower Shantaveny: landlord Sir Hugh Stewart M.P., agent Marbel Mann. One-third of the above townland is mountain, remainder under cultivation. Average rent per acre from 22s to 30s. In general the inhabitants are wealthy, much better than the former townlands; turbary plenty. The rent is chiefly made by the farmers on the west side of the townland by turf, on the east and north side by butter, corn and potatoes. March 29th 1834.

Millix

Townland of Millix: landlord Colonel Verner, agent Captain Crossley, Aghnahoo. Two-sevenths of the above townland is cultivated. The mountain part of the townland is not rented by the acre but let in portions, from 4 to 6 pounds each portion, which is sufficient to keep 3 cows, giving potatoes and corn to the farmer. The lowlands of the townland is pretty good ground, soil very good; let by the acre, average rent per acre is from 20s to 28s. The farmers make their rent chiefly by butter, pigs and potatoes. March 18th 1834.

Richmond

Townland of Richmond: landlord Reverend James Graham, vicar, parish of Errigal Keerogue, agent George Wilcock, Dungannon. The above townland is entirely cultivated. Rent very high, from 30s to 38s per acre, soil pretty good. The farmers make their rent by butter, corn and potatoes. The townland of Richmond is glebe land. The children of the above townland is instructed in the national school of Ballygawley. March 28th 1834.

Tullybryan

Townland of Tullybryan: landlord John Moutray Esquire, agent John Dale of Augher. The above townland is entirely cultivated, ground extremely good, soil capital. Rent very high in proportion, from 36s to 2 pounds per acre, no bog. The children of the above townland is educated in the national school of Ballygawley. The rent is chiefly made by corn, butter, pigs, hay and potatoes.

Notes on Townlands I

Garvaghy, Altclogfin and Brackagh

Townland of Garvaghy has 7 different qualities of rocks and quarries, viz. sandstone, conglomerate. The chief and only manufacture is linen and labour; manure: mud, lime and dung mixed together. The soil is a cold, [?] mountainy and gravelly black and red clay. Produces corn and potatoes with a few fields of flax; proprietor Sir Hugh Stewart. Plenty of bog, the half is mountain. Leases of lives, and part of this townland for ever.

Townland of Altclogfin the same.

Townland of Brackagh the same as Garvaghy.

The north east side is a cold, uncultivated black soil covered with bent grass; proprietor Lieutenant-Colonel Verner; leases of lives.

Rarogan

Townland of Rarogan: the greater part is mountain. The cultivated portion is a light black soil, very poor. Produces corn and potatoes. Mr William Spear, proprietor. Nothing but labour. Dung, mud and lime; no leases.

Clananelly, Bloomhill and Kilgreen

Townland of Clananelly produces corn, potatoes and a few fields of flax, a very bad crop of either. The south east side of this townland is in a state of high cultivation, being the seat of Mr Spear, the owner of the townland. No leases, no bogs, a little mountain. Soil a light black clay towards the mountain, which part is covered with tumbling freestone rocks. It has 1 excellent limestone quarry. Proprietor Mr John Spear of Enniskillen.

Townland of Bloomhill is in a state of high cultivation, being the seat of Mr Simpson <Simson>, the proprietor; has no bog, has 1 excellent limestone quarry, light clay soil.

Townlands of Upper and Lower Kilgreen: the same as Clananelly, proprietor Mr Simpson of Bloomhill.

Fernamerna and Gort

Townlands of Fernamerna and Gort: the half is mountain, the other half is a very poor, light mountain soil covered with tumbling rocks of freestone and conglomerate. In Gort is the ruins of an old Roman Catholic church, built by a man the name of Saint Keeran. Linen and labour is the only manufacture.

Other Townlands

Townlands of Upper and Lower Foremas belongs to Lieutenant-Colonel Verner, part leases and part none. Chief manufacture is weaving and labour. A light black soil; mud, lime and dung for manure.

Townland of Dunmoile belongs to Sir Hugh Stewart. Plenty of bog. Produce: corn, potatoes, a few fields of flax; a light, black clay soil. Leases of lives. Manufacture and manure the same as Foremas.

Townland of Lurganbuy the same, belongs to Colonel Verner; the greater part is mountain.

Townlands of Altamoscan and Fallgherin the same. The people in all these townlands are in a despicable way of living, through heavy rent and cesses <sesses>.

Notes on Townlands II

Altcloghfin

Townland of Altcloghfin: a compact mountain townland, lying in the north west of the parish and about 4 miles north west of the town of Ballygawley. It is nearly 2 miles long from east to west and 1 and a half from north to south. About two-fifths is cultivated, the remaining three-fifths being mountain heather and bog. The surface is high, sloping westwards from the mountain, the highest point of which is 965 feet above the level of the sea. It lies north of the mail coach road, about half a mile from which it is traversed by a good mountain [road] leading to Sixmilecross. Another road from Ballygawley also leads across the mountain into the centre of the townland, where it ends. The soil is light and gravelly, oats, flax and potatoes being the principal produce. The inhabitants [are] poor small farmers. On the western [2 words illegible] boundary there is a corn mill and kiln.

Altamoskan

Townland Altamoskan, at the north west of the parish and about 5 miles north west of Ballygawley. It is a very retired and wild townland, two-thirds of it being wild mountain heather. The soil is light and gravelly. It is thinly inhabited, principally by small farmers; well supplied with fuel. Produces oats and potatoes, no wheat. 2 forts or mounds.

Altnagore

Townland Altnagore is about 1 and a quarter miles north east of Ballygawley, by the road to the nearest part of it. It is situated in the east of the parish. It is a long and narrow townland about 1 and three-quarter miles long and a quarter mile broad. It is principally under cultivation, but having some heathy and bog-land towards the north.

Anaghilla

Anaghilla, 177 acres 3 roods 21 and a half perches. There are several tracts of bog and marsh land in it. 2 forts and a small limestone quarry on the road to Augher.

Parish of Errigal Keerogue

Ballygawley

Townland Ballygawley: a Presbyterian meeting house, a corn mill and brewery. Townlands have been set off for a perpetual cure and a church recently built in the adjacent townland Richmond, close to the town. The whole of this townland is occupied intown parks by the inhabitants of Ballygawley.

Ballylagan

Ballylagan, 158 acres 2 roods 14 perches. An extensive bog on its western boundary, 1 fort or mound.

Ballymackelroy

Townland Ballymackelroy, in the north centre of the parish, is about 2 and a half miles north west of Ballygawley by a road direct to the mountain, the nearest point of the townland, at the Roman Catholic chapel, being about 1 and three-quarter miles. About three-quarters of this townland is mountain heather, all of which is in the north of it. Surface hilly and uneven, produces oats, potatoes and flax, soil inclined to be light. There are several gravel pits in it. Farmers are middling well-off, plenty of turf.

Ballynana

Ballynana, a townland of 201 acres 1 rood 22 perches. A large proportion of this townland on its western boundary is bog. A limestone quarry on the road to Augher and some fir planting.

Ballynasagart

Townland Ballynasagart, all under cultivation. Contains abundance of limestone which is quarried in several places. A new church has recently been erected in the townland, close to the site of the old church which has been pulled town. Contains 2 old mounds or forts.

Bloomhill

Bloomhill, a small townland of 74 acres 23 perches, farmed by Thomas Simpson Esquire, who resides in the parish. It lies on a gentle acclivity, sloping from north to south, and contains [blank] acres of fir plantations.

Brackagh

Townland of Brackagh: about 5 miles north west of Ballygawley on the mail coach road. It is hilly, sloping from the north towards its southern boundary. It comprises much rough pasture-land. The soil is light and gravelly, producing oats, flax and potatoes. Small farms, but the inhabitants and farmers are more comfortable than their north western neighbours of the mountain. The mail coach road traverses it in its whole extent for about 1 and a quarter miles. An old mound called the Hanging Fort, from its peculiar situation overhanging the mail coach road, is in this townland.

Carran

Carran, townland of 99 acres 1 rood 35 perches, all under cultivation. A limestone quarry on its eastern boundary, a fort or mound in its centre.

Cavey

Townland Cavey, a long and narrow townland situated in the east centre of the parish and about 1 mile north west of Ballygawley, on the mail coach road to Derry. In the northern extremity is some heathy and bog-land, the southern portion being cultivated. It contains an ancient fort, also a freestone quarry from which Ballygawley House was built.

Cleanally

Cleanally, a townland of 254 acres 31 perches. It is a compact townland about 1 and a quarter miles long and mean breadth three-eighths of a mile. Its general surface slopes from north at 690 feet above the sea to 219 feet [above the] water at its southern boundary. It is traversed by the old road from Ballygawley to Augher. Mr Spears, who resides in the townland, holds a large portion in his own hands which he farms. There is a corn mill and corn kiln near the road, belonging to the same person; see Field Name Book.

Coolagery

Coolagery, a small townland pleasantly situated on Martray lough on the east boundary of the parish and about half a mile north east of Ballygawley. Grounds have lately been laid out and planted for the site of a house by Captain Stewart, the proprietor, of which the stabling and outhouses only have yet been built. It is all under cultivation.

Crew

Crew, townland of 189 acres 1 rood 25 perches. Contains limestone which is quarried at the southern extremity of the parish. It is all under cultivation. Contains 1 old fort.

Crossbuy

Crossbuy, a townland of 95 acres 3 roods 17 perches. An extensive bog on its south western boundary. The new road from Ballygawley to Augher traverses it.

Cullenbrone

Cullenbrone townland, 324 acres 1 rood 15 perches, a rich and valuable townland in a good state of cultivation. It is well fenced, with trees very generally planted on the fences; a small plantation on the side of the road leading to Aughnacloy. Several brickfields and 2 mounds which are planted. At its northern extremity is an extensive bog.

Culnaha

Culnaha, a small townland on the western boundary of the parish, of 171 acres 36 perches. It is situated 2 and three-quarter miles north east of Augher and about 3 and a quarter miles west of Ballygawley. It is a straggling townland, of which the southern portion is all under cultivation. The centre is rocky rough ground with patches of reclaimed land interspersed. At the north western extremity it is also cultivated. The surface is hilly and the soil light, producing oats, flax and potatoes. There is a bog on its northern boundary which supplies fuel to the inhabitants; also a tuck mill for beetling flax.

Derrymene

Derrymene townland, 203 acres 2 roods 5 perches, a rich and valuable townland. An extensive wood at its southern extremity near the Blackwater river, a small bog at its northern end and several limestone quarries.

Drumcork

Drumcork, a townland of 87 acres 21 perches, all under cultivation.

Drumcullion

Drumcullion, 183 acres 2 roods 39 perches. An extensive flow bog on its eastern boundary. A country road runs through its centre, communicating with the farmhouses on its route. There is a fort at its northern end.

Drumnamitta

Drumnamitta, a townland of 112 acres 1 rood 1 perch, situated about 3 and a quarter miles north west of Ballygawley, on the mail coach road to Omagh and Derry in the centre of the parish. With the exception of 3 small patches of potato and oat land, it is entirely mountain heather and rough pasture. It is churchland held under the see of Armagh by Saville Spear Esquire.

Dunmoyle

Townland Dunmoyle, at the north of the parish, about 5 miles from Ballygawley. About two-fifths is mountain heather, the remainder is cultivated and inhabited by poor farmers. Soil and produce the same as Fallaghearn.

Errigal

Errigal, a townland of 570 acres 1 rood 6 perches, situated due west of Ballygawley about 3 miles and the same distance east of Augher. It is about 2 miles long from north to south and averages half a mile in breadth from east to west, comprising a large extent of mountain heather and bog at its northern extremity, interspersed with patches of cultivated land. Towards the south it is principally under cultivation, producing oats, flax and potatoes, the soil being light and stony. The northern and mountain portion is high and flat, lying between 600 and 700 feet above the level of the sea. From about the centre of the townland the descent is tolerably regular towards the south, from the trigonometrical station 676 feet above the sea to the southern boundary at 196 feet. There are 2 small mounds or forts towards the southern boundary.

Feddin

Feddin, townland of 119 acres 3 roods 22 perches; an extensive bog on its eastern extremity. Limestone quarried on its southern boundary. 2 old forts or mounds.

Fernamenagh

Fernamenagh, a townland of 103 acres 1 rood 15 perches, about 1 mile in length, its greatest breadth being little more than a quarter of a mile. Its surface is very uneven and hilly but the general slope is from north to south, the highest point, at the trigonometrical station, being 690 feet above the sea, 279 feet at the road near Bloomhill. At its northern extremity there is some mountain heather, the remainder being under cultivation. See Field Name Book.

Findrum

Findrum, a long and narrow townland in the east

Parish of Errigal Keerogue

of the parish, the southern and nearest point being about half a mile from Ballygawley. It is all under cultivation, with the exception of a very few acres of heathy land at its northern extremity.

Foremas

Lower Foremas, at the north west corner of the parish and about 6 and a half miles from Ballygawley. All cultivated, no bog. Contains a corn mill and kiln, 3 forts, a sandstone quarry. [Insert note: no.1 [Lower Foremas ?] about 3 and a half miles north to south, 4 miles east to west].

Upper Foremas, at the north of the parish and about 6 miles from Ballygawley. About two-thirds rough pasture and turf bog, the remainder is cultivated.

Fullaghearn

Townland Fullaghearn, at the north centre of the parish, about 4 miles from Ballygawley. A school (see account in Private Bremner's descriptions). A very wild and heathery tract of country, the cultivated portion in particular very hilly and uneven, about nine-tenths waste land. Soil light and gravelly; produce potatoes, flax and oats.

Garvaghey

Townland of Garvaghey: this extensive townland contains 1,533 acres 3 roods 35 perches; is situated about 4 and a half miles north west of Ballygawley on the mail coach road, which traverses its centre. It is of an irregular form, its length from east to west being 2 and a quarter miles, from north to south about 1 and a half miles. It comprises a large tract of mountain heather and bog-land, with patches of cultivated land scattered through almost every part of it. The soil is light and gravelly, with an admixture of red sandstone and sand which gives the soil a reddish tinge. Produce: oats, flax and potatoes. The townland is intersected by a small river to which the surface slopes on each side from north and south. A Roman Catholic chapel is situated in the centre of the townland and on the river a corn mill has recently been erected.

Glenchuil

Townland of Glenchuil, in the centre of the parish, is about 2 and a quarter [miles] west of Ballygawley by the mail coach road. About half of this townland is rough, heathy mountain land. There is 1 national school on the north side of the mail coach road, about 300 links after crossing the boundary between Sess Kilgreen and Glenchuil. The mail coach road from Dublin to Londonderry runs through the north side of this townland. The soil is light about the centre of this townland, but good and well cultivated at the east end. There is 1 ancient fort in this townland and one built lately and walled in.

There is a man buried <burried> in the latter. When this man, Mr Neely, died, he was buried in the old churchyard of Ballynasagart, but according to the accounts of the people he returned to his dwelling house several times; and, from a request that he had made before he died and while building this fort, that he should be laid in it, they thought it was from that he came back; and they afterwards removed him from the churchyard to the above-mentioned fort and he has not appeared since. There are several very respectable families in this townland [crossed out: and not poor]. It is well supplied with water. Some planting at the east end of the townland.

Gort

Gort, a townland of 297 acres 39 perches, situated about 3 miles west of Ballygawley in the west centre of the parish. Its length from north to south is about 2 and a quarter miles and mean breadth about 350 yards. It is principally mountain heather, very little more than a quarter being under cultivation, which is all at its southern extremity. The surface of the mountain portion is high and flat, of the southern, hilly. [The] soil partakes of the gravelly quality of the parish. The ruins of an old church of great antiquity are situated towards the south of the townland, of which the 4 walls only are standing. The burial ground is still in use by the Roman Catholics. A school under the new Education Board is situated near the old church. A good road extends in its whole extent along its western boundary. The mail coach road traverses its northern extremity and the road from Ballygawley to Augher communicates with its southern end.

Grange

Townland Grange, 338 acres 1 rood 36 perches. This is a long townland, traversed in a south west direction by the mail coach road and north east by the road to Dungannon. It is all under cultivation and is productive of all kinds of grain, contains abundance of limestone, contains 1 old fort.

Greenhill Demesne

Greenhill Demesne, in the centre of the parish and about 1 and a half miles north west of Ballygawley, on the mail coach road to Derry. Ballygawley House, the residence of Sir Hugh Stewart, M.P. for county Tyrone, is situated in this demesne, a large portion of which is occupied by the grounds and plantations surrounding it. The Roman Catholic chapel is also in this townland.

Half Town

Half Town, 76 acres 1 rood 7 perches. A small bog at its eastern end. There is a small school near the centre of the townland.

Keady

Keady, 212 acres 2 roods 32 perches; there is a large bog on its western boundary.

Kilgreen Lower

Lower Kilgreen, a small townland of 88 acres 23 perches, situated about 3 and a half miles due west of Ballygawley and 2 and three-quarter miles north of Augher. It lies on a slope falling from north to south towards a good road which traverses it from east to west. Its soil is light and gravelly and produces oats and potatoes. It contains a good deal of rough furzy pasture.

Kilgreen Upper

Townland Upper Kilgreen: a small townland of 73 acres 2 roods 15 perches on the western boundary of the parish. It is about 2 and a half miles north of Augher and 4 miles west of Ballygawley. Its surface is hilly, falling towards its river boundary on the west. The soil is light and gravelly and produces oats and potatoes. It is principally under cultivation but is intersected in the centre from north to south by a tract of rocky and rough pasture-land. It is traversed by a good road from north to south. It contains a small bog of about 1 acre. Proprietor Mr Simpson of Bloomhill.

Killymorgan

Killymorgan, a long and narrow townland in the east of the parish and about half a mile north of Ballygawley. It is 1 and a half miles long, its greatest breadth being about a qaurter of a mile. It is all under cultivation with the exception of about 1 and a half acres of heathy land at its northern extremity. It is well supplied with limestone for agricultural purposes.

Knockbrack

Townland Knockbrack, about 2 and three-quarter [miles] west of Ballygawley, thinly inhabited, only 4 houses in the townland. It is a small townland, about four-sixths of which are mountain heather, soil light. It is situated in the west centre of the parish.

Knockoney

Knockoney, a very long and narrow townland in the east of the parish, and about half a mile north of Ballygawley. It is about 2 miles in length and little more than a quarter of a mile broad at any point. It is principally under cultivation, there being some high heathy land at its northern extremity. There is a schoolhouse on a good mountain road which traverses the townland from north to south.

Lettery

Lettery, townland of 182 acres 1 rood 32 perches, all under cultivation.

Lisgonnell

Lisgonnell, a small townland lying north and close to the town of Ballygawley, all under cultivation.

Lisnabunny

Lisnabunny, 56 acres 3 roods 18 perches, see Field Name Book.

Lisnawery

Lisnawery: 96 acres 3 roods 30 perches, an extensive bog at its northern extremity. Its surface is hilly. A circular fort planted towards its southern end.

Lismore

Lismore, 311 acres 35 perches, a rich and valuable townland. At its southern extremity, on the Blackwater river, is a very extensive wood. An old square castle on the road to Aughnacloy, of which the walls alone are standing; a fort towards its northern end. All under cultivation with the exception of a small bog.

Lurganboy

Townland Lurganboy, at the north east corner of the parish, 4 and a half miles north from Ballygawley. Contains much mountain heather and waste-lands. Thinly inhabited, principally by small and poor farmers. A small school at the

Parish of Errigal Keerogue

north west corner of the parish. It is well supplied with turf for fuel.

Millix

Townland Millix is about 2 and a half miles north from Ballygawley and to the centre of the townland [parish], the nearest part being about 1 mile north east. It is a very wild mountain townland. For about 1 and a half miles from the north toward[s] the south is mountain heather. There is 1 ancient fort in this townland. The mountain part is moderately level but high, average height about 800 feet above the sea, and from the south end of the mountain it descends gradually towards the south extremity of the townland. There are several gravel pits in this townland. The inhabitants at the south are a great deal more comfortable and clean than those of the north of the townland. About two-sevenths of the townland are under cultivation, principally at the southern end of it, where limestone abounds and is extensively quarried. It is situated on the eastern boundary of the parish. It is 2 and three-quarter miles long and 1 mile broad on the mountain.

Rarogan

Townland of Rarogan: a townland on the western boundary of the parish, about 4 miles west of Ballygawley and 3 and a quarter north of Augher. It consists principally of mountain heather and bog-land, about a third only being under cultivation. Its surface is flat and soil light and gravelly, producing oats and potatoes. At the southern extremity there is a small school under the new Education Board. It is traversed by a good road from north to south.

Richmond

Townland Richmond, 266 acres 3 roods 4 perches. The mail coach road to Derry runs through the town. The new church built within its boundary and close to the town of Ballygawley.

Roughan

Roughan, 257 acres 3 roods 19 perches. Extensive bogs on its western and north western boundaries, a schoolhouse and 1 fort or mound.

Rough Hill

Rough Hill, 59 acres 2 roods 22 perches, a subdivision of Lisnawery. A marsh bounds its western side. There is a circular plantation in its centre and a corn mill at its south east extremity close to the river.

Sess

Sess, a townland of 70 acres 2 roods 32 perches. An extensive bog at its southern extremity.

Sess Kilgreen

Townland Sess Kilgreen is situated in the centre of the parish and about 1 and three-quarter miles on the mail coach road to Derry; 1 ancient fort, good land.

Shantavney

Townland of Irish or Upper Shantavney, in the north centre of the parish, is about 2 and a half miles from Ballygawley in a north west direction. About five-sevenths of this townland is mountain heather, the highest part of which is Shantavney, 1,035 feet above the sea, and the highest point in the parish. The cultivated part of this townland is pretty well inhabited [by] poor farmers holding small farms. It is well supplied with turf. The soil is of a light description. There is a very fine spa well towards the top of the mountain, about 3,000 links on the north side of the trigonometrical station and 1,200 links west of a small lough.

The townland of Scotch or Lower Shantavney is situated in the centre of the parish. This townland is about 2 and a half miles north west by west from Ballygawley. About a half is mountain heather and bog. The cultivated land is pretty well inhabited. There is a freestone quarry at the side of a by-road near the west end of the townland. The inhabitants seem to be a little more comfortable than Irish Shantavney, but not a school or place of worship in the 2 townlands. Soil is of a light and gravelly nature. There are several gravel pits in this townland, which denotes that the soil is gravelly as well as light. The produce of those 2 Shantavneys are oats, flax and potatoes. The farms are not small and the inhabitants are more wealthy than in Irish Shantavney; 1 fort. Nearly the whole townland lies north of the mail coach road from Dublin to Derry, which skirts its southern boundary in its whole extent.

Ternaskea

Ternaskea, a long and narrow townland in the east of the parish and about 1 mile north and by east of Ballygawley. It is a little more than 2 miles in length and its average breadth about a quarter of a mile. Upwards of two-thirds under cultivation, the remainder being heathy mountain land. It contains several gravel pits for the repair of the roads and abundance of limestone extensively quarried to the south, and 1 fort or mound.

Tullybryan

Tullybryan, townland of 150 acres 1 rood 28 perches. An extensive bog on its western boundary. All under cultivation. An old fort in the centre of the townland.

Tullyglush

Townland Tullyglush, in the north centre of the parish, about 2 and one-eighth miles north by west of Ballygawley: about three-quarters is mountain heather and the remainder very light and gravelly. Produces oats and potatoes. The inhabitants are few and poor and very badly clothed. Surface is not very uneven. It is a very poor townland. It is situated high on the mountain, the general altitude being from 600 to 800 feet above the sea.

Tullylinton

Tullylinton, in the centre of the parish and about 1 mile west of Ballygawley, on the mail coach road; 1 fort.

Notes on Townlands III, by Private Bremner

MEMOIR WRITING

Instructions from Lieutenant Stotherd

Bremner, you will get all the information you can from the inhabitants of the townlands you have been employed in, by order of Lieutenant Stotherd, Royal Engineers.

TOWNLAND DIVISIONS

Altamuskan

There are no public works on this townland. No place of worship with the exception of a Roman Catholic altar immediately on the mearing of Altamuskan and Fallagherin. The ground hilly and high, soil not able to carry wheat. The inhabitants of which are generally employed weaving, the greater number <noumber> of which are Roman Catholics.

Fallagherrin

There are no public works on this townland. There is an excellent <exlent> schoolhouse supported and built by the Misses Montgomery of Bath, the teacher's salary <sallary> very low, not exceeding 12 pounds per annum, together with about 1 English acre of very bad land. No place of public worship, the inhabitants chiefly Roman Catholic.

Lower Foremas

Townland of Lower Foremas: there is no public <publick> schools in the townland of Lower Foremas, or any public buildings. There is a corn mill and kiln. No place of worship, the inhabitants are generally Roman Catholics <Catholicks>.

Upper Foremas

There are no public works or public schools in this townland. The soil in general light, not capable of growing wheat, the inhabitants of which are generally employed weaving. The greater number are Roman Catholics.

Upper or Irish Shantavney

This townland, with the exception of cultivated patches, is chiefly mountain, but of such a nature that the greater part could be cultivated if money would be expended on this townland. Towards the top of the mountain there is a spa <spaw> well worthy the attention of the mineralogist. The few inhabitants chiefly Roman Catholic.

Townlands and Proprietors

[Insert addition: Parish of Errigal Keerogue or Ballinasaggart].

Altclofin, 225 acres arable, 336 acres mountain, Sir J. Stewart, resident.
Altnamuscan or Barnasroan, 200 acres arable, 68 acres mountain, [blank] Verner Esquire.
Anahilla, 80 acres arable, J.C. Moutray, resident.
Atnagore, 90 acres arable, 188 acres mountain.
Ballygawley, 60 acres arable, Sir J. Stewart.
Ballylagan, 81 acres arable, Mr Moore.
Ballymacelroy, 125 acres arable, 94 acres mountain.
Ballynard, 77 acres arable.
Ballynasaggart, 95 acres arable, J.C. Moutray Esquire.
Bracca, 200 acres arable, 60 acres mountain.
Carnan, 60 acres arable.

Parish of Errigal Keerogue

Cass, 37 acres arable, J.C. Moutray Esquire.
Cavey, 54 acres arable.
Cess Kilgreen, 36 acres arable, Sir J. Stewart.
Clenally, 100 acres arable, 46 acres mountain, see of Armagh.
Coolgeary, 84 acres arable, Sir J. Stewart.
Crew, 114 acres arable.
Crossley, 48 acres arable.
Cullenbrone, 180 acres arable.
Culnaha, 70 acres arable, 26 acres mountain, see of Armagh.
Derrymeen, 115 acres arable, J.C. Moutray Esquire.
Drumcork, 53 acres arable; Drumcullion, 85 acres arable, J.C. Moutray Esquire.
Dunmoyle, 183 acres arable, 101 acres mountain, Sir J. Stewart.
Errigal, 120 acres arable, 121 acres mountain, see of Armagh.
Fallagheran, 95 acres arable, 281 acres mountain, Mr Moore.
Fedden, 65 acres arable, J.C. Moutray Esquire.
Fendrum, 93 acres arable, 35 acres mountain, Sir J. Stewart.
Fernamenagh, 100 acres arable, 76 acres mountain, see of Armagh.
Foremass, 611 acres arable, 92 acres mountain, [blank] Verner Esquire.
Garvaghey, 218 acres arable, 419 acres mountain, Mr Moore.
The glebe of the parish of Errigal Keerogue, 155 acres arable.
Glenchull, 170 acres arable, 73 acres mountain, J.C. Moutray Esquire.
Gort, 40 acres arable, 80 acres mountain, Glebe of Errigal Keerogue.
Grange, 186 acres arable, Mr Moore.
Keady, 110 acres arable, Mr Moore.
Killgreen and Ragogan, 118 acres arable, 110 acres mountain, see of Armagh.
Killymorgan 115 acres arable, Sir J. Stewart.
Knockenny, 138 acres arable, 52 acres mountain, Sir J. Stewart.
Lettery, 100 acres arable, J.C. Moutray Esquire.
Lisgonnell, 62 acres arable, Sir J. Stewart.
Lismore, 200 acres arable, J.C. Moutray Esquire.
Lisnawerry, 125 acres arable, J.C. Moutray Esquire.
Lurganboy, 80 acres arable, 115 acres mountain, [blank] Verner Esquire.
Millix, 83 acres arable, 121 acres mountain, [blank] Verner Esquire.
Roghan Hill, 120 acres arable, Mr Moore.
Shantavney Uppertown, 80 acres arable, 400 acres mountain, [blank] Verner Esquire.
Tullybryan, 85 acres arable, J.C. Moutray Esquire.
Tullyglush, 150 acres arable, 40 acres mountain, Sir J. Stewart.
Tullylinton, 108 acres arable, J.C. Moutray Esquire.
Turnaskea, 122 acres arable, 53 acres mountain, Sir J. Stewart.

Parish of Kildress, County Tyrone

Statistical Report by Lieutenant C. Bailey, October 1833

NATURAL STATE AND NATURAL FEATURES

Locality

[Insert note: Addressed to Lieutenant-colonel Colby, Royal Engineers, commanding].

The parish of Kildress is situated in the county of Tyrone and barony of Dungannon, a rectory in the diocese of Armagh, the rights of presentation being vested in the lord primate. It is bounded on the north by the parish of Lissan, on the east by the parish of Derryloran, on the south east and south by the parish of Desertcreat and in the west by the parishes of Termonmaguirk and Badoney. [It] is divided into 57 townlands containing 26,251 statute acres.

Surface and Soil

It is a mountainous district, particularly the northern part of the parish which presents a very bleak and wild appearance. Large projecting rocks scattered over the surface and rising above the heather indicate a country little subject to cultivation. In the south east corner the soil is strong clay capable of producing wheat, but the mountain land is of a sharp gravelly nature yielding but very indifferent crops of oats and potatoes.

PRODUCTIVE ECONOMY

Agriculture

Not more than one-half of the parish is under cultivation. The farms vary in size from 3 to 20 acres Irish measure. Lowland lets at from 15s to 20s and mountain land at from 5s to 10s per acre, but if incapable of cultivation is generally let by the lump at about 9d per acre for grazing. Many farms near the mountains have a portion of unreclaimed land allotted to each for fuel and grazing, the size governed by the quantity of arable land.

Land Reclamation

In a great part of the parish such mountain ground as is capable of cultivation has been divided into farms of 20 acres, each free from rent for the first 3 years to cover the expense of reclaiming the land and of building a house, and at the expiration of that time to enter upon a lease for 21 years, generally at the rate of from 2s to 5s per acre. This requires a small capital which in some instances is expended before the land is brought into a state to make any return.

Crops

The usual crops are oats, potatoes and flax. Wheat is sometimes grown upon the best land. About 1 ton of wheat, 6 bushels of oats or 250 bushels of potatoes are considered fair average crops per acre on the lowland; the average mountain crops would not be much above half. Flax is generally sown only in small quantities: a peck of seed will yield from 3 to 4 stones of flax.

Manure

The land is manured with stable dung or lime mixed with bog; however, but very little lime is made use of in the mountains. It is usual for the inhabitants to take turf to Cookstown, a distance of perhaps 6 or 8 miles, and to load back with lime. The turf is readily disposed of at 10d per gauge, which will purchase a barrel of lime.

Markets and Fairs

Cookstown is the only market for all kinds of agricultural produce. Oats fetch from 6d to 9d per stone, potatoes generally from 6d to 1s per bushel, flax 5s per stone of 16 lbs. There are 2 fairs held at Gortin during the year, viz. on the first Monday after old Midsummer day and on the first Wednesday after old Hallow day, and another is held at Charlestown in the townland of Tullynacross on the first Monday of every month, both for the sale of mountain stock.

Manufacture

The only manufacture carried on is that of linen. A bleaching establishment belonging to Mr Irwin is situated in the townland of Drimleagh. A great many of the inhabitants derive their chief support from spinning and weaving. For the last few years linen has been selling at a very low rate, but just now it obtains a better price. It is disposed of at Cookstown and Moneymore.

MODERN TOPOGRAPHY

Roads and Communications

The principal roads intersecting the parish are kept in tolerably good order; they are repaired

Parish of Kildress

with gravel which is easily obtained. It is in contemplation to make a new line of road through Killucan and Drumshanbo and, passing by Oaklands demesne, to Cookstown, for the purpose of facilitating the communication between Omagh and this part of the country.

NATURAL FEATURES

Rivers

The northern extremity is bounded by the Broaghderagh river, dividing the parishes of Kildress and Lissan. There is rather a considerable river (called the Kildress river) which takes its rise in Camlough in the townland of Evishanoran, flows east through the centre of the parish, being increased in its course by several tributary streams, and eventually empties itself into Lough Neagh. It abounds with trout, and a few salmon run up during the spawning season and are frequently killed.

PRODUCTIVE ECONOMY

Quarries

There are excellent limestone quarries in Gortnagross and Lower Kildress. The lime is burnt with coals brought from Drumglass colliery, where they are purchased at 3d ha'penny per cwt and cost 3d per cwt drawing. The lime is sold at 10d per barrel. These quarries contain a great many fossil shells. A limestone quarry was opened in Tullyroan but it is worked out. Limestone is still to be found in that townland but it is not abundant.

Very excellent freestone is found in Lower Kildress. The stone used in building Oaklands House was procured from a quarry near the river in the north west corner of this townland. It is very white and is raised in large blocks. There is an indication of limestone in 2 or 3 places in Lower Kildress and in Oaklands demesne.

MODERN TOPOGRAPHY

Places of Worship

The parish church is situated in the townland of Clare. There are 2 Roman Catholic chapels, one in Killernan and another in Dunamoe. There is also a Presbyterian meeting house in the townland of Tamlaght.

SOCIAL ECONOMY

Inhabitants

The country is not thickly populated. The inhabitants in the mountains are for the most part Roman Catholics speaking the Irish language. They are generally very poor. [Signed] C. Bailey, Lieutenant Royal Engineers, October 30th, 1833.

Memoir by G. Scott

MEMOIR WRITING

Memoir Writing

Memo: A considerable portion of this parish in Mr Ormsby['s] district.

NATURAL FEATURES

Hills

The north and south west part of this parish is mountainous, with a very small portion of arable land. The few patches of land that are reclaimed appear only to produce bad crops, but to the more eastern end of the parish the ground is well cultivated and produces good crops. The mountains are large with long falls, the steep side being to the north.

Lakes

There are some small lakes throughout the parish which are of little or no consequence. The edges are generally marsh and difficult to be approached by cattle. They are but little use to the country people. As the water is mostly deep, it prevents their steeping flax.

Rivers

Killucan water takes its rise at the western end of the parish and is greatly increased by tributary streams. Its depth varies from 1 to 10 feet. The breadth is quite uncertain, as the banks are low. In many places it is broad, in others very narrow. In the winter season it overflows its banks but does [not ?] effect any serious injury, as the flats adjoining are chiefly kept for meadow.

Bogs

There is a quantity of bog in this parish but not much wood. The poor cottiers exchange a load of turf for limestone. The depth is generally 3 or 4 feet. The landlords mostly let the uncultivated mountain to persons rent free for the first 3 years, provided they build a stone house of certain dimensions and reclaim an allotted portion of ground.

Modern Topography

Public Buildings

Church, meeting house, chapel, chapel.

Church

A substantial building erected in the year 1818, cost 1,600 pounds granted by Board of First Fruits. It would accommodate about 400 persons. There are 350 persons generally in attendance; dimensions 60 feet by 30 feet. It is surrounded by a neat plantation.

Meeting House

Situated in the townland of Tamlaght: it is a plain neat building and of a better description than the generality of meeting houses. Erected in the year 1828, cost between 500 pounds and 350 pounds, paid by general subscription. It would accommodate about 250 persons, average number in attendance 180; dimensions 60 feet by 33 feet.

Roman Catholic Chapels

Situated in the townland of Dunnamore, erected about the year 1828, paid by subscription, cost about 60 pounds. It would accommodate 260 persons, the full number generally in attendance. It is a little off of the high road from Cookstown to Gortin. Previous to the erection of this chapel, service was performed at an old ruin of a chapel in the townland of Roisbrack.

In the townland of Killeenan: the date of erection, cost or by whom paid cannot be ascertained. It is supposed to be upwards of 150 years old. Service is still performed in it, but it is in very bad repair.

Communications

The following main roads pass through the parish: from Cookstown to Gortin 9 miles; from Cookstown to Mountfield 9 miles; from Cookstown to Pomeroy 1 mile. The road from Cookstown to Gortin and Pomeroy is in good repair, average breadth 34 feet. The other road from Cookstown to Mountfield has of late been greatly improved, in consequence of its being the intended road for the new coach to run upon from Cookstown to Omagh, average breadth 44 feet.

General Appearance and Scenery

Ancient: none.

The eastern end of the parish is well cultivated, produces good oats and other crops. The scenery is mountainous and the northern and western part of the parish is a large tract of wild mountain, with nothing but a few miserable cabins and small patches of cultivated ground to relieve it.

Social Economy

Habits of the People

The cottages throughout the country are generally made of stone cemented with lime. In the lower end of the parish they are mostly clean and in many cases surrounded with trees. They have 2 or more windows with good panes of glass in them. In the wild part of this parish the landlords, in order to get good houses on their estates, give the uncultivated land rent free for 3 years, provided they build a good stone house of such dimensions that may be agreed upon.

Religion

The majority of persons in this parish appear to be Catholics.

Schools

[Table contains the following headings: townland, number of pupils subdivided by religion and sex, religion of master, how supported, when established].

Killeenan: Protestants 4, Catholics 62, boys 48, girls 18, total 66; master a Catholic, receives 1d per week from each scholar; established 1827.

Tamlaght: Protestants 19, Catholics 31, boys 27, girls 23, total 50; master a Catholic; supported solely by the children, the master receives 1d a week from each; established 1830.

Productive Economy

Mills

In the townland of Corkhill there are mills belonging to S. Gorring. Diameter 20 feet, breadth of wheel 4 feet, overshot wheel, fall of water 4 feet. There are 3 others belonging to the same person, same dimensions, in the adjoining townland of Wellbrook.

In the townland of Derryseele there is a mill belonging to Mr Guick. Dimensions of wheel 14 feet, breadth 2 and a half feet, fall of water 8 feet, breast wheel.

Office Copy of Memoir

Natural Features

Hills

The most elevated points within this parish are in

Parish of Kildress

the townlands of Ballynasolus and Beleernamore, situated near the northern extremity. The height of the former is 1,241 and the latter 1,253 feet above the level of the sea. The mountainous character extends from north to south, comprising the entire western portion. The average height of the eastern portion is about 350 feet.

Lakes

The north western part of the parish contains several lakes. The largest within the parish boundary is Camlough, which extends over 14 acres 1 rood 16 perches. In the immediate vicinity of Camlough are 2 other lakes which contain respectively 9 acres 3 roods 24 perches and 6 acres 2 roods 14 perches. Loughbracken, which is divided between Kildress and Desertcreat, extends over 27 acres 26 perches, of which 14 acres 1 rood 9 perches belong to Kildress. One-half mile northwards of Loughbracken is a fifth, the extent of which is 8 acres 1 rood 8 perches.

Rivers

The Owenkillew or Broaghderg river rises in the northern side of the above-mentioned mountain and flows in a westerly direction, forming the parish boundary on the north. It subsequently assumes the name of the Strule river and, uniting with the Derg, forms the Mourne river.

The Kildress or Ballinderry river rises in Camlough and flows eastward through the centre of the parish, being increased in its course by several tributary streams. It eventually empties itself into Lough Neagh.

MODERN TOPOGRAPHY

Towns, Public Buildings and Gentlemen's Seats

Towns: none; Oritor, a little hamlet on the eastern boundary; Charlestown.

Public buildings: the church, situated in the townland of Clare; the Presbyterian meeting house in Tamlaght; Roman Catholic chapel in Killvern; Roman Catholic chapel in Dunamore.

Gentlemen's seats: the rectory, Oaklands, Wellbrook.

Bleach Greens, Manufactories and Mills

Bleaching establishment in Drimleagh, the property of Mr [blank] Irvine.

Communications

The main roads of this district are those which lead from Cookstown to Strabane and from Cookstown to Omagh. Of the former, there are 8 and a half miles within this parish and of the latter, 9 miles.

Parish of Killeeshil <Killeshell>, County Tyrone

Statistical Report by Lieutenant G. Dalton, July 1834

NATURAL STATE

Name

The following are various modes of spelling the name of this parish: Killeeshil, county map; Killeshell, Beaufort's Map of Ireland; Killeshill, *Carlisle's Topographical dictionary*; Killeshill, *Irish ecclesiastical register*, 1824; Killishal, House of Commons *Report on the population of Ireland*; Killeshill, *McEvoy's Statistical survey*; Killishill, *McEvoy's Statistical survey*.

Locality

Is in the county Tyrone and western portion of the barony of Dungannon, is bounded on the north by Termonmaguirk <Tarmonmaguirk>, on the east by Donaghmore and on the south and west by Aghaloo parish. Contains 9,598 English acres, of which 7,200 are cultivated, 2,394 are bog and mountain ground, and 4 water. It is valued at 350 pounds per annum to the county cess.

NATURAL FEATURES

Hills

This parish is hilly and lies at a great height above the sea. The principal hills are in Cranlome townland, height 911 feet and in Ballynahaye townland, height 821 feet.

Bogs

There are several patches of bog used for fuel as well as a great extent of mountain ground, the edges of which are used for fuel and thus gradually brought into cultivation.

Climate

From the ground being high and on the side of a mountain district, the climate is cold and the different crops are ripened at least 1 month later than those in the eastern portions of the barony [insert footnote: which side?].

NATURAL HISTORY

Zoology

The mountainous portions of the parish abound with game, principally hares and red grouse which, however, are becoming more scarce as population and cultivation increase.

MODERN TOPOGRAPHY

Towns

There is no town or even village belonging to this parish and the inhabitants carry the produce of their farms to the neighbouring markets of Ballygawley and Dungannon.

Gentlemen's Seats

The only gentlemen's seats are those of Captain Crossley <Crosslee>, agent to Colonel Verner M.P., in Aghnahoe townland and the Glebe House in Killeeshil townland. Near the former are some small but thriving plantations belonging to Colonel Verner.

Mills

There are 3 corn mills in this parish, one in Mullyroddan townland, one in Ennish and a third in Farriter, on the high road from Dungannon to Ballygawley.

Communications

The high road from Dungannon to Omagh through Ballygawley traverses the parish from east to west for 3 and a half miles. It is in moderately good repair but is very injudiciously laid out, and its direction might be easily altered so as to avoid several of the steep hills over which it now passes.

There are also several by-roads, the two principal of which branch off north and south from the above-named high road and traverse the parish for a considerable length. They are, generally speaking, in good repair, being principally formed of gravel, in which the country abounds. These roads are also kept in repair at the expense of the county.

General Appearance and Scenery

The general appearance of this parish is that of a wild and open country with round bare hills having little or no wood, and the fields on them divided by low and broken hedgerows, whilst the valleys are generally patches of bog. This

Parish of Killeeshil

particularly applies to the centre, whilst the north is nearly all mountain heath and the south, which lies lower, is richer and better land.

SOCIAL ECONOMY

Local Government

Captain Crossley of Aghnahoe House is the only magistrate residing in the parish and there is a party of 10 of the constabulary force. Illicit distillation is carried on to a considerable extent among the uncultivated hills and the spirit is constantly offered for sale in Dungannon and Ballygawley.

Religion

The population is about 5,000, of which one half are Roman Catholics and the other half comprises all the different sects of the reformed religions.

Habits of the People

The cottages are generally composed of stone, there not being much clay land. They are of poor and uncomfortable appearance when compared with those of parishes in the eastern part of the barony. The custom of Beal Tinne prevails.

Emigration

There are, every year, some families who emigrate to America and also single men who go over to England and Scotland to assist in the harvest. It is not uncommon for a young man who has been fortunate in his service in America to send back at the end of a few years a sufficient sum to enable the rest of his family to join him there.

PRODUCTIVE ECONOMY

Hand-spinning and Weaving

Hand-spinning and weaving of coarse linen is carried on throughout the parish, but is far less profitable than it was formerly.

Fairs and Markets

There are no markets held within the parish. The inhabitants attend the neighbouring ones at Ballygawley, Dungannon, Clogher and Aughnacloy, and sometimes carry their linen for sale to Omagh.

Cultivation

Cultivation has much improved within the last 20 years and the farmers are beginning to set an increased value on manure and particularly on lime, in the use of which the landlords of those townlands which are partly cultivated and partly mountain heath are giving some assistance, by either giving it to their tenants or allowing them to purchase it at their kilns at reduced prices. Potatoes, oats and flax are the common crop and a little barley and wheat is occasionally sown. In general the farms are not more than from 6 to 8 acres in size, though some of the better farmers hold from 20 to 30 acres. The principal proprietors are Colonel Verner M.P. and James Goff Esquire, neither of whom reside in the parish. [Insert query: Where do they reside?].

Cattle

The common Irish breed of both cattle and pigs prevails and hardly any horses are bred.

General Remarks

This parish, when compared with those of Donaghmore and Clonfeacle <Clonfeckle> which bound it to the east, has a bleak and wild appearance and is in every sense a much poorer country. There is very little planting.

SOCIAL ECONOMY

Ecclesiastical Summary

Name Killeeshil, diocese Armagh, province Armagh, rectory, is not a union; patron Archbishop of Armagh, incumbent Reverend John Young; extent of glebe Killeeshil townland. The townland of Glencull in Aghaloo parish was formerly the glebe and was exchanged with Lord Charlemont for Killeeshil townland in the year 1771. The tithes belong to the rector. They were compounded for on the 13th May 1828 under the Tithe Composition Act, at the annual sum of 300 pounds. [Signed] George Dalton, Lieutenant Royal Engineers, 31 July 1834.

Table of Schools

[Table contains the following headings: townland, number of pupils divided by religion and sex, how supported, when established].

Killeeshil, 58 Protestants, 115 Catholics, 99 males, 74 females, 173 total pupils; Mr Goff allows 1d each per week for 20 girls and 20 pounds a year to the teacher, the present one receiving from Erasmus Smith's bounty 30 pounds yearly, from which 10 pounds per annum is deducted for a superannuated teacher. The scholars have, besides this, to pay from 1d to 2s per week; established 1820.

Backets, 26 Protestants, 64 Catholics, 74 males, 16 females, 90 total pupils; Colonel Verner subscribes 7 pounds per annum to the teacher and the scholars pay from 1d to 2d per week; established 1823.

Mulnahunch, 25 Protestants, 15 males, 10 females, 25 total pupils; the Kildare Street Society give 2 pounds per annum and James Goff Esquire 8 pounds; the scholars have to pay from 1d to 2d per week for instruction; established 1820.

Shonkey, 73 males, 31 females, 94 Protestants, 10 Catholics, 104 total pupils; National Board pays 10 pounds per annum, the remainder is paid by the children; established 1821.

Stewartstown, 47 males, 30 females, 70 Protestants, 7 Catholic, 77 total pupils; [from] Association for Discountenancing Vice 8 pounds per annum, the remainder is paid by the children; established 1814.

Infant school in the town of Stewartstown, 25 males, 65 females, 75 Protestants, 15 Catholics, 90 total pupils; [supported by] private subscription; established 1835 [sic].

In the town of Stewartstown, 22 males, 44 females, 36 Protestants, 30 Catholics, 66 total pupils; National Board pays 10 pounds per annum and the children pay the rest; established 1830.

Office Copy of Draft Memoir

NATURAL FEATURES

Hills

This parish is exceedingly hilly, the western and northern portions occupying the eastern and north eastern sides of Shantavny mountain. The highest points within the parish boundary are Oranloone, 911 feet, Ballynahaye, 820 and Edenfore, 814 feet above the level of the sea.

Lakes

There are 2 inconsiderable lakes or ponds in the south western side of the parish, in Lurgancullion townland. Their united extent is about 5 acres.

Rivers

The Ballyreagh water, the source of which is in the adjoining parish of Pomeroy, flows from north to south through the western portion of Killeeshil. It then enters Errigal Trough parish, passing to the south of Ballygawley. From thence to its junction with the Blackwater on the confines of the county it is called the Ballygawley water.

The Oona river rises in the townland of Altaghish in the parish of Donaghmore and runs in a south easterly direction to the Blackwater, with which it unites at a point at about quarter of a mile west of Battleford bridge.

Bogs

All the valleys throughout the parish contain fields of bog of greater or less extent and the northern portion is principally mountain bog.

MODERN TOPOGRAPHY

Towns, Public Buildings and Gentlemen's Seats

Towns: none.

Public buildings: the church in Killeeshil townland; the meeting house in Lisfearty; the Roman Catholic chapel in Aghaginduff.

Gentlemen's seats: Aghnahoe, the residence of Captain Crossley, agent to Colonel Verner; the Glebe House in Killeeshil townland.

Bleach Greens, Manufactories and Mills

There is neither bleach green nor manufactory in the parish. There are 4 corn mills, 2 in Mullyroddan, 1 in Ennish and 1 in Farriter townland, and also a flax mill in Mullyroddan; Ballyreagh mill.

Communications

The high road from Dungannon to Enniskillen, which also leads to Omagh through Ballygawley, traverses the parish from east to west for 3 and a quarter miles. It is in moderately good repair but is very injudiciously laid out. Its direction might be easily altered so as to avoid several of the steep hills over which it now passes. There are also several by-roads. They are kept in tolerable repair, being principally formed of gravel with which the country abounds. The roads are universally kept in repair at the expense of the county.

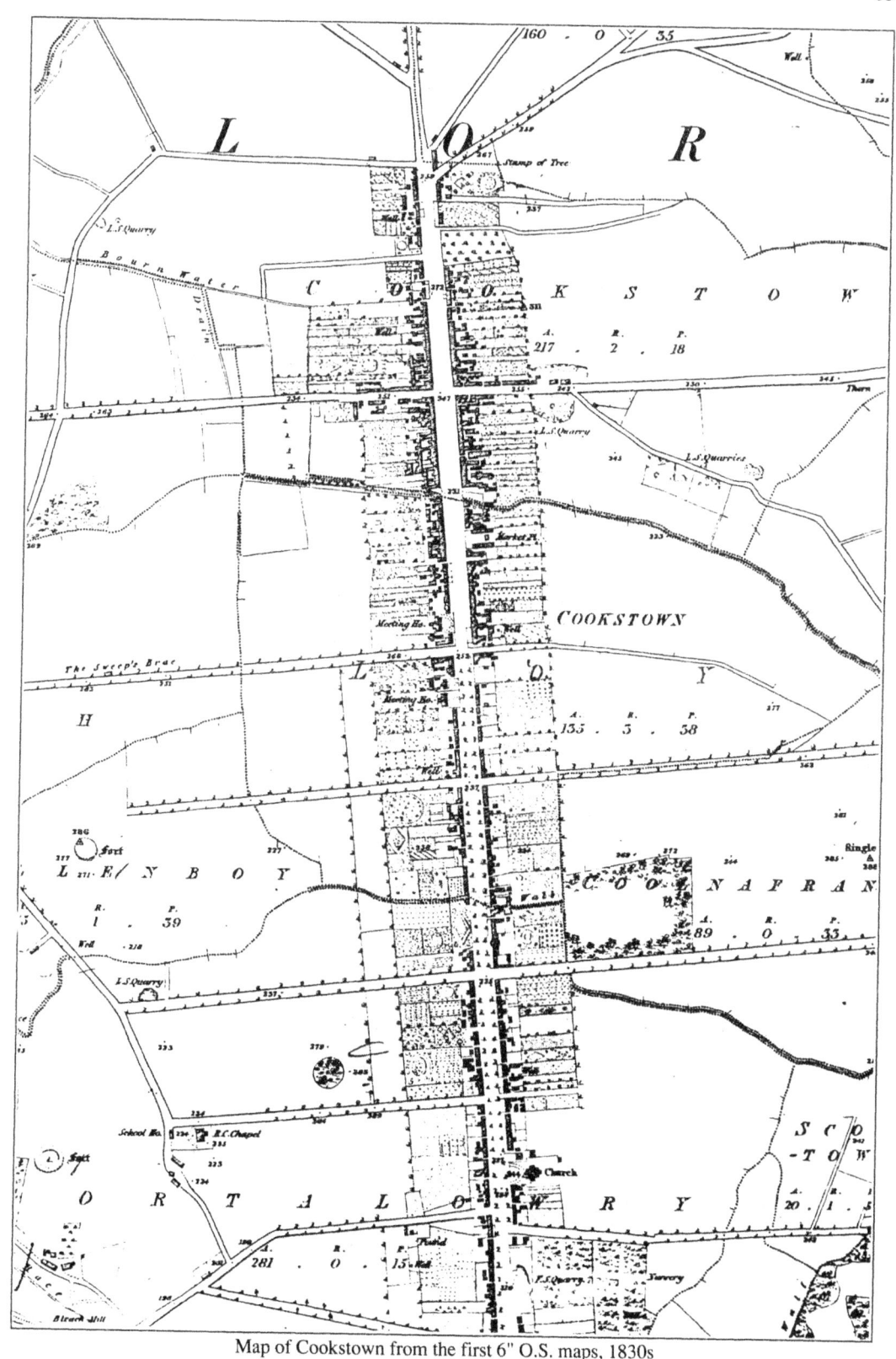

Map of Cookstown from the first 6" O.S. maps, 1830s

Parish of Killyman, County Tyrone

Memoir by George Scott, 1835

Natural Features

Hills

The hills in this parish are all sand, plain and of various shapes. They are slightly connected between the streams but do not form any principal ridge. The highest is in the townland of Drumkee, being 194 feet above the level of the sea. The country surrounding this parish is quite of the same description. The sides of the hills facing south are not so uniformly steep as the sand country about Cloughmills.

Lakes and Rivers

Lakes: none.

The River Blackwater is the boundary of the parish and divides the county from the county Armagh. It flows into Lough Neagh. In this parish it takes a south east direction. Its average breadth is 40 feet, depth from 7 to 10 feet. It takes its rise at [blank]. It is navigable for lighters and small boats. At this side there are but few, if any, mills turned by its waters. In this parish there are not any rapids, and the fall appears to be very gentle. It does not overflow to any great extent. When it does it soon subsides without any artificial means. After a flood it leaves a light sand, which is neither injurious or beneficial to the soil. The scenery of its banks are not in the least interesting.

A small portion of the River Torrent flows through this parish into the Blackwater. About 2 miles of the canal also passes through the parish, for particulars vide Memoir of [blank].

This parish is well supplied with springs.

Weather Journal for July 1835

[Table gives date, state of weather at morning, noon and afternoon, with wind direction].

1st: fair, fine, fair, south.
2nd: fine, fine, fair, south east.
3rd: cloudy, fine, fair, south east.
4th: cloudy, [?] gale, showers, south west.
5th: wet, fine, fair, south west.
6th: wet, showers, showers, south west.
7th: wet, wet, very wet, south west.
8th: wet, wet, showers, south west.
9th: wet, fair, fair, north west.
10th: wet, showers, showers, west.
11th: wet, wet, wet, south west.
12th: wet, fair, wet, north west.
13th: wet, showers, fair, west.
14th: fair, fair, fine, south west.
15th: fair, fair, fine, south west.
16th: showers, wet, wet, south west.
17th: showers, fair, wet, south west.
18th: showers, wet, fair, south west.
19th: showers, fair, fine, south west.
20th: fair, fine, fine, east.
21st: fair, fine, fine, east.
22nd: fine, fine, fine, south east.
23rd: fine, fine, fine, west.
24th: fine, fine, fine, north.
25th: fine, fine, fine, north.
26th: fine, fine, fine, north.
27th: very fine, fine, fine, west.
28th: very fine, fine, fine, west.

Bogs

There are many detached portions of bog in this parish of very small extent, Derrytresk bog being the largest, containing about 5 square miles, 55 feet above the level of the sea; the nearest river Blackwater. Black oak is found embedded at the edges of the bog. They are not broken at the same height, or do the stumps remain upright. The timber is found at various depths from the surface of the bog without any particular layers. The depth of this bog is from 20 to 30 feet, but the countrymen are not in the habit of cutting it more than 10 or 15 feet, it being very inconvenient throwing the turf over a high bank. The description of bog is light and not considered the best description. It contains a few islands, indiscriminately dispersed through it, the highest being 114 feet above the level of the sea.

Woods

Woods: none, [nor] are there evidences of any having ever existed.

Climate

Showers are most frequent in this parish, as mist rises off of the lake, and it is said that it frequently rains in this and the adjoining parish when there is not any in the valley. The ripening of the crops is much the same as mentioned in former Memoirs. For state of weather, vide opposite page.

Modern Topography

Public Buildings

Towns: none.

Parish of Killyman

Public buildings: church, meeting house, Society of Friends' meeting house, Roman Catholic chapel.

Society of Friends' Meeting House

The Society of Friends' meeting house in the townland of Grange, a very plain building with 12 windows. The aisle would accommodate 300 persons, the gallery 100 persons. Erected in the year 1819, cost 1,000 pounds, paid by the Society of Quakers, dimensions of building 54 feet by 36.

Roman Catholic Chapel

The Roman Catholic chapel in the townland of Cavan, erected in the year 1786, dimensions <dimentions> 60 feet by 24. The aisle would contain about 300 persons, the gallery about 60. Extremely plain building and the interior very much out of repair, cost cannot be ascertained.

Gentlemen's Seats

Grange House, the residence of Miss Thompson; Grange Park, the residence of H. Handcock; Loyd House, the residence of [blank] Loyd; the residence of the Reverend [blank] O'Sulivan.

Mills

Corn mill, townland of Drumaspil, diameter of wheel 14 feet, breadth 2 feet, fall of water 10 feet, undershot wheel.

Corn mill, townland of Tempanroe, diameter of wheel 16 and a half feet, breadth 6 and a half feet, fall of water 8 feet, undershot wheel.

Bleach mill, townland of [blank], diameter of wheel 14 feet, breadth of wheel 3 feet 6 inches, fall of water 7, overshot wheel.

There are not any disputes about the supply of water, fishing etc.

Communications

There are many leading roads through this parish but not any coach roads. Their average breadth is from 26 to 30 feet. They are made to run over hill and hollow, and exceedingly bad roads for carts. They are kept in pretty good order at the expense of the county. The crossroads are not unnecessarily numerous, but kept in bad order.

The portion of canal passing through this parish is not more than 3 miles; for particulars vide Memoir of Clonoe and Tullyniskan.

ANCIENT TOPOGRAPHY

Monuments

There are neither monuments or buildings of any ancient date in this parish.

MODERN TOPOGRAPHY

General Appearance and Scenery

The scenery of this parish is dull and monotonous. It is merely a succession of sandhills of various heights. From the top of one nearly the whole parish may be seen. Generally speaking, there is a farmhouse on the top of each hill, surrounded with a few small trees. The smooth slopes with the different hue of the various crops give a fertile appearance, but by no means picturesque <picturesk>.

SOCIAL ECONOMY

Local Government

No town in this parish. There is not any illicit distilling carried on in this parish, neither are insurances very frequent. Dispensaries: none.

Schools

[Table contains the following headings: townland, number of pupils subdivided by religion and sex, religion of master, how supported, when established].

Drumard: Protestants 26, all boys, total 26; master a Protestant. The master is supported solely by the parents of the children, who pay 1d per week; established 1825.

Grange: Protestants 31, Presbyterians 2, Catholics 8, Quakers 4, boys 7, girls 38, total 45; mistress a Protestant. The mistress receives 5 pounds from the London Hibernian Society, 4 pounds from the Ladies' Society and 1d per week from children. The schoolhouse cost 64 pounds, erected by subscriptions and donations; established 1813.

Tamlaghtmore: Protestants 73, Presbyterians 5, Catholics 16, boys 63, girls 31, total 94; master a Protestant. The master receives 5 pounds from Mr Loyd and 1d per week from each child. This schoolhouse cost 30 pounds, erected at the expense of Mr Loyd; established 1819.

Religion

The people in this parish are almost all Protestants and Presbyterians. I should scarcely think there were 1 dozen exceptions.

Habits of the People

There are some cottages made of stone, but the majority made of mud, generally thatched, 2 or 3 small glass windows, mostly 1-storey, with 2 rooms. I do not think there is much attention paid to comfort or cleanliness. There are some exceptions where there are good slated houses and frequently clean. The chief food potatoes, oatmeal and bacon; chief fuel turf, which they can easily procure at the lower end of the parish, but those that have not carts carry it in sacks. In many parts of this parish I observed men who had a cartload of potatoes bringing them about, selling by retail to the poorer classes. Longevity, average 56 years. Usual number in a family average 6 children, very early marriage none. Their chief amusement handball. The old customs of fire on St John's Eve are nearly if not quite extinct. The costume similar to the description in Memoir of Lisburn.

Remarkable Events

This parish has always been remarkable for the Killyman Orangemen.

PRODUCTIVE ECONOMY

Fishing

The only fishing is for amusement in the river, where a few small fish of various descriptions are caught.

MODERN TOPOGRAPHY

Public Buildings and Gentlemen's Seats

Towns: none.

The church is situated in the southern portion of the parish. It is a handsome building. About three-eighths of a mile south of the church is a meeting house. The Roman Catholic chapel is situated about half a mile north of the church.

Gentlemen's seats: Tamlaghmore, the seat of Richard Lloyd Esquire; Derrygally demesne.

Bleach Greens, Manufactories and Mills

Bleach green in Drummuck townland; beetling engine in Dungorman; paper manufactory in Tarlaghan.

Communications

There are 3 leading roads, viz. from Dungannon to Portadown, from Coalisland to Moy and from Coalisland to Portadown. The former traverses the parish from east to west and the 2 latter from north to south.

Office Copy of Draft Memoir

NATURAL FEATURES

Hills

The highest point within the parish boundary is in Drumanagh townland, and it is only 196 feet above the level of the sea.

Lakes

On the western [side?] is a lake which extends over 14 acres 2 roods 16 perches.

Rivers

The Blackwater bounds the parish on the south for 3 and one-eighth miles, and there are 19 acres 3 roods 13 perches of its area included within the parish boundary. The Torrent river flows on the northern boundary and empties into the Blackwater at the north eastern extremity of the parish.

Bogs

There is an extensive tract of bog situate between the Blackwater and Torrent rivers.

Parish of Lissan, County Tyrone

Office Copy of Memoir

NATURAL FEATURES

Hills

The southern part of the parish forms the secondary features of Slievegallion in the county of Londonderry. The extreme height on the southern extremity of Lissan is 1,278 feet above the level of the sea. South eastward from this point there is a fall of about 780 feet in 2 and a half miles to the parish boundary. Further in the same direction rises the mountains of Beleermanon and Ballynasolus, situated in the northern extermity of Kildress parish. Eastward of these is Fir mountain in Lissan parish, the height of which [is] 1,188 feet.

Lakes

Lough Fea is situated towards the centre of the parish. Its length is about 1,540 yards and breadth 730, and it extends over 129 acres 3 roods 19 perches, of which 59 acres 3 roods 21 perches are in the county Tyrone and 69 acres 3 roods 38 perches in the county Londonderry. It is a picturesque sheet of water surrounded by mountains [and] contains some good trout and pike.

Rivers

The Broughderg or Owenkillew river rises in Broughderg townland in the south west of the parish, at a height of about 800 feet above the sea. It runs in a westerly direction across the county and unites with the Strule on the southern side of Stewartstown. This stream is subject to very great floods, sometimes inundating the valley through which it runs.

Bogs

There is but little bog to be met with in the lower parts of the parish, but the surface of the mountains is principally composed of rough boggy soil which produces a coarse herbage and is generally grazed by young cattle.

Woods

See the description Lissan demesne, as there are none on the part situated in the county Tyrone except these.

MODERN TOPOGRAPHY

Public Buildings

Towns: none.
  Public buildings: none that I know of. I mean there are none in the Tyrone part of the parish.

Gentlemen's Seats

Lissan demesne, the seat of Thomas Staples Esquire: the part of this demesne contained in the county is very beautiful, but see a further description in the part of the parish contained in the county Derry. The woods are extensive and contain a great deal of old timber, together with several young plantations [of] larch, Scotch fir and oak.

Communications

The principal road is that leading from Cookstown to Derry. It traverses the parish from south east to north west for 6 miles, very hilly and in very bad repair, average breadth 40 feet. At a distance of 1 and a half miles from Cookstown a road branches off to the north east leading to Moneymore, and 3 miles further from Cookstown a second road branches off which leads to Dungiven.

Parish of Pomeroy, County Tyrone

Statistical Report by Lieutenant C. Bailey,
April 1834

Geography or Natural State

Name and Locality

[Insert footnote: To Lieutenant-colonel Colby, Royal Engineers, commanding].

The customary, and indeed the only mode of spelling the name, is Pomeroy. I am not aware of the derivation, or of any localities to support it. The peasantry in pronouncing the word lay the emphasis on the last syllable. The parish of Pomeroy is situated in the barony of Dungannon and county of Tyrone, bounded on the north by the parish of Desertcreat, on the east by a small portion of Tullyniskan <Tullaniskan> parish, on the south east and south by the parish of Donaghmore, and on the west by the parish of Donaghmore. It is almost 8 miles in length by 4 in breadth, containing 15,950 acres, two-thirds of which are under cultivation. The remainder consists of bog and unreclaimed mountain land.

Natural Features

Hills

The hills in the western side of the parish, called Cappagh mountain, Barrack mountain, Cranogue, Altmore, Gortnagarn (from the name of the townland in which situated), are not isolated but form part of a general mountain district. Their height above the sea is from 946 to 570 feet.

Bogs

There are great number of detached bogs from 1 to 100 acres in extent. Most of them contain fir and oak timber. The turbary is from 4 to 8 feet thick, resting upon a substratum of clay, or more generally of grey sand.

Modern Topography

Town of Pomeroy

The town of Pomeroy is situated in the north west corner of the parish, on the road leading from Cookstown to Omagh. Its general appearance is bleak and miserable in the extreme. It consists of 1 small street. The houses are built with a species of sandstone slate procured in the immediate neighbourhood, and generally thatched. There are a few slated houses, but all very bad and dirty. A meeting house and Roman Catholic chapel are within the town. There are also 2 schools, one under the Board of Education and the other supported by Robert Lowry Esquire, for the use of his tenantry. A grain market is held every Tuesday and a fair on the second Tuesday of every month (custom free) for the sale of mountain stock, pigs, provisions and yarn. A few horses are sold but they are of a very bad description. The town is not likely soon to improve as the tenements are mostly held under perpetuity leases by a very poor class of people.

Productive Economy

Manufacturing

The only manufactory carried on is that of linen. There are 5 corn mills situated in the townlands of Killey, Munderrydoe, Galbally, Killmore and Crossdernot.

Modern Topography

Communications

The principal roads passing through the parish are those leading from Dungannon and Cookstown (through Pomeroy) to Omagh. They are made and repaired at the expense of the county but are not kept in very good order.

The mountain road from Dungannon to Omagh (passing through Altmore and thus avoiding Pomeroy) is much newer, but the road is not so good. Carriages generally go through Pomeroy. There certainly appears to be a greater number of roads than necessary. This evil arises in great measure from the difficulty of stopping up the old roads, owing to the number of houses still existing upon them to which a communication must be kept open.

Scenery

The scenery is wild, but not by any means picturesque or interesting. The great want of wood and hedgerows gives the country a cold and bleak appearance.

Social Economy

Local Government

A party of 4 police constables is stationed in the town of Pomeroy. Petty sessions are held there

Parish of Pomeroy

every fortnight. The nearest magistrates are Robert Lowry of Pomeroy, Esquire and James Lowry of Rockdale, Esquire. Illicit distilling is carried to a great extent and has very much increased lately. The spirit meets a ready sale at about 6s per gallon.

Poor

There is no provision whatever for the poor or infirm, nor any charitable endowments.

Cottages

The cottages are built with rough stones or mud, thatched, 1-storey high and divided into 2 or 3 rooms. They are for the most part very dirty and uncomfortable.

Emigration

Emigration prevails to a considerable extent and generally to America. But few persons go to England for harvest work. They do not take over their families but return home again in time to dig their potato crops.

PRODUCTIVE ECONOMY

Linen

A great deal of hand-spinning and weaving is carried on in the cottages, principally narrow webs of coarse linen which sell at 7d or 8d per yard. It is not profitable: a good weaver can only earn about 5s per week and a spinner must work hard to earn 2d per day.

Landholdings and Proprietors

The parish is divided into 48 townlands, these again into farms of from 4 to 40 Irish acres, generally held under leases of 3 lives or 31 years, or 1 life or 21 years; and as the leases fall in, the land is let at the yearly rent of 1 pound per statute acre. The principal proprietors are Robert Lowry of Pomeroy, Esquire, James Lowry of Rockdale, Esquire, Edward Litton of Dublin, Esquire and the Reverend James Lowry of Clogherny.

Most of the tenants hold direct from the head landlords, average rent of the best land 30s, middling 18s per Irish acre. The mountain land is let by the lump and, taking good and bad together, generally amounts to about 10s per Irish acre. In addition to the rent some of the landlords exact a number of duty days (according to the size of the holding) for drawing turf and setting potatoes. The farmers are poor and till the land for subsistence only and not for profit. No land is let in conacre. Cottiers are usually given as much land as they are able to manure for potatoes.

Agriculture

The fields are small, badly shaped and enclosed with banks of earth. The soil in the lower part of the parish is a stiff reddish clay resting upon limestone.

In the upper or mountain part it is of a cold gravelly nature. The land is manured with stable dung or a composition of soil and bog mixed with a little lime. A great deal of limestone is brought from Shivey, parish Desertcreat, procured at the quarry for 2d ha'penny a car-load and burned at home with turf. The common wheel car is the usual mode of conveyance. Average produce per statute acre: wheat 15 cwt, oats 40 bushels, potatoes 200 bushels. Flax sown only in small quantities; a peck of seed will produce about 4 stones of flax. Wheat fetches from 7s 6d to 8s per cwt, oats 7d to 8d per stone and potatoes 10d per bushel.

Grazing

There is very little grazing in the lowlands and what the mountains afford is not good.

Wages

Farm labourers are paid from 8d to 1s per day. Cottiers get a house and a small piece of ground, for which they give so many days work in the week in lieu of money.

Cattle

The breed of cattle, horses and pigs is bad. Jobbers buy them up and take them to market. There is a regular system of jobbing through the whole of this country. Every small farmer deals more or less in cattle.

Uses made of the Bogs

The bogs are used wholly as fuel. A good deal of turf is taken to Dungannon and is sold at about 1s or 1s 2d per gauge, or cubical yard.

Fishing

The rivers contain a great quantity of small trout, which are killed with a fly or taken by the country people in nets.

Fairs and Markets

There are no fairs or markets within the parish

except at Pomeroy. Those in the neighbourhood usually attended are Dungannon, Cookstown and Stewartstown. [Signed] C. Bailey, Lieutenant Royal Engineers, 18th April 1834.

Office Copy of Draft Memoir

NATURAL FEATURES

Hills

The hills on the western side of the parish form a part of the Tyrone chain of mountains. The principal points are Cappagh mountain, 946 feet, Shane Barnard's Sentry Box, 901 feet, Barrack mountain, 865 feet, Altmore, 750 feet, Gortnagarn, 696 feet.

Lakes and Rivers

Lakes: none of importance.

The source of the Torrent river is a small lake situated on the western side of the parish, at an elevation of 800 feet above the level of the sea. The general direction of its course is south east to the Blackwater, with which it unites at a point about 1 mile north of Verner's bridge.

The source of the Cloghfin river is in Crannogue townland, about a mile north of that of the Oona. It flows in a westerly direction and, uniting with the Termonmaguirk river near Deverny bridge, forms the Camowen river.

Parish of Tamlaght, County Tyrone

Notes on Coagh

PRODUCTIVE ECONOMY

Town of Coagh: Remarks on Livestock

Having attended the fairs and examined into the various kinds and prices of stock during my stay in this town, the following remarks may serve as a check on the field returns for the neighbouring townlands.

There is a regular monthly fair held on the second Friday of each month, wherein are offered for sale in the open streets an extensive assortment of cattle, sheep, goats and hogs, part of which I have witnessed sold at the following prices, viz. lowland milch cows from 5 pounds to 14 pounds; highland milch cows from 4 pounds to 7 pounds; lowland dry heifers 2 years old, from 3 pounds to 8 pounds; highland dry heifers 3 years old, from 2 pounds 10s to 5 pounds 10s; lowland calves 1 year old, from 1 pound 10s to 3 pounds; highland calves 1 year old, from 15s to 1 pound 10s. Fatted cattle are seldom or never sold in this town. I am told that farmers who feed cattle for beef take them to Cookstown, Moneymore or Magherafelt. Bull calves are but seldom reared by the farmers; therefore they are never to be seen in the fairs of this town.

There is no horses offered for sale in it. The supply of sheep is not so extensive as that of cattle. They are as follows: large lowland sheep for breeding from 1 to 2 years old, 1 pound to 1 pound 10s; large lowland lambs 5 months old, 10s to 15s. The supply of goats is also but small. They are as follows: a large milch goat of 2 years old, 7s 6d to 10s; young goats or kids 1s to 2s 6d. Always a large supply of pigs: young pigs in creels from 6 to 10 weeks old, called "sneens", 5s to 7s 6d; young pigs running about, from 12 weeks to 15 weeks, 10s to 16s; young pigs from 6 to 12 months, 1 pound to 1 pound 10s; pigs aged from 12 to 18 months, 2 pounds to 3 pounds; pigs aged from 2 years old, 3 pounds 10s to 4 pounds 10s. They are all sold alive in this town. There is no pork market.

Provision of Goods

There is sometimes a small supply of farming implements: old wooden ploughs 15s to 1 pound, common harrows 6s to 9s, brake harrows 9s to 12s, box barrows 7s 6d to 10s, turf barrows 2s 6d to 3s 4d, hand barrows 1s 10d to 2s 6d. The quantities of yarn are more extensive than the qualities. It is chiefly 2 hanks and 6 cuts to the lb, selling from 4d to 4d ha'penny per hank and 3 hanks to the lb, generally at 4d ha'penny per hank. It is purchased by the weavers of the neighbouring parishes.

Always a large supply of earthenware, brought from the parishes of Killyman and Ballyscullion, for which there is an extensive demand. Pedlar's goods on covered stands. Meal and potatoes not offered for sale as there is no provision market. Merchants for purchase of cattle come from Dungannon, Cookstown, Draperstown, Maghera, Magherafelt and Moneymore. Cattle are bought for sale from the parishes of Lissan, Magherafelt, Maghera, Artrea, Ballinderry, Arboe, Tamlaght, Ballyclog, Donaghenry, Derryloran, Glenoe and Killyman.

There was an attempt made to establish a weekly market in this town, but it proved a complete failure, Stewartstown, Cookstown and Magherafelt being so convenient; and they also being celebrated markets, the farmers still attended them with their goods, thus affording no inducement to the merchants for purchase in Coagh that they declined coming, and therefore it entirely fell away.

The loss of a weekly market is not materially felt by the inhabitants, as the shopkeepers and tradespeople are a very respectable class. They do not derive their entire support from their establishments, having, in general, farms in the immediate vicinity of the town; and also the poorer class can purchase from the former on the most reasonable terms. Their shops are always well supplied with goods of the best quality, wheatmeal, oatmeal, flour and bran in constant supply in the grocers' shops. Potatoes can be had by retail from the shops and also from the neighbouring farmers. The prices as established in Cookstown market on Saturday generally regulate the sale in Coagh during the ensuing week. The farmers send into the shops, in exchange for their groceries, fresh butter and eggs, which keeps up a good supply in the shops for persons who have to purchase. This town has also its butcher and baker.

Taking the town collectively, it is well supplied with everything necessary for food and raiment. Fresh pullans and eels daily from Lough Neagh. Also a good and constant supply in the shops of: foundry agricultural spades 16 by 6 inches, at from 2s to 2s 6d; foundry turf spades 16 by 3 and a half inches, at from 1s 10d to 2s 4d; foundry shovels without handles, at from 1s 3d to 1s 5d; handles for the above turned at from 3d to 6d; scythe <sythe> hooks at from 6d to 9d; teethed hooks at from 5d to 7d; meadow scythes patent at from 4s 6d to 7s 6d; meadow scythes common at from 3s 6d to 5s 6d. Steel, iron, iron hoop, deal <dale> in planks and boards. [Signed] John Hanna, 12th June 1840, Coagh; received 29th June 1840 [initialled] JBH.

Corn Mills

[Table contains the following headings: townland, proprietor, date established, water and steam power, number of attendants, time employed, capacity of mill, supply of water, whether tenants are bound, by toll or mulcture, remarks].

No.1, Coagh, proprietor Duncan Storey, established time immemorial, rebuilt in 1750; water power, 2 wheels: 1st, diameter 14 and two-third feet; 2nd, diameter 14 and two-third feet; width of buckets: 1st, 3 and a half feet; 2nd, 2 and a half feet; both undershot; 4 attendants, 2 employed by proprietor, 2 by customers; 6,000 cwt of oats, produces 3,000 cwt of meal; 2,240 cwt of wheat, produces 1,600 cwt of meal; the mill is constantly employed from November to May and works occasionally during the remainder of the year, say two-thirds of the time; mill could grind 18,000 cwt of oats, 8,000 cwt of wheat; supply of water all year; are tenants bound: no; oats pays one-thirtieth grain, wheat one-sixteenth grain; is the work of the mill stationary or not: stationary. It is considered that this mill would not be increasing nor stationary but for the work got from the dealers <dalers> in meal. [Signed] John Hanna, 12th June 1840.

Flax Mills

[Table contains the following headings: townland, proprietor, date of establishment, dimensions and type of wheel, number of attendants, time employed, water supply, quantity of flax scutched per diem, greatest quantity it could scutch in time employed, number of stocks and rollers, charge per stone for scutching, from 10 cwt of raw or unbeetled flax how much beetled, from 18 cwt of beetled flax how much scutched, work of mill, remarks].

Urbal, proprietor Thomas Duff, established 1836, rebuilt in 1838; diameter of wheel 15 feet, width of buckets 3 and a quarter feet, undershot; 6 men employed for 3 months, 3 men for 3 months, 2 women constantly, number of weeks 24, 6 days in the week; does the supply of water continue longer: all year; does it cease working for want of materials: yes; flax scutched per annum: 1,944 stones of 16 lbs; could scutch 3,000 stone; 6 stocks <stoucks>, 1 set of rollers, charges 9d per stone for scutching; can't tell how much beetled flax from 10 cwt unbeetled; 3 cwt of scutched flax from 10 cwt of beetled; is work of mill increasing or not: increasing. It is considered that farmers are sowing more flax within the 2 last years, which increases the work.

Coagh, proprietor John Magee, established 1818; diameter of wheel 14 feet, width of buckets 3 and a third feet, undershot; 6 men employed 5 months, 3 men employed 4 months, 2 females constantly; number of weeks 36; 6 days in the week; does the supply of water continue longer: all year; does it cease working for lack of materials: yes; flax scutched per year: 2,736 stones of 16 lbs; could scutch 5,000 stone; 6 stocks, 1 set of rollers, 9d per stone for scutching; can't tell how much beetled flax from 10 cwt unbeetled; 3 cwt scutched flax from 10 cwt beetled; is work of the mill increasing or not: increasing. It is considered that the establishment of the flax factory in this part of the country has increased the demand for flax, and therefore farmers are sowing more flax.

[Insert note on attendants in Coagh: In each of those mills there are 6 stocks, but when work gets slack there is not so great a demand, therefore the number is reduced. So, it is to be understood that there has been 6 men employed for a number of months and that when the work got slack, there was only 3 men employed, thus leaving 3 stocks idle]. 12th June 1840.

Hotels and Inns: Coagh

[Table contains the following headings: proprietor, when established, number of coffee rooms, number of private sitting rooms, number of sleeping rooms, saddle horses, gigs, jaunting cars, post chaises, public cars, public coaches, remarks].

Proprietor Walter Duff, established 1829, 1 coffee room, 2 private sitting rooms, 3 sleeping rooms.

Proprietor William McIntire, established 1818, 2 private sitting rooms, 4 sleeping rooms, 1 saddle horse, 1 jaunting car. [Signed] John Hamilton, 27th and 28th May 1840; lodged in William Vance's, Coagh. Forwarded 24th June 1840, [signed] J. Hanna.

Table of Occupations

[Printed table contains the following headings:

Parish of Tamlaght

number and name, profession, trade or business, grade, total in family, aid from family, other assistants, livestock and other stock, remarks].

[Printed footnotes: NB 1. The master by whom a clerk, journeyman, apprentice, servitor or labourer is employed (where such persons are not lodged in the master's house) will be shown by the street letter and number of the master being appended to the name of the clerk etc. in the column of names. 2. The entries of denominations to be by the initials of the word, thus, m = master, c = clerk, j = journeyman. [*Numbers of household given as fractions which may indicate adults to children eg. females 1/4 = 1 female adult to 4 female children*].

Occupations: Townlands adjacent to Coagh

[Townland of Urbal: all master craftsmen, stock mostly on Field Book].

1, Michael Donnelly, carter, family: 1/2 males, 1/4 females, 1 carrier's cart, rest of stock on Field Book.

2, James McCombs, carter, family: 1/1 males, 2/0 females, 1 carrier's cart, rest of stock on Field Book.

3, Thomas Clendinning, shoemaker, family: 2/4 males, 1/1 females, family aid 1 male journeyman, 1 female servitor, stock on Field Book.

4, John Cowdan, shoemaker, family: 1/4 males, 1/2 females, family aid 1 female servitor, stock on Field Book.

5, William Kilpatrick, scutcher, family: 2/0 males, 1/2 females, stock on Field Book, works at the scutch mill in [Coagh ?].

6, John Henderson, shoemaker, Coagh, family: [3/1 ?] males, [1/2 ?] females, family aid 2 male apprentices, lives with his father, no.12 Field Note Book, the apprentices are his brothers.

7, Thomas Robinson, baker, Coagh, family: 1 males, 1/2 females, no stock.

8, John Spence, process server, Coagh, family: 1/1 males, 1/1 females, stock on Field Book.

9, Joseph Young, sawyer, Coagh, family: 1/2 males, 3/1 females, stock on Field Book.

10, James Latimer, blacksmith, Coagh, family: 1/2 males, females 1/2, stock on Field Book.

11, Robert Young, carpenter, family: 2/1 males, 1/1 females, 1 male journeyman, stock on Field Book.

12, William John Cowan, farmer, not working, family: [?] 2/0 males, 1/2 females, 1 female domestic labourer, 1 private car, rest of stock on Field Book.

13, Robert Crooks, scutcher, not working, family: 1/1 males, 1/0 females, stock on Field Book.

14, John Cairns, scutcher, family: 1/1 males, 1/1 females, stock on Field Book.

15, James Wilkinson, scutcher, family: 1/3 males, 1/2 females, stock on Field Book.

16, Thomas McAlister, shoemaker, family: 2/2 males, 1/1 females, family aid 1 male journeyman, 1 female servitor, stock on Field Book.

17, John Fearson, publican, family: 1/0 males, 1/0 females, stock on Field Book.

Townland of Drumconway: 2 master craftsmen, stock on Field Book.

1, Andrew Bree, carpenter, family: 3/2 males, 1/1 females, stock on Field Book.

2, Alexander MacBree, grocer, family: 2/0 males, 1/3 females, stock on Field Book.

Observer's signature: Archibald Thompson, 28th to 30th May, 3th and 4th June 1840; forwarded 24 June 1840 [signed] J. Hanna.

Occupations: Hanover Street, Coagh

[All master craftsmen, all workers lodged in the house].

1, William Robinson, woollen draper, family: 1/0 males, 3/0 females, family aid 1 female servitor, others 1 female domestic labourer, g Book no.1.

2, William Downing, draper and farmer, family: 1/0 males, 1 female domestic labourer, farmer no.1 Field Book.

3, Walter Duff, hotelkeeper, family: 1/0 males, 1 male domestic labourer, 1 female domestic labourer, g Book no.3.

4, William George, publican, family: 1/0 males, g Book no.4.

5, Sarah Ann McCleland, dressmaker, family: 1/0 females, no garden or stock.

6, John Thompson, farmer and wheelwright, family: 1/1 males, 2/0 females, farmer no.3 Field Book.

7, Maria Thompson, dressmaker, and 8, Anna Thompson, dressmaker, daughters to no.6.

9, William John Howard, farmer and publican, family: 1/3 males, 1/1 females, 1 female domestic labourer, 1 private car, g Book no.6.

10, James Gibson, woollen draper, family: 1/3 males, 1/1 females, 2 male apprentices, 1 male labourer, 2 female domestic labourers, 1 public car, 1/1 private cars g [gig ?], g Book no.7.

11, William McConnol, lodging house keeper, family: 1/0 males, 1/3 females, 1 spinning wheel, no stock or garden.

12, John Keightly, publican, family: 1/0 males, others 1 female domestic labourer, g Book no.8.

13, William McCormick, physician and surgeon, family: 1/0 males, 1/0 females, others 1 male labourer, 1 female domestic labourer, 1 private carriage, 1 private car g [gig ?], g Book no.9.

14, James Ekin, farmer and grocer, family: 1/0 males, 1/0 females, others 2 male apprentices, 1 female domestic labourer, farmer no.4 Field Book.

15, James McIntire, farmer and publican, family: 3/1 males, 2/0 females, family aid 2 male servitors, 1 female servitor, others 2 male labourers, 1 female domestic labourer, 1 public car, g Book no.11.

16, John Ekin, farmer and grocer, family: 1/1 males, 1/5 females, others 2 female domestic labourers, 1 private car, farmer no.5 Field Book.

17, Eliza Hamilton, lives private <privet>, family: 2/0 females, others 1 female domestic labourer, 1 private car, farmer no.6 Field Book.

18, James Slogs, grocer, family: 1/0 males, 2/0 females, others 1 male apprentice, 1 female domestic labourer, g Book no.14.

19, Daniel Campbell, lives private, family: 1/0 males, others 1 female domestic labourer, g Book no.15.

20, Ann Brown, lives private, family: 2/0 females, farmer no.7 Field Book.

NB The public cars entered against nos 10 and 15: the one against no.10 is a hearse and no.15 a post car. Observer's signature: John Hamilton, date 27th to 29th May 1840.

21, William Vance, lives private, family: 1/0 males, lodged with no.20 this street.

22, Samuel Vance, constable, family: 1/2 males, 1/2 females, no stock.

23, Henery Kane, subconstable, family: 1/0 males, no stock.

24, William [?] Rat, subconstable, family: 1/0 males, no stock.

25, James Johnson, subconstable, family: 1/0 males, no stock.

26, John McGee, farmer, family: 1/0 males, 1/1 females, farmer no.8 Field Book.

27, July Hamilton, dressmaker, family: 1/0 [females], 1 female apprentice, lodged with no.26 this street.

28 James Galway, butcher, family: 1/0 males, 1/0 females, 1 male labourer, g Book no.17.

29, William Vance, blue dyer <dier>, family: 1/0 males, 1/1 females, g Book no.18.

30, Thomas Hardy, glazier and painter, family: 1/2 males, 1/2 females, no garden or stock.

31, James Sampson, surgeon, family: 1/3 males, 2/2 females, 1 female domestic labourer, 1 private car, farmer no.9 Field Book.

32, Jane Sampson, haberdasher, wife to no.31 this street.

33, Alicia Newtown, lady, family: 0/1 males, 2/0 females, 3 female domestic labourers, 1 male labourer not lodging in the house, 2 private cars, farmer no.10 Field Book.

34, John Fields, land steward, family: 1/0 males, stop[s] in the house with no.33 this street.

34[a], Duncan Storey, miller, family: 2/2 males, 1/1 females, family aid 1 male apprentice, 1 other male apprentice, 2 male labourers not lodging in the house, farmer no.12 Field Book.

35, Nancy Storey, keeper of post office, daughter to no.34 this street.

Occupations: Kettel's Entry, Coagh

1, Daniel Ward, labourer, family: 2/0 males, 2/0 females, 2 spinning wheels, no garden or stock, works to any person.

2, John Ward, labourer, son to no.1 this street, works to any person.

3, John McPeake, labourer, family: 1/1 males, 1/1 females, lodged with no.1 this street, works to any person.

4, Patrick McEldoon, labourer, family: 2/1 males, 2/0 females, 2 spinning wheels, no stock or garden, works [to any] person.

5, William McEldoon, labourer, son to no.4 this street, works to any person.

6, Hugh McCala, process server, master, family: 1/1 males, 3/0 females, 2 spinning wheels, no stock or garden.

7, Elen McCala, dressmaker, master, daughter to no.6 this street.

8, James Malon, hackler, master, family: 1/3 males, 2/2 females, family aid 1 female apprentice, 2 spinning wheels, no stock or garden.

Occupations: George Street, Coagh

[Masters unless stated].

1, James McClain, shoemaker, family: 3/1 males, 1/1 females, family aid 2 male apprentices, 1 spinning wheel, no stock or garden.

2, Edmund Bell, grocer, family: 1/0 males, 1/0 females, no stock or garden.

3, James Alexander, grocer, family: 2/0 males, family aid 1 male apprentice, g Book no.23.

4, James Graham, carpenter, family: 1/2 males, 1/0 females, g Book no.24.

5, William Cowdan, shoemaker, family: 1/0 males, 1/1 females, 1 male apprentice lodging in the house, g Book no.25.

6, Robert Cowan, grocer, family: 1/2 males, 1/1 females, 1 male apprentice and 1 female domestic labourer lodging in the house, 1 private car, Field Book no.13, farmer.

Parish of Tamlaght

7, Robert Blackwood, carpenter, family: 2/0 males, 3/3 females, family aid 1 male journeyman, Field Book no.12, farmer.

8, Margret Blackwood, bonnetmaker, daughter to no.7 this street.

9, Thomas Walker, broker, family: 1/0 males, 1/0 females, g Book no.28.

10, Mathew Conlin, tailor, family: 1/3 males, 1/2 females, g Book no.29.

11, William Ferguson, publican, family: 1/2 males, 1/0 females, g Book no.30.

12, William Wilson, lives private, family: 1/0 males, 2/0 females, g Book no.31.

13, Duncan Higans, shoemaker, family: 1/1 males, 4/1 females, g Book no.32.

14, Rachel Higans, dressmaker, sister to no.13 this street.

Observer's signature: John Hamilton, date 30th May and 1st June 1840.

15, Catherin Higans, shoebinder, sister to no.13 this street.

16, Margot Kenedy, lady, family: 1/0 females, 1 female domestic labourer lodging in the same house, g Book no.33.

17, James Dunseith, tailor, family: 1/3 males, 1/2 females, 1 spinning wheel, no stock or garden.

18, William Simpson, butcher, family: 1/3 males, 1/1 females; stock: 0/1 hogs, 1 spinning wheel, no garden.

19, Daniel O'Hara, mason, family: 1/2 males, 2/0 females, g Book no.35.

20, Bernard O'Hara, labourer, master, family: 1/1 females, 1 loom, 1 spinning wheel, no stock or garden.

21, Walter Young, schoolmaster, family: 1/0 females, g Book no.36.

22, James Falkner, tailor, family: 2/0 males, 4/0 females, family aid 1 male journeyman, g Book no.37.

23, Betty Hamilton, lodging house keeper, family: 1/0 females, g Book no.38.

24, Eliza Saly Malon, dressmaker, family: 1/3 females, 2 female apprentices not lodging in the house, lodged with no.23 this street.

25, Elen Falkner 24D, apprentice dressmaker, daughter to no.22 this street.

26, James Kane, reedmaker, family: 1/0 males, 1/0 females, g Book no.39.

27, William Riddel, blacksmith, family: 1/2 males, 1/2 females, 1 male journeyman lodging in the house, g Book no.40.

28, Alexander Hemans, wheelwright, family: 1/2 males, 1/2 females, farmer no.15 Field Book.

29, James Minow, labourer, family: 1/0 males, 2/0 females, g Book no.41.

30, Margot Campbell, spinner, family: 1/0 females, lodged with no.29 this street.

31, Alex Cowden, shoemaker, family: 1/0 males, 2/0 females, g Book no.42.

32, John O'Neill, hackler, family: 1/2 males, 1/2 females, g Book no.43.

33, Saly Eldertin, spinner, family: 1/0 males, 1/0 females, g Book no.44.

34, William Eldertin, weaver, son to no.33 this street.

Observer's signature: John Hamilton, date 1st and 2nd June 1840.

35, Peter McLaughlin, nailor, family: 2/2 males, 1/2 females, family aid 1 male apprentice, g Book no.45.

36, Fill McGarvey, trade labourer, grade labourer, family: 1/2 males, 1/2 females, g Book no.46.

Occupations: Ann Street, Coagh

[Masters except those whose trade is labourer].

1, James McDade, tailor, family: 3/1 males, 2/0 females, family aid 1 male journeyman, 1 male apprentice, stock: 0/1 hogs, 2 spinning wheels, garden in townland of Urbal.

2, Hugh Malon, labourer, family: 2/0 males, 1/0 females, stock: 0/1 hogs, 1 spinning wheel, garden in townland of Urbal, works to any person.

3, James Malon, shoemaker, son to no.2 this street.

4, Joseph Belsher, labourer, family: 3/0 males, 1/1 females, family aid 2 male servitors, 1 spinning wheel, no stock or garden.

5, Richard Hamilton, nailor, family: 1/3 males, 1/2 females, no stock, 1 spinning wheel, garden in townland of Urbal.

6, Charles Hamilton, nailor, family: 1/0 males, 1/0 females, no stock, 1 spinning wheel, garden in townland of Urbal.

Occupations: Catherin Street, Coagh

[Masters except those whose trade is labourer].

1, Hugh McEldoon, labourer, family: 1/0 males, 1/1 females, 1 spinning wheel, no stock or garden, works to any person.

2, Hugh McErlane, labourer, family: 1/1 males, 1/0 females, 1 spinning wheel, no stock or garden, works to any person.

3, Mary Dofin, schoolmistress, family: 1/0 females, no stock or garden.

4, Saly Minow, spinner, family: 0/1 males, 1/1 females, 1 spinning wheel, no stock or garden.

5, John Laghery, letter carrier from Coagh to Moneymore, family: 1/0 males, lodged with no.4 this street.

6, Elidia Donaghy, labourer, family: 1/1 females, 1 spinning wheel, lodged with no.4 this street.

7, Susana Tailer, lady, family: 1/0 females, 1 female domestic labourer lodging in the house, no stock or garden.

8, Arthur Carr, cooper, family: 2/0 males, 2/1 females, family aid 1 male apprentice, 2 spinning wheels, no stock or garden.

9, Thomas O'Neill, blacksmith, family: 1/0 males, 1/0 females, 1 male apprentice lodging in the house, 1 spinning wheel, no stock or garden.

10, John McIver, tailor, family: 1/2 males, 1/1 females, 1 male journeyman lodging in the house, 1 spinning wheel, no stock or garden.

Observer's signature: John Hamilton, date 2nd and 3rd June 1840.

11, Arthur McEldoon, shoemaker, family: 4/0 males, 4/0 females, family aid 2 male journeymen and 1 male apprentice, 3 spinning wheels, no stock or garden.

12, Eliza McEldoon, shoebinder, daughter to no.11 this street.

Observer's signature: John Hamilton, date June 3rd.

Occupations: Townlands of Tamlaght, County Londonderry

[All masters except no.4].

1, Archibald Cook, shoemaker, family: 1/3 males, 1/2 females, farmer, stock taken on Field Book.

2, Reverend M. Carpendale, rector, family: 1/3 males, 2/4 females, [crossed out: 2 male domestic labourers] and 5 female domestic labourers lodging in the house, 1 private carriage, 1 private car, stock on Field Book.

3, Patrick Morgan, shoemaker, family: 2/0 males, 1/0 females, family aid 1 male journeyman, 1 male journeyman lodging in the house, stock on Field Book.

4, James Young, scutcher, journeyman, farmer's son, works to Mr Magee, Coagh.

5, Samuel Young, shoemaker, works in his father's.

6, John Degney, mason, family: 1/2 males, 1/1 females, farmer, stock on Field Book.

7, Givan Hamilton, yarn and cloth gauger, family: 3/1 males, 2/1 females, farmer, stock on Field Book.

8, Jackson Fields, parish schoolmaster, family: 1/3 males, 1/0 females, cottier, stock on Field Book. 18th May 1840.

Townland of Ballygonybeg: no trades but weavers.

Occupations: Townlands of Tamlaght, County Tyrone

[All masters].

Townland of Mullaghtirony: 1, Robert Coulter, water keeper, family: 1/2 males, 1/4 females, cottier, stock on Field Book. 28th May 1840.

Townland of Aghaveagh: 1, William Edmondson, carpenter, family: 1/0 males, 4/0 females, farmer, stock on Field Book.

2, Hugh Gilbreath, thatcher, family: 1/2 males, 2/1 females, cottier, stock on Field Book.

Observer's signature: John Hanna, date 4th June 1840.

Notebook entitled "Weaving and Trades" completed by John Hanna, June 1840

MEMOIR WRITING

Memoir Writing

Forwarded June 24th 1840 [signed] J. Hanna received 29th June 1840 [initialled] JBH.

PRODUCTIVE ECONOMY

Linen Weavers: Townland of Aghaveagh

[Printed table contains the following headings: townland, name of weaver, denomination of weft length of web [52 yards]; price of linen and cotton yarn per lb of hank, price of woollen yarn per hank; number of independent and dependent looms; number of hanks per web of linen, cotton and woollen cloth; number of webs woven per annum; price of cloth per yard; number of weeks employed per annum; grade of weaver; independent weavers' markets; Field Book reference; dependent weavers: wage per week, by whom employed, proprietor and commission, how employed remainder of the year. Denomination 10/28, each weaver has 1 loom, markets Cookstown and Moneymore, all independent weavers unless indicated, all master weavers].

Weaver no.1, John Wilson; warp hanks 4d weft hanks 4d; warp hanks 26/2.8, weft hanks 28 2.10; weaves 20 webs per annum, cloth priced 6 per yard, employed weaving 45 weeks per annum reference F2.

Weaver no.2, John Long; warp hanks 4d, weft hanks 4d; warp hanks 26/2.8, weft hanks 26/2.8 weaves 19 webs per annum, cloth priced 6d per yard, employed weaving 40 weeks per annum reference F8.

Weaver no.3, James Owens; warp hanks 4d weft hanks 4d; warp hanks 26/2.8, weft hanks 2

Parish of Tamlaght

2.8; weaves 22 webs per annum, cloth priced 6d farthing per yard, employed weaving 45 weeks per annum; reference F10.

Weaver no.4, Andrew Taylor; warp hanks 4d ha'penny, weft hanks 4d; warp hanks 26/2.10, weft hanks 28/3.0; weaves 20 webs per annum, cloth priced 6d ha'penny per yard, employed weaving 34 weeks per annum; reference F11.

Weaver no.5, William Vance; warp hanks 4d ha'penny, weft hanks 4d; warp hanks 26/2.8, weft hanks 27/2.10; weaves 18 webs per annum, cloth priced 6d farthing per yard, employed weaving 40 weeks per annum; reference F13.

Weaver no.6, Robert Campbell; warp hanks 4d ha'penny, weft hanks 4d; warp hanks 26/2.8, weft hanks 26/3.0; weaves 12 webs per annum, cloth priced 6d farthing per yard, employed weaving 15 weeks per annum; reference F14.

Weaver no.7, William Campbell; warp hanks 4d ha'penny, weft hanks 4d; warp hanks 26/2.8, weft hanks 26/3.0; weaves 12 webs per annum, cloth priced 6d farthing per yard, employed weaving 15 weeks per annum; reference F14.

Weaver no.8, Robert Owens; warp hanks 4d ha'penny, weft hanks 4d; warp hanks 26/2.8, weft hanks 27/3.0; weaves 22 webs per annum, cloth priced 6d farthing per yard, employed weaving 45 weeks per annum; reference C15.

Weaver no.9, John Owens; warp hanks 4d ha'penny, weft hanks 4d, dependent loom; warp hanks 26/2.10, weft hanks 29/3.8; weaves 24 webs per annum, cloth priced 7d per yard, employed weaving 45 weeks per annum; wages 5s per week, working for William Downing, Coagh; reference S15,

Weaver no.10, James Leech; warp hanks 4d ha'penny, weft hanks 4d; warp hanks 26/2.8, weft hanks 27/3.0; weaves 18 webs per annum, cloth priced 6d farthing per yard, employed weaving 36 weeks per annum; reference C15.

Weaver no.11, William Dunlop; warp hanks 4d ha'penny, weft hanks 4d; warp hanks 26/2.10, weft hanks 26/3.0; weaves 16 webs per annum, cloth priced 6d ha'penny per yard, employed weaving 38 weeks per annum, reference F15.

Weaver no.12, William Carnaghan; warp hanks 4d ha'penny, weft hanks 4d; warp hanks 26/3.0, weft hanks 28/4.0; weaves 24 webs per annum, cloth priced 6d 3 farthings per yard, employed weaving 40 weeks per annum; reference F16.

Weaver no.14, William Sands; warp hanks 4d ha'penny, weft hanks 4d; warp hanks 26/3.0, weft hanks 28/4.0; weaves 26 webs per annum, cloth priced 6d 3 farthings per yard, employed weaving 45 weeks per annum; reference F17.

Weaver no.15, Thomas Sands; warp hanks 4d ha'penny, weft hanks 4d; warp hanks 26/3.0, weft hanks 28/4.0; weaves 25 webs per annum, cloth priced 6d 3 farthings per yard, employed weaving 45 weeks per annum; reference F17.

Weaver no.16, Alexander Gibson; warp hanks 4d ha'penny, weft hanks 4d; warp hanks 26/2.10, weft hanks 26/3.0; weaves 24 webs per annum, cloth priced 6d farthing per yard, employed weaving 40 weeks per annum, reference F18.

Weaver no.17, Samuel Gibson; warp hanks 4d farthing, weft hanks 4d; warp hanks 26/2.10, weft hanks 26/3.0; weaves 30 webs per annum, cloth priced 6d farthing per yard, employed weaving 52 weeks per annum, reference F18.

Weaver no.18, James Quin; warp hanks 4d, weft hanks 4d; warp hanks 26/2.10, weft hanks 27/3.0; weaves 26 webs per annum, cloth priced 6d farthing per yard, employed weaving 45 weeks per annum; reference F19.

Weaver no.19, Henry Quin; warp hanks 4d, weft hanks 4d; warp hanks 26/2.10, weft hanks 27/3.0; weaves 26 webs per annum, cloth priced 6d farthing per yard, employed weaving 45 weeks per annum; reference F19.

Weaver no.20, William Montgomery; warp hanks 4d ha'penny, weft hanks 4d farthing; warp hanks 26/2.10, weft hanks 29/4.0; weaves 36 webs per annum, cloth priced 6d 3 farthings per yard, employed weaving 40 weeks per annum, markets Moneymore, Cookstown and Magherafelt; reference F22.

Weaver no.21, Joseph Montgomery; warp hanks 4d ha'penny, weft hanks 4d farthing; warp hanks 26/2.10, weft hanks 29/4.0; weaves 36 webs per annum, cloth priced 6d 3 farthings per yard, employed weaving 40 weeks per annum, markets Moneymore, Cookstown and Magherafelt; reference F22.

Weaver no.22, James Montgomery; warp hanks 4d farthing, weft hanks 4d; warp hanks 26/2.8, weft hanks 27/3.6; weaves 36 webs per annum, cloth priced 6d ha'penny per yard, employed weaving 50 weeks per annum, markets Moneymore, Cookstown and Magherafelt; reference F25.

[Signed] John Hanna, 2nd to 4th June 1840.

Linen Weavers: Townland of Ballygoneybeg

[Each weaver has 1 independent loom, markets Cookstown, Moneymore and Magherafelt, no dependent weavers, all master weavers].

Weaver no.1, James Ferguson, denomination 12/32; warp hanks 5d, weft hanks 5d; warp hanks 40/3.4, weft hanks 39/5.0; weaves 18 webs per annum, cloth priced 10d farthing per yard, employed weaving 46 weeks per annum; weaves constantly; reference F2.

Weaver no.2, Peter Mantavna, denomination 12/32; warp hanks 5d ha'penny, weft hanks 5d; warp hanks 40/3.0, weft hanks 40/3.6; weaves 10 webs per annum, cloth priced 10d ha'penny per yard, employed weaving 35 weeks per annum, farming the remainder of the year; reference F5.

Weaver no.3, George Mantavna, denomination 10/28; warp hanks 4d farthing, weft hanks 4d; warp hanks 26/2.10, weft hanks 26/2.10; weaves 16 webs per annum, cloth priced 6d per yard, employed weaving 30 weeks per annum, farming the remainder of the year; reference F5. May 20th 1840.

Linen Weavers: Townland of Coagh

[Denomination 9/28, each weaver has 1 independent loom; markets Cookstown, Moneymore and Magherafelt; no dependent weavers; all master weavers except no.3].

Weaver no.1, William Eldertin; warp hanks 4d farthing, weft hanks 4d; warp hanks 26/2.7, weft hanks 26/3.0; weaves 30 webs per annum, cloth priced 6d per yard, employed weaving 46 weeks per annum; weaves constantly.

Weaver no.2, John Charlton; warp hanks 4d farthing, weft hanks 4d farthing; warp hanks 26/3.0, weft hanks 26/3.6; weaves 16 webs per annum, cloth priced 6d farthing per yard, employed weaving 30 weeks per annum, farming the remainder of the year; reference F22.

Weaver no.3, William Charlton; warp hanks 4d farthing, weft hanks 4d farthing; warp hanks 26/3.0, weft hanks 26/3.6; weaves 12 webs per annum, cloth priced 6d farthing per yard, employed weaving 30 weeks per annum, apprentice weaver, farming the remainder of the year; reference F22.

Weaver no.4, Robert Charlton; warp hanks 4d farthing, weft hanks 4d farthing; warp hanks 26/2.8, weft hanks 26/3.6; weaves 19 webs per annum, cloth priced 6d farthing per yard, employed weaving 29 weeks per annum, farming the remainder of the year; reference F23.

Weaver no.5, William Charlton; warp hanks 4d farthing, weft hanks 4d farthing; warp hanks 26/2.8, weft hanks 26/3.6; weaves 19 webs per annum, cloth priced 6d farthing per yard, employed weaving 30 weeks per annum, farming the remainder of the year; reference F23.

Weaver no.6, Robert Ferguson; warp hanks 4d farthing, weft hanks 4d; warp hanks 26/3.0, weft hanks 26/2.8; weaves 27 webs per annum, cloth priced 6d farthing per yard, employed weaving 40 weeks per annum, farming the remainder of the year; reference C2.

Weaver no.7, George Millar; warp hanks 4d, weft hanks 4d; warp hanks 26/2.8, weft hanks 26/3.0; weaves 30 webs per annum, cloth priced 6d per yard, employed weaving 45 weeks per annum; weaves constantly; reference F51.

Weaver no.8, Edward [?] Willison; warp hanks 4d ha'penny, weft hanks 4d; warp hanks 26/2.10, weft hanks 26/3.0; weaves 16 webs per annum, cloth priced 6d farthing per yard, employed weaving 28 weeks per annum, farming the remainder of the year; reference F32.

Weaver no.9, William [?] McCollinn; warp hanks 4d farthing, weft hanks 4d; warp hanks 26/2.8, weft hanks 26/3.0; weaves 12 webs per annum, cloth priced 6d farthing per yard, employed weaving 28 weeks per annum, farming the remainder of the year; reference F33.

Weaver no.10, Robert Simpson; warp hanks 4d farthing, weft hanks 4d; warp hanks 26/2.9, weft hanks 26/3.0; weaves 27 webs per annum, cloth priced 6d farthing per yard, employed weaving 43 weeks per annum, weaves constantly; reference C4.

Weaver no.11, Hugh Taylor; warp hanks 4d ha'penny, weft hanks 4d; warp hanks 26/2.10, weft hanks 26/3.0; weaves 12 webs per annum, cloth priced 6d per yard, employed weaving 27 weeks per annum, farming the remainder of the year; reference F35.

Weaver no.12, David Berryman; warp hanks 4d, weft hanks 4d; warp hanks 26/3.0, weft hanks 26/3.0; weaves 27 webs per annum, cloth priced 6d per yard, employed weaving 48 weeks per annum, farming the remainder of the year; reference F39.

[Signed] John Hamilton, 2nd to 5th June 1840. Lodged in William Vance's, Coagh; forwarded June 24 1840, [signed] J. Hanna.

Linen Weavers: Townland of Drumconway

[Denomination 10/28, warp hanks 4d farthing, weft hanks 4d; warp hanks per web 26/2.6; each weaver has 1 independent loom; markets Cookstown, Magherafelt and Moneymore].

Weaver no.1, James Ford; weft hanks 25/2.10; weaves 36 webs per annum, cloth priced 6d farthing per yard, son to farmer no.1; weaves constantly.

Weaver no.2, Hugh Wates; weft hanks 25/2.10; weaves 36 webs per annum, cloth priced 6d farthing per yard, farmer no.9; weaves occasionally.

Weaver no.3, Samuel Bell; weft hanks 26/3.0; weaves 26 webs per annum, cloth priced 6d ha'penny per yard, farmer no.10; weaves occasionally.

Weaver no.4, Robert Bell; weft hanks 26/3.0; weaves 36 webs per annum, cloth priced 6d ha'penny per yard, son to farmer no.10; weaves constantly.

Weaver no.5, Peter Devlin; weft hanks 25/2.10; weaves 36 webs per annum, cloth priced 6d farthing per yard, journeyman to farmer no.11; weaves constantly.

Weaver no.6, William Hunter Junior; weft hanks 25/2.10; weaves 30 webs per annum, cloth priced 6d farthing per yard, son to farmer no.24; weaves occasionally.

Weaver no.7, Robert Henderson; weft hanks 26/3.0; weaves 36 webs per annum, cloth priced 6d ha'penny per yard, cottier no.1; weaves constantly.

Weaver no.8, William Bridget; weft hanks 26/3.0; weaves 36 webs per annum, cloth priced 6d ha'penny per yard, cottier no.6; weaves constantly.

[Signed] Archibald Thompson, 2nd to 4th June 1840, lodging in Mr Vance's, Coagh.

Linen Weavers: Townland of Drumard

[All master weavers, denomination 10/28 unless indicated; warp hanks 4d unless indicated; warp hanks 26/2.8 unless indicated; cloth priced 6d per yard unless indicated; each weaver has 1 independent loom, markets Cookstown and Moneymore].

Weaver no.1, James Gibson; denomination 12/32; warp hanks 4d ha'penny, weft hanks 4d; warp hanks 37/2.9, weft hanks 37/4.6; weaves 17 webs per annum, cloth priced 9d 3 farthings per yard; employed 46 weeks per annum; weaves constantly; reference F1.

Weaver no.2, William Rollins; weft hanks 28/3.4; weaves 6 webs per annum, employed weaving 13 weeks per annum, farming the remainder of the year; reference F4.

Weaver no.3, John Rollins; weft hanks 28/3.4; weaves 8 webs per annum, employed weaving 18 weeks per annum, farming the remainder of the year; reference F5.

Weaver no.4, Henry Hogg; weft hanks 27/3.0; weaves 14 webs per annum, employed weaving 28 weeks per annum, farming the remainder of the year; reference F11.

Weaver no.5, John Happer; warp hanks 26/2.10; weft hanks 28/3.4; weaves 18 webs per annum, employed weaving 36 weeks per annum, farming the remainder of the year; reference F6.

Weaver no.6, Henry Spear; weft hanks 27/3.2; weaves 3 webs per annum, cloth priced 6d farthing per yard, employed weaving 6 weeks per annum, farming the remainder of the year; reference F14.

Weaver no.7, Robert Spear; weft hanks 27/3.2; weaves 4 webs per annum, cloth priced 6d farthing per yard, employed weaving 8 weeks per annum, farming the remainder of the year; reference F15.

Weaver no.8, Henry Hamilton; weft hanks 27/3.8; weaves 26 webs per annum, employed weaving 40 weeks per annum, farming the remainder of the year; reference F16.

Weaver no.9, James Hamilton; weft hanks 27/3.8; weaves 28 webs per annum, employed weaving 40 weeks per annum; farming the remainder of the year; reference F16.

Weaver no.10, William Leech; weft hanks 27/3.4; weaves 32 webs per annum, employed weaving 52 weeks per annum, weaves constantly; reference F20.

Weaver no.11, William Manow; weft hanks 27/3.4; weaves 30 webs per annum, employed weaving 52 weeks per annum, weaves constantly; reference C to F20.

Weaver no.12, Philip McIlvanan; weft hanks 27/3.2; weaves 12 webs per annum, employed weaving 15 weeks per annum, labouring the remainder of the year; reference C to F21.

Weaver no.13, Robert Devlin; weft hanks 26/3.0; weaves 20 webs per annum, employed weaving 36 weeks per annum, farming the remainder of the year; reference F22.

Weaver no.14, John Devlin; weft hanks 26/3.0; weaves 12 webs per annum, employed weaving 26 weeks per annum, farming the remainder of the year; reference F23.

Weaver no.15, Hugh Devlin; weft hanks 26/3.0; weaves 14 webs per annum, employed weaving 35 weeks per annum, farming the remainder of the year; reference F24.

I have remarked that the above denominations were generally woven in this neighbourhood. I enquired of several weavers the reason why. I am told that the farmers are anxious to have a great crop of flax, and that they sow it on the potato ground. The flax is coarse in consequence and the yarn cannot be spun fine. [Signed] John Hanna, 18th June 1840, forwarded 11th July 1840.

Linen Weavers: Townland of Mullaghtironey

[Each weaver has 1 independent loom, markets

Cookstown and Moneymore, no dependent weavers, all master weavers].

Weaver no.1, Thomas Campbell, denomination 10/28; warp hanks 4d, weft hanks 4d; warp hanks 26/2.10, weft hanks 26/3.0; weaves 30 webs per annum, cloth priced 6d farthing per yard, employed weaving 46 weeks per annum; weaves constantly; reference F6.

Weaver no.2, James Kane, denomination 12/32; warp hanks 5d, weft hanks 4d 3 farthings; warp hanks 40/3.0, weft hanks 40/5.6; weaves 18 webs per annum, cloth priced 10d ha'penny per yard, employed weaving 46 weeks per annum, farming the remainder of the year; reference F14.

Weaver no.3, Robert Coulter, denomination 12/32; warp hanks 5d, weft hanks 4d 3 farthings; warp hanks 40/3.0, weft hanks 41/6.0; weaves 18 webs per annum, cloth priced 10d ha'penny per yard, employed weaving 46 weeks per annum, waterkeeper the remainder of the year; reference C15.

[Signed] John Hanna, 26th to 28th May 1840; forwarded June 24 1840.

Linen Weavers: Townland of Sessia

Thomas Bradley; denomination 10/28; warp hanks 4d farthing, weft hanks 4d, 1 independent loom; warp hanks 26/2.6, weft hanks 24/2.10; weaves 30 webs per annum, cloth priced 6d farthing per yard; markets Cookstown, Magherafelt and Moneymore; son to farmer no.2, weaves constantly.

[Signed] Archibald Thompson, June 5th 1840, lodging in Mr Vance's, Coagh. This townland is part of the parish of Arboe [initialled] JH. Forwarded June 24th 1840, J. Hanna.

Linen Weavers: Townland of Tamlaght

[Each weaver has 1 independent loom, markets Cookstown, Moneymore and Magherafelt; no dependent weavers, all master weavers].

Weaver no.1, George Walker, denomination 10/28: warp hanks 4d farthing, weft hanks 4d; warp hanks 26/2.8, weft hanks 26/3.0; weaves 12 webs per annum, cloth priced 6d ha'penny per yard; denomination 12/32; warp hanks 5d farthing, weft hanks 5d; warp hanks 40/3.6, weft hanks 41/5.0; weaves 4 webs per annum, cloth priced 10d ha'penny per yard; employed weaving 36 weeks per annum, farming the remainder of the year; reference F4.

Weaver no.2, George Irvine, denomination 12/32: warp hanks 5d farthing, weft hanks 5d; warp hanks 40/3.6, weft hanks 41/5.6; weaves 6 webs per annum, cloth priced 10d ha'penny per yard; denomination 10/28: warp hanks 4d farthing, weft hanks 4d; warp hanks 26/2.8, weft hanks 26/3.0; weaves 11 webs per annum, cloth priced 6d ha'penny per yard; employed weaving 39 weeks per annum, farming the remainder of the year; reference F5.

Weaver no.3, Mathew Taylor, denomination 12/32; warp hanks 5d ha'penny, weft hanks 5d; warp hanks 40/3.0, weft hanks 41/3.6; weaves 12 webs per annum, cloth priced 10d ha'penny per yard, employed weaving 30 weeks per annum, farming the remainder of the year; reference F11.

Weaver no.4, Hugh Hamilton, denomination 10/28; warp hanks 4d farthing, weft hanks 4d; warp hanks 26/2.8, weft hanks 26/2.10; weaves 30 webs per annum, cloth priced 6d farthing per yard, employed weaving 48 weeks per annum; weaves constantly; reference F22. May 18th 1840.

Linen Weavers: Townland of Urbal

[All independent weavers, each with with 1 loom, markets Cookstown, Stewartstown and Moneymore].

Weaver no.1, William Ranfrew; denomination 10/28; warp hanks 4d farthing, weft hanks 4d; warp hanks 26/3.6, weft hanks 25/2.10; weaves 26 webs per annum, cloth priced 6d farthing per yard, cottier no.1; occasionally labouring.

Weaver no.2, Thomas Wilkinson; denomination 10/28; warp hanks 4d farthing, weft hanks 4d; warp hanks 26/2.6, weft hanks 25/2.10; weaves 20 webs per annum, cloth priced 6d farthing per yard, cottier no.2; occasionally labouring.

Weaver no.3, Harry Bell; denomination 10/28; warp hanks 4d farthing, weft hanks 4d; warp hanks 26/2.6, weft hanks 26/3.0; weaves 30 webs per annum, cloth priced 6d farthing per yard, half-brother to farmer no.11; weaves constantly.

Weaver no.4, Thomas Ferguson; denomination 9/28; warp hanks 4d, weft hanks 4d; warp hanks 23/2.3, weft hanks 23/2.6; weaves 26 webs per annum, cloth priced 5d ha'penny per yard, son to farmer no.27; weaves constantly.

Weaver no.5, Samuel Ferguson; denomination 9/28; warp hanks 4d, weft hanks 4d; warp hanks 23/2.3, weft hanks 23/2.6; weaves 26 webs per annum, cloth priced 5d ha'penny per yard, son to farmer no.27; weaves constantly.

Weaver no.6, Joseph Eldertin; denomination 10/28; warp hanks 4d ha'penny, weft hanks 4d; warp hanks 26/2.6, weft hanks 26/3.0; weaves 30 webs per annum, cloth priced 6d ha'penny per yard, farmer no.43; weaves pretty constantly.

[Signed] Archibald Thompson, 27th to 29th May 1840, lodging in Mr Vance's, Coagh.

Parish of Tamlaght

Statistical Information for Aghaveagh, May and June 1840

Aghaveagh: Farmers, Acreages and Crops

[Printed form no.1, with additional handwritten columns, contains the following headings: farmer's number and name; size of farm, number of acres tillage, pasture, meadow, waste; number of acres under various crops, order of rotation; acres under orchards [*described in fractions which is suggested as acreage over number of years planted i.e. 1/50 = 1 acre, 50 years planted*], acres reclaimed since 1830, informant, kind and quantity of drainage].

Farmer no.1, Widow <Wido> Gilmore; 34 acres, 22 tillage, 2 pasture, 3 and three-quarters meadow, 5 bog: 2 wheat, 12 oats, 3 potatoes, half an acre flax, half an acre vetches, 1 turnips, 3 clover; rotation: 1 oats, 2 potatoes or turnips, 3 oats, wheat or vetches with clover sown, 4 flax or oats with clover cut, 5 grass, 6 grass; acres under orchard: 1 acre, 50 years planted; drainage: [diagram of drainage system, 40 by 40, 6 10/200].

Farmer no.2, James Wilson; 8 acres, 3 tillage, 2 and seven-eighths pasture, 2 meadow: 1 and three-quarters oats, 1 potatoes, a quarter acre flax; rotation: 1 oats, 2 potatoes, 3 oats or flax, 4 oats, 5 grass, 6 grass, 7 grass.

Farmer no.3, Widow Vance; 3 acres, 1 and five-eighths tillage, 1 and a quarter pasture: 1 oats, half an acre potatoes, one-eighth acre flax; rotation: 1 oats, 2 potatoes, 3 oats or flax, 4 oats, 5 grass, 6 grass.

Farmer no.4, John Arnold; 11 and a half acres, 8 and a quarter tillage, 1 and seven-eighths pasture, 1 and a quarter meadow: half an acre wheat, one-eighth acre rye, 4 oats, 2 and a half potatoes, half an acre flax, one-eighth acre turnips, half an acre clover; rotation: 1 oats, 2 potatoes or turnips, 3 potatoes or oats with wheat or rye and clover sown, 4 oats with clover cut, 5 grass, 6 grass.

Farmer no.5, Samuel Dool; 11 and a half acres, 7 and three-quarters tillage, 2 and a half pasture, 1 meadow: a quarter acre rye, 3 and a half oats, 2 potatoes, three-quarter acres flax, one-eighth acre vetches, one-eighth acre turnips, 1 acre clover; rotation: 1 oats, 2 potatoes or turnips, 3 rye, flax, vetches or oats with clover sown, 4 oats with clover cut, 5 grass, 6 grass.

Farmer no.6, John Vance; 14 acres, 10 and seven-eighths tillage, 3 pasture: a quarter or a half an acre rye, 6 and a half oats, 3 and a half potatoes, half an acre vetches, one-eighth acre turnips; rotation: 1 potatoes or turnips, 2 oats, rye or vetches, 3 oats or vetches, 4 grass, 5 grass, 6 grass; acres under orchard: a quarter acre, 6 years planted.

Farmer no.7, Alexander Gray; 17 and a half acres, 2 and a quarter tillage, 5 pasture, 6 meadow, 4 bog: 1 oats, 1 potatoes, a quarter acre flax; rotation: 1 potatoes, 2 oats or flax, 3 potatoes.

Farmer no.8, John Long; 4 and a quarter acres, 1 and seven-eighths tillage, 1 and three-quarters pasture, half an acre meadow: three-quarter acres oats, 1 potatoes, one-eighth acre flax; rotation: 1 potatoes, 2 oats or potatoes, 3 grass, 4 grass.

Farmer no.9, William Danagh; 8 and three-quarter acres, 4 and a half tillage, 3 and a half pasture, half an acre meadow: half an acre wheat, 1 and a quarter oats, 2 potatoes, half an acre flax, a quarter acre clover; rotation: 1 potatoes, 2 wheat, oats or flax with clover sown, 3 oats with clover cut, 4 grass, 5 grass; acres under orchard: one-eighth acre, 40 years planted.

Farmer no.10, Robert Owens; 7 and a quarter acres, 4 and a quarter tillage, 2 and seven-eighths pasture: 2 oats, 1 and a half potatoes, three-quarter acres flax; rotation: 1 potatoes, 2 oats or flax, 3 oats, 4 grass, 5 grass.

Farmer no.11, Andrew Wright, farmer and weaver; 3 acres, tillage: 2 oats, 1 potatoes; rotation: 1 potatoes, 2 oats, 3 potatoes etc.

Farmer no.12, Widow Davison; 3 acres, 1 and a quarter tillage, 1 and five-eighths pasture: half an acre oats, half an acre potatoes, one-eighth acre flax, one-eighth acre clover; rotation: 1 potatoes, 2 oats or flax with clover sown, 3 oats with clover cut, 4 grass, 5 grass.

Farmer no.13, William Vance, farmer and weaver; 17 acres, 8 and three-eighths tillage, 1 acre pasture, 1 acre meadow, 6 acres s [soft?] bog: one-eighth acre rye, 4 and three-quarters oats, 2 and a half potatoes, 1 acre flax; rotation: 1 potatoes, 2 oats, rye or flax, 3 oats, 4 grass, 5 grass; acres under orchard: one-thirty-second of an acre, 10 years planted; 1 acre reclaimed since 1830.

Farmer no.14, Robert Campbell; 11 and a quarter acres, 7 tillage, 4 pasture: 4 oats, 3 potatoes; rotation: 1 oats, 2 potatoes, 3 oats or flax, 4 grass, 5 grass.

Farmer no.15, William Dunlop; 18 acres, 11 and three-eighths tillage, 5 and a quarter pasture, 1 acre meadow: half an acre wheat, one-eighth acre rye, 4 and a half oats, 5 potatoes, 1 acre flax, one-eighth acre vetches, one-eighth acre turnips; rotation: 1 potatoes, 2 wheat or oats with turnips, rye or potatoes, 3 oats or vetches, 4 grass, 5 grass; 2 acres reclaimed since 1830.

Farmer no.16, William Carnaghan, farmer and weaver; 1 acre, tillage: three-quarter acres oats, a quarter acre potatoes; rotation: 1 potatoes, 2 oats, 3 potatoes or oats.

Farmer no.17, James Sands; 3 and a quarter acres, 2 and a half tillage, three-quarter acres pasture: 1 and a half oats, 1 potatoes; rotation: 1 potatoes, 2 oats or flax, 3 oats, 4 grass, 5 grass.

Farmer no.18, William Gibson; 12 and a quarter acres, 7 and one-eighth tillage, 4 pasture, 1 acre scrog; half an acre wheat, 4 oats, 2 and a quarter potatoes, a quarter acre flax, one-eighth acres vetches; rotation: 1 oats, 2 potatoes, 3 wheat, oats or potatoes, 4 oats or vetches, 5 grass, 6 grass; 2 acres reclaimed since 1830; drainage: [diagram of drainage system, 40 20, 1 2/12].

Farmer no.19, Widow Quin; 2 acres, 1 and fifteen-sixteenths tillage: 1 and one-eighth oats, three-quarter acres potatoes, one-sixteenth acre flax; rotation: 1 potatoes, 2 oats or flax, 3 potatoes.

Farmer no.20, William Edminson, farmer and carpenter; 9 and a quarter acres, 4 and a quarter tillage, 3 and one-eighth pasture, 2 acres meadow: 2 and a half oats, 1 and a quarter potatoes, half an acre flax; rotation: 1 potatoes, 2 oats or potatoes, 3 oats, 4 grass, 5 grass; acres under orchard: a quarter acre, 8 years planted.

Farmer no.21, Widow Edminson; 7 acres, 4 and seven-eighths tillage, 1 pasture, 1 meadow: a quarter acre wheat, 3 oats, 1 and a half potatoes, one-eighth acre flax; rotation: 1 potatoes, 2 oats, wheat or flax, 3 oats, 4 grass, 5 grass.

Farmer no.22, William Montgomery; 15 acres, 9 and a quarter tillage, 4 and a half pasture, 1 acre meadow: a quarter acre wheat, one-eighth acre rye, 5 oats, 3 potatoes, one-eighth acre flax, three-quarter acres clover; rotation: 1 potatoes, 2 oats or flax with rye or wheat and clover sown, 3 oats with clover cut, 4 grass, 5 grass; acres under orchard: half an acre, 100 years planted; 1 acre reclaimed since 1830; drainage: [diagram of drainage system, 36 by 24, 3 4/100].

Farmer no.23, Alexander Hamilton; 8 acres, 5 and three-eighths tillage, 2 and a half pasture: three-quarter acres wheat, 2 oats, 2 potatoes, one-eighth acre flax, half an acre clover; rotation: 1 potatoes, 2 oats, flax or wheat with clover sown, 3 oats with clover cut and clover sown for grazing, 4 grass, 5 grass; acres under orchard: a quarter acre, 70 years planted.

Farmer no.24, William Smith; 5 acres, 3 and a quarter tillage, 1 and five-eighths pasture: 1 and a half oats, 1 and a half potatoes, a quarter acre flax; rotation: 1 potatoes, 2 oats or flax, 3 oats, 4 grass, 5 grass, 6 grass; acres under orchard: a quarter acre, 60 years planted.

Farmer no.25, William Smith Junior; 5 acres, 3 tillage, 1 and seven-eighths pasture: 1 and three-quarters oats, 1 potatoes, a quarter acre flax; rotation: 1 potatoes, 2 oats or flax, 3 oats, 4 grass, 5 grass, 6 grass.

Farmer no.26, Thomas Read; 2 and three-quarter acres, 1 and thirteen-sixteenths tillage, fifteen-sixteenths pasture: 1 oats, three-quarter acres potatoes, one-sixteenth acre flax; rotation: 1 potatoes, 2 oats or flax, 3 oats, 4 grass, 5 grass.

Farmer no.27, Samuel Jamison; 25 acres, 11 and a half tillage, 10 and a half pasture, 1 and a half meadow, 1 acre waste: 1 wheat, 5 oats, 3 potatoes, 1 flax, a quarter acre vetches, one-eighth acre turnips, 1 and one-eighth clover; rotation: 1 oats, 2 potatoes or turnips, 3 wheat with oats or flax and clover sown, 4 oats or vetches with clover cut, 5 grass, 6 grass.

Farmer no.28, William J. Mackey Esq., proprietor of townland, 20 acres unenclosed bog: information from Tithe Book.

Statute acres 370.24 equals 287 and a half acres Cunningham. Totals: 153 and a quarter acres tillage, 69 and five-sixteenths pasture, 22 and a half acres meadow, 37 acres waste. Tillage: 6 and a quarter wheat, 1 rye, 78 and five-eighths oats, 48 and a quarter potatoes, 8 and five-eighths flax, 1 and five-eighths vetches, 1 and five-eighths turnips, 7 and a quarter clover, [total] 153 and a quarter acres.

There are a great many roads through this townland which I consider will fully account for the deficiency in the acreage [initialled] J.H.

Field observer's signature: John Hanna, date 2nd to 5th June 1840.

Aghaveagh: Farmers' Stock and Implements

[Printed form no.2, with additional handwritten columns, contains the following headings: farmer's number, irrigation, horses and other livestock, looms, implements of husbandry. Handwritten additions to printed table: horses for pleasure 18 pounds; for agriculture, old 10 to 15 pounds, young 5 pounds; for transport none; asses none; cattle, old 10 to 15 pounds, young 1 to 3 pounds; sheep 25s, goats 6s 6d; hogs, old 3 to 4 pounds, young 5s 6d to 15s; geese old 3s to 3s 6d, ducks old 6d to 9d, turkeys old 3s to 3s 6d, hens old 5d to 9d, beehives none; ploughs, iron 4 pounds, wood 1 pound to 30s; harrows none, breaks 10s to 14s, rollers 30s to 50s, drill hoes 1 pound, carts 3 to 5 pounds, wheel cars 30s, slide cars none, threshing machines none, corn fans 2 pounds, spinning wheels 8s to 14s; linen looms 2 pounds to 2 pounds 10s; box barrows 8s 6d to 12s,

Parish of Tamlaght

turf barrows 2s to 3s, agricultural spades 2s to 2s 2d, agricultural shovels 15d to 30d, scythe hooks 7d to 9d, teethed hooks 5d to 7d].

Numbers of animals are given as fractions which may relate to mature or young stock e.g. 2/1 agricultural horses = 2 horses, 1 foal. In the case of agricultural spades, 2/1 indicates 2 agricultural spades and 1 turf spade. All looms are for linen].

Farmer no.1, inundated; 2 pleasure horses, 2/1 agricultural horses, 7/6 cattle, 6/0 hogs, 4/16 geese, 4/10 ducks, 4/2 turkeys, 3/10 hens, 1 iron and 1 wooden plough, 2 breaks, 1 roller, 1 drill hoe, 2 carts, 1 corn fan, 3 spinning wheels, 1 unemployed loom, 1 box barrow, 4 turf barrows, 2/2 agricultural spades, 2 agricultural shovels, 2 scythe hooks, 4 teethed hooks.

Farmer no.2, inundated; 1/0 cattle, 1/0 hogs, 3/4 ducks, 2/6 hens, 1 spinning wheel, 1 employed loom, 1 box barrow, 1 turf barrow, 1/1 agricultural spades, 1 agricultural shovel, 2 teethed hooks.

Farmer no.3, grass let, 2/0 hens, 1 spinning wheel, 1/0 agricultural spades, 1 agricultural shovel, 1 teethed hook.

Farmer no.4, 1/0 agricultural horses, 2/1 cattle, 1/0 hogs, 2/6 geese, 4/8 ducks, 2/11 hens, 1 wooden plough, 1 break, 1 cart, 2 spinning wheels, 1 box barrow, 4 turf barrows, 2/1 agricultural spades, 2 agricultural shovels, 2 teethed hooks.

Farmer no.5, inundated; 1/0 agricultural horses, 1/1 cattle, 2/0 hogs, 2/9 geese, 1/7 ducks, 4/3 hens, 1 wooden plough, 1 break, 1 cart, 2 spinning wheels, 1 unemployed loom, 1 box barrow, 2 turf barrows, 2/1 agricultural spades, 1 agricultural shovel, 4 teethed hooks.

Farmer no.6, 1/0 agricultural horses, 3/0 cattle, 2/12 hogs, 1/6 geese, 2/4 ducks, 2/12 turkeys, 3/6 hens, 1 improved wooden plough, 1 break, 1 roller, 1 cart, 2 spinning wheels, 1 unemployed loom, 1 box barrow, 2 turf barrows, 2/1 agricultural spades, 2 agricultural shovels, 4 teethed hooks.

Farmer no.7, inundated; lives in Ballynaragan, parish Arboe, grazes his cattle occasionally on this farm.

Farmer no.8, 1/0 cattle, 2 spinning wheels, 1 employed loom, 1 box barrow, 2/0 agricultural spades, 1 agricultural shovel, 2 teethed hooks.

Farmer no.9, 1/0 agricultural horses, 3/0 cattle, 2/0 hogs, 4/6 ducks, 2/10 hens, 1 wooden plough, 1 break, 1 cart, 1 spinning wheel, 1 unemployed loom, 1 turf barrow, 2/0 agricultural spades, 2 agricultural shovels, 1 teethed hook.

Farmer no.10, 2/0 cattle, 2/0 hogs, 4/10 ducks, 2/6 hens, 2 spinning wheels, 1 employed and 1 unemployed loom, 2/0 agricultural spades, 1 agricultural shovel, 2 teethed hooks.

Farmer no.11, 1 goat, 3/5 ducks, 4/8 hens, 1 spinning wheel, 1 employed and 1 unemployed loom, 1/0 agricultural spades, 1 agricultural shovel, 1 teethed hook.

Farmer no.12, 1/0 cattle, 1/0 hogs, 2/7 ducks, 6/3 hens, 1 spinning wheel, 1 box barrow, 1 turf barrow, 2/0 agricultural spades, 1 agricultural shovel, 4 teethed hooks.

Farmer no.13, 1 agricultural horse, 2/1 cattle, 2/0 hogs, 2/10 ducks, 3/10 turkeys, 3/6 hens, 1 wooden plough, 1 break, 1 cart, 4 spinning wheels, 1 employed and 1 unemployed loom, 1 box barrow, 1 turf barrow, 2/0 agricultural spades, 4 agricultural shovels, 2 teethed hooks.

Farmer no.14, 2/0 agricultural horses, 2/0 cattle, 1/0 sheep, 2/0 hogs, 2/9 geese, 2/9 ducks, 4/0 hens, 1 improved wooden plough, 1 break, 1 cart, 1 wheel car, 3 spinning wheels, 2 employed looms, 2 turf barrows, 2/1 agricultural spades, 1 agricultural shovel, 4 teethed hooks.

Farmer no.15, 1/0 agricultural horses, 4/0 cattle, 3/0 hogs, 1/3 geese, 5/0 ducks, 3/0 turkeys, 4/6 hens, 1 improved wooden plough, 1 break, 1 cart, 3 spinning wheels, 1 employed and 1 unemployed loom, 1 box barrow, 2 turf barrows, 2/1 agricultural spades, 1 agricultural shovel, 4 teethed hooks.

Farmer no.16, 1/0 hogs, 2/0 ducks, 2/0 hens, 3 spinning wheels, 1 employed and 1 unemployed loom, 1 agricultural spade, 1 agricultural shovel, 1 teethed hook.

Farmer no.17, 1/0 cattle, 1/0 hogs, 1/9 ducks, 4/6 hens, 1 spinning wheel, 2 employed looms, 2/0 agricultural spades, 2/0 agricultural shovels, 4 teethed hooks.

Farmer no.18, 1/0 agricultural horses, 2/1 cattle, 1/0 hogs, 7/9 ducks, 1/0 hens, 1 iron plough, 1 break, 1 cart, 2 spinning wheels, 2 employed looms, 1 box barrow, 2/1 agricultural spades, 3 agricultural shovels, 4 teethed hooks.

Farmer no.19, 2/0 goats, 7/0 ducks, 4/0 hens, 2 spinning wheels, 2 employed looms, 2/0 agricultural spades, 3 teethed hooks.

Farmer no.20, irrigation by rivulet, 1/0 cattle, 2/0 goats, 2/0 hogs, 6/0 ducks, 2/0 hens, 1 wooden plough, 1 break, 1 wheel car, 3 spinning wheels, 1 box barrow, 3/0 agricultural spades, 3 agricultural shovels, 1 scythe hook, 3 teethed hooks.

Farmer no.21, 1/0 cattle, 1/0 hogs, 2/7 ducks, 1/4 hens, 1 spinning wheel, 1 box barrow, 2/0 agricultural spades, 1 agricultural shovel, 3 teethed hooks.

Farmer no.22, inundated, 2/0 agricultural

horses, 2/1 cattle, 1/0 hogs, 9/5 ducks, 4/6 hens, 1 iron and wooden plough, 1 break, 2 carts, 2 spinning wheels, 2 employed looms, 1 box barrow, 2 turf barrows, 5/1 agricultural spades, 2 agricultural shovels, 2 scythe hooks, 3 teethed hooks.

Farmer no.23, 1/0 agricultural horses, 1/0 cattle, 3/1 hogs, 3/0 ducks, 2/4 hens, 1 wooden plough, 1 cart, 1 spinning wheels, 1 unemployed loom, 1 box barrow, 2/0 agricultural spades, 1/0 agricultural shovels, 1 teethed hook.

Farmer no.24, 1 agricultural horse, 1/0 cattle, 1/0 hogs, 4/0 ducks, 3/11 hens, 1 wooden plough, 1 break, 1 cart, 1 spinning wheel, 1 employed loom, 2/0 agricultural spades, 1 agricultural shovel, 1 teethed hook.

Farmer no.25, 1/0 cattle, 1/0 hogs, 2/6 ducks, 2/0 hens, 1 spinning wheel, 1 unemployed loom, 1/0 agricultural spades, 1 agricultural shovel, 2 teethed hooks.

Farmer no.26, 1/0 cattle, 1/0 hogs, 4/0 hens, 1 spinning wheel, 1 unemployed loom, 1 box barrow, 1/0 agricultural spades, 1/0 agricultural shovels, 1 teethed hook.

Farmer no.27, 2/1 agricultural horses, 4/2 cattle, 6/2 sheep, 1/0 hogs, 7/22 geese, 4/6 ducks, 2/11 hens, 1 iron plough, 1 wooden plough, 1 break, 1 cart, 1 wheel car, 1 spinning wheel, 1 box barrow, 2 turf barrows, 4/1 agricultural spades, 2 agricultural shovels, 1 scythe hook, 2 teethed hooks.

Note: no.1 has 2 horses for sale. Her son is in the habit of purchasing young horses in autumn and feeding them for a year, and then selling them, but those horses are not worked. I therefore have entered them in the column of "pleasure horses." The young horse entered in the column of "agricultural horses" is a foal reared from one of the agricultural horses.

Field observer's signature: John Hanna, date 2nd to 5th June 1840.

Aghaveagh: Cottiers' Stock and Implements

[Printed form no.3, with additional handwritten columns, contains the following headings: cottier number, farmer's number, cottier's name and occupation, horses and other livestock, other stock and implements of husbandry, looms, yearly rent].

Cottier no.1, farmer no.1, John Sampson, labourer; 1/0 hogs, 4/2 hens, 1 spinning wheel, 1 teethed hook; rent 2 pounds.

Cottier no.2, Thomas Dawlis, labourer; 1/0 hogs, 2/0 hens, 1 spinning wheel, 1/0 agricultural spades, 1 agricultural shovel, 1 teethed hook; rent 2 pounds.

Cottier no.3, farmer no.7, William Kilpatrick, labourer; 1/0 hogs, 4/10 ducks, 2/6 hens, 1 spinning wheel, 1 box barrow, 1/0 agricultural spades, 1/0 agricultural shovels, 1 teethed hook; rent 4 pounds.

Cottier no.4, farmer no.15, James Owens, labourer; 3/0 ducks, 4/6 hens, 2 spinning wheels, 1/0 agricultural spades, 1/0 agricultural shovels, 2 teethed hooks; rent 50s.

Cottier no.5, James Leech, labourer and weaver; 1/0 hogs, 2/7 ducks, 1 spinning wheel, 1 employed linen loom, 1/0 agricultural spades; rent 3 pounds.

Cottier no.6, Ann [McKnow or McKeown ?], spinner; 3/6 ducks, 4/6 hens, 3 spinning wheels, 1 turf barrow, 1/0 agricultural spades, 3 teethed hooks; rent 3 pounds.

Cottier no.7, farmer no.18, Hugh Gilbreath, thatcher; 2/0 hogs, 3/0 hens, 2 spinning wheels, 1 turf barrow, 2/0 agricultural spades, 1 agricultural shovel, 1 teethed hook; rent 30s.

Cottier no.8, farmer no.21, John Neal, labourer; 1/0 hogs, 4/0 ducks, 2/6 hens, 1 spinning wheel, 1 agricultural spade, 1 agricultural shovel, 2 teethed hooks; rent 56s.

Cottier no.9, farmer no.26, Robert Whinerey, labourer; 1 spinning wheel, 1/0 agricultural spades, 1/0 agricultural shovels, 1 teethed hook; rent 28s.

Cottier no.10, farmer no.27, Nancy Rea, spinner; 1/0 hogs, 4/11 ducks, 3/0 hens, 1 spinning wheel, 1 agricultural spade, 2 agricultural shovels, 2 teethed hooks; rent 40s.

Cottier no.11, John Dimond, labourer; 1/0 hogs, 5/10 ducks, 2/0 hens, 1 spinning wheel, 1 agricultural spade, 1 agricultural shovel, 1 teethed hook; rent 20s.

Field observer's signature: John Hanna, date 2nd to 5th June 1840.

Aghaveagh: Labour and Proprietors

[Printed form no.4, with additional handwritten columns, contains the following headings: farmer's number; labour from family, house servants, constant labourers, occasional labourers, with number of days in spring, summer and autumn; head landlord, immediate landlord and tenure; tenant direct (t), subtenant from t (t2), subtenant from t2 (t3); yearly rent per acre; occasional labour of farmer and family, observations on other duties, spring wells, water pumps. Head landlord William Thomas Mackey Esq., immediate landlord the same, direct tenants].

[*In the tables numbers in household are sometimes represented as fractions, probably indicating older and younger members; and several*

Parish of Tamlaght

abbreviations are used, probably indicating occupation: thus n = non-working, s = spinner, t = thatcher, w = weaver].

Farmer no.1, family: 2/0 males, 5s/0 females, 1 male house servant, 2 male constant labourers; occasional labour: 4 males for 10 days in spring, for 12 days in autumn; family labour: 2 females for 6 days in spring, for 10 days in autumn; 1 female domestic duties constantly, 2 labours and spins, the rest spins constantly; rent per acre 1 pound 1s; 1 spring well.

Farmer no.2, family: 1,1w/0 males, 1/0 females; family labour: 1 male for 10 days in spring, for 12 days in autumn; 1 female for 10 days in autumn; female spinning, weaver weaving; rent per acre 1 pound 3s 6d.

Farmer no.3, family: 1/0 females; occasional labour: 1 male for 14 days in spring, for 8 days in autumn; family labour: this woman is constantly employed attending to her little farm; rent per acre 1 pound 3s 6d.

Farmer no.4, family: 1/0 males, 2/1n females; 1 male house servant; occasional labour: 1 male for 8 days in spring, for 14 days in autumn; family labour: 2 females for 10 days in spring, for 4 days in summer, for 14 days in autumn; females domestic duties and spinning, males farm constantly; rent per acre 1 pound 2s 6d; 1 spring well.

Farmer no.5, family: 2/1 males, 2/0 females; family labour: 1 female for 10 days in spring, for 4 days in summer, for 12 days in autumn; 1 female domestic duties and spinning, 1 farms and spins, males farm constantly; rent per acre 1 pound 2s 6d.

Farmer no.6, family: 1/0 males, 1/0 females; 1 male house servant; occasional labour: 1 male for 24 days in spring, 3 males for 12 days in autumn; 1 female for 24 days in spring, 3 females for 18 days in autumn; family labour: 1 female domestic duties and spinning, 1 farms and spins, male farms constantly; rent per acre 1 pound 2s 6d.

Farmer no.7, lives in Ballynacreagan; occasional labour: 2 males for 15 days in spring, 1 male for 10 days in summer, 4 males for 15 days in autumn; 2 females for 6 days in autumn; the work done by hired persons, farmer employed on his other farm; rent per acre 1 pound 3s 6d.

Farmer no.8, family: 1,1w/0 males, 2/0 females; family labour: 1 male for 10 days in spring, for 4 days in summer, for 20 days in autumn; 2 females for 6 days in spring, for 3 days in summer, for 10 days in autumn; male weaves and the females spin and attend to the domestic duties the rest of the time; rent per acre 1 pound.

Farmer no.9, family: 1/0 males, 1/2n females; occasional labour: 1 male for 40 days in spring, 2 males for 14 days in autumn; family labour: 1 female for 14 days in spring, for 4 days in summer, for 20 days in autumn; male farms constantly, female spins and attends to domestic duties; rent per acre 1 pound 3s.

Farmer no.10, family: 2,1w/2n males, 2/1 females; occasional labour: 1 male for 12 days in spring, for 16 days in autumn; 2 females for 12 days in spring, for 6 days in summer, for 14 days in autumn; 2 males farm, 1 weaves and farms, females spin and attend to domestic duties; rent per acre 1 pound.

Farmer no.11, family: [crossed out: 1 old],1w/0 males, 1/3n females; family labour: 1 male for 40 days in spring, for 15 days in summer, for 60 days in autumn; 1 female for 14 days in spring, for 4 days in summer, for 16 days in autumn; old man works none, weaver weaves the remainder, female spins; rent per acre 2 pound 2s.

Farmer no.12, family: 1/2n females; occasional labour: 1 male for 11 days in spring, for 6 days in summer, for 14 days in autumn; this woman attends constantly to her farm; rent per acre 1 pound 3s.

Farmer no.13, family: 2,1w/0 males, 3/2 females; family labour: 1 male for 20 days in spring, for 10 days in summer, for 30 days in autumn; 2 females for 6 days in spring, for 4 days in summer, for 18 days in autumn; 1 female domestic duties, 2 spin the remainder, 1 male weaver the remainder; rent per acre 17s 6d; 1 spring well.

Farmer no.14, family: 1,2w/0 males, 2/0 females; tenure 31 years, 3 lives; family labour: 2 males for 30 days in spring, for 14 days in summer, for 50 days in autumn; 1 female for 4 days in spring, for 3 days in summer, for 12 days in autumn; 1 female domestic duties, 1 spins, males weaving and labouring their farm in Mullaghtirony; rent per acre 1 pound 8s; 1 spring well.

Farmer no.15, family: 3,1w/0 males, 3/3n females; occasional labour: 2 males for 10 days in spring, for 12 days in autumn; family labour: 1 male for 10 days in spring, for 4 days in summer, for 16 days in winter; 2 females for 10 days in spring, for 10 days in summer, for 18 days in autumn; 1 female domestic duties, 2 spin, 1 male weaving and labouring, 3 males farm constantly; rent per acre 1 pound 2s 6d; 1 spring well.

Farmer no.16, family: 1w/0 males, 3s/0 females; family labour: 1 male for 8 days in spring, for 6 days in summer, for 8 days in autumn; 3 females for 4 days in spring, for 6 days in summer, for 10 days in autumn; females spin, males weave the remainder; rent per acre 1 pound 5s.

Farmer no.17, family: 1,2w/0 males, 1/3n females; family labour: 1 male for 10 days in spring, for 2 days in summer, for 11 days in autumn; 1 female for 8 days in autumn; females spin, males weave the remainder; rent per acre 1 pound 5s.

Farmer no.18, family: 2,2w/4n males, 2/3n females; family labour: 1 male for 14 days in spring, for 6 days in summer, for 10 days in autumn; 2 females for 4 days in spring, for 6 days in summer, for 12 days in autumn; females spin, males weave the remainder; rent per acre 1 pound 3s; 1 spring well.

Farmer no.19, family: 2w/2n males, 2/3n females; family labour: 2 males for 6 days in spring, for 4 days in summer, for 10 days in autumn; 2 females for 14 days in spring, for 4 days in summer, for 12 days in autumn; females spin, males weave the remainder; rent per acre 1 pound 3s.

Farmer no.20, family: 3,[crossed out: 1]/0 males, 4/0 females; occasional labour: 3 males for 6 days in spring, 2 males for 4 days in autumn; family labour: 3 females for 30 days in spring, for 20 days in summer, for 40 days in autumn; 1 female domestic duties constantly, 3 females spin the remainder of the year; trade farms none; rent per acre 1 pound 7s; 1 spring well.

Farmer no.21, family: 0/2 males, 1/2n females; occasional labour: 1 male for 4 days in spring, for 10 days in autumn; family labour: 1 female for 20 days in spring, for 16 days in summer, for 60 days in autumn; 1 female domestic duties, spins the remainder of the year; rent per acre 1 pound 9s.

Farmer no.22, family: 4,2w/0 males, 2/0 females; family labour: 2 males for 18 days in spring, for 10 days in summer, for 18 days in autumn; 1 female for 10 days in spring, for 10 days in summer, for 14 days in autumn; 1 female domestic duties constantly, 1 spins the remainder, weavers weave the remainder; rent per acre 1 pound 9s.

Farmer no.23, family: 1/1n males, 1/1n females, 1 female house servant; occasional labour: 1 male for 10 days in spring, for 12 days in autumn; family labour: 1 female for 10 days in autumn; 1 female domestic duties constantly, 1 female spins the remainder, male farms constantly; rent per acre 1 pound 5s.

Farmer no.24, family: 1,[crossed out: 1]w/2 males; weaver weaves constantly; rent per acre 1 pound 1s.

Farmer no.25, family: 1 male, 1 female; occasional labour: 1 male for 4 days in autumn; family labour: 1 female for 4 days in spring, for 6 days in summer, for 10 days in autumn; female atttends to domestic duties constantly and spins the remainder; rent per acre 1 pound 1s.

Farmer no.26, family: 1/1n males, 1/2n females; tenure 3 lives; family labour: females attend to domestic duties constantly; rent per acre 1 pound 8s 6d.

Farmer no.27, family: 2,1[crossed out:w]/0 males, 1/0 females; 1 male house servant; occasional labour 2 males for 10 days in spring, 1 male for 14 days in summer, 2 males for 20 days in autumn; 3 females for 10 days in summer, 2 females for 6 days in autumn; tenure 3 lives; family labour: 1 male for 30 days in spring, for 20 days in summer, for 100 days in autumn; female attends to domestic duties constantly, his 2 sons farm constantly, himself occasionally; rent per acre 1 pound 5s.

[Insert footnote, no.27: the master of this place has a farm in county Armagh, where part of his family reside. He goes back and forth betwixt the 2 farms [initialled] JH].

Field observer's signature: John Hanna; date 2nd to 5th June 1840.

Aghaveagh: Manures

[Printed form no.5, with additional handwritten columns, contains the following headings: farmer's number, use of dung, bog, lime, clay, compost loads, lime-kilns, compost weight, days employed, where made up].

[*Days employed are represented as fractions, e.g. 1/2, which may mean the number of people employed and days worked*].

Farmer no.1, dung: 36 tons per acre, 2s 8d per ton, 9 cwt per load, carried from farmyard, 2 persons employed for 1 and a half days; lime: 25 barrels per acre, 8d per barrel, 10 and a quarter cwt per load, carried 3 and a quarter Irish miles, 2 persons employed for 2 days; clay: 3d per ton, 9 cwt per load, carried from townland, 1 person employed for 7 days; compost loads: 60 loads dung, 100 loads clay; 9 cwt of compost from heap to the field, 2 persons employed for 6 days; made up at the house.

Farmer no.4, dung: 30 tons per acre, 2s 6d per ton, 8 cwt per load, carried from farmyard, 1 person employed for 4 days; bog: 2d per ton, 8 cwt per load, carried from townland, 1 person employed for 4 days; lime: 20 barrels per acre, 8d per barrel, 10 and a quarter cwt per load, carried 3 and a quarter Irish miles, 1 person employed for 3 days; clay: 3d per ton, 8 cwt per load, carried from townland, 1 person employed for 4 days; compost loads: 40 loads dung, 30 loads bog, 100 loads clay; 8 cwt of compost from heap to the field, 1 person employed for 13 days; made up at the house.

Parish of Tamlaght

Farmer no.15, dung: 35 tons per acre, 2s 6d per ton, 8 cwt per load, carried from farmyard, 1 person employed for 3 days; bog: 2d per ton, 8 cwt per load, carried from townland, 1 person employed for 6 days; lime: 30 barrels per acre, 8d per barrel, 10 and a quarter cwt per load, carried 3 and a half Irish miles, 1 person employed for 3 and a quarter days; clay: 3d per ton, 8 cwt per load, carried from townland, 1 person employed for 5 days; compost loads: 45 loads dung, 60 loads bog, 120 loads clay; 8 cwt of compost from heap to the field, 1 person employed for 11 days; made up at the house.

Farmer no.18, dung: 35 tons per acre, 2s 6d per ton, 8 cwt per load, carried from farmyard, 1 person employed for 4 days; bog: 2d per ton, 8 cwt per load, carried from townland, 1 person employed for 4 days; lime: 25 barrels per acre, 8d per barrel, 10 and a quarter cwt per load, carried 3 and a half Irish miles, 1 person employed for 2 and a half days; clay: 2d per ton, 8 cwt per load, carried from townland, 1 person employed for 4 days; compost loads: 36 loads dung, 50 loads bog, 200 loads clay; 8 cwt of compost from heap to the field, 1 person employed for 13 days; made up at the house.

Farmer no.27, dung: 28 tons per acre, 2s 4d per ton, 8 cwt per ton, carried from farmyard, 1 person employed for 4 days; bog: 2d per ton, 8 cwt per load, carried from townland, 1 person employed for 6 days; lime: 25 barrels per acre, 8d per barrel, 10 and a quarter cwt per load, carried 3 and a quarter Irish miles, 1 person employed for 3 days; clay: 2d per ton, 8 cwt per load, carried from townland, 1 person employed for 6 days; compost loads: 40 loads dung, 60 loads bog, 18 barrels of lime, 120 loads clay; 8 cwt of compost from heap to the field, 1 person employed for 10 days; made up at the house.

Farmers no.1, no.3, no.15, no.18: dung used alone and in compost, bog in compost, lime alone, clay in compost.

Farmer no.27: dung used alone and in compost, bog in compost, lime alone and in compost, clay in compost.

Description of acre: Cunningham.

Lime: number of bushels per barrel 4, weight per barrel 230 lbs.

Dung got in farmyard, bog in townland, clay in townland, lime at Tamnalanan, parish of Donaghenry.

Aghaveagh: Seed and Produce

[Printed form no.6 contains the following headings: farmer's number, quantity of seed and produce per Cunningham acre of wheat, barley (rye), oats, potatoes, flax, vetches, turnips, mangel wurzle, hay, clover; values of seed and measure, produce and time of sowing and harvest, observations].

Farmer no.1, wheat: 14 stones seed, 140 produce; oats: 18 stones seed, 160 produce; potatoes: 25 bushels seed, 200 produce; flax: 3 and a half bushels seed, 6 cwt produce; vetches: 3 and a half bushels seed, 10 tons produce; turnips: 2 lbs seed, 20 tons produce; clover: 1 bushel of hay seed to 10 lbs of clover seed, 12 tons produce; observations: level moory land, well cultivated.

Farmer no.4, wheat: 14 stones seed, 150 produce; rye: 12 stone seed, 110 produce; oats: 18 stones seed, 150 produce; potatoes: 26 bushels seed, 250 produce; flax: 3 and a half bushels seed, 5 and a half cwt produce; turnips: 2 and a half lbs seed, 18 tons produce; clover: 1 bushel of hay seed to 10 lbs of clover seed, 10 tons produce; observations: level, moory land, well cultivated.

Farmer no.15, wheat: 14 stones seed, 140 produce; rye: 12 stone seed, 118 produce; oats: 18 stones seed, 140 produce; potatoes: 25 bushels seed, 260 produce; flax: 3 and a half bushels seed, 6 cwt produce; vetches: 3 and a half bushels seed, 12 tons produce; turnips: 2 lbs seed, 25 tons produce; observations: south west aspect, red clay, well cultivated.

Farmer no.18, wheat: 14 stones seed, 130 produce; oats: 18 stones seed, 140 produce; potatoes: 25 bushels seed, 300 produce; flax: 3 and a half bushels seed, 6 and a half cwt produce; vetches: 3 and a half bushels seed, 10 tons produce; observations: south aspect, red clay, well cultivated.

Farmer no.27, wheat: 14 stones seed, 140 produce; oats: 18 stones seed, 140 produce; potatoes: 28 bushels seed, 250 produce; flax: 3 and a half bushels seed, 6 cwt produce; vetches: 3 and a half bushels seed, 12 tons produce; turnips: 2 and a half lbs seed, 18 tons produce; clover: 1 and a half bushels of hay seed to 8 lbs of clover seed, 12 tons produce; observations: east aspect, gravelly clay, well cultivated.

[Information from] farmer no.27. Wheat: value of seed 1s 4d to 1s 8d per stone, value of produce 1s 4d to 1s 6d per stone; time of sowing 1st to 20th November, time of harvest 20th August to 20 September.

Rye: value of seed 11d to 13d per stone, value of produce 10d to 13d per stone; time of sowing 1st December to 1st February, time of harvest 20th August to 10 September.

Oats: value of seed 11d to 14d per stone, value of produce 9d to 14d per stone; time of sowing

17th March to 10th April, time of harvest 1st September to 1st October.

Potatoes: value of seed 2d ha'penny to 3d ha'penny, value of produce 2d ha'penny to 3d ha'penny; time of sowing 10th April to 17th May, time of harvest 16th October to 1st December.

Flax: value of seed 12s 6d to 14s per bushel, value of produce 45s 6d to 50s per cwt; time of sowing 20th April to 12th May, time of harvest 25th July to 12th August.

Vetches: value of seed 7s 6d to 9s per bushel, value of produce 5d to 7d per cwt; time of sowing 1st November to 1st April, time of harvest 1st July to 12th August.

Turnips: value of seed 12d to 18d per lb, value of produce 6d to 8d per cwt; time of sowing 20th May to 12th June, time of harvest 1st November to 1st January.

Hay: value of seed 2s 6d to 5s per bushel.

Clover: value of seed 13d to 15d per lb, value of produce 6d to 7d per cwt; time of sowing 1st April to 1st May, time of harvest 10th June to 12th August.

Kind of acre: Cunningham.

Note: I have here returned the price of potatoes at 3d ha'penny, as it is the general price of produce until a few weeks past. They are at present selling at 4d ha'penny per stone, and about 2 weeks ago were so high as 5s 4d but only for about 1 week [initialled JH].

Field observer's signature: John Hanna, dated 2nd to 5th June 1840.

Aghaveagh: Table of Trades

[Printed form no.7 contains the following headings: name, trade, kind, rank, wages].

William Edmonson, carpenter, master, wages 2s per day.

Hugh Gilbreath, thatcher, master, wages 1s per day.

Field observer's signature: John Hanna, dated 2nd to 5th June 1840.

Aghaveagh: Condition of Cottiers

[Printed form no.8, with additional handwritten columns, contains the following headings: number of apartments, whether whitewashed, type of house, roof and chimney, number and type of windows, floor, beds, furniture, quality of clothes, area of garden. None are whitewashed, all stone and lime, with straw roofs, dry clay floors. Beds and clothes good unless stated. *Furniture is recorded by abbreviations without a key: t = table; c = chair; s = settle beds; ew = earthenware; tc = [ticking clock ?]; d = dresser].*

No.1, brick chimney, 2 lead windows, furniture: s, tc, ew; clothes bad; garden one-sixteenth of an acre.

No.2, brick chimney, 2 lead windows; furniture: s, tc, ew; garden one-sixteenth of an acre.

No.3, brick chimney, 2 lead windows; furniture: t, s, c, d, tc, ew; garden one-eighth of an acre.

No.4, mud chimney, 3 lead windows; furniture: t, s, c, d, tc, ew; garden a quarter of an acre.

No.5, mud chimney, 2 lead windows; furniture: t, s, c, d, tc, ew; garden one-sixteenth of an acre.

No.6, mud chimney, 2 lead windows; furniture: t, s, c, d, tc, ew; garden one-eighth of an acre.

No.7, brick chimney, 3 lead windows; furniture: t, s, t, c, d, ew; garden one-sixteenth of an acre.

No.8, brick chimney, 1 sash, 1 lead window; furniture: t, s, tc, ew; garden one-sixteenth of an acre.

No.9, 1 apartment, brick chimney, 1 lead window; furniture: s, tc, ew; clothes bad; garden one-sixteenth of an acre.

No.10, brick chimney, 2 lead windows, furniture: t, s, c, d, tc, e [ew ?]; garden a quarter of an acre.

No.11, 1 apartment, brick chimney, 2 sash windows; furniture: t, s, c, d, tc, e [ew ?]; garden one-sixteenth of an acre.

Field observer's signature: John Hanna, date 2nd to 5th June 1840.

Aghaveagh: Summary of Economy

[Form 9] Surface: a quarter part of it is level and three-quarters hilly.

Soils, kind: moory land (reclaimed from bog), red clay and red gravelly clay; depth from 5 to 14 inches.

Subsoil, kind: bog, blue clay and red sand mixed with gravel; depth, unknown.

Exposure: to all winds.

Springs: 7 spring wells.

Drainage: a few drains made with loose stones to within 10 inches of the surface.

Irrigation: part by a rivulet and part inundated by the overflow of the same.

Implements: iron, wooden and wooden improved ploughs, spades, 16 by 6 inches, nosed shovels <shovils>, scythe and teethed hooks.

Acres reclaimed since 1830: 6 acres.

Mills, corn: none; mills, flax: none; mills, fulling: none.

Quarries, kind of: none; application of: none.

Communications: a branch road from the Coagh and Stewartstown road passes through the

Parish of Tamlaght

townland to the Diamond <Dimond> of Arboe and a branch road from the Arboe and Cookstown road passes through the townland to Coagh, all in good repair.

Markets: Cookstown, Stewartstown, Coagh and Moneymore.

Breed of horses: Irish; breed of cattle: Irish and half bred from Durham and Irish; breed of sheep: large lowland; breed of hogs: Irish and half bred from Irish and Dutch.

Woods or plantations: 2 and twenty-one thirty-second acres of orchards; kind: apple, pear, cherry and plum <plumb> trees; when first planted: 6, 8, 10, 40, 50, 60, 90 and 100 years; present return: no fruit sold by any of them; it is all [consumed] by their own families and presented to their relatives.

Lime-kilns: none; manufactures: none.

Kinds of crops cultivated, oats: blanter, Poland, potatoe and tartanan; wheat: red and white, and golden drop; potatoes: cups, red and white Downs, copper dunns and kilties; flax: Riga and Dutch, a little New York; vetch: spring vetch; turnips: yellow Aberdeen, Swedish and white Norfolk.

Field observer's signature: John Hanna; residence: William Vance's, Coagh; 2nd to 5th June 1840.

[Insert addition: farmer's name and acres, where got: Tithe Book and John Arnold, cess applotter. Natural meadow, quantity per acre: 2 and three-quarter tons; time of harvest: from August 20th to September 30th; price per ton: 2 pounds 5s per ton; kind of acre: Cunningham; fences, kind of; soil and subsoil, faced with stones and planted with whitethorn; turf, where got: in townland; rent per acre, rough or waste land: same as arable, arable land from 1 pound to 2 pounds 2s; rough or waste land, kind of: spent bog and scraggy <scragey> land].

Statistical Information for Coagh, May and June 1840

Coagh: Farmers, Acreages and Crops

[Form 1, same as Aghaveagh except that it inquires about acres reclaimed since 1840. *The formula for orchards and plantations differs from previous table and we have represented 17/1p as 17 years old, 1 acre planted*].

Farmer no.1, William Dorning, farmer and drover, not working; 5 and quarter acres, 2 and three-quarters tillage, 2 and a half pasture: 1 and a half oats, 1 potatoes, a quarter acre flax; rotation: 1 potatoes, 2 oats or flax, 3 oats, 4 grass, 5 grass.

Farmer no.2, Mathew George, farmer, not working; 2 and quarter acres, tillage, oats; rotation: 1 oats, 2 potatoes, 3 wheat, 4 oats, 5 grass, 6 grass, 7 grass.

Farmer no.3, John Thompson, farmer and wheelwright; 7 acres, 5 tillage, 2 pasture: 1 wheat, 2 and a half oats, 1 potatoes, half an acre clover; rotation: 1 oats, 2 potatoes, 3 wheat or oats, 4 oats with clover sown, 5 grass with clover cut, 6 grass; drainage: [diagram of drainage system, 30 by 30, 10 4/100].

Farmer no.4, James Ekin, farmer and grocer, not working; 17 and quarter acres, 11 and three-quarters tillage, 1 pasture, 4 meadow, half an acre waste: 2 and a half wheat, 7 and quarter oats, 2 potatoes; rotation: 1 oats, 2 potatoes, 3 oats or wheat, 4 oats with clover sown for grass, 5 grass, 6 grass, 7 grass; drainage: [diagram of drainage system, 32 by 18, 2 6/35].

Farmer no.5, John Ekin, farmer and grocer, not working; 7 acres, 5 tillage, 1 pasture, 1 waste: 3 oats, 2 potatoes; rotation: 1 oats, 2 potatoes, 3 oats or wheat, 4 oats with clover sown for grass, 5 grass, 6 grass, 7 grass; acres under orchard: 17 years, 1 acre.

Farmer no.6, Eliza Hamilton, lives private; 7 acres, 4 tillage, 3 pasture: 3 oats, 1 potatoes; rotation: 1 oats, 2 potatoes, 3 oats, 4 oats with clover sown for grass, 5 grass, 6 grass, 7 grass.

Farmer no.7, Tom Brown, farmer, not working; 1 and a half acres, three-quarter acres tillage, three-quarter acres pasture: half an acre oats, a quarter acre potatoes; rotation: 1 oats, 2 potatoes, 3 oats, 4 grass, 5 grass, 6 grass.

Farmer no.8, John McGee, farmer, 5 acres, tillage: 2 oats, 1 potatoes, 2 flax; rotation: 1 oats, 2 potatoes, 3 flax, 4 oats, 5 grass, 6 grass, 7 grass; drainage: [diagram of drainage system, 30 by 24, 5 5/100].

Farmer no.9, James Sampson, surgeon, not working; 4 acres, 2 and a half tillage, 1 and a half pasture: 1 and quarter wheat, 1 potatoes, a quarter acre clover; rotation: 1 oats, 2 potatoes, 3 wheat, 4 oats with clover sown, 5 grass with clover cut, 6 grass; drainage: [diagram of drainage system, 30 by 30, 3 4/20].

Farmer no.10, Eliza Newtown, lady, not working; 11 acres, 7 and three-eighths tillage, 1 and five-eighths pasture, 2 meadow: one-eighth acre wheat, 2 and a half oats, 1 and a quarter potatoes, 3 and a half hay; rotation: 1 oats, 2 potatoes, 3 oats or wheat, 4 oats with hay sown, 5 grass with hay cut, 6 grass; land steward <stewart>; drainage:

[diagram of drainage system, 50 by 12, 20 62/200].

Farmer no.11, Duncan Storey, miller, not working; 8 and quarter acres, 6 and three-quarters tillage, 1 and a half pasture: 2 and quarter oats, 3 and half potatoes, 1 flax; rotation: 1 potatoes, 2 flax or oats, 3 oats with clover sown for grass, 4 grass, 5 grass, 6 grass; acres under orchard: 7 years, a quarter acre; drainage: [diagram of drainage system, 30 by 24, 7 2/70].

Farmer no.12, Robert Backwood, carpenter, not working; 2 and three-quarter acres, 1 and three-quarters tillage, 1 pasture: 1 and three-quarters oats; rotation: 1 potatoes, 2 oats, 3 oats, 4 grass, 5 grass, 6 grass.

Farmer no.13, Robert Cowan, grocer, not working; 6 and a half acres, tillage: three-quarter acres wheat, 3 and a half oats, 2 potatoes, a quarter acre clover; rotation: 1 potatoes, 2 wheat or oats, 3 oats with clover sown, 4 grass with clover cut, 5 grass over grass; drainage: [diagram of drainage system, 30 by 30, 4 2/40].

Farmer no.14, Lewis Quin [15 written above], grocer and publican, not working; 1 acre, tillage: half an acre oats, half an acre potatoes; rotation: 1 potatoes, 2 oats, 3 potatoes.

Farmer no.15, Alexander Slemons, wheelwright; 3 and quarter acres, 2 and quarter tillage, 1 pasture: 1 and a half oats, three-quarter acres potatoes; rotation: 1 potatoes, 2 oats, 3 oats, 4 grass, 5 grass.

Farmer no.16, Lily Devlin, labourer; [crossed out: one-eighth acre, tillage, potatoes]; rotation: 1 potatoes.

Farmer no.17, Henery Hagin, sawyer; [crossed out: one-eighth acre, tillage, potatoes]; rotation: 1 potatoes.

Farmer no.18, Thomas Dobson, labourer; [crossed out: one-eighth acre, tillage, potatoes]; rotation: 1 potatoes.

Farmer no.19, Mary Johnson, spinner, not working; [crossed out: one-eighth acre, tillage, potatoes]; rotation: 1 potatoes.

Farmer no.20, Thomas Young, labourer; [crossed out: half an acre, pasture]; not laboured.

Farmer no.21, Hugh Holly, farmer; [crossed out: half an acre, tillage, potatoes]; rotation: potatoes.

Farmer no.22, John Charlton, farmer and weaver; 3 acres, tillage: 1 and three-quarters oats, 1 potatoes, a quarter acre flax; rotation: 1 potatoes, 2 oats or flax, 3 oats, clover.

Farmer no.23, Robert Charlton, farmer and weaver; 3 acres, 2 and quarter tillage, three-quarter acres pasture: 1 oats, 1 potatoes, one-eighth acre flax, one-eighth acre clover; rotation: 1 potatoes, 2 oats or flax, 3 oats with clover sown, 4 grass with clover cut twice, 5 grass.

Farmer no.24, David Graham, farmer; 13 acres, 6 and a half tillage, 6 and a half pasture: 4 and quarter oats, 1 and quarter potatoes, a quarter acre flax; rotation: 1 oats, 2 potatoes, 3 oats or flax, 4 oats with clover sown, 5 grass with clover cut twice, 6 grass, 7 grass; acres under orchard: 11 years, one-eighth of an acre; drainage: [diagram of drainage system, 24 by 24, 1 1/10].

Farmer no.25, John McGucken, farmer;, 2 and a half acres, tillage: 1 wheat, three-quarter acres oats, three-quarter acres potatoes; rotation: 1 potatoes, 2 wheat, 3 oats.

Farmer no.26, [Terence or Birine?] McGucken, farmer, not working; 3 acres, tillage: half an acre wheat, 1 and five-eighths oats, three-quarter acres potatoes, one-eighth acre flax; rotation: 1 potatoes, 2 wheat, oats or flax, 3 oats.

Farmer no.27, James Gibson, farmer; 2 and a half acres, 1 and three-eighths tillage, 1 and one-eighth pasture, three-quarter acres oats, half an acre potatoes, one-eighth acre flax; rotation: 1 potatoes, 2 oats or flax, 3 oats, 4 grass, 5 grass.

Farmer no.28, John Gibson, farmer; [crossed out: three-quarters of an acre, half an acre tillage, a quarter acre waste: half an acre potatoes]; rotation: 1 potatoes.

Farmer no.29, George McGucken, farmer; 6 and three-quarter acres, 4 and quarter tillage, 2 and a half pasture: three-quarter acres oats, 2 and a half potatoes, 1 flax; rotation: 1 oats, 2 potatoes, 3 oats or flax, 4 oats, 5 grass, 6 grass, 7 grass.

Farmer no.30, Samuel Harkness [27 written above], farmer; 5 and a half acres, 2 and a half tillage, 2 pasture, 1 meadow: 2 and a half oats; rotation: 1 oats, 2 potatoes, 3 oats, 4 oats, 5 grass, 6 grass, 7 grass.

Farmer no.31, Charles Millar, farmer; 2 acres, tillage: 1 and quarter oats, three-quarter acres potatoes; rotation: 1 potatoes, 2 oats, 3 oats.

Farmer no.32, John Wilkison, farmer; 7 acres, 4 and three-quarters tillage, 2 and quarter pasture: 3 oats, 1 and a half potatoes, a quarter acre flax; rotation: 1 potatoes, 2 oats or flax, 3 oats, 4 grass, 5 grass.

Farmer no.33, John McCollum, farmer; 6 acres, 3 and a quarter tillage, 1 and a half pasture, 1 and quarter waste: 2 oats, 1 and one-eighth potatoes, one-eighth acre flax; rotation: 1 potatoes, 2 oats or flax, 3 oats, 4 grass, 5 grass; drainage: [diagram of drainage system, 30 by 30, 7 4/150].

Farmer no.34, Samuel Crooks, farmer; 25 acres, 10 tillage, 11 and quarter pasture, three-quarters of an acre meadow, 3 waste: 1 and quarter barley,

Parish of Tamlaght

5 oats, 2 and three-quarters potatoes, a quarter acre flax, three-quarter acres clover; rotation: 1 oats, 2 potatoes, 3 barley, flax or oats with clover sown, 4 oats with clover cut, 5 grass, 6 grass, 7 grass; acres under orchard: 20 years, half an acre; 2 acres reclaimed since 1840; drainage: [diagram of drainage system, 30 by 30, 2 3/150].

Farmer no.35, Sarah Montgomery, farmer; 2 and a half acres, 2 tillage, half an acre pasture: 1 and quarter oats, three-quarter acres potatoes; rotation: 1 potatoes, 2 oats, 3 oats, 4 grass.

Farmer no.36, James Bettie, carman, not working; 15 and three-quarter acres, 6 tillage, 6 and quarter pasture, half an acre meadow, 3 waste: 4 oats, 2 potatoes; rotation: 1 potatoes, 2 oats, 3 oats, 4 grass, 5 grass, 6 grass; acres under orchard: 120 years, a quarter acre.

Farmer no.37, James Montgomery, farmer, not working; 17 acres, 7 and three-quarters tillage, 9 and quarter pasture: 5 and a half oats, 2 potatoes, a quarter acre flax; rotation: 1 oats, 2 potatoes, 3 oats or flax, 4 oats, 5 grass, 6 grass, 7 grass; acres under orchard: 15 years, half an acre; 5 acres reclaimed since 1840; drainage: [diagram of drainage system, 30 by 30, 10 5/130].

Farmer no.38, Jane Taylor, farmer and spinner; 5 and a half acres, 3 and three-quarters tillage, 1 and three-quarters pasture: 2 and quarter oats, 1 and a quarter potatoes, a quarter acre flax; rotation: 1 potatoes, 2 oats or flax, 3 oats, 4 grass, 5 grass; 1 acre reclaimed since 1840.

Farmer no.39, Robert Berryman, farmer; 13 acres, 8 and a half tillage, 4 and a half pasture: three-quarter acres wheat, 5 oats, 2 and a half potatoes, a quarter acre flax; rotation: 1 oats, 2 potatoes, 3 wheat, oats or flax, 4 oats, 5 grass, 6 grass.

Farmer no.40, William Montgomery, farmer; 3 acres, 1 and a half tillage, 1 and a half pasture: 1 oats, half an acre potatoes; rotation: 1 potatoes, 2 oats, 3 oats, 4 grass, 5 grass.

Farmer no.41, James Walker, farmer; 14 and three-quarter acres, 7 tillage, 4 and quarter pasture, half an acre meadow, 3 waste: 4 and a half oats, 2 potatoes, half an acre flax; rotation: 1 oats, 2 potatoes, 3 oats or flax, 4 oats, 5 grass, 6 grass; acres under orchard: 200 [sic] acres; drainage: [diagram of drainage system, 30 by 30, 3 1/20].

Farmer no.42, Eliza Stewart, farmer; 3 and a half acres, 1 and three-quarters tillage, 1 and quarter pasture, half an acre waste: 1 oats, half an acre potatoes, a quarter acre flax; rotation: 1 potatoes, 2 oats or flax, 3 oats, 4 grass, 5 grass.

Farmer no.43, Robert Hogg, farmer and horse dealer, not working; 28 acres, 13 tillage, 11 and a half pasture, 3 and a half scrog: 9 and a half oats, 3 and a half potatoes; rotation: 1 oats, 2 potatoes, 3 oats, 4 oats with clover sown for grass, 5 grass, 6 grass, 7 grass; drainage: [diagram of drainage system, 30 by 30, 2 4/50].

Farmer no.44, Thomas Gerty, farmer; 5 acres, 3 and a half tillage, 1 and half pasture: 2 and a half oats, 1 potatoes; rotation: 1 potatoes, 2 oats, 3 oats, 4 grass, 5 grass.

Farmer no.45, Whaley Johnson, farmer; 19 acres, 8 and a half tillage, 10 and a half pasture: half an acre wheat, 5 and a half oats, 2 and quarter potatoes, a quarter acre flax; rotation: 1 oats, 2 potatoes, 3 wheat, flax or oats, 4 oats, 5 grass, 6 grass, 7 grass; acres under orchard: 8 years, a quarter acre; drainage: [diagram of drainage system, 30 by 30, 7 4/100].

Farmer no.46, James Wilkinson [45 written above], farmer; 5 and quarter acres, 3 and quarter tillage, 2 pasture: 2 and quarter oats, 1 potatoes; rotation: 1 potatoes, 2 oats, 3 oats, 4 grass, 5 grass.

Farmer no.47, John George [45 written above], lives private; 6 acres, pasture, not laboured.

Farmer no.48, James Wilson, farmer; 5 and three-quarter acres, 3 and five-eighths tillage, 2 and one-fifth pasture, one-eighth waste: half an acre wheat, 1 and a half oats, 1 and one-fifth potatoes, half an acre flax; rotation: 1 potatoes, 2 oats or flax, 3 oats, 4 grass, 5 grass; 1 acre reclaimed since 1840.

Farmer no.49, John Lagan, farmer; 5 and three-quarter acres, 3 and three-quarters tillage, 2 pasture: a quarter acre wheat, 2 oats, 1 and quarter potatoes, a quarter acre flax; rotation 1 potatoes, 2 wheat, oats or flax, 3 oats, 4 grass, 5 grass.

Farmer no.50, James Gibbins, farmer; 10 and three-quarter acres, 6 and quarter tillage, 4 and a half pasture: 4 oats, 2 potatoes, a quarter acre flax; rotation: 1 potatoes, 2 oats or flax, 3 oats, 4 grass, 5 grass.

Farmer no.51, John Ferson, farmer and publican; 4 acres, tillage: 3 oats, 1 potatoes; rotation: 1 potatoes, 2 oats, 3 oats, 4 oats, 5 grass, 6 grass.

Farmer no.52, John Hopkins, farmer; 1 acre, pasture, not laboured.

Farmer no.53, William Lenox Conyngham Esquire [37 written above], gentleman, not working; 127 and a half acres, waste: bog, [?] woods and plantings; acres under orchard: 15 years, 6 and a half acres.

Gardens brought from Garden Notebook, 6 and a half acres.

(Statute 606 and [?] nine-tenth acres equals Cunningham 470).

[Totals] farms: 194 and one-eighth acres tillage, 115 and one-eighth acres pasture, 8 and three-quarter acres meadow, 145 and a half acres waste: 9 and one-eighth acres wheat, 1 and quarter acres barley, 113 and three-eighth acres oats, 56 and a quarter acres potatoes, 8 and a half acres flax, 3 and a half acres hay, 2 and one-eighth acres clover.

Gardens: 1 and a half acres tillage, half an acre pasture, a quarter acre waste: 1 and a half acres potatoes; on this book.

Coagh: Farmers' Stock and Implements

[Prices added to form no.2: horses for pleasure 30 to 50 pounds, for agriculture 14 pounds to 20 pounds, for transport 18 pounds, asses 1 pound, cattle 6 pounds 10s to 12 pounds, sheep 15s to 25s, goats 5s to 7s 6d, hogs 1 pound to 1 pound 10s, geese 2s, ducks 6d to 8d, turkeys 2s, hens 6d, beehives none; iron ploughs 5 pounds, wooden ploughs 1 pound 10s, harrows 7s 6d, breaks 15s to 1 pound, rollers 12s to 1 pound 8s, drill hoes 1 pound 8s, carts 4 pounds 10s to 5 pounds, wheel cars 3 pounds, slide cars none, threshing machines none, corn fans 2 pounds to 3 pounds, spinning wheels 12s to 16s, employed linen looms 2 pounds 10s, unemployed linen looms 2 pounds 5s].

[Insert alternative prices: agricultural horses 10 pounds, cattle 1 to 2 pounds 10s, sheep 5s to 15s, goats 2s, hogs 10s to 15s, geese 6d, ducks 3d, turkeys 6d, hens 2d, box barrows 9s to 12s, turf barrows 2s 6d to 3s 6d, agricultural spades 2s to 2s 6d, agricultural shovels 1s 6d to 2s, scythe hooks 10d to 1s 4d, teethed hooks 5d to 7d].

[Insert footnote: Turf spades given as denominator to agricultural spades, price 1s 10d to 2s 2d [*e.g. 2/1 agricultural spades = 2 agricultural spades and 1 turf spade*].

Farmer no.1, 1/0 agricultural horses, 1/2 cattle, 2/0 hens, 1 cart, 1 box barrow, 2/0 agricultural spades, 1 agricultural shovel, 2 scythe hooks, 1 teethed hook.

Farmer no.2, lives in Tralee, parish Artrea.

Farmer no.3, 1/0 agricultural horses, 1/1 cattle, 0/1 hogs, 1 wooden plough, 1 break, 1 cart, 1 box barrow, 3/1 agricultural spades, 2 agricultural shovels, 3 scythe hooks, 1 teethed hook.

Farmer no.4, 2/2 agricultural horses, 2/1 cattle, 3/0 hens, 1 iron plough, 2 breaks, 2 carts, 1 corn fan, 1 spinning wheel, 2 box barrows, 1/0 agricultural spades, 2 agricultural shovels, 2 scythe hooks, 1 teethed hook; no water supply.

Farmer no.5, 1/0 agricultural horses, 2/1 cattle, 5/0 hens, 1 iron plough, 1 break, 1 cart, 1 corn fan, 1 box barrow, 2/0 agricultural spades, 2 agricultural shovels, 2 scythe hooks, 2 teethed hooks.

Farmer no.6, 1/0 agricultural horses, 1/1 cattle, 4/17 geese, 6/5 ducks, 8/9 hens, 1 cart, 1 box barrow, 1/0 agricultural spades, 1 agricultural shovel, 2 scythe hooks.

Farmer no.7, 1/0 cattle, 1/0 agricultural spades, 1 agricultural shovel.

Farmer no.8, 1/0 agricultural horses, 1/1 cattle, 1/0 hens, 1 iron plough, 1 break, 1 cart, 1 spinning wheel, 1 turf barrow, 1/0 agricultural spades, 1 agricultural shovel, 2 scythe hooks, 1 teethed hook.

Farmer no.9, 1/0 agricultural horses, 1/0 cattle, 0/1 hogs, 8/0 ducks, 6/7 hens, 1 break, 1 drill hoe, 1 cart, 1 box barrow, 1/0 agricultural spades, 2 agricultural shovels, 1 scythe hook, 1 teethed hook.

Farmer no.10, 1/0 pleasure horses, 2/0 agricultural horses, 5/1 cattle, 1/4 sheep, 1/9 hogs, 2/0 ducks, 1/0 turkeys, 12/0 hens, 1 iron plough, 1 break, 1 roller, 4 carts, 1 corn fan, 2 box barrows, 4 turf barrows, 1/0 agricultural spades, 2 agricultural shovels; no water supply.

Farmer no.11, 1/0 agricultural horses, 2/2 cattle, 0/4 hogs, 49/15 ducks, 2/0 hens, 1 wooden plough, 2 carts, 1 spinning wheel, 2 box barrows, 3 turf barrows, 3/1 agricultural spades, 2 agricultural shovels, 2 scythe hooks, 2 teethed hooks.

Farmer no.12, 1/0 cattle, 2/0 hens, 2 spinning wheels, 1 turf barrow, 1/0 agricultural spades, 1 agricultural shovel.

Farmer no.13, 1/0 agricultural horses, 2/0 cattle, 0/2 hogs, 1/0 turkey, 7/8 hens, 1 wooden plough, 1 break, 1 cart, 1 corn fan, 2 box barrows, 1 turf barrow, 2/0 agricultural spades, 2 agricultural shovels, 2 scythe hooks, 1 teethed hook.

Farmer no.14, lives in Derrycrin Eglish, parish of Ballinderry.

Farmer no.15, 1/0 asses, 1/1 cattle, 1/0 goats, 0/1 hogs, 1/9 geese, 2/0 hens, 1 wheel car, 1 spinning wheel, 1/0 agricultural spades, 1 agricultural shovel, 2 scythe hooks.

Farmer no.16, 1 spinning wheel.

Farmer no.17, 0/1 hogs, 2/0 hens, 2 spinning wheels, 1 agricultural spade.

Farmer no.18, 1 spinning wheel, 1/0 agricultural spades, 1 agricultural shovel, 2 scythe hooks.

Farmer no.19, 1 spinning wheel.

Farmer no.20, lives in Tamlaght.

Farmer no.21, 3/9 hens, 1 spinning wheel, 1/0 agricultural spades, 1 agricultural shovel, 1 teethed hook.

Farmer no.22, 3/7 ducks, 3/0 hens, 2 spinning wheels, 2 employed linen looms, 1 turf barrow,

Parish of Tamlaght

2/0 agricultural spades, 1 agricultural shovel, 2 scythe hooks, 1 teethed hook.

Farmer no.23, 1/0 agricultural horses, 1/0 cattle, 6/0 ducks, 2/0 hens, 1 wooden plough, 1 cart, 2 spinning wheels, 2 employed linen looms, 2/0 agricultural spades, 2 agricultural shovels, 2 scythe hooks, 2 teethed hooks.

Farmer no.24, 1/0 agricultural horses, 2/0 cattle, 1/0 hogs, 4/6 hens, 3/9 geese, 4/0 ducks, 1 wooden plough, 1 break, 1 cart, 2 spinning wheels, 1 unemployed loom, 1/1 agricultural spades, 1 agricultural shovel, 2 scythe hooks, 2 teethed hooks.

Farmer no.25, 1/0 agricultural horses, 1/0 cattle, 2/5 hens, 1 cart, 1 spinning wheel, 1/0 agricultural spades, 1 agricultural shovel, 2 scythe hooks.

Farmer no.26, 3/12 ducks, 4/12 hens, 1 spinning wheel, 1/0 agricultural spades, 1 agricultural shovel, 1 scythe hook, 2 teethed hooks.

Farmer no.27, 1/0 cattle, 1/0 hens, 1 spinning wheel, 1 box barrow, 1/0 agricultural spades, 1 agricultural shovel, 2 scythe hooks.

Farmer no.28, 1 box barrow, 1/0 agricultural spades, 1 agricultural shovel.

Farmer no.29, lives in Drumconway.

Farmer no.30, lives in Drumconway; no water supply.

Farmer no.31, 2/0 ducks, 4/7 hens, 2 spinning wheels, 1 employed linen loom, 1 turf barrow, 0/1 agricultural spades, 1 agricultural shovel, 2 scythe hooks, 1 teethed hook.

Farmer no.32, 1/0 agricultural horses, 1/0 cattle, 4/5 geese, 4/5 ducks, 6/5 hens, 1 wooden plough, 1 cart, 2 spinning wheels, 1 employed linen loom, 2 turf barrows, 2/1 agricultural spades, 1 agricultural shovel, 2 scythe hooks, 2 teethed hooks.

Farmer no.33, 1/0 cattle, 0/1 hogs, 4/0 ducks, 3/7 hens, 2 spinning wheels, 1 employed linen loom, 1 turf barrow, 1/0 agricultural spades, 1 agricultural shovel, 2 scythe hooks, 3 teethed hooks.

Farmer no.34, 2/0 agricultural horses, 5/1 cattle, 1/11 sheep, 0/1 hogs, 4/24 geese, 5/4 ducks, 1/7 turkeys, 6/12 hens, 1 iron plough, 1 break, 1 drill hoe, 1 cart, 1 wheel car, 1 corn fan, 3 spinning wheels, 1 box barrow, 2 turf barrows, 3/1 agricultural spades, 2 agricultural shovels, 4 scythe hooks, 3 teethed hooks; no water supply.

Farmer no.35, 0/2 hogs, 3/0 hens, 1 spinning wheel, 1 unemployed linen loom, 1 turf barrow, 1/1 agricultural spades, 1 agricultural shovel, 2 teethed hooks.

Farmer no.36, 3 transport horses, 2/1 cattle, 0/1 hogs, 4/0 ducks, 3/10 hens, 1 wooden plough, 1 cart, 1 box barrow, 2/0 agricultural spades, 2 agricultural shovels, 2 scythe hooks, 3 teethed hooks; no water supply.

Farmer no.37, 1/0 agricultural horses, 3/2 cattle, 1/1 goats, 0/2 hogs, 3/9 geese, 5/7 ducks, 0/3 turkeys, 6/8 hens, 1 wooden plough, 1 harrow, 1 break, 1 cart, 1 corn fan, 4 spinning wheels, 3 turf barrows, 2/2 agricultural spades, 1 agricultural shovels, 2 scythe hooks, 4 teethed hooks.

Farmer no.38, 1/0 agricultural horses, 1/0 cattle, 3/0 hens, 1 harrow, 1 cart, 3 spinning wheels, 1 employed linen loom, 2/1 agricultural spades, 1 agricultural shovel, 2 scythe hooks, 3 teethed hooks.

Farmer no.39, 1/0 agricultural horses, 3/2 cattle, 10/0 ducks, 2/0 hens, 1 wooden plough, 1 break, 1 cart, 2 spinning wheels, 1 employed linen loom, 2 turf barrows, 3/1 agricultural spades, 2 agricultural shovels, 3 scythe hooks, 3 teethed hooks.

Farmer no.40, lives in Aghaveagh.

Farmer no.41, 1/0 agricultural horses, 2/2 cattle, 2/11 geese, 7/0 ducks, 5/11 hens, 1 wooden plough, 1 break, 1 cart, 2 spinning wheels, 2 turf barrows, 2/1 agricultural spades, 2 agricultural shovels, 3 scythe hooks, 2 teethed hooks; no water supply.

Farmer no.42, 1/0 cattle, 1/0 goats, 4/0 hens, 2 spinning wheels, 1 turf barrow, 1/0 agricultural spades, 1 agricultural shovel, 2 scythe hooks, 1 teethed hook.

Farmer no.43, 4/0 pleasure horses, 2/0 agricultural horses, 2/2 cattle, 2/2 sheep, 3/14 hogs, 6/5 ducks, 1/7 turkeys, 6/0 hens, 1 wooden plough, 1 break, 2 carts, 1 spinning wheel, 1 box barrow, 2/0 agricultural spades, 2 agricultural shovels, 2 scythe hooks, 2 teethed hooks.

Farmer no.44, 1/1 cattle, 0/1 hogs, 2/10 geese, 5/0 ducks, 4/10 hens, 1 cart, 2 spinning wheels, 2 turf barrows, 2/1 agricultural spades, 1 agricultural shovel, 1 scythe hook, 3 teethed hooks.

Farmer no.45, 2/0 agricultural horses, 1/0 cattle, 4/8 geese, 5/0 ducks, 5/6 hens, 1 wooden plough, 1 break, 1 cart, 1 wheel car, 2 spinning wheels, 1 unemployed linen loom, 2 turf barrows, 2/1 agricultural spades, 2 agricultural shovels, 3 scythe hooks, 2 teethed hooks.

Farmer no.46, 2/0 turkeys, 5/0 hens, 1 spinning wheel, 1/0 agricultural spades, 1 agricultural shovel, 2 scythe hooks.

Farmer no.47, lives in Cookstown.

Farmer no.48, 2/1 cattle, 3/2 sheep, 2/0 goats, 0/2 hogs, 4/0 hens, 1 wooden plough, 1 harrow, 1 cart, 1 spinning wheel, 2 turf barrows, 2/1 agricultural spades, 1 agricultural shovel, 1 scythe hook, 2 teethed hooks.

Farmer no.49, 1/0 agricultural horses, 1/0 cattle, 2/1 goats, 0/2 hogs, 5/0 ducks, 3/7 hens, 1 wooden plough, 1 break, 1 cart, 2 spinning wheels, 1 unemployed linen loom, 2 turf barrows, 3/1 agricultural spades, 2 agricultural shovels, 2 scythe hooks.

Farmer no.50, 2/0 agricultural horses, 2/0 cattle, 1/8 hogs, 2/7 geese, 6/0 ducks, 3/0 hens, 1 wooden plough, 1 break, 2 carts, 1 corn fan, 1 spinning wheel, 1 box barrow, 2 turf barrows, 2/1 agricultural spades, 2 agricultural shovels, 1 scythe hook, 2 teethed hooks.

Farmer no.51, lives in Urbal.

Farmer no.52, lives in Tamlaght.

Coagh: Cottiers' Stock and Implements

[Form 3]

Cottier no.1, farmer no.26, Hugh McGuckan, labourer; 2/0 hens, 1 spinning wheel, 1/0 agricultural spades, 1 agricultural shovel, 2 teethed hooks; yearly rent 12s.

Cottier no.2, farmer no.30, Robert Ferguson, weaver; 1/0 hens, 1 spinning wheel, 1 unemployed linen loom, 1/0 agricultural spades, 1 agricultural shovel, 2 scythe hooks; yearly rent 2 pounds.

Cottier no.3, farmer no.28, James Irwin, labourer; 3/5 hens, 1 spinning wheel, 1/0 agricultural spades, 1 agricultural shovel, 1 scythe hook, 1 teethed hook; yearly rent 2 pounds.

Cottier no.4, farmer no.40, Robert Simpson, labourer; 2/0 hens, 2 spinning wheels, 1 employed linen loom, 1 turf barrow, 1/1 agricultural spades, 1 agricultural shovel, 3 scythe hooks, 1 teethed hook; yearly rent 2 pounds 10s.

Cottier no.5, farmer no.40, Alexander Simpson, labourer; 1/0 goats, 3/6 ducks, 5/8 hens, 1 spinning wheel, 1/0 agricultural spades, 1 agricultural shovel, 2 scythe hooks, 2 teethed hooks; yearly rent 2 pounds 10s.

Cottier no.6, farmer no.34, John Wilkson, labourer; 2/0 ducks, 2/0 hens, 1 spinning wheel, 1 unemployed linen loom, 1/0 agricultural spades, 1 agricultural shovel, 2 scythe hooks; yearly rent 2 pounds 10s.

Cottier no.7, farmer no.50, Robert Dougherty, carpenter; 2/8 ducks, 3/6 hens, 1 spinning wheel; yearly rent 4 pounds.

Cottier no.8, farmer no.34, John McGuigan, labourer; 4/0 hens, 1 spinning wheel, 1/0 agricultural spades, 1 agricultural shovel, 2 scythe hooks; yearly rent 2 pounds 10s.

Cottier no.9, farmer no.37, Thomas Anderson, labourer; 4/0 ducks, 5/7 hens, 2 spinning wheels, 2 turf barrows, 1/1 agricultural spades, 1 agricultural shovel, 2 scythe hooks, 1 teethed hook; yearly rent 2 pounds 10s.

Field observer's signature: John Hamilton, date 3rd to 5th June 1840.

Coagh: Labour and Proprietors

[Form 4. Head landlord is William Lenox Conyngham. All are direct tenants].

Farmer no.1, family: 1/0 males, 1 male house servant; occasional labour: 2 males for 24 days in spring, 1 male for 12 days in summer, 2 males for 20 days in autumn; 1 female for 10 days in spring, for 10 days in summer, 2 females for 7 days in autumn; family non-working; immediate landlord William Lenox Conyngham, tenure at will, 2 pounds yearly rent per acre; 1 spring well.

Farmer no.2, lives in Tralee; occasional labour: 1 male for 13 days in spring, for 3 days in summer, 2 males for 9 days in autumn; immediate landlord Alexander Ferguson by lease, tenure at will, 2 pounds yearly rent per acre.

Farmer no.3, family: 1t/0 males, 2t/0 females; occasional labour: 2 males for 45 days in spring, 1 male for 18 days in summer, 3 males for 20 days in autumn; 2 females for 7 days in spring, [blank] for 3 days in summer, 3 females for 7 days in autumn; family labour: 1 male for 4 days in spring, [blank] for 3 days in summer, [blank] for 7 days in autumn; male at his trade and females at their trade constantly; immediate landlord William Lenox Conyngham, tenure perpetuity, 8 pounds yearly rent per acre.

Farmer no.4, family: 1t/0 males, 2 male house servants; occasional labour: 2 males for 24 days in spring, 3 males for 12 days in summer, 4 males for 20 days in autumn; 1 female for 2 days in spring, 5 females for 7 days in summer, 3 females for 15 days in autumn; family non-working, immediate landlord William Lenox Conyngham, tenure perpetuity, 7s yearly rent per acre.

Farmer no.5, family: 1t/1 males, 0/6 females, 2 male house servants; family non-working, immediate landlord William Lenox Conyngham, tenure 61 years and 1 life, 1 pound 8s yearly rent per acre.

Farmer no.6, family: 0/2 females, 1 male house servant; occasional labour: 2 males for 15 days in spring, 1 male for 7 days in summer, 3 males for 4 days in autumn; 1 female for 12 days in spring, 2 females for 7 days in summer, 4 females for 12 days in autumn; family non-working, immediate landlord William Lenox Conyngham, tenure 61 years and 1 life, 1 pound 8s yearly rent per acre.

Farmer no.7, family: 0/2 females; occasional labour: 1 male for 17 days in spring, for 8 days in

Parish of Tamlaght

summer, 2 males for 6 days in autumn; family non-working, immediate landlord William Lenox Conyngham, tenure at will, 2 pounds yearly rent per acre.

Farmer no.8, family: 1/3 males, 1s/1 females, 1 male house servant; occasional labour: 1 female for 3 days in spring, 6 females for 8 days in summer, 3 females for 6 days in autumn; occasional labour: 2 males for 48 days in spring, [blank] for 30 days in summer, [blank] for 30 days in autumn; this is all the labour done on this farm by male servants; the remainder of their time in the townland of Tamlaght flax mill, female spinning, cooking constantly; immediate landlord Daniel McGee by perpetuity, tenure at will, 2 pounds yearly rent per acre.

Farmer no.9, family: 1t/3 males, 0/4 females, 1 male house servant; occasional labour: 2 females for 7 days in autumn; this family non-working, male servant constantly labouring in farm and garden; immediate landlord James Hogg by lease, tenure 21 years and 2 lives, 2 pounds yearly rent per acre.

Farmer no.10, family: 0/1 males, 0/2 females; occasional labour: 6 males for 10 days in spring, 4 males for 13 days in summer, for 12 days in autumn; 2 females for 7 days in spring, 1 female for 6 days in summer, 2 females for 11 days in autumn; family non-working, immediate landlord William Lenox Conyngham, tenure perpetuity, 5s 6d yearly rent per acre.

Farmer no.11, family: 0/3 males, 1/1 females, 1 male house servant; occasional labour: 2 males for 12 days in spring, 1 male for 6 days in summer, for 20 days in autumn; 1 female for 18 days in spring, 3 females for 13 days in autumn; family non-working, immediate landlord William Lenox Conyngham, tenure 32 years, 1 pound 10s yearly rent per acre.

Farmer no.12, family: 0/2 males, 0/6 females; occasional labour: 2 males for 4 days in spring, 1 male for 2 days in summer, for 15 days in autumn; family non-working, immediate landlord William Lenox Conyngham, tenure at will, 2 pounds yearly rent per acre.

Farmer no.13, family: 0/3 males, 0/2 females, 1 male house servant; occasional labour: 2 males for 12 days in spring, 3 males for 9 days in autumn; 1 female for 12 days in spring, 2 females for 18 days in autumn; family non-working, immediate landlord William Lenox Conyngham, tenure 21 years and 2 lives, 2 pounds yearly rent per acre.

Farmer no.14, lives in Derrycrin Eglish; occasional labour: 2 males for 10 days in spring, 1 male for 2 days in summer, 2 males for 7 days in autumn; 1 female for 5 days in spring, 2 females for 5 days in autumn; family non-working, immediate landlord Alexander Ferguson by lease, tenure at will, 2 pounds 5s yearly rent per acre.

Farmer no.15, family: 1t/2 males, 1s/2 females; occasional labour: 1 male for 8 days in spring, [blank] for 2 days in summer, [blank] for 7 days in autumn; 1 female for 5 days in spring, 2 females for 8 days in autumn; family labour: 1 male for 18 days in spring, [blank] for 6 days in summer, [blank] for 7 days in autumn; male working at his trade, female constantly spinning, cooking; immediate landlord William Lenox Conyngham, tenure 21 years and 1 life, 1 pound 7s yearly rent per acre.

Farmer no.16, family: 1s/2 females; family labour: 1 female for 6 days in spring, [blank] for 2 days in summer, [blank] for 5 days in autumn; female spinning and labouring to the neighbouring farmer; immediate landlord Daniel McGee by perpetuity, tenure at will, 6 pounds yearly rent per acre.

Farmer no.17, family: 2t/1 males, 2s/0 females; family labour: 2 males for 2 days in spring; 2 females for 1 day in summer, [blank] for 2 days in autumn; males working at their trade, females spinning; immediate landlord Daniel McGee, tenure at will, 6 pounds yearly rent per acre; 1 spring well.

Farmer no.18, family: 1/4 males, 1s/2 females; family labour: 1 male for 5 days in spring, [blank] for 2 days in summer, [blank] for 3 days in autumn; 1 female for 3 days in autumn; this is all the labour done on this land by this family; immediate landlord Daniel McGee by perpetuity, tenure at will, 6 pounds yearly rent per acre.

Farmer no.19, family: 1/4 males, 1s/2 females; occasional labour: 1 male for 4 days in spring, for 2 days in autumn; 1 female for 1 day in spring, 2 females for 1 day in autumn; family non-working; immediate landlord Daniel McGee by perpetuity, tenure at will, 6 pounds yearly rent per acre.

Farmer no.20, lives in Tamlaght, non-working; immediate landlord Daniel McGee by perpetuity, tenure at will, 2 pounds 10s yearly rent per acre.

Farmer no.21, family: 1/0 males, 1s/0 females; family labour: 1 male for 12 days in spring, [blank] for 2 days in summer, [blank] for 10 days in winter; [blank] females for 6 days in spring, [blank] for 3 days in summer, [blank] for 10 days in autumn; male labouring to other farms, female spinning; immediate landlord William Lenox Conyngham, tenure at will, 2 pounds yearly rent per acre.

Farmer no.22, family: 2w/1 males, 2s/3 females; family labour: 2 males for 24 days in spring, [blank] for 12 days in summer, [blank] for 20 days in autumn; 2 females for 30 days in spring, [blank] for 7 days in summer, [blank] for 12 days in autumn; males weaving, females spinning; immediate landlord Mary Hogg, tenure at will, 1 pound 15s yearly rent per acre.

Farmer no.23, 2w/1 males, 2s/2 females; family labour: 2 males for 27 days in spring, [blank] for 7 days in summer, [blank] for 24 days in autumn; 2 females for 12 days in spring, [blank] for 10 days in summer, [blank] for 10 days in autumn; males weaving, females spinning; immediate landlord Mary Hogg, tenure at will, 1 pound 15s yearly rent per acre.

Farmer no.24, family: 1/0 males, 2s/2 females, 1 male house servant; family labour: 2 females for 7 days in spring, [blank] for 10 days in summer, [blank] for 12 days in autumn; male constantly labouring on farm, females spinning; immediate landlord William Lenox Conyngham, tenure at will, 1 pound 5s yearly rent per acre.

Farmer no.25, family: 1/2 males, 1s/2 females; family labour: 1 female for 6 days in spring, [blank] for 2 days in summer, [blank] for 4 days in autumn; male constantly labouring on farm and making turf, females spinning; immediate landlord William Lenox Conyngham, tenure at will, 1 pound 10s yearly rent per acre.

Farmer no.26, family: 1/1 males, 1s/1 females; family labour: 1 male for 72 days in spring, [blank] for 18 days in summer, [blank] for 48 days in autumn; 1 female for 24 days in spring, [blank] for 6 days in summer, [blank] for 15 days in autumn; this is all the labour done by this family on this farm; immediate landlord William Lenox Conyngham, tenure at will, 1 pound 10s yearly rent per acre; 1 spring well.

Farmer no.27, family: 1/0 males, 1s/0 females; family labour: 1 male for 24 days in spring, [blank] for 8 days in summer, [blank] for 27 days in autumn; 1 female for 10 days in spring, [blank] for 2 days in summer, [blank] for 10 days in autumn; this is all the labour done on this farm by this family; immediate landlord William Lenox Conyngham, tenure 21 years and 1 life, 1 pound yearly rent per acre.

Farmer no.28, family: 1/0 males; family labour: 1 male for 12 days in spring, [blank] for 6 days in summer, [blank] for 10 days in summer; this is all the labour done on this farm by this family; immediate landlord William Lenox Conyngham, tenure 21 years and 1 life, 1 pound yearly rent per acre.

Farmer no.29, lives in Drumconway; occasional labour: 3 males for 10 days in spring, 2 males for 10 days in autumn; 2 females for 4 days in summer; family labour: 1 male for 50 days in spring, [blank] for 20 days in summer, [blank] for 40 days in autumn; 2 females for 12 days in spring, [blank] for 14 days in summer, [blank] for 28 days in autumn; this is all the labour done by this man or family on this farm; immediate landlord William Lenox Conyngham, tenure 21 years and 1 life, 1 pound yearly rent per acre.

Farmer no.30, lives in Drumconway; occasional labour: 2 males for 6 days in spring, for 4 days in autumn; 1 female for 4 days in summer, 2 females for 3 days in autumn; family labour: 1 male for 4 days in spring, [blank] for 4 days in summer, [blank] for 8 days in autumn; this is all the labour done by this man on this farm; immediate landlord William Lenox Conyngham, tenure 21 years and 1 life, 1 pound yearly rent per acre.

Farmer no.31, family: 1,1w/0 males, 2s/0 females; family labour: 1 male for 65 days in spring, [blank] for 20 days in summer, [blank] for 30 days in autumn; 2 females for 10 days in spring, [blank] for 3 days in summer, [blank] for 10 days in autumn; this is all the labour done on this farm by this family; immediate landlord Daniel McGee by perpetuity, tenure at will, 3 pounds yearly rent per acre.

Farmer no.32, 1,1w/4 males, 2s/1 females; family labour: 1 male for 18 days in spring, [blank] for 18 days in autumn; 2 females for 18 days in spring, [blank] for 7 days in summer, [blank] for 12 days in autumn; 1 male weaving and 1 male constantly labouring on the farm and making turf, females spinning; immediate landlord Daniel McGee by perpetuity, tenure at will, 2 pounds yearly rent per acre.

Farmer no.33, family: 1,1w/4 males, 2s/1 females; family labour: 1 male for 30 days in spring, [blank] for 15 days in summer, [blank] for 24 days in autumn; 2 females for 12 days in spring, [blank] for 8 days in summer, [blank] for 9 days in autumn; 1 male weaving and 1 male constantly labouring on farm and making turf, females spinning; immediate landlord William Lenox Conyngham, tenure at will, 18s yearly rent per acre.

Farmer no.34, family: 3/1 males, 3s/4 females; occasional labour: 3 males for 7 days in spring, 2 males for 6 days in summer, 4 males for 7 days in autumn; 2 females for 12 days in spring, 3 females for 12 days in autumn; family labour: 3 females for 18 days in spring, [blank] for 10 days in summer, [blank] for 15 days in autumn; males

Parish of Tamlaght

constantly labouring on farm and making turf and females spinning; immediate landlord William Lenox Conyngham, tenure 21 years and 2 lives, 1 pound yearly rent per acre; 1 spring well.

Farmer no.35, family: 1s/0 females; occasional labour: 3 males for 7 days in spring, 2 males for 4 days in summer, 4 males for 5 days in autumn; family labour: 1 female 22 days in spring, [blank] for 12 days in summer, [blank] for 14 days in autumn; female spinning; immediate landlord William Lenox Conyngham, tenure 21 years and 2 lives, 10s yearly rent per acre.

Farmer no.36, family: 1t,1/0 males, 0/3 females; 1 male working at his trade and 1 male constantly labouring on his farm, females constantly cooking and washing; immediate landlord William Lenox Conyngham, tenure 21 years and 2 lives, 10s yearly rent per acre.

Farmer no.37, family: 0/1 males, 2s/0 females, 1 male house servant, 1 male constant labourer; occasional labour: 3 males 12 days in spring, 1 male for 18 days in summer, 5 males for 7 days in autumn; 2 females for 10 days in spring, 3 females for 10 days in autumn; male non-working, females constantly spinning and cooking; immediate landlord William Lenox Conyngham, tenure 21 years and 2 lives, 16s yearly rent per acre; 1 water pump, [value] 4 pounds.

Farmer no.38, family: 1,1w/0 males, 3s,1t/0 females; family labour: 1 male for 12 days in spring, [blank] for 7 days in summer, [blank] for 18 days in autumn; 3 females for 9 days in spring, [blank] for 4 days in summer, [blank] for 7 days in autumn; 1 male weaving and 1 male constantly labouring on farm and making turf, female spinning; immediate landlord William Lenox Conyngham, tenure at will, 18s yearly rent per acre.

Farmer no.39, family: 2,1w/1 males, 2s/2 females; family labour: 1 male for 12 days in spring, [blank] for 6 days in summer, [blank] for 12 days in autumn; 2 females for 11 days in spring, [blank] for 7 days in summer, [blank] for 10 days in autumn; 1 male weaving, 2 males constantly labouring on the farm and making turf, female spinning; immediate landlord William Lenox Conyngham, tenure at will, 1 pound yearly rent per acre.

Farmer no.40, lives in [blank]; this labour is all done by this man's family: immediate landlord William Lenox Conyngham, tenure at will, 1 pound 10s yearly rent per acre.

Farmer no.41, family: 2/0 males, 2s/0 females; occasional labour: 1 male for 1 day in spring, 2 males for 4 days in autumn; family labour: 2 females for 30 days in spring, [blank] for 18 days in summer, [blank] for 27 days in autumn; males constantly labouring on farm and making turf, females spinning; immediate landlord William Lenox Conyngham, tenure at will, 1 pound 1s yearly rent per acre; 1 spring well.

Farmer no.42, family: 2s/0 females; occasional labour: 2 males for 12 days in spring, 1 male for 10 days in autumn; family labour: 2 females for 13 days in spring, [blank] for 12 days in summer, [blank] for 15 days in autumn; females spinning; immediate landlord William Lenox Conyngham, tenure at will, 1 pound yearly rent per acre.

Farmer no.43, family: 0/3 males, 0/2 females, 2 male house servants; occasional labour: 2 males for 9 days in spring, 4 males for 10 days in autumn; 2 females for 18 days in spring, 1 female for 10 days in summer, 5 females for 10 days in autumn; family non-working, immediate landlord William Lenox Conyngham, tenure 21 years and 1 life, 1 pound 2s 9d yearly rent per acre; 1 water pump, [value] 6 pounds per acre.

Farmer no.44, family: 1,1s/1 males, 2s/1 females; family labour: 1 male for 15 days in spring, [blank] for 6 days in summer, [blank] for 12 days in autumn; 2 females for 12 days in spring, [blank] for 6 days in summer, [blank] for 14 days in autumn; 1 male works at his trade and 1 constantly labouring on farm and making turf, females spinning; immediate landlord William Lenox Conyngham, tenure 21 years and 1 life, 1 pound 1s yearly rent per acre; 1 spring well.

Farmer no.45, family: 2/0 males, 2s females; occasional labour: 1 male for 7 days in autumn; 2 females for 28 days in spring, [blank] for 12 days in summer, [blank] for 30 days in autumn; males constantly labouring on farm and making turf, females spinning; immediate landlord William Lenox Conyngham, tenure 21 years and 1 life, 1 pound yearly rent per acre.

Farmer no.46, family: 1/2 males, 1s/1 females; family labour: 1 female for 18 days in spring, [blank] for 9 days in summer, [blank] for 15 days in autumn; males constantly labouring on farm and making turf, females spinning; immediate landlord William Lenox Conyngham, tenure at will, 1 pound yearly rent per acre.

Farmer no.47, lives in Cookstown; males constantly labouring on farm and making turf, females spinning; immediate landlord William Lenox Conyngham, tenure by perpetuity, 10s yearly rent per acre.

Farmer no.48, family: 1/0 males, 1s/0 females; family labour: 1 female for 18 days in spring, [blank] for 12 days in autumn; male constantly labouring on farm and making turf, females spinning; immediate landlord William Lenox Conyngham, tenure 21 years and 1 life, 18s yearly rent per acre.

Farmer no.49, family: 1/4 males, 2s/2 females; family labour: 2 females for 7 days in spring, [blank] for 5 days in summer, [blank] for 8 days in autumn; male constantly labouring on farm and making turf, females spinning; immediate landlord William Lenox Conyngham, tenure 21 years and 1 life, 18s yearly rent per acre.

Farmer no.50, family: 1/2 males, 1s/3 females, 1 male house servant; occasional labour: 2 females for 4 days in spring, for 7 days in autumn; male constantly labouring on farm and making turf, female constantly spinning; immediate landlord William Lenox Conyngham, tenure 21 years and 1 life, 1 pound 1s yearly rent per acre; 1 water pump, [value] 5 pounds.

Farmer no.51, lives in Urbal; family labour: none on this farm; immediate landlord William Lenox Conyngham, tenure at will, 2 pounds yearly rent per acre.

Farmer no.52, lives in Tamlaght; immediate landlord William Lenox Conyngham, tenure at will, 2 pounds 10s yearly rent per acre.

Farmer no.53 [blank], tenure perpetuity, not let.

Coagh: Manures

[Form 5. Distances in Irish miles].

Farmer no.3, dung: 32 tons per acre, 2s per ton, 8 cwt per load, carried from farmyard, 4 days employed; bog: 9 cwt per load, carried from townland, 6 days employed; lime: 12d per barrel, 8 cwt per load, half a mile carried, 1 day employed; clay: 9 cwt per load, carried from townland, 3 days employed; compost loads: 100 bog, 6 lime, 94 clay; 8 cwt of compost, 4 days employed, made up in the field.

Farmer no.10, dung: 34 tons per acre, 2s 1d per ton, 8 cwt per load, carried from farmyard, 4 days employed.

Farmer no.24, dung: 30 tons per acre, 2s per ton, 6 cwt per load, carried from farmyard, 4 days employed.

Farmer no.34, dung: 32 tons per acre, 2s per ton, 8 cwt per load, carried from farmyard, 4 days employed; bog: 9 cwt per load, carried from townland, 2 days employed; lime: 12d per barrel, 8 cwt per load, carried from townland, a quarter of a day employed; clay: 9 cwt per load, carried from farmyard, 4 days employed; compost loads: 60 bog, 4 lime, 120 clay; lime-kilns 1, 60 barrels of lime burned per annum; 8 cwt of compost, 6 days employed, made up in the field.

Farmer no.39, dung: 30 tons per acre, 2s per ton, 7 cwt per load, carried from farmyard, 5 days employed; bog: 8 cwt per load, carried from townland, 3 days employed; lime: 12d per barrel, 8 cwt per load, 1 and a half miles carried, 2 days employed; clay: 9 cwt per load, carried from townland, 3 days employed; compost loads: 95 bog, 6 lime, 95 clay; lime-kilns 1, no barrels of lime burnt per annum; 8 cwt of compost, 6 days employed, made up at the house.

Farmer no.45, dung: 31 tons per acre, 2s per ton, 7 cwt per load, carried from farmyard, 4 days employed; bog: 8 cwt per load, carried from townland, 5 days employed; lime: 12d per barrel, 8 cwt per load, carried from townland, a quarter of a day employed; clay: 8 cwt per load, carried from townland, 3 and a half days employed; compost loads: 100 bog, 4 lime, 100 clay; lime-kilns 1, 20 barrels of lime burnt per annum; 7 cwt of compost, 10 days employed, made up at the house.

No.3: dung used alone, bog, lime and clay used only in compost; no.10: dung used alone; no.24: dung used alone; no.34: dung used alone, bog, lime and clay used only in compost; no.39: dung used alone, bog, lime and clay used only in compost; no.45: dung used alone, bog, lime and clay used only in compost.

Kind of acre: Cunningham.

Lime: number of buckets per barrel 4, weight per barrel 28 lbs.

Dung farmyard, bog townland, clay townland, lime Ruskey Lower and limestone Ballyvally, and lime townland.

Coagh: Seed and Produce

[Form 6]

Farmer no.3, wheat: 14 stones seed, 140 produce; oats: 18 stones seed, 140 produce; potatoes: 24 bushels seed, 230 produce; clover: 2 bushels hay seed, 10 lbs clover seed, 14 tons produce; clay and loam, well laboured.

Farmer no.10, wheat: 14 stones seed, 140 produce; oats 18 stones seed, 150 produce; potatoes: 24 bushels seed, 280 produce; hay: 2 bushels hay seed, 6 bushels clover seed, 2 and a quarter tons produce; clay and loam, well laboured.

Farmer no.24, oats: 20 stones seed, 130 produce; potatoes 26 bushels seed, 230 produce; flax: 3 bushels seed, 6 and a half cwt produce; clover: 14 lbs clover seed, 13 tons produce; clay, well laboured.

Farmer no.34, barley: 14 stones seed, 160 produce; oats: 18 stones seed, 130 produce; potatoes: 24 bushels seed, 250 produce; flax: 3 and a half bushels seed, 6 and a half cwt produce; clover: 1

Parish of Tamlaght

Statistical table for Coagh

bushel hay seed, 10 lbs clover seed, 16 tons produce; clay, loam and bog, well laboured.

Farmer no.39, wheat: 14 stones seed, 140 produce; oats: 18 stones seed, 140 produce; potatoes 24 bushels seed, 240 produce; flax: 3 bushels seed, 6 cwt produce; clay, loam and bog, well laboured.

Farmer no.45, wheat: 14 stones seed, 140 produce; oats: 18 stones seed, 140 produce; potatoes: 24 bushels seed, 270 produce; flax: 3 bushels seed, 6 cwt produce; clay and loam, well laboured.

Farmer no.50, oats: 18 stone seed, 140 produce; potatoes: 26 bushels seed, 280 produce, flax: 3 bushels seed, 6 cwt produce; clay and loam, well laboured.

Kind of acre Cunningham.

[Prices] Wheat: value of seed 1s 10d per stone, value of produce 1s 3d per stone; time of sowing 1st November to 1st January, time of harvest 25th August to 20th September.

Barley: value of seed 1s 8d per stone, value of produce 12d per stone; time of sowing 21st April to 1st May, time of harvest 10th August to 21st August.

Oats: value of seed 1s 2d per stone, value of produce 12d per stone; time of sowing 20th March to 20th April, time of harvest 25th August to 1st October.

Potatoes: value of seed 3d ha'penny per stone, value of produce 5d per stone; time of sowing 20th April to 1st June, time of harvest 1st November to 1st January.

Flax: value of seed 14s per bushel, value of produce 54s per cwt; time of sowing 1st May to 12th May, time of harvest 1st August to 20th August.

Hay: value of seed 2s per bushel, value of produce 2s 9d per cwt; time of sowing 20th March to 12th May, time of harvest 1st July to 12th July.

Clover: value of seed 12d per lb, value of produce 4d per cwt; time of sowing 20th March to 12th May, time of harvest 10th May to 1st September.

Field observer's signature: John Hamilton, date 3rd to 6th June 1840.

Coagh: Table of Trades

[Form 7]
John Charlton, weaver, master.
William Charlton, weaver, apprentice.
Robert Charlton, weaver, master.
William Charlton, weaver, master.
Robert Ferguson, weaver, master.

George Millar, weaver, master.
Allan Wilkinson, weaver, master.
William McCollman, weaver, master.
Robert Simpson [?] Junior, weaver, master.
Robert Dougherty, carpenter, master, 2s a day.
Hugh Taylor, weaver, master.
Sarah Taylor, schoolmistress, 20 pounds per annum.
Daniel Berryman, weaver, master.
James Garty, mason, master, 2s per day.
Field observer's signature: John Hamilton, date 3rd to 5th June 1840.

Coagh: Condition of Cottiers

[Form 8. Houses have 2 apartments except no.6, none are whitewashed, all with straw roofs, brick chimneys, clay floors, good beds and good clothes. *All have the same furniture, which is recorded by abbreviations without a key: t = table, s = settle bed, c = chair, d = dresser, tn = tinware, ew = earthenware*].

Cottier no.1, 2 apartments, mud house, 2 lead windows, gardens none.
Cottier no.2, 2 apartments, mud house, 3 lead windows, garden one-eighth of an acre.
Cottier no.3, 2 apartments, mud house, 3 lead windows, garden one-eighth of an acre.
Cottier no.4, 2 apartments, mud house, 2 lead windows, garden one-eighth of an acre.
Cottier no.5, 2 apartments, house stone and lime, 2 glazed and 2 lead windows, garden one-eighth of an acre.
Cottier no.6, 3 apartments, house stone and lime, 5 glazed windows, garden one-sixteenth of an acre.
Cottier no.7, 2 apartments, house stone and lime, 3 lead windows, garden one-sixteenth of an acre.
Cottier no.8, 2 apartments, house stone and lime, 3 lead windows, garden one-sixteenth of an acre.
Field observer's signature: John Hamilton, date 3rd to 5th June 1840.

Coagh: Summary of Economy

[Form 9]
Surface: hilly and uneven.
Soils, kind: clay, loam and bog; depth: from 6 to 24 inches.
Subsoil, kind: clay, sand and gravel; depth: 10 feet in parts, the rest unknown.
Exposure: to all winds.
Springs: 8 spring wells and 6 water pumps.
Drainage: 1,145 perches of drains, part made by placing stones in an angular form in the bottom of the drain, then throwing in the loose stones on the top, and part made by throwing in the loose stone.
Irrigation: not practised, as there is no supply of water.
Implements: iron and wooden ploughs common, wooden and brake harrows, spades 16 by 6 inches, common hosed shovels, scythe and teethed reaping hooks.
Acres reclaimed since 1830: 7 and a half acres.
Mills, corn: 1; mills, flax: 1; mills, fulling: none.
Quarries, kind of: 2, limestone quarry not worked for the last 20 years as they were prohibited.
Quarries, application of: stone used for lime when worked.
Communications: there are leading roads from this town to Cookstown, Stewartstown, Moneymore, Magherafelt, Battery, parish Arbo and to Magherafelt by Ballinderry bridge, all in good order.
Markets: Stewartstown, Magherafelt, Cookstown and Moneymore.
Breed of horses: Irish; breed of cattle: Irish Durhams and half-bred Devonshires; breed of sheep: sort [south ?] of Ireland; breed of hogs: half-bred Irish and Dutch called belties.
Woods or plantations: (23 acres woods) 7 and a half acres planting, (2 and three-eighth acres orchard); kind: oak, ash, alder, firs, birch, sycamore. Orchard: apple, pears and cherry trees; when first planted: in the years 1820, 1823, 1825, 1829, 1832 and 1833; present return: no timber cut or sold, no fruit sold. The fruit is all used by the farmers.
Lime-kilns: 3 kilns for farmers' own use.
Manufactures: 2 brickfields.
Kind of crops cultivated, oats: potato, Poland, august, blanter and black tarterum oats; barley: common barley; wheat: red and yellow <yalow> Kent wheat; potatoes: cups, lumpers, Cork reds, farmers, downs and kidney blacks; flax: Dutch, New York and Riga; hay: rye grass; turnips [blank]; clover: red and white clover.
Field observer's signature: John Hamilton, residence William Vance's, Coagh, date: June 6th 1840.
[Insert addition: Farmer's name and acres, where got: from Walter [or Watter] Young, cess applotter. Natural meadow: quantity per acre 2 and a half tons per acre; time of harvest from 1st August to 1st September; price per ton 2s 6d per cwt. Kind of acre: Cunningham. Fences, kind of:

Parish of Tamlaght

soil only and soil set with thorns, good. Turf, where got: in townland and in Drumconway. Rent per acre: rough or waste land, arable land: from 5s 6d to 6 pounds per acre, rough and arable <arabel>. Rough or waste land, kind of: woods, planting, scrogs and bog].

Coagh: Lime and Manufacture

Estimate of 1 lime-kiln containing 25 barrels of 4 bushels to the barrel of 228 lbs per barrel, 5 tons of raw stones at 10d per ton, 4s 2d; carting the stones from Ballydawley, 1 horse 2 days at 3s per day, 6s; breaking the stones and filling the kiln, 1 man 4 days at 10d per day, 3s 4d; 14 carts of turf at 1s per cart, 14s; [total] 1 pound 7s 6d. Samuel Crooks, informant.

Statistical Information for Coagh Gardens, May and June 1840

Coagh Gardens: Farmers, Acreages and Crops

[Form 1. Rotation of crops: in potatoes and vegetables constantly. Informant the farmer in each case].

Farmer no.1, William Robinson, woollen draper, not working; 24 perches, tillage: 6 vegetables, 18 potatoes.

Farmer no.2, William Downing, draper and farmer, not working; 24 perches, tillage: 12 vegetables, 12 potatoes.

Farmer no.3, Walter Duff, hotel keeper, not working; 24 perches, tillage: 12 vegetables, 12 potatoes; acres under orchard: 11 acres, 24 years planted.

Farmer no.4, William George, publican, not working; 12 perches, tillage: 6 vegetables, 6 potatoes.

Farmer no.5, John Thompson, farmer and wheelwright; 5 perches, tillage, vegetables.

Farmer no.6, William John Howard, farmer and publican; 5 perches, tillage, vegetables.

Farmer no.7, James Gibson, woollen draper, not working; 18 perches, tillage: 6 vegetables, 12 potatoes.

Farmer no.8, John Kightley, publican, not working; 5 perches, tillage, potatoes.

Farmer no.9, William McCormick, surgeon and physican, not working; 24 perches, tillage: 12 vegetables, 12 potatoes; acres under orchard: 1 acre, 24 years planted.

Farmer no.10, James Ekin, farmer and grocer, not working; 48 perches, tillage: 14 vegetables, 34 potatoes.

Farmer no.11, William McIntire, farmer and publican; 10 perches, waste.

Farmer no.12, John Ekin, farmer and grocer, not working; 12 perches, tillage, vegetables.

Farmer no.13, Eliza Hamilton, lives private, not working; 12 perches, tillage, potatoes.

Farmer no.14, James Sloss, grocer, not working; 35 perches, tillage: 6 vegetables, 29 potatoes.

Farmer no.15, Daniel Campbell, lives private, not working; 35 perches, tillage, potatoes.

Farmer no.16, John McGan, farmer; 48 perches, tillage: 8 vegetables, 40 potatoes.

Farmer no.17, James Galway, butcher, not working; 18 perches, tillage: 1 vegetables, 17 potatoes.

Farmer no.18, William Vance, blue dyer; 18 perches, tillage: 2 vegetables, 16 potatoes.

Farmer no.19, Robert Hogg, farmer, not working; 36 perches, tillage: 2 vegetables, 34 potatoes; acres under orchard: 6 acres, 32 years planted.

Farmer no.20, James Sampson, surgeon, not working; 45 perches, tillage: 10 vegetables, 34 potatoes.

Farmer no.21, Alicia Newtown, lady, not working; 45 perches, 22 tillage, 23 waste: 22 vegetables; land steward.

Farmer no.22, Duncan Storey, miller, not working; 45 perches, 35 tillage, 10 waste: 6 vegetables, 29 potatoes.

Farmer no.23, James Alexander, grocer, not working; 10 perches, 5 tillage, 5 waste: 5 potatoes.

Farmer no.24, James Graham, carpenter, not working; 15 perches, 13 tillage, 2 waste: 13 potatoes.

Farmer no.25, William Cowden, shoemaker, not working; 30 perches, 27 tillage, 3 waste: 4 vegetables, 23 potatoes.

Farmer no.26, Robert Cowan, grocer, not working; 25 perches, 20 tillage, 5 waste: 20 vegetables.

Farmer no.27, Robert Blackwood, carpenter, not working; 16 perches, tillage: 2 vegetables, 14 potatoes.

Farmer no.28, Thomas Walker, broker, not working; 16 perches, 14 tillage, 2 waste: 14 potatoes.

Farmer no.29, Matthew Conlin, tailor, not working; 38 perches, 36 tillage, 2 waste: 36 potatoes.

Farmer no.30, William Ferguson, publican; 38 perches, 34 tillage, 4 waste: 4 vegetables, 30 potatoes.

Farmer no.31, William Wilson, lives private, not working; 25 perches, tillage: 2 vegetables, 23 potatoes.

Farmer no.32, Duncan Higans, shoemaker, not working; 38 perches, tillage: 4 vegetables, 34 potatoes.

Farmer no.33, Marget Kenedy, lady, not working; 38 perches, tillage: 12 vegetables, 26 potatoes.

Farmer no.34, Thomas Ferguson, farmer; 20 perches, 18 tillage, 2 waste: 2 vegetables, 16 potatoes.

Farmer no.35, Daniel O'Hara, mason, not working; 10 perches, tillage: 2 vegetables, 8 potatoes.

Farmer no.36, Walter Young, schoolmaster, not working; 10 perches, tillage: 3 vegetables, 7 potatoes.

Farmer no.37, James Faulkner, tailor, not working; 10 perches, 8 tillage, 2 waste: 2 vegetables, 6 potatoes.

Farmer no.38, Betty Hamilton, lodging house keeper, not working; 10 perches, 7 tillage, 3 waste: 1 vegetables, 6 potatoes.

Farmer no.39, James Kane, reed maker, not working; 10 perches, 8 tillage, 2 waste: 2 vegetables, 6 potatoes.

Farmer no.40, William Riddel, blacksmith, not working; 15 perches, 12 tillage, 3 waste: 4 vegetables, 8 potatoes.

Farmer no.41, John Minow, labourer, 26 perches, tillage, potatoes; in potatoes constantly.

Farmer no.42, Alex Cowden, shoemaker, not working; 26 perches, tillage, potatoes; in potatoes constantly.

Farmer no.43, John O'Neill, hackler, not working; 20 perches, tillage, potatoes; in potatoes constantly.

Farmer no.44, Saly Eldertin, spinner, not working; 20 perches, tillage, potatoes; in potatoes constantly.

Farmer no.45, Patrick Laughlin, nailor, not working; 18 perches, tillage, potatoes; in potatoes constantly.

Farmer no.46, Fill McGarvey, labourer; 18 perches, tillage, potatoes; in potatoes constantly.

Summary: size of farms 1,050 perches, 972 tillage, 78 waste, 223 vegetables, 748 potatoes. The total of the gardens is taken to Field Book.

Coagh Gardens: Farmer's Stock and Implements

[Form 2]

Farmer no.1, 1 box barrow, 1/0 agricultural spades, 1 agricultural shovel.

Farmer no.2, stock on Field Book no.1.

Farmer no.3, 1/0 agricultural horses, 1/0 hogs, 2/0 turkeys, 2/0 hens, 1 box barrow, 2/0 agricultural spades, 3 agricultural shovels, 2 scythe hooks.

Farmer no.4, 0/1 hogs.

Farmer no.5, stock in Field Notebook no.3.

Farmer no.6, 1/0 agricultural horses, 1/0 cattle, 0/1 hogs, 4/0 hens, 0/1 agricultural spades.

Farmer no.7, 1/0 agricultural horses, 2/0 cattle, 0/1 hogs, 1 cart, 1/0 agricultural spades, 1 agricultural shovel, 1 scythe hook.

Farmer no.8, [blank].

Farmer no.9, 1/0 pleasure horses, 1/0 agricultural horses, 1/0 cattle, 6/0 hens, 1 wooden plough, 1 break, 1 cart, 1 box barrow, 2 turf barrows, 2/0 agricultural spades, 1/0 agricultural shovels, 2 scythe hooks.

Farmer no.10, stock on Field Book no.4.

Farmer no.11, 1/0 pleasure horses, 3/0 agricultural horses, 4/5 cattle, 1/0 goats, 4/0 hogs, 4/18 geese, 8/10 ducks, 1/7 turkeys, 12/15 hens, 2 ploughs, 2 breaks, 1 roller, 1 drill hoe, 5 carts, 1 corn fan, 1 box barrow, 4 turf barrows, 4/2 agricultural spades, 3 agricultural shovels, 4 scythe hooks, 2 teethed hooks.

Farmer no.12, stock on Field Book no.5.

Farmer no.13, stock on Field Book no.6.

Farmer no.14, 1/0 cattle, 1 hog, 2/0 hens, 1 box barrow, 1/0 agricultural spades, 1 agricultural shovel.

Farmer no.15, 1 spinning wheel.

Farmer no.16, stock on Field Book no.8.

Farmer no.17, 1/0 asses, 1/0 cattle, 1/0 goats, 2/0 hogs, 1/0 agricultural spades, 1 agricultural shovel.

Farmer no.18, 1/1 agricultural spades, 1 agricultural shovel.

Farmer no.19, stock on Field Book no.43.

Farmer no.20, stock on Field Book no.9.

Farmer no.21, stock on Field Book no.10.

Farmer no.22, stock on Field Book no.11.

Farmer no.23, [blank].

Farmer no.24, 1 spinning wheel.

Farmer no.25, 1/0 cattle, 1 spinning wheel, 1/0 agricultural spades, 1 agricultural shovel.

Farmer no.26, stock on Field Book no.13.

Farmer no.27, stock on Field Book no.12.

Farmer no.28, [blank].

Farmer no.29, 1 spinning wheel, 1/0 agricultural spades.

Farmer no.30, 8/0 hens, 1 spinning wheel, 1 unemployed linen loom, 1/0 agricultural spades, 1 agricultural shovel.

Farmer no.31, 1/0 geese, 2 spinning wheels.

Farmer no.32, [blank].

Farmer no.33, 1/0 cattle, 1/0 hens, 1 box barrow.

Farmer no.34, lives in Urbal.

Farmer no.35, 3/0 hens, 2 spinning wheels, 1

unemployed linen loom, 1 turf barrow, 1/0 agricultural spades, 1 agricultural shovel.

Farmer no.36, 1/0 hens, 1 spinning wheel.
Farmer no.37, 3 spinning wheels.
Farmer no.38, 0/1 hogs, 1 spinning wheel.
Farmer no.39, 1 spinning wheel.
Farmer no.40, 1 spinning wheel, 1 box barrow.
Farmer no.41, 2 spinning wheels, 1/0 agricultural spades, 1 agricultural shovel, 1 scythe hook.
Farmer no.42, 0/1 hogs, 2 spinning wheels.
Farmer no.43, 1 spinning wheel.
Farmer no.44, 1 spinning wheel, 1 employed linen loom.
Farmer no.45, 1 spinning wheel.
Farmer no.46, 1 spinning wheel, 1/0 agricultural spades, 1 agricultural shovel, 2 scythe hooks.

Coagh Gardens: Labour and Proprietors

[Form 4. Head landlord William Lenox Conyngham Esquire; direct tenants unless indicated].

Farmer no.1, occasional labour: 1 male for 8 days in spring, for 1 day in summer, for 4 days in autumn; 1 female for 1 day in spring, for 2 days in autumn; family non-working; immediate landlord John Weir, by perpetuity, tenure at will, 12 pounds 10s yearly rent per acre.

Farmer no.2, occasional labour: 1 male for 10 days in spring, for 2 days in summer, for 7 days in autumn; 1 female for 3 days in autumn; family non-working; immediate landlord William Lenox Conyngham, tenure 61 years and 3 lives, 13 pounds yearly rent per acre.

Farmer no.3, occasional labour: 1 male for 14 days in spring, for 4 days in summer, for 12 days in autumn; 1 female for 2 days in spring, for 4 days in autumn; family non-working; immediate landlord William Lenox Conyngham, tenure 61 years and 3 lives, 14s 6d yearly rent per acre.

Farmer no.4, occasional labour: 1 male for 7 days in spring, for 2 days in summer, 2 males for 3 days in autumn; family non-working; immediate landlord Alex Firenson, by lease, tenure at will, 15 pounds yearly rent per acre.

Farmer no.5, occasional labour: 1 male for 7 days in spring, for 3 days in summer, 2 males for 3 days in autumn; works now in his own garden; immediate landlord William Lenox Conyngham, tenure perpetuity, 10s yearly rent per acre.

Farmer no.6, occasional labour: 1 male for 5 days in spring, for 2 days in summer, for 5 days in autumn; family non-working; immediate landlord Samuel McGill Esq., by perpetuity, tenure at will, 10 pounds yearly rent per acre.

Farmer no.7, occasional labour: 1 male for 10 days in spring, 2 males for 3 days in summer, for 6 days in autumn; family non-working; immediate landlord Marget McIntire, by perpetuity, tenure 14 years, 8 pounds yearly rent per acre.

Farmer no.8, occasional labour: 1 male for 2 days in spring, for 1 day in summer, for 2 days in autumn; family non-working; immediate landlord Samuel McGill Esq., by perpetuity, tenure at will, 10 pounds yearly rent per acre.

Farmer no.9, occasional labour: 2 males for 8 days in spring, 1 male for 5 days in summer, 2 males for 8 days in autumn; 1 female for 2 days in spring, 2 females for 3 days in summer; family non-working; immediate landlord William Lenox Conyngham, tenure 61 years and 3 lives, 18s yearly rent per acre.

Farmer no.10, occasional labour: 2 males for 13 days in spring, 1 male for 7 days in summer, 2 males for 8 days in autumn; 1 female for 4 days in summer, for 4 days in autumn; family non-working; immediate landord William Lenox Conyngham, tenure perpetuity, 1 pound yearly rent per acre; 1 water pump, [value] 4 pounds.

Farmer no.11; family non-working; immediate landlord William Lee, by perpetuity, tenure 21 years and 1 life, 30 pounds yearly rent per acre.

Farmer no.12, occasional labour: 1 male for 7 days in spring, for 4 days in summer, for 6 days in autumn; family non-working; immediate landlord William Lenox Conyngham, tenure perpetuity, 10s yearly rent per acre; 1 water pump, [value] 5 pounds.

Farmer no.13, occasional labour: 1 male for 8 days in spring, for 2 days in summer, 2 males for 3 days in autumn; family non-working; immediate landlord William Lenox Conyngham, tenure perpetuity, 10s yearly rent per acre.

Farmer no.14, occasional labour: 2 males for 10 days in spring, 1 male for 3 days in summer, 2 males for 5 days in autumn; 1 female for 3 days in autumn; family non-working; immediate landlord James Hogg, by lease, tenure perpetuity, 17 pounds yearly rent per acre.

Farmer no.15, occasional labour: 3 males for 5 days in spring, 1 male for 1 day in summer, 2 males for 5 days in autumn; 1 female for 2 days in autumn; family non-working; immediate landlord William Lenox Conyngham, tenure perpetuity, 9s yearly rent per acre.

Farmer no.16, occasional labour: 2 males for 10 days in spring, 1 male for 2 days in summer; family labour: 1 male for 3 days in spring, for 10 days in summer; this is all the labour done in this garden by this family; immediate landlord William

Lenox Conyngham, tenure at will, 12 pounds yearly rent per acre.

Farmer no.17, occasional labour: 1 male for 5 days in spring, for 1 day in summer, for 5 days in autumn; family non-working; immediate landlord Mrs Hogg, by lease, tenure at will, 4 pounds 17s yearly rent per acre.

Farmer no.18, family labour: 1 male for 10 days in spring, for 3 days in summer, for 7 days in autumn; male does all the labour of this garden; immediate landlord Mrs Hogg, tenure at will, 4 pounds 17s yearly rent per acre.

Farmer no.19, occasional labour: 2 males for 6 days in spring, 1 male for 2 days in summer, for 4 days in autumn; 1 female for 4 days in autumn; family non-working; immediate landlord William Lenox Conyngham, tenure 61 years and 3 lives.

Farmer no.20, family labour: 1 male for 18 days in spring, [blank] for 7 days in summer, [blank] for 12 days in autumn; family non-working; this labour that is given is done by a man, to be taken from his labour on farm; immediate landlord William Lenox Conyngham, tenure 21 years and 1 life, 5 pounds yearly rent per acre.

Farmer no.21, occasional labour: 2 males for 12 days in spring, 1 male for 12 days in summer, for 18 days in autumn; 1 female for 10 days in summer; family non-working; immediate landlord William Lenox Conyngham, tenure perpetuity, 15s yearly rent per acre; 1 water pump, [value] 5 pounds.

Farmer no.22, non-working; tenure 32 years, immediate landlord William Lenox Conyngham, 2 pounds yearly rent per acre.

Farmer no.23, occasional labour: 1 male for 3 days in spring, for 1 day in summer, for 1 day in autumn; family non-working; immediate landlord Thomas Duff, by perpetuity, tenure 10 years, 12 pounds yearly rent per acre.

Farmer no.24, occasional labour: 1 male for 6 days in spring, for 1 day in summer, 2 males for 1 day in autumn; family non-working; immediate landlord Mathew George, by perpetuity, tenure at will, 4 pounds 10s yearly rent per acre.

Farmer no.25, occasional labour: 1 male for 20 days in spring, for 2 days in summer, for 7 days in autumn; 1 female for 5 days in autumn; family non-working; immediate landlord Mary Crookshanks, by perpetuity, tenure at will, 4 pounds 12s 3d ha'penny yearly rent per acre.

Farmer no.26, occasional labour: 2 males for 12 days in spring, 1 male for 10 days in summer, 2 males for 7 days in autumn; 1 female for 5 days in summer; family non-working; immediate landlord William Lenox Conyngham, tenure 31 years and 3 lives, 13 pounds yearly rent per acre; 1 spring well.

Farmer no.27, occasional labour: 1 male for 4 days in spring, for 2 days in autumn; 1 female for 1 day in summer; family non-working; immediate landlord William Lenox Conyngham, tenure perpetuity, 5s yearly rent per acre.

Farmer no.28, occasional labour: 1 male for 5 days in spring, for 1 day in summer, for 2 days in autumn; family non-working; immediate landlord Robert Blackwood Esq., by perpetuity, tenure at will, 7 pounds yearly rent per acre.

Farmer no.29, occasional labour: 1 male for 8 days in spring, for 5 days in autumn; family non-working; immediate landlord William Lenox Conyngham, tenure at will, 7 pounds yearly rent per acre.

Farmer no.30, family labour: 1 male for 12 days in spring, [blank] for 6 days in summer, [blank] for 7 days in autumn; this is the labour done by this man; immediate landlord William Lenox Conyngham, tenure at will, 6 pounds 16s 6d yearly rent per acre; 1 spring well.

Farmer no.31, occasional labour: 1 male for 6 days in spring, for 4 days in autumn; 1 female for 2 days in summer; family non-working; immediate landlord William Lenox Conyngham, tenure at will, subtenant, 4 pounds yearly rent per acre.

Farmer no.32, occasional labour: 1 male for 8 days in spring, for 2 days in summer, for 6 days in autumn; 1 female for 2 days in autumn; family non-working; immediate landlord William Lenox Conyngham, tenure at will, 3 pounds 10s yearly rent per acre.

Farmer no.33, occasional labour: 2 males for 6 days in spring, 1 male for 4 days in summer, for 8 days in autumn; 1 female for 2 days in summer; family non-working; immediate landlord William Lenox Conyngham, tenure perpetuity, 10s yearly rent per acre.

Farmer no.34, occasional labour: 1 male for 7 days in spring, for 1 day in summer, for 5 days in autumn; family non-working; immediate landlord William Lenox Conyngham, tenure 31 years and 3 lives, 15s yearly rent per acre.

Farmer no.35, occasional labour: 1 male for 2 days in spring, for 2 days in summer, for 1 day in autumn; family non-working; immediate landlord William Lenox Conyngham, tenure at will, 2 pounds 10s yearly rent per acre.

Farmer no.36, occasional labour: 1 male for 4 days in spring, for 1 day in summer, for 2 days in autumn; family non-working; immediate landlord William Lenox Conyngham, tenure at will, 2 pounds 10s yearly rent per acre.

Parish of Tamlaght

Farmer no.37, occasional labour: 1 male for 3 days in spring, for 1 day in summer, for 2 days in autumn; family non-working; immediate landlord William Lenox Conyngham, tenure at will, 2 pounds 2s yearly rent per acre.

Farmer no.38, occasional labour: 1 male for 2 days in spring, for 2 days in autumn; family non-working; immediate landlord William Lenox Conyngham, tenure at will, 2 pounds 2s yearly rent per acre.

Farmer no.39, occasional labour: 1 male for 3 days in spring, for 1 day in summer, for 2 days in autumn; family non-working; immediate landlord William Lenox Conyngham, tenure 21 years and 1 life, 4s 6d yearly rent per acre.

Farmer no.40, occasional labour: 1 male for 4 days in spring, for 1 day in summer, for 3 days in autumn; family non-working; immediate landlord William Lenox Conyngham, tenure 21 years and 1 life, 2 pounds yearly rent per acre.

Farmer no.41, family labour: 1 male for 4 days in spring, [blank] for 1 day in summer, [blank] for 2 days in autumn; this is all the labour done on this garden by this man or family; immediate landlord James Brown, by perpetuity, tenure at will, 4 pounds yearly rent per acre.

Farmer no.42, occasional labour: 1 male for 3 days in spring, for 2 days in autumn; 1 female for 2 days in autumn; family non-working; immediate landlord James Brown, by perpetuity, tenure at will, 4 pounds yearly rent per acre.

Farmer no.43, occasional labour: 1 male for 2 days in spring, for 1 day in summer, for 2 days in autumn; family non-working; immediate landlord James Brown, by perpetuity, tenure at will, 4 pounds yearly rent per acre.

Farmer no.44, occasional labour: 1 male for 2 days in spring, for 2 days in autumn; family non-working; immediate landlord James Brown, by perpetuity, tenure at will, 4 pounds yearly rent per acre.

Farmer no.45, occasional labour: 1 male for 2 days in spring, for 2 days in autumn; family non-working; immediate landlord James Brown, tenure at will, 4 pounds yearly rent per acre.

Farmer no.46, family labour: 1 male for 2 days in spring, [blank] for 1 day in summer, [blank] for 2 days in autumn; this is all the labour done by this man and family in this garden; immediate landlord James Brown, tenure at will, 3 pounds 6s yearly rent per acre.

Coagh Gardens: Manures

Manures given in Field Book.

Coagh Gardens: Seed and Produce

Quantity of seed and of produce per acre: seed and produce given in Field Book.

Value of seed and measure, value of produce, time of sowing, time of harvest: this given in Field Book.

Field observer's signature: John Hamilton, date 2nd June 1840.

Coagh Gardens: Table of Trades

Trades given in town table.

Field observer's signature: John Hamilton, date 2nd June 1840.

Coagh Gardens: Condition of Cottiers

Cottiers in Field Book.

Field observer's signature: John Hamilton, date June 2nd 1840.

Coagh Gardens: Summary of Economy

This given in Field Book.

Field observer's signature: John Hamilton, residence William Vance's, Coagh, date 2nd June 1840.

Statistical Information for Drumard, May and June 1840

Drumard: Farmers, Acreages and Crops

[Form 1. Information from farmer in each case].

Farmer no.1, Widow Gibson, farmer; 5 acres, 3 and five-sixteenths tillage, 1 and five-eighths pasture: 2 and a quarter oats, 1 potatoes, one-sixteenth of an acre flax; rotation: 1 potatoes, 2 oats or flax, 3 oats, 4 grass, 5 grass.

Farmer no.2, Samuel Bell, farmer; 7 and a half acres, 5 and a quarter tillage, three-eighth acres pasture [rough ?], three-quarter acres meadow, 1 waste [written above: s [soft ?] bog]: three-quarter acres wheat, 2 and a half oats, 1 and a half potatoes, a quarter acre flax, a quarter acre hay; rotation: 1 oats, 2 wheat, 3 potatoes, 4 oats or flax, 5 oats; drainage: [diagram of drainage system, 36 by 30, 2 10/60].

Farmer no.3, John Booth, farmer; 23 and a quarter acres, 17 and three-eighths tillage, 2 and half pasture, 3 meadow: 3 wheat, one-eighth acre barley, 8 oats, 4 potatoes, a quarter acre flax, half an acre turnips, 1 and a half clover; rotation: 1 oats, 2 potatoes or turnips, 3 wheat or barley, 4 oats or flax with clover sown, 5 grass with clover cut, 6 grass; acres under orchard: half an acre, 18 years planted; drainage: [diagram of drainage system, 36 by 24, 5 6/100].

Farmer no.4, William Rollins, farmer and weaver; 2 and a half acres, 1 and nine-sixteenths tillage, seven-eighth acres pasture: 1 oats, half an acre potatoes, one-sixteenth acre flax; rotation: 1 oats, 2 potatoes, 3 oats or flax, 4 oats, 5 grass, 6 grass.

Farmer no.5, John Rollins, farmer and weaver; 2 and three-quarter acres, 1 and nine-sixteenths tillage, seven-eighth acres pasture: 1 oats, half an acre potatoes, one-sixteenth acre flax; rotation: 1 oats, 2 potatoes, 3 oats or flax, 4 oats, 5 grass, 6 grass.

Farmer no.6, James Happer, farmer; 6 and a half acres, 3 and nine-sixteenths tillage, 2 and three-quarters pasture: a quarter acre wheat, 1 and three-quarters oats, 1 and quarter potatoes, a quarter acre flax, one-sixteenth acre clover; rotation: 1 potatoes, 2 oats or flax, 3 oats with clover sown, 4 grass with clover cut, 5 grass.

Farmer no.7, John Hamilton, farmer and thatcher; 2 acres, 1 and five-sixteenths tillage, five-eighth acres pasture: three-quarter acres oats, half an acre potatoes, one-sixteenth acre flax; rotation: 1 potatoes, 2 oats or flax, 3 oats, 4 grass, 5 grass.

Farmer no.8, James Hamilton, farmer; 4 and a half acres, 2 and a half tillage, seven-eighth acres pasture: 1 and a quarter oats, three-quarter acres potatoes, a quarter acre flax, a quarter acre clover; rotation: 1 potatoes, 2 oats or flax, 3 oats with clover sown, 4 clover cut, 5 grass, 6 grass.

Farmer no.9, John McIldoon, farmer; 29 and a half acres, 22 and a quarter tillage, 5 and a half pasture, 1 meadow: 4 wheat, 9 oats, 5 potatoes, a quarter acre flax, 3 hay, 1 clover; rotation: 1 oats, 2 potatoes, 3 wheat or oats, 4 oats or flax with clover sown and hay sown, 5 clover cut and hay cut, 6 grass; acres under orchard: half an acre, 9 years planted; half an acre reclaimed since 1830; drainage: [diagram of drainage system, 36 by 30, 12 40/500].

Farmer no.10, John Hamilton, farmer; 30 acres, 14 and a half tillage, 11 and a half pasture, 2 meadow, 1 waste: 8 oats, 3 and a half potatoes, 1 flax, 1 hay, 1 clover; rotation: 1 oats, 2 potatoes, 3 oats or flax, 4 oats with clover sown and hay sown, 5 clover cut and hay cut, 6 grass; 3 acres reclaimed since 1830; drainage: [diagram of drainage system, 40 by 36, 14 60/410].

Farmer no.11, Henry Hogg, farmer and weaver; 4 acres, 2 and seven-eighths tillage, 1 pasture: 1 and a half oats, 1 potatoes, a quarter acre flax, one-eighth acre clover; rotation: 1 oats, 2 potatoes, 3 oats or flax, 4 oats with clover sown, 5 grass with clover cut, 6 grass.

Farmer no.12, Robert Lennon, farmer; 10 acres, 7 and a quarter tillage, 2 pasture, half an acre meadow: 1 wheat, 4 oats, 1 and a half potatoes, a quarter acre flax, half an acre clover; rotation: 1 oats, 2 potatoes, 3 oats or flax, 4 oats with clover sown, 5 clover cut, 6 grass; half an acre reclaimed since 1830.

Farmer no.13, William Townsend, farmer; 4 acres, 2 and seven-eighths tillage, 1 pasture: 1 and a half oats, 1 potatoes, one-eighth acre flax, a quarter acre clover; rotation: 1 oats, 2 potatoes, 3 oats or flax, 4 oats with clover sown, 5 clover cut, 6 grass.

Farmer no.14, William Spear, farmer and weaver; 4 and a half acres, 2 and a half acres tillage, 1 and seven-eighths pasture: half an acre wheat, 1 oats, three-quarter acres potatoes, a quarter acre flax; rotation: 1 oats, 2 potatoes, 3 wheat, oats or flax, 4 oats, 5 grass, 6 grass.

Farmer no.15, Robert Spear, farmer and weaver; 4 and a half acres, 3 tillage, 1 and three-eighths pasture: 1 wheat, 1 oats, three-quarter acres potatoes, a quarter acre flax; rotation: 1 oats, 2 potatoes, 3 wheat, oats or flax, 4 oats, 5 grass, 6 grass.

Farmer no.16, Widow Hamilton, farmer; 1 and a half acres, tillage: 1 oats, half an acre potatoes; rotation: 1 potatoes, 2 oats.

Farmer no.17, Robert Ferguson, farmer; 7 acres, 4 and a half acres tillage, 1 and a quarter pasture, 1 meadow: 2 and a half oats, 1 potatoes, half an acre flax, half an acre clover; rotation: 1 oats, 2 potatoes, 3 oats or flax, 4 oats with clover sown, 5 clover cut, 6 grass; acres under orchard: a quarter acre, 14 years planted.

Farmer no.18, William Wallace [? Wallan], farmer; 4 acres, tillage: 2 oats, 1 and a half potatoes, half an acre flax; rotation: 1 oats, 2 potatoes, 3 oats or flax, 4 oats, sown alternately.

Farmer no.19, John Bell, farmer; 9 and a quarter acres, 5 and a half tillage, 3 and three-quarters pasture: three-quarter acres wheat, 3 oats, 1 and a half potatoes, a quarter acre flax; rotation: 1 oats, 2 potatoes, 3 oats or wheat, 4 oats or flax, 5 grass, 6 grass.

Farmer no.20, William Leech, farmer; 10 acres, 5 and a half tillage, 4 and a quarter pasture: 3 and a half oats, 1 and three-quarters potatoes, a quarter acre flax; rotation: 1 oats, 2 potatoes, 3 oats or flax, 4 oats, 5 grass, 6 grass; acres under orchard: a quarter acre, 45 years planted.

Farmer no.21, Widow Johnston, farmer; 36 acres, 22 and three-quarters tillage, 8 and a quarter pasture, 4 meadow: 5 wheat, 10 oats, 4 potatoes, half an acre flax, a quarter acre turnips, 2 hay, 1 and a half clover; rotation: 1 oats, 2 potatoes or turnips, 3 wheat, flax or oats with clover

Parish of Tamlaght

sown and hay sown, 4 oats with hay cut and clover cut, 5 grass, 6 grass; acres under orchard: one-eighth acre, 16 years planted; half an acre reclaimed since 1830; drainage: [diagram of drainage system, 40 by 30, 7 20/300].

Farmer no.22, Robert Devlin, farmer and weaver; 4 acres, 2 and three-quarters tillage, 1 and one-eighth pasture: 1 and a half oats, 1 potatoes, one-eighth acre flax, one-eighth acre clover; rotation: 1 oats, 2 potatoes, 3 oats or flax with clover sown, 4 oats with clover cut, 5 grass.

Farmer no.23, John Devlin [22 written above], farmer and weaver; 2 acres, tillage: 1 and a quarter oats, three-quarter acres potatoes; rotation: 1 potatoes, 2 oats, 3 potatoes.

Farmer no.24, Hugh Devlin, farmer and weaver; 2 acres, tillage: 1 oats, three-quarter acres potatoes, a quarter acre flax; rotation: 1 potatoes, 2 oats or flax, 3 oats, 4 potatoes.

Farmer no.25, Widow Hamilton, farmer; 5 acres, 2 and a half tillage, 1 and seven-eighths pasture, half an acre meadow: 1 and three-quarters oats, half an acre potatoes, one-eighth acre flax, one-eighth acre clover; rotation: 1 oats, 2 potatoes, 3 oats or flax with clover sown, 4 oats with clover cut, 5 grass, 6 grass.

Undivided bog 30 acres, waste; roads 1 and a quarter acres; [total] statute acres 409 = plantation acres 252 and a half: 144 and eleven-sixteenths tillage, 55 and a quarter pasture, 12 and three-quarters meadow, 32 waste: 16 and a quarter wheat, one-eighth barley, 72 oats, 36 and three-quarters potatoes, 6 and one-eighth flax, three-quarter acres turnips, 6 and a quarter hay, 6 and three-sixteenths clover.

[Insert addition: o.m. 421 and a quarter statute acres].

Nos.4 and 5, William and John Rollins, are brothers. Their holdings is 1 farm. They crop it jointly and divide the produce in autumn.

Major Rynd, the proprietor, had this townland surveyed a few weeks ago. I went to the surveyor Mr Robert Turk in order to compare the survey he had taken. He'd not got it calculated but he states that there is only 31 and a quarter acres under undivided bog and roads and he considers that the farms must answer for the deficiency. I could obtain no more.

Field observer's signature: John Hanna, date 9th to 11th and 17th to 19th June 1840.

Drumard: Farmers' Stock and Implements

[Form 2. Additional prices added to table: horses for pleasure 20 pounds, horses for agriculture 7 pounds to 14 pounds; cattle: old 4 pounds to 9 pounds, young 15s to 30s; sheep 1 pound; hogs: old 1 pound to 3 pounds, young 5s to 20s; geese: old 20d to 3s 2d, young 15d to 20d; ducks: old 7d to 9d, young 5d to 7d; turkeys: old 2s 6d to 3s 4d, young 15d to 20d; hens: old 5d to 7d, young 5d to 8d; beehives 15s; ploughs: iron 4 pounds, wooden 20s to 30s; harrows 7s 6d, breaks 9s to 14s, rollers 30s to 2 pounds, drill hoes 15s to 1 pound, carts 3 pounds to 5 pounds, wheel cars 20s to 2 pounds, corn fans 2 pounds 5s, spinning wheels 8s to 14s 6d, employed and unemployed linen looms 2 pounds to 50s, box barrows 9s to 12s, turf barrows 2s 6d to 3s 6d, agricultural spades 2s to 2s 2d, agricultural shovels 15d to 18d, scythe hooks 7d to 9d, teethed hooks 5d to 8d].

Farmer no.1, 1/0 agricultural horses, 4/0 ducks, 4/10 hens, 1 wooden plough, 1 cart, 1 spinning wheel, 1 employed linen loom, 1 box barrow, 2/0 agricultural spades, 1 agricultural shovel, 3 teethed hooks.

Farmer no.2, 1/0 agricultural horses, 1/1 cattle, 2/0 hogs, 1 wooden plough, 1 break, 1 cart, 1 spinning wheel, 1 unemployed linen loom, 2 turf barrows, 2/1 agricultural spades, 1 agricultural shovel, 2 teethed hooks.

Farmer no.3, 3/0 agricultural horses, 4/2 cattle, 5/0 hogs, 6/0 geese, 3/9 ducks, 6/10 hens, 1 wooden and 1 iron plough, 2 breaks, 1 roller, 3 carts, 1 corn fan, 3 spinning wheels, 1 box barrow, 3 turf barrows, 4/2 agricultural spades, 1 agricultural shovel, 4 teethed hooks; irrigation: inundated.

Farmer no.4, 1/0 cattle, 1/0 hens, 1 spinning wheel, 1 employed linen loom, 1 agricultural spade, 1 agricultural shovel, 2 teethed hooks.

Farmer no.5, 1/0 cattle, 1 spinning wheel, 1 employed linen loom, 1 agricultural spade, 1 agricultural shovel, 2 teethed hooks.

Farmer no.6, 1/0 cattle, 6/0 ducks, 3/0 hens, 3 spinning wheels, 1 employed linen loom, 2 unemployed linen looms, 1 box barrow, 2 turf barrows, 2/1 agricultural spades, 1 agricultural shovel, 2 scythe hooks, 1 teethed hook.

Farmer no.7, 1/0 cattle, 4/8 ducks, 4/0 hens, 3 spinning wheels, 1 box barrow, 1 turf barrow, 2/1 agricultural spades, 1 agricultural shovel, 2 teethed hooks.

Farmer no.8, 1/0 agricultural horses, 1/0 cattle, 3/4 ducks, 2/7 hens, 1 wooden plough, 1 break, 1 cart, 1 spinning wheel, 1 unemployed linen loom, 1 box barrow, 2 turf barrows, 1/2 agricultural spades, 1 agricultural shovel, 1 scythe hook, 1 teethed hook.

Farmer no.9, 1/0 pleasure horses, 3/1 agricultural horses, 3/1 cattle, 1/0 sheep, 4/0 hogs, 4/18 geese, 4/14 turkeys, 10/18 hens, 3 beehives, 3 wooden improved ploughs, 3 breaks, 1 roller, 1 drill hoe, 2 carts, 2 wheel cars, 1 corn fan, 3/3 idle spinning wheels, 2 unemployed linen looms, 3 box barrows, 4 turf barrows, 4/2 agricultural spades, 3 agricultural shovels, 5 scythe hooks, 5 teethed hooks; irrigation: not required.

Farmer no.10, 3/0 agricultural horses, 7/1 cattle, 3/0 sheep, 1/0 hogs, 2/11 geese, 2/1 hens, 1 iron plough, 2 breaks, 1 roller, 1 drill hoe, 3 carts, 1 corn fan, 1 spinning wheel, 2 box barrows, 3 turf barrows, 5/2 agricultural spades, 3 agricultural shovels, 3 scythe hooks, 3 teethed hooks.

Farmer no.11, 1/0 cattle, 1/0 hogs, 4/6 hens, 2 spinning wheels, 1 employed linen loom, 1 box barrow, 1 agricultural spade, 1 agricultural shovel, 1 scythe hook, 1 teethed hook.

Farmer no.12, 1/0 agricultural horses, 2/1 cattle, 2/1 hogs, 3/7 geese, 7/14 hens, 1 wooden plough, 1 break, 1 cart, 4 spinning wheels, 1 unemployed linen loom, 2 box barrows, 4 turf barrows, 2/1 agricultural spades, 3 agricultural shovels, 3 scythe hooks, 2 teethed hooks.

Farmer no.13, 1/1 cattle, 1/0 hogs, 2/6 hens, 1 spinning wheel, 1 unemployed linen loom, 1/0 agricultural spades, 1 agricultural shovel, 2 teethed hooks.

Farmer no.14, 1/0 agricultural horses, 1/0 cattle, 2/0 hogs, 3/0 ducks, 2/4 hens, 1 wooden plough, 1 break, 1 cart, 1 spinning wheel, 1 employed linen loom, 2 turf barrows, 1/2 agricultural spades, 1 agricultural shovel, 2 scythe hooks.

Farmer no.15, 1/0 agricultural horses, 1/0 cattle, 2/0 hogs, 2/6 hens, 1 wheel car, 1 spinning wheel, 1 employed linen loom, 3 turf barrows, 1/0 agricultural spades, 1 agricultural shovel, 1 scythe hook, 1 teethed hook.

Farmer no.16, 1/0 cattle, 6/0 ducks, 6/0 hens, 2 employed linen looms, 2 turf barrows, 2/1 agricultural spades, 1 agricultural shovel, 3 teethed hooks.

Farmer no.17, 1/0 agricultural horses, 1/0 cattle, 1/0 hogs, 2/10 ducks, 4/3 hens, 1 wooden plough, 1 break, 1 wheel car, 2 spinning wheels, 1 box barrow, 1 turf barrow, 1/1 agricultural spades, 1 agricultural shovel, 1 scythe hook, 2 teethed hooks.

Farmer no.18, 1/0 hogs, 1 spinning wheel, 1 unemployed linen loom, 1 box barrow, 2 turf barrows, 4 agricultural spades, 1 agricultural shovel, 2 scythe hooks, 2 teethed hooks.

Farmer no.19, 1/0 agricultural horses, 1/1 cattle, 3/9 hens, 1 wooden plough, 1 break, 1 cart, 2 spinning wheels, 1 box barrow, 3 turf barrows, 1/1 agricultural spades, 1 agricultural shovel, 2 scythe hooks.

Farmer no.20, 1 agricultural horse, 2/0 cattle, 0/2 hogs, 7/6 ducks, 3/10 hens, 1 wooden plough, 1 break, 1 roller, 1 cart, 2 spinning wheels, 1 employed linen loom, 1 unemployed linen loom, 1 box barrow, 2 turf barrows, 2/1 agricultural spades, 1 agricultural shovel, 1 scythe hook, 4 teethed hooks.

Farmer no.21, 3/0 agricultural horses, 6/3 cattle, 4/6 hogs, 3/12 geese, 9/14 ducks, 6/10 hens, 1 iron and 1 wooden improved plough, 2 breaks, 1 roller, 1 drill hoe, 3 carts, 1 corn fan, 1 spinning wheel, 2 box barrows, 4 turf barrows, 4/2 agricultural spades, 3 agricultural shovels, 3 scythe hooks.

Farmer no.22, 1/0 agricultural horses, 1/0 cattle, 2/0 hogs, 3/11 ducks, 6/4 hens, 1 wooden plough, 1 harrow, 1 cart, 1 spinning wheel, 1 employed linen loom, 2 turf barrows, 2/1 agricultural spades, 1 agricultural shovel, 3 teethed hooks.

Farmer no.23, 1/0 hogs, 1 spinning wheel, 1 employed linen loom, 1/0 agricultural spades, 1 agricultural shovel, 2 teethed hooks.

Farmer no.24, 1/0 cattle, 1/0 hogs, 2 spinning wheels, 1 employed linen loom, 1/0 agricultural spades, 1 agricultural shovel, 1 teethed hook.

Farmer no.25, 1/0 cattle, 1/2 hogs, 3/9 ducks, 7/2 hens, 2 spinning wheels, 1 unemployed linen loom, 1 box barrow, 2 turf barrows, 2/1 agricultural spades, 1 agricultural shovel, 2 teethed hooks.

Field observer's signature: John Hanna, date 9th to 11th and 17th to 19th June 1840.

Drumard: Cottiers' Stock and Implements

[Form 3]

[Crossed out: William Wallace [Wallan ?], labourer, William Townsend, labourer]. Those men [named] by Mr Hamilton, no.10, as his cottiers and when I came to them to get their information, I found them to be tenants 2 [subtenants]; see nos 12 and 18, Form 1.

Cottier no.1, farmer no.10, William Little, labourer; 1/0 goats, 1/0 hogs, 3/0 ducks, 4/6 hens, 2 spinning wheels, 1/0 agricultural spades, 1 agricultural shovel, 2 scythe hooks; 50s rent per annum.

Cottier no.2, farmer no.10, James McCord, labourer; 1/0 hogs, 6/2 ducks, 2/7 hens, 1 spinning wheel, 1/0 agricultural spades, 1 agricultural shovel, 1 teethed hook; 50s rent per annum.

Cottier no.3, farmer no.20, William Monroe, weaver; 1/0 hogs, 2 spinning wheels, 1 employed linen loom, 1 turf barrow, 1/0 agricultural spades, 1 agricultural shovel, 2 teethed hooks; 40s rent per annum.

Cottier no.4, farmer no.21, Philip McIlvenan, weaver; 1/0 hogs, 3/0 ducks, 2/0 hens, 1 spinning

Parish of Tamlaght

wheel, 1 employed linen loom, 1 box barrow, 2 turf barrows, 2/0 agricultural spades, 1 agricultural shovel, 1 scythe hook, 1 teethed hook; 50s rent per annum.

Cottier no.5, farmer no.21, James Hamilton, labourer; 2/0 hogs, 6/9 ducks, 5/14 hens, 2 spinning wheels, 1 unemployed linen loom, 1/1 agricultural spades, 1 agricultural shovel, 2 scythe hooks; 50s rent per annum.

Field observer's signature: John Hanna, date 9th to 11th, 17th to 19th June 1840.

Drumard: Labour and Proprietors

[Form 4. Head landlord is Major Thomas Rynd, tenure at will in each case, direct tenants unless indicated].

Farmer no.1, family: 2/0 males, 1/0 females; family labour: 1 female for 10 days in summer, [blank] for 20 days in autumn; female attends to domestic duties and spins; immediate landlord Major Thomas Rynd, 1 pound 3s yearly rent per acre; 1 spring well.

Farmer no.2, family: 2/0 males, 1/0 females, 1 male house servant; family labour: 1 female for 10 days in spring, [blank] for 14 days in summer, [blank] for 18 days in autumn; female attends to domestic duties and spins; immediate landlord Major Thomas Rynd, 1 pound 3s yearly rent per acre; 1 spring well.

Farmer no.3, family: 2/0 males, 3/1 females, 2 male house servants; occasional labour: 3 males for 14 days in spring, 2 for 6 days in summer, 4 for 18 days in autumn; family labour: 2/1 females for 10/4 days in spring, [blank] for 8/4 days in summer, [blank] for 20/14 days in autumn; 1 female at domestic duties continually and spins the remainder; 1 little girl goes to school the remainder; immediate landlord Major Thomas Rynd, 1 pound 4s 6d yearly rent per acre; 1 spring well.

Farmer no.4, family: 1w/2n males, 1/2n females; family labour: 1 male for 60 days in spring, [blank] for 20 days in summer, [blank] for 200 [sic] days in autumn; 1 female for 4 days in spring, [blank] for 6 days in summer, [blank] for 12 days in autumn; male weaves, female domestic duties and spins; immediate landlord Major Thomas Rynd, 1 pound 1s yearly rent per acre; 1 spring well.

Farmer no.5, family: 1w/1n males, 1/3n females; family labour: 1 male for 60 days in spring, [blank] for 20 days in summer, [blank] for 200 [sic] days in autumn; [blank] females for 4 days in spring, [blank] for 6 days in summer, [blank] for 12 days in autumn; male weaves, female domestic duties and spins; immediate landlord Major Thomas Rynd, 1 pound 1s yearly rent per acre.

Farmer no.6, family: 2, 1w/1n males, 3/2n males; family labour: 1 male for 30 days in spring, [blank] for 8 days in summer, [blank] for 8 days in autumn; 2 females for 10 days in spring, [blank] for 8 days in summer, [blank] for 14 days in autumn; 1 male weaves, 1 female domestic duties constantly, the others spin; immediate landlord Major Thomas Rynd, 1 pound 5s 2d yearly rent per acre; 1 spring well.

Farmer no.7, family: 1t/2n males, 4 females; family labour: 1 male for 40 days in spring, [blank] for 10 days in summer, [blank] for 100 days in autumn; 3 females for 4 days in spring, [blank] for 6 days in summer, [blank] for 12 days in autumn; 1 thatches, 1 female domestic duties constantly, the others spin; immediate landlord Major Thomas Rynd, 1 pound 5s 2d yearly rent per acre.

Farmer no.8, family: 2 males, 1/2n females; family labour: 1 female for 3 days in spring, [blank] for 5 days in summer, [blank] for 18 days in autumn; female attends to domestic duties and spins the remainder of time; immediate landlord Major Thomas Rynd, 1 pound 5s 2d yearly rent per acre; 1 spring well.

Farmer no.9, family: 2/0 males, 4/0 females, 3 male house servants; occasional labour: 6 males for 40 days in spring, 2 for 10 days in summer, 8 for 30 days in autumn; 3 females for 30 days in autumn; family labour: 3 males for 10 days in spring, [blank] for 12 days in summer; 3 females for 60 [40] days in spring, [blank] for 10 days in summer, [blank] for 30 days in autumn; female attends to domestic duties constantly, the other spins the remainder; immediate landlord Major Thomas Rynd, 1 pound 3s yearly rent per acre; 1 [?] metal water pump, [value] 10 pounds.

Farmer no.10, family: 1/0 males, 2/0 females, 2 male house servants, 2 female house servants; occasional labour: 6 males for 16 days in spring, 4 for 10 days in summer, 6 for 20 days in autumn; family labour: 1 female for 10 days in spring, [blank] for 10 days in summer, [blank] for 20 days in autumn; 1 female attends to domestic duties, 1 female spins the remainder; immediate landlord Major Thomas Rynd, 1 pound 5s 2d yearly rent per acre; 1 spring well, 1 water pump, wood, [value] 10 pounds.

Farmer no.11, family: 1w/0 males, 3 females; family labour: 1 male for 50 days in spring, [blank] for 20 days in summer, [blank] for 100 days in autumn; 3 females for 6 days in spring, [blank] for 10 days in summer, [blank] for 40 days in autumn; females spin the remainder, male weaves; immediate landlord Mr Hamilton, no.10, subtenant, 2 pounds yearly rent per acre.

Farmer no.12, family: 1/2n males, 1/1n females, 1 male house servant, 1 female house servant; occasional labour: 2 males for 12 days in spring, 1 for 10 days in summer, 3 for 12 days in autumn; family labour: 1 female for 14 days in spring, [blank] for 16 days in summer, [blank] for 30 days in autumn; 1 female spins, attends to domestic duties the remainder of time; immediate landlord Major Thomas Rynd, 1 pound 3s yearly rent per acre; 1 spring well.

Farmer no.13, family: 1/0 males, 1/2n females; family labour: 1 female for 13 days in spring, [blank] for 6 days in summer, [blank] for 20 days in autumn; 1 female spins and attends to domestic duties the remainder of time; immediate landlord Mr Hamilton, no.10, subtenant, 2 pounds yearly rent per acre.

Farmer no.14, family: 1/0 males, 1/0 females; family labour: 1 male for 70 days in spring, [blank] for 20 days in summer, [blank] for 120 days in autumn; 1 female for 6 days in spring, [blank] for 8 days in summer, [blank] for 20 days in autumn; 1 female spins and attends to domestic duties, male weaves; immediate landlord Major Thomas Rynd, 1 pound 3s yearly rent per acre; 1 spring well.

Farmer no.15, family: 1 males, 1/1n females; family labour: 1 male for 70 days in spring, [blank] for 20 days in summer, [blank] for 120 days in autumn; 1 female for 4 days in spring, [blank] for 6 days in summer, [blank] for 10 days in autumn; 1 female spins and attends to domestic duties the remainder, male weaves; immediate landlord Major Thomas Rynd, 1 pound 3s yearly rent per acre.

Farmer no.16, family: 2w/0 males, 1 old female; family labour: 2 males for 3 days in spring, [blank] for 4 days in summer, [blank] for 4 days in autumn; 1 female spins constantly, male weaves; immediate landlord Major Thomas Rynd, 1 pound 5s yearly rent per acre; 1 spring well.

Farmer no.17, family: 1/0 males, 3/0 females, 1 male house servant; family labour: 2 females for 14 days in spring, [blank] for 12 days in summer, [blank] for 30 days in autumn; 1 female spins and attends to domestic duties constantly, 2 farm and spin occasionally; immediate landlord Major Thomas Rynd, 1 pound 3s yearly rent per acre; 1 spring well.

Farmer no.18, family: 1/0 males, 3/0 females; family labour: 2 females for 25 days in spring, [blank] for 6 days in summer, 3 for 36 days in autumn; 1 female spins most constantly at domestic duties, 2 spin and farm occasionally; immediate landlord Mr Hamilton, no.10, subtenant, 2 pounds yearly rent per acre.

Farmer no.19, family: 1/1 males, 3/1n females; occasional labour: 4 males for 8 days in spring, 2 for 4 days in summer, 3 for 9 days in autumn; family labour: 2 females for 18 days in spring, [blank] for 11 days in summer, [blank] for 25 days in autumn; 1 female domestic duties constantly, 2 spins and farms occasionally; immediate landlord Major Thomas Rynd, 1 pound 3s yearly rent per acre; 1 spring well.

Farmer no.20, family: 2,1w/2n,1 males, 3/0 females; family labour: 2 females for 10 days in spring, [blank] for 4 days in summer, [blank] for 30 days in autumn; 1 female domestic duties constantly, 2 spin, male weaver weaves constantly; immediate landlord Major Thomas Rynd, 1 pound 3s yearly rent per acre; 1 spring well.

Farmer no.21, family: 2/0 males, 1/0 females, 2 male house servants, 2 female house servants, 1 constant male labourer; occasional labour: 4 males for 20 days in spring, 2 for 10 days in summer, 6 for 18 days in autumn; 2 females for 18 days in spring, for 12 days in summer, for 30 days in autumn; family labour: female attends to domestic duties constantly, males farm constantly; immediate landlord Major Thomas Rynd, 1 pound 3s yearly rent per acre; 1 spring well.

Farmer no.22, family: 1,1w/0 males, 1/0 females; family labour: 1 male for 14 days in spring, [blank] for 6 days in summer, [blank] for 18 days in summer; 1 female for 10 days in spring, [blank] for 7 days in summer, [blank] for 12 days in autumn; female attends domestic duties the remainder, weaver weaves the remainder; immediate landlord Major Thomas Rynd, 1 pound 3s yearly rent per acre.

Farmer no.23, family: 1w/2n males, 2/0 females; family labour: 1 male for 30 days in spring, [blank] for 10 days in summer, [blank] for 50 days in autumn; 2 females for 4 days in spring, [blank] for 6 days in summer, [blank] for 8 days in autumn; male farms and weaves occasionally, females spin the remainder; immediate landlord Major Thomas Rynd, 1 pound 3s yearly rent per acre.

Farmer no.24, family: 1w/1n males, 1/1n females; family labour: 1 male for 18 days in spring, [blank] for 6 days in summer, [blank] for 24 days in autumn; 1 female for 11 days in spring, [blank] for 4 days in summer, [blank] for 17 days in autumn; male farms and weaves occasionally, females spin the remainder; immediate landlord

Parish of Tamlaght

Major Thomas Rynd, 1 pound 3s yearly rent per acre.

Farmer no.25, family: 2/0 males, 2/0 females; family labour: 2 females for 14 days in spring, [blank] for 10 days in summer, [blank] for 20 days in autumn; females spin and attend to domestic duties the remainder of the time; immediate landlord Major Thomas Rynd, 1 pound 3s yearly rent per acre.

Field observer's signature: John Hanna, date 9th to 11th, 17th to 19th June 1840.

Drumard: Manures

[Form 5]

Farmer no.2, dung: 2s 4d per ton, carried from townland; bog: 1d ha'penny per ton, 8 cwt per load, carried from townland, 1 person employed for 3 days; lime: 8d per barrel, 8 and a half cwt per load, 4 and a half miles carried, 1 person employed for 4 days; clay: 3d per ton, 8 cwt per load, carried from townland, 1 person employed for 6 days; compost loads: 50 dung, 100 bog, 20 barrels of lime, 100 clay; 8 cwt of compost carried from the heap to the field, 1 person employed for 11 days, made at the house.

Farmer no.3, dung: 29 tons per acre, 2s 4d per ton, 8 cwt per load, carried from townland, 1 person employed for 4 days; bog: 2d per ton, 8 cwt per load, carried from townland, 1 person employed for 10 days; lime: 8d per barrel, 10 and a quarter cwt per load, 4 and a half miles carried, 1 person employed for 6 days; clay: 3d per ton, 8 cwt per load, carried from townland, 1 person employed for 10 days; compost loads: 45 dung, 100 bog, 25 barrels of lime, 100 clay; 8 cwt of compost carried from the heap to the field, 1 person employed for 12 days, made at the house.

Farmer no.9, dung: 36 tons per acre, 2s 6d per ton, 8 cwt per load, carried from farmyard, 2 people employed for 2 days; bog: 2d per ton, 8 cwt per load, carried from townland, 3 people employed for 7 days; lime: 8d per barrel, 10 cwt per load, 4 and a half miles carried, 1 person employed for 10 days; clay: 3d per ton, 8 cwt per load, carried from townland, 3 people employed for 10 days; compost loads: 40 dung, 120 bog, 20 barrels of lime, 200 clay; 8 cwt of compost carried from the heap to the field, 3 people employed for 6 days, made at the house.

Farmer no.21, dung: 35 tons per acre, 2s 4d per ton, 8 cwt per load, carried from farmyard, 3 people employed for 1 and a half days; bog: 2d per ton, 8 cwt per load, carried from townland, 3 people employed for 4 days; lime: 15 barrels per acre, 8d per barrel, 10 and a quarter cwt per load, 4 and a half miles carried, 3 people employed for 2 days; clay: 2d per ton, 8 cwt per load, carried from townland, 3 people employed for 5 days; compost loads: 50 dung, 100 bog, 15 barrels of lime, 120 clay; 8 cwt of compost carried from the heap to the field, 3 people employed for 4 days, made at the house.

Dung used alone and in compost; bog used in compost; lime used in compost, and by no.21 it is used alone and in compost; clay used in compost.

Description of acre: plantation.

Lime: number of bushels per barrel 4, weight of barrel 230 lbs.

Dung got in farmyard, bog in townland, clay in townland, lime in Tamnalanan, parish of Donaghenry.

Drumard: Seed and Produce

[Form 6]

Farmer no.2, wheat: 18 stones seed, 180 produce; oats: 21 stones seed, 160 produce; potatoes: 25 bushels seed, 300 produce; flax: 4 bushels seed, 9 cwt produce; hay and clover [bracketed together] 4 bushels hay seed, 12 lbs clover seed, produce 3 tons; general observations: level aspect, red clay and moory land.

Farmer no.3, wheat: 18 stones seed, 170 produce; barley: 16 stones seed, 150 produce; oats: 22 stones seed, 150 produce; potatoes; 26 bushels seed, 280 produce; flax: 4 bushels seed, 8 and a half cwt produce; turnips: 2 and a half lbs seed, 26 tons produce; hay: 3 bushels hay seed, 14 lbs clover seed, 18 tons produce; general observations: level aspect, red clay and moory land.

Farmer no.9, wheat: 18 stones seed, 160 produce; oats: 24 stones seed, 200 produce; potatoes: 25 bushels seed, 400 produce; flax: 4 bushels seed, 8 cwt produce; hay: 3 bushels hay seed, 10 lbs clover seed, 4 tons produce; clover: 3 bushels hay seed, 10 lbs clover seed, 18 tons produce; general observations: sou' west aspect, red, heavy and gravelly clay.

Farmer no.21, wheat: 18 stones seed, 180 produce; oats: 21 stones seed, 200 produce; potatoes: 25 bushels seed, 350 produce; flax: 4 bushels seed, 8 cwt produce; turnips: 2 and a half lbs seed, 30 tons produce; hay: 3 bushels hay seed, 8 lbs clover seed, 4 and a half tons produce; clover: 3 bushels hay seed, 8 lbs clover seed, 18 tons produce; general observations: a hill sloping down to all points, good.

It is to be understood that the forced hay and clover are sowed at the same time together and part cut green and part reserved for hay [initialled] JH.

Description of acre: plantation.

[Information from] farmer no.21. Wheat: value of seed 1s 4d to 1s 6d per stone, value of produce 1s 4d to 1s 6d per stone; time of sowing 25th October to 20th December, time of harvest 25th August to 25th September.

Barley: value of seed 12d to 1s 3d per stone, value of produce 12d to 1s 3d per stone; time of sowing 1st April to 10th April, time of harvest 25th August to 1st October.

Oats: value of seed 9d to 14d per stone, value of produce 9d to 14d per stone; time of sowing 20th March to 10th April, time of harvest 10th September to 10th October.

Potatoes: value of seed 3d ha'penny to 4d ha'penny per stone, value of produce 3d ha'penny to 4d ha'penny per stone; time of sowing 20th April to 20th May, time of harvest 10th October to 10th November.

Flax: value of seed 12s 6d to 14s per bushel, value of produce 40s to 45s per cwt; time of sowing 17th April to 10th May, time of harvest 1st August to 17th August.

Vetches: none.

Turnips: value of seed 14d to 18d per lb, value of produce 6d to 8d per cwt; time of sowing 15th May to 10th June, time of harvest 1st November to 1st January.

Mangle-wurzle: none.

Hay: value of seed 3s 6d to 4s 6d per bushel, value of produce 2s to 2s 8d per cwt; time of sowing 9th April to 1st May, time of harvest 25th June to 20th July.

Clover: value of seed 10d to 13d per lb, value of produce 6d to 6d ha'penny per cwt; time of sowing 1st April to 1st May, time of harvest 10th June to 1st October.

Field observer's signature: John Hanna, date 9th to 11th, 17th to 19th June 1840.

Drumard: Table of Trades

[Form 7]

John Hamilton, thatcher, master, wages 15d per day; family: 1/2 males, 4/0 females; his stock etc. is entered on townland book.

Field observer's signature: John Hanna, date 9th to 11th, 17th to 19th June 1840.

Drumard: Condition of Cottiers

[Form 8. No houses are whitewashed, all have straw roofs, clay, dry floors, with good beds and and good clothes. *All have the same furniture, which is recorded by abbreviations without a key: t = table, s = settle bed, c = chair, d = dresser, ew = earthenware, tc = [ticking clock ?].*

No.1, 2 apartments, mud house, mud and brick chimney, 4 lead windows, one-eighth of an acre garden.

No.2, 2 apartments, mud house, brick chimney, 4 lead windows, one-eighth of an acre garden.

No.3, 2 apartments, mud house, brick chimney, 3 lead windows, one-sixteenth of an acre garden.

No.4, 3 apartments, stone house, brick chimney, 5 lead windows, a quarter of an acre garden.

No.5, 3 apartments, stone house, brick chimney, 4 lead windows, a quarter of an acre garden.

Field observer's signature: John Hanna, date 9th to 11th, 17th to 19th June 1840.

Drumard: Summary of Economy

[Form 9]

Surface: hilly and uneven.

Soils, kind: heavy red clay, red gravelly clay and boggy clay in various parts of townland; depth: from 5 to 15 inches.

Subsoil, kind: red gravel, blue clay and bog in various parts of the townland; depth: unknown.

Exposure: to all winds.

Springs: 14 spring wells and 2 water pumps.

Drainage: it is well drained with drains of about 3 feet deep, filled with loose stones.

Irrigation: not considered needful, the land is naturally damp.

Implements: wooden, wooden improved and iron ploughs, spades 16 by 6 inches, hosed shovels, scythe and teethed hooks.

Acres reclaimed since 1830: 4 and a half plantation acres.

Mills, corn: none; flax: none; fulling: none.

Quarries, kind of: none.

Communications: a branch road from the Coagh and Maghery road by Arboe passes through the townland to the Coagh and Stewartstown road, in good repair.

Markets: Stewartstown, Cookstown and Coagh.

Breed of horses: Irish; breed of cattle: Irish and a few half bred from Irish and Devonshire; breed of sheep: large lowland; breed of hogs: Belties, half bred from Dutch and Irish.

Woods or plantations: none; kind: 1 and five-sixth plantation acres of orchard, apple, plum <plumb> and cherry trees; when first planted: 9, 14, 16, 18 and 45 years ago; present return: all used by farmers' families or presented to their friends.

Lime-kilns: none.

Manufactures: 1 brickfield for farmers' own use.

Kind of crops cultivated, oats: potato, blanter, Poland; wheat: red and white; potatoes: cups for the standing crop, red downs, black downs and copper downs for the early crop; flax: New York, Riga and Dutch; turnips: white Norfolk, yellow Aberdeen and Swedish.

[Insert addition: Farmers' names and acres, where got: from Tithe Composition Book and compared with Mr John Hamilton's, no.10, return for cess applotting the townland. Natural meadow: quantity per acre 3 tons; time of harvest 25th August to 25th September; price per ton 40s to 45s. Kind of acre: plantation. Fences, kind of: mounds of the various soils and subsoils found with whitethorns and stone. Turf, where got: in the townland. Rent per acre, rough or waste land, arable land: rough and arable land rented together, at from 21s to 25s per acre for tenant direct, subtenant at 2 pounds. Rough or waste land, kind of: spent bog].

Statistical Information for Drumconway, May and June 1840

Drumconway: Farmers, Acreages and Crops

[Form 1. Informant the farmer in each case].

Farmer no.1, Thomas Ford, farmer; 5 acres, 3 tillage, 2 pasture: 2 oats, 1 potatoes; rotation: 1 potatoes, 2 oats, 3 oats with hay sown for grazing, 4 grass, 5 grass, 6 grass.

Farmer no.2, Widow McGuckan, farmer, not working; 2 and a half acres, 1 and five-eighths tillage, seven-eighths pasture: 1 and one-eighth oats, half an acre potatoes; rotation: 1 potatoes, 2 oats, 3 oats with hay sown for grazing, 4 grass, 5 grass, 6 grass.

Farmer no.3, Hugh McGuckan, farmer; 2 and a half acres, 1 and a half tillage, 1 pasture: 1 oats, half an acre potatoes; rotation: 1 potatoes, 2 oats, 3 oats with hay sown for grazing, 4 grass, 5 grass, 6 grass.

Farmer no.4, Thomas Duff, farmer; 16 and three-quarter acres, 9 and a quarter tillage, 6 pasture, 1 and a quarter meadow, a quarter acre waste: 1 and a quarter wheat, 5 oats, 2 and a half potatoes, half an acre flax; rotation: 1 oats, 2 potatoes, 3 oats, flax or wheat, 4 oats with hay sown for grazing, 5 grass, 6 grass, 7 grass; acres under orchards: one-sixth of an acre, 40 years planted; plantation: one-sixteenth of an acre, 14 years planted; drainage: [diagram of drainage system 33 4/500].

Farmer no.5, George McGuckan, farmer, not working; 7 and three-quarter acres, 2 tillage, 4 and three-quarters pasture, half an acre meadow, half an acre waste: 1 and a half oats, half an acre flax; rotation: 1 oats, 2 potatoes, 3 oats or flax, 4 oats with hay sown for grazing, 5 grass, 6 grass, 7 grass.

Farmer no.6, George McGuckan, farmer; 13 acres, 8 and a half tillage, 4 and a quarter pasture, a quarter acre waste: half an acre wheat, 5 oats, 2 and three-quarters potatoes, a quarter acre flax; rotation: 1 oats, 2 potatoes, 3 oats, flax or wheat, 4 oats with hay sown for grazing, 5 grass, 6 grass, 7 grass.

Farmer no.7, Samuel Harkness, farmer; 3 and a half acres, tillage: 2 and a quarter oats, 1 and a quarter potatoes; rotation: 1 oats, 2 potatoes, 3 oats with clover sown, 4 clover cut twice, 5 grass.

Farmer no.8, Robert Duff, farmer; 26 and a half acres, 16 and a quarter tillage, 5 and a half pasture, 2 and a quarter meadow, 2 and a half waste: 3 wheat, 7 oats, 4 potatoes, half an acre flax, a quarter acre turnips, 1 and a half hay; rotation: 1 oats, 2 potatoes or turnips, 3 oats, wheat or flax with hay sown, 4 oats with hay cut and hay sown for grazing, 5 grass, 5 grass; acres under orchard: half an acre, 14 years planted; half an acre reclaimed since 1830; drainage: [diagram of drainage system 30 6/400].

Farmer no.9, Hugh Wates, farmer and weaver; 5 and a half acres, 3 tillage, 1 and a half pasture, 1 waste: 2 oats, 1 potatoes; rotation: 1 oats, 2 potatoes, 3 oats, 4 oats with hay sown for grazing, 5 grass; half an acre reclaimed since 1830.

Farmer no.10, Thomas Bell, farmer and weaver; 5 and a half acres, 3 tillage, 1 pasture, half an acre meadow, 1 waste: half an acre wheat, 1 and a quarter oats, 1 potatoes, a quarter acre flax; rotation: 1 oats, 2 potatoes, 3 wheat, oats or flax with clover sown, 4 clover cut twice, 5 grass; acres under orchard: one-eighth of an acre, 10 years planted; plantation: one-sixteenth of an acre, 4 years planted; half an acre reclaimed since 1830.

Farmer no.11, Robert Bell Senior, farmer; 26 and a quarter acres, 12 and three-quarters tillage, 10 pasture, 2 meadow, 1 and a half waste: 2 and a half wheat, 6 oats, 3 potatoes, a quarter acre flax, 1 clover; rotation: 1 oats, 2 potatoes, 3 wheat, oats or flax with clover sown, 4 oats with clover cut twice and hay sown for grazing, 5 grass, 6 grass; acres under orchard: a quarter acre, 10 years planted; plantation: one-eighth of an acre, 4 years planted; 1 acre reclaimed since 1830; drainage: [diagram of drainage system, 30 5/90].

Farmer no.12, Samuel Smith, farmer, not working; 13 acres, 3 and a half tillage, 3 and a half pasture, 1 waste: 1 wheat, 5 oats, 2 potatoes, half an acre flax; rotation: 1 oats, 2 potatoes, 3 wheat, flax or oats, 4 oats with hay sown for grazing, 5 grass, 6 grass; acres under orchard: a quarter acre, 40 years planted; 2 acres reclaimed since 1830.

Farmer no.13, James Ekin, farmer; 15 acres, 10 tillage, 4 pasture, 1 waste: 1 and a half wheat, 5 and a half oats, 2 and a half potatoes, half an acre flax; rotation: 1 oats, 2 potatoes, 3 wheat, flax or oats, 4 oats with hay sown for grazing, 5 grass, 6 grass; 1 acre reclaimed since 1830.

Farmer no.14, Hugh Stuart, farmer; 29 and a half acres, 20 and three-quarters tillage, 8 and a half pasture, a quarter acre waste: 3 wheat, 11 oats, 5 potatoes, a quarter acre flax, three-quarters of an acre hay, three-quarters of an acre clover; rotation: 1 oats, 2 potatoes, 3 wheat or flax with hay sown and clover sown, 4 oats with hay cut and clover cut twice and hay sown for grazing, 5 grass, 6 grass; half an acre reclaimed since 1830; drainage: [diagram of drainage system, 33 5/60].

Farmer no.15, William McInty [figures 14/20 written beside name], publican, not working; 20 acres, 15 tillage, 3 pasture, 2 meadow: 2 wheat, 9 oats, 4 potatoes; rotation: 1 oats, 2 potatoes, 3 wheat or oats, 4 oats with hay sown for grazing, 5 grass, 6 grass; 1 acre reclaimed since 1830.

Farmer no.16, James Quinn, pensioner, not working; 3 acres, 2 tillage, 1 pasture: 1 and a quarter oats, three-quarters of an acre potatoes; rotation: 1 potatoes, 2 oats, 3 oats, 4 grass, 5 grass, 6 grass.

Farmer no.17, George Skiffington, farmer; 4 and three-quarter acres, 3 and three-quarters tillage, half an acre pasture, half an acre waste: half an acre wheat, 2 oats, 1 and a quarter potatoes; rotation: 1 potatoes, 2 wheat or oats, 3 oats with hay sown for grazing, 4 grass, 5 grass; 1 acre reclaimed since 1830.

Farmer no.18, Alexander [Mackreed?], farmer and grocer; 14 acres, 8 tillage, 5 and a half pasture, half an acre waste: 1 acre wheat, 5 oats, 2 potatoes; rotation: 1 oats, 2 potatoes, 3 oats or wheat, 4 oats with hay sown for grazing, 5 grass, 6 grass, 7 grass; acres under orchard: a quarter acre, 8 years planted.

Farmer no.19, Andrew Bridget, farmer; 8 and a quarter acres, 6 and a quarter tillage, three-quarters of an acre pasture, 1 and a quarter waste: 4 oats, 2 potatoes, a quarter acre flax; rotation: 1 potatoes, 2 oats or flax, 3 oats with hay sown for grazing, 4 grass, 5 grass.

Farmer no.20, David Murdock, farmer; 11 acres, 9 tillage, 1 pasture, 1 waste: half an acre wheat, 4 and a half oats, 2 and a half potatoes, 1 and a half clover; rotation: 1 oats, 2 potatoes, 3 oats or wheat with clover sown, 4 oats with hay sown for grazing and clover cut twice, 5 grass, 6 grass; half an acre reclaimed since 1830.

Farmer no.21, Robert Murdock, farmer; 10 acres, 8 tillage, 1 and three-quarters pasture, a quarter acre waste: 1 and a half wheat, 3 and a half oats, 2 potatoes, 1 clover; rotation: 1 oats, 2 potatoes, 3 wheat or oats with clover sown, 4 oats with hay sown for grazing and clover cut twice, 5 grass, 6 grass.

Farmer no.22, Andrew Bell, farmer and carpenter; 19 acres, 11 and a half tillage, 6 pasture, 1 meadow, half an acre waste: 1 acre wheat, 7 oats, 3 potatoes, half an acre clover; rotation: 1 oats, 2 potatoes, 3 oats or wheat with clover sown, 4 oats with hay sown for grazing and clover cut twice, 5 grass, 6 grass, 7 grass; 3 and a half acres reclaimed since 1830; drainage: [diagram of drainage system, 33 5/300].

Farmer no.23, Robert Bell Junior, farmer; 43 acres, 24 and three-quarters tillage, 13 and three-quarters pasture, 2 and a half meadow, 2 waste: 3 wheat, 15 oats, 5 and three-quarters potatoes, 1 flax; rotation: 1 oats, 2 potatoes, 3 flax, oats or wheat, 4 oats with hay sown for grazing, 5 oats with grass, 6 grass, 7 grass, 8 grass; 3 acres reclaimed since 1830; drainage: [diagram of drainage system, 30 9/500].

Farmer no.24, William Hunter, farmer, not working; 7 acres, 3 and three-quarters tillage, three-quarters pasture, 2 and a half waste: 2 and a half oats, 1 and a quarter potatoes; rotation: 1 potatoes, 2 oats, 3 oats with hay sown for grazing, 4 grass; 4 acres reclaimed since 1830.

[Totals]: undivided bog 102 acres, roads 1 and a half acres; statute acres 536.8 equals Cunningham 415 and three-quarters: 195 and five-eighths tillage, 86 and seven-eighths pasture, 12 meadow, 119 and three-quarters waste: 22 and three-quarters wheat, 109 and three-eighths oats, 51 and a half potatoes, 4 and three-quarters flax, a quarter acre turnips, 2 and a quarter hay, 4 and three-quarters clover.

[Insert note at top of page: OM 539 and a half statute acres].

Field observer's signature: Archibald Thompson, date 2nd to 4th June 1840.

Drumconway: Farmers' Stock and Implements

[Prices added to printed form no.2, with additions from foot of columns: Horses for agriculture 7 pounds to 14 pounds, [insert addition: 6 pounds], cattle 6 pounds to 8 pounds [insert addition: 7s 6d to 2 pounds], sheep 1 pound to 1 pound 10s [insert addition: 5s], goats 12s to 1 pound 15s, hogs 2

Parish of Tamlaght

pounds to 4 pounds, geese 2s, ducks 8d, turkeys 2s 6d, hens 6d, iron ploughs 4 pounds 4s, wooden ploughs 1 pound 10s, breaks 18s, rollers 1 pound, carts 5 pounds 10s to 6 pounds 10s, wheel cars 3 pounds, corn fans 2 pounds 15s, spinning wheels 9s, linen looms employed 2 pounds 10s, unemployed 1 pound 15s, box barrows 10s, turf barrows 4s, agricultural spades 2s 4d, turf spades 2s 9d, agricultural shovels 1s 8d, scythe hooks 9d, teethed hooks 5d].

Farmer no.1, 1/0 agricultural horses, 1/0 cattle, 0/1 hogs, 4/8 ducks, 4/9 hens, 1 wooden plough, 1 break, 1 cart, 1 spinning wheel, 1 employed linen loom, 1 box barrow, 2/1 agricultural spades, 1 agricultural shovel, 2 scythe hooks, 1 teethed hook.

Farmer no.2, 1/0 cattle, 0/1 hogs, 3/5 ducks, 4/8 hens, 1 spinning wheel, 1/0 agricultural spades, 1 agricultural shovel, 1 scythe hook, 1 teethed hook.

Farmer no.3, 1/0 cattle, 0/2 hogs, 4/5 ducks, 3/5 hens, 3 spinning wheels, 1 turf barrow, 1/1 agricultural spades, 1 agricultural shovel, 1 scythe hook, 1 teethed hook.

Farmer no.4, 2/1 agricultural horses, 3/2 cattle, 2/3 hogs, 6/12 geese, 6/12 ducks, 4/9 turkeys, 6/8 hens, 1 iron plough, 1 break, 1 roller, 1 cart, 1 wheel car, 1 spinning wheel, 2 turf barrows, 2/1 agricultural spades, 2 agricultural shovels, 2 scythe hooks, 1 teethed hook; irrigation: yes.

Farmer no.5, 1/0 agricultural horses, 4/1 cattle, 1/2 hogs, 2/10 geese, 3/9 ducks, 6/12 hens, 1 wooden plough, 1 break, 1 cart, 3 spinning wheels, 1 box barrow, 1 turf barrow, 1/1 agricultural spades, 1 agricultural shovel, 1 scythe hook, 2 teethed hooks.

Farmer no.6, 1/0 agricultural horses, 3/2 cattle, 0/2 hogs, 3/9 geese, 5/9 ducks, 3/6 turkeys, 4/0 hens, 1 wooden plough, 1 break, 1 cart, 1 spinning wheel, 1 box barrow, 1 turf barrow, 2/1 agricultural spades, 1 agricultural shovel, 2 scythe hooks, 1 teethed hook.

Farmer no.7, 2/1 cattle, 0/1 hogs, 4/8 ducks, 5/0 hens, 1 break, 2 spinning wheels, 1 unemployed linen loom, 1/0 agricultural spades, 1 agricultural shovel, 1 scythe hook, 1 teethed hook.

Farmer no.8, 2/1 agricultural horses, 4/2 cattle, 2/2 hogs, 6/15 geese, 6/10 ducks, 4/10 turkeys, 3/9 hens, 1 iron plough, 1 break, 1 roller, 2 carts, 2 spinning wheels, 1 box barrow, 1 turf barrow, 2/1 agricultural spades, 2 agricultural shovels, 2 scythe hooks, 1 teethed hook.

Farmer no.9, 1/0 cattle, 0/1 hogs, 5/0 hens, 1 corn fan, 3 spinning wheels, 1 employed linen loom, 1 turf barrow, 2/1 agricultural spades, 1 agricultural shovel, 2 scythe hooks, 1 teethed hook.

Farmer no.10, 1/0 cattle, 3/6 ducks, 6/10 hens, 2 spinning wheels, 2 employed linen looms, 1 box barrow, 2 turf barrows, 2/1 agricultural spades, 1 agricultural shovel, 2 scythe hooks, 2 teethed hooks.

Farmer no.11, 2/0 agricultural horses, 4/2 cattle, 1/2 sheep, 1/3 hogs, 4/12 geese, 7/10 ducks, 4/9 turkeys, 7/0 hens, 1 wooden plough, 1 break, 1 cart, 2 spinning wheels, 1 box barrow, 2 turf barrows, 3/1 agricultural spades, 2 agricultural shovels, 4 scythe hooks, 1 teethed hook.

Farmer no.12, 1/0 agricultural horses, 2/2 cattle, 0/1 hogs, 2/8 geese, 6/8 ducks, 5/11 hens, 1 wooden plough, 1 break, 1 cart, 3 spinning wheels, 1 box barrow, 2 turf barrows, 2/2 agricultural spades, 2 agricultural shovels, 2 scythe hooks, 2 teethed hooks.

Farmer no.13, 2/0 agricultural horses, 3/1 cattle, 2/4 hogs, 4/12 geese, 6/12 ducks, 5/9 turkeys, 9/0 hens, 1 iron plough, 1 break, 1 roller, 2 carts, 1 corn fan, 1 spinning wheel, 1 box barrow, 2 turf barrows, 2/1 agricultural spades, 2 agricultural shovels, 3 scythe hooks, 1 teethed hook.

Farmer no.14, 2/0 agricultural horses, 4/4 cattle, 0/3 hogs, 3/14 geese, 6/10 ducks, 4/11 turkeys, 8/15 hens, 1 iron plough, 1 break, 2 carts, 1 corn fan, 2 spinning wheels, 1 box barrow, 2 turf barrows, 2/2 agricultural spades, 2 agricultural shovels, 2 scythe hooks, 2 teethed hooks.

Farmer no.15, lives in Coagh.

Farmer no.16, 1/0 cattle, 2/3 ducks, 6/0 hens, 1/0 agricultural spades, 1 agricultural shovel, 1 scythe hook.

Farmer no.17, 1/0 cattle, 0/1 hogs, 3/9 ducks, 4/8 hens, 1 spinning wheel, 1 unemployed linen loom, 1 turf barrow, 1/1 agricultural spades, 1 agricultural shovel, 1 scythe hook.

Farmer no.18, 1/0 agricultural horses, 3/2 cattle, 0/2 hogs, 8/0 ducks, 5/12 hens, 1 wooden plough, 1 break, 1 cart, 1 spinning wheel, 1 box barrow, 1 turf barrow, 2/1 agricultural spades, 2 agricultural shovels, 2 scythe hooks, 2 teethed hooks.

Farmer no.19, 1/0 agricultural horses, 2/0 cattle, 0/2 hogs, 6/8 geese, 6/7 ducks, 4/6 hens, 1 wooden plough, 1 roller, 1 cart, 1 spinning wheel, 1 unemployed linen loom, 1 box barrow, 1 turf barrow, 2/1 agricultural spades, 2 agricultural shovels, 2 scythe hooks, 1 teethed hook.

Farmer no.20, 1/0 agricultural horses, 2/2 cattle, 1/2 hogs, 8/10 ducks, 7/11 hens, 1 wooden plough, 1 break, 1 cart, 1 spinning wheel, 2/0 agricultural spades, 2 agricultural shovels, 2 scythe hooks.

Farmer no.21, 1/0 agricultural horses, 2/0 cattle, 1/8 hogs, 7/0 ducks, 6/0 hens, 1 wooden plough, 1 break, 1 wheel car, 1 spinning wheel, 1 employed linen loom, 1 unemployed linen loom, 1 box barrow, 1 turf barrow, 2/1 agricultural spades, 1 agricultural shovel, 2 scythe hooks.

Farmer no.22, 2/0 agricultural horses, 4/3 cattle, 2/4 hogs, 8/14 geese, 9/0 ducks, 8/12 hens, 1 wooden plough, 1 break, 2 carts, 1 corn fan, 1 spinning wheel, 1 box barrow, 2 turf barrows, 4/2 agricultural spades, 2 agricultural shovels, 3 scythe hooks, 2 teethed hooks.

Farmer no.23, 2/0 agricultural horses, 5/4 cattle, 3/4 sheep, 2/8 hogs, 9/15 geese, 10/0 ducks, 4/12 turkeys, 8/20 hens, 1 iron plough, 1 wooden plough, 2 breaks, 1 roller, 2 carts, 1 corn fan, 1 spinning wheel, 1 box barrow, 2 turf barrows, 4/2 agricultural spades, 3 agricultural shovels, 4 scythe hooks, 3 teethed hooks.

Farmer no.24, 1/0 agricultural horses, 1/0 cattle, 4/12 hogs, 10/0 geese, 8/0 turkeys, 6/10 hens, 1 wooden plough, 1 break, 1 cart, 2 spinning wheels, 1 employed linen loom, 1 box barrow, 1 turf barrow, 2/1 agricultural spades, 2 agricultural shovels, 2 scythe hooks, 3 teethed hooks.

Field observer's signature: Archibald Thompson, date 2nd to 4th June 1840.

Drumconway: Cottiers' Stock and Implements

[Form 3]

Cottier no.1, farmer no.4, Robert Henderson, weaver; 3/5 ducks, 4/0 hens, 1 spinning wheel, 1 employed linen loom, 1/0 agricultural spades, 1 agricultural shovel, 2 pounds 5s yearly rent.

Cottier no.2, farmer no.14, John Donnelly, labourer; 4/0 ducks, 3/9 hens, 2 spinning wheels, 1/0 agricultural spades, 1 agricultural shovel, 2 pounds 5s yearly rent.

Cottier no.3, Terence Quin, weaver; 3/0 ducks, 5/0 hens, 1 spinning wheel, 1 employed linen loom, 1/0 agricultural spades, 1 agricultural shovel, 1 scythe hook, 2 pounds yearly rent.

Cottier no.4, farmer no.15, James Reid, not able to work; 4/12 hens, 2 spinning wheels, 1/0 agricultural spades, 1 agricultural shovel, 2 pounds 10s yearly rent.

Cottier no.5, Peter McIntyre, labourer; 2 hens, 2 spinning wheels, 1/0 agricultural spades, 1 agricultural shovel, 1 scythe hook, 2 pounds yearly rent.

Cottier no.6, farmer no.23, William Bridget, weaver; 3/0 ducks, 4/10 hens, 1 spinning wheel, 1 employed linen loom, 1/0 agricultural spades, 1 agricultural shovel, 1 scythe hook, 2 pounds 10s yearly rent.

Cottier no.7, Sarah Ann Ferguson, spinner; 4/0 ducks, 5/0 hens, 2 spinning wheels, 1/0 agricultural spades, 1 agricultural shovel, 2 pounds yearly rent.

Cottier no.8, John MacBreen, labourer; 3/10 hens, 1 spinning wheel, 1 agricultural spade, 1 agricultural shovel, 1 scythe hook, 2 pounds 10s yearly rent.

Field observer's signature: Archibald Thompson, date 2nd to 4th June 1840.

Drumconway: Labour and Proprietors

[Form 4. Head landlord William Lenox Conyngham, immediate landlord William Lenox Conyngham in each case].

Farmer no.1, family: 2/1w males, 0/2 females; occasional labour: 1 female for 8 days in spring, 2 females for 8 days in autumn; males constantly employed, no female labour; tenure at will, 1 pound 2s yearly rent per acre; 1 spring well.

Farmer no.2, family: 1/0 males, 0/1 females; occasional labour: 1 female for 4 days in spring, for 8 days in autumn; family labour: 1 male for 24 days in spring, for 15 days in summer, for 18 days in autumn; male rest of time working for others, no female labour; tenure at will, 1 pound 2s yearly rent per acre.

Farmer no.3, family: 1/1 males, 1s/4 females; family labour: 1 male for 20 days in spring, for 15 days in summer, for 18 days in autumn; 1 female for 6 days in spring, for 6 days in summer, for 9 days in autumn; male rest of time working for others, females spins; tenure at will, 1 pound 2s yearly rent per acre.

Farmer no.4, family: 1/0 males, 0/2 females, 1 male house servant; occasional labour: 2 males for 14 days in spring, 3 males for 15 days in autumn; 2 females for 12 days in spring, for 12 days in summer, 3 females for 15 days in autumn; male constantly employed, no female labour; tenure at will, 1 pound 4s yearly rent per acre.

Farmer no.5, family: 1/0 males, 2s/2 females; family labour: 1 male for 12 days in spring, for 8 days in summer, for 12 days in autumn; 2 females for 4 days in spring, for 6 days in summer, for 15 days in autumn; male rest of time working on farm in parish of Coagh, female spins, washes etc.; tenure at will, 1 pound 4s yearly rent per acre; 1 water pump, [value] 3 pounds.

Farmer no.6, family: 1/1 males, 0/2 females, 1 male house servant, 1 female house servant; occasional labour: 2 males for 12 days in spring, for 14 days in autumn; 2 females for 12 days in autumn; male constantly employed, no female labour;

Parish of Tamlaght 119

tenure 21 years and 1 life, 1 pound 4s yearly rent per acre.

Farmer no.7, family: 1/0 males, 1s/2 females; family labour: 1 male for 40 days in spring, for 18 days in summer, for 30 days in autumn; 1 female for 12 days in spring, for 12 days in summer, for 18 days in autumn; male working occasionally in townland of Coagh, female spins; tenure 21 years and 1 life, 1 pound 1s yearly rent per acre.

Farmer no.8, family: 1/1 males, 0/3 females, 1 male house servant, 1 female house servant; occasional labour: 4 males for 16 days in spring, 2 males for 16 days in summer, 4 males for 20 days in autumn; 2 females for 15 days in spring, for 15 days in summer, 3 females for 20 days in autumn; male constantly employed, no female labour; tenure 31 years and 2 lives, 1 pound 2s yearly rent per acre.

Farmer no.9, family: 1,1w/0 males, 1s/5 females; family labour: 1w/1 males for 18/12 days in spring, 1/1 males for 12/12 days in spring, 1 in summer, 1/1 males for 18/12 days in autumn; 1 female for 12 days in spring, for 12 days in summer, for 15 days in autumn; 1 male weaves occasionally; 1 male and old man occasionally idle; female cooks; tenure at will, 1 pound 7s yearly rent per acre.

Farmer no.10, family: 1w,1/1w,1 males, 2/2 females; family labour: 1w/1 males for 10/20 days in spring, 1/1 males for 10/20 days in summer, for 12/20 days in autumn; 2 females for 8 days in spring, for 9 days in summer, for 10 days in autumn; 1 male weaves, 1 rest of time making turf, ditching, females attend weavers etc.; tenure 21 years and 2 lives, 10s 6d yearly rent per acre; 1 spring well.

Farmer no.11, family: 3/1 males, 2s/1 females; occasional labour: 2 males for 10 days in autumn; family labour: 2 females for 20 days in spring, for 18 days in summer, for 20 days in autumn; males constantly employed, females spin, work; tenure 31 years and 3 lives, 10s 6d yearly rent per acre.

Farmer no.12, family: 2/1 males, 2s/1 females; occasional labour: 2 males for 12 days in autumn; family labour: 2 females for 15 days in spring, for 12 days in summer, for 15 days in autumn; males constantly employed, females spin, work; tenure at will, 1 pound 1s yearly rent per acre; 1 spring well, [?] 4 water pumps.

Farmer no.13, family: 1/1 males, 0/1 females, 1 male house servant, 1 female house servant; occasional labour: 2 males for 10 days in spring, 3 males for 12 days in autumn; 1 female for 12 days in spring, 2 females for 10 days in summer, 3 females for 15 days in autumn; male constantly employed, no female labour; tenure 21 years and 1 life, 1 pound yearly rent per acre; 1 water pump, [value] 2 pounds 10s.

Farmer no.14, family: 1/0 males, 0/2 females, 1 male house servant, 2 female house servants; occasional labour: 4 males for 20 days in spring, 3 males for 15 days in summer, 4 males for 35 days in autumn; 2 females for 20 days in spring, 3 females for 20 days in summer, 4 females for 20 days in autumn; male constantly employed, no female labour; tenure 21 years and 1 life, 1 pound 2s yearly rent per acre; 1 spring well.

Farmer no.15: lives in Coagh; occasional labour: 3 males for 30 days in spring, 2 males for 20 days in summer, 4 males for 30 days in autumn; 2 females for 20 days in spring, for 20 days in summer, 4 females for 30 days in autumn; tenure 21 years and 1 life, 1 pound 2s yearly rent per acre.

Farmer no.16, family: 0/1 males, 0/1 females; occasional labour: 2 males for 9 days in spring, 1 male for 9 days in summer, 2 males for 9 days in autumn; 1 female for 6 days in spring, for 8 days in summer, 2 females for 9 days in autumn; tenure at will, subtenant, 2 pounds 2s yearly rent per acre.

Farmer no.17, family: 1/3 males, 0/2 females; occasional labour: 1 male for 8 days in spring, for 12 days in autumn; 1 female for 8 days in spring, 2 females for 12 days in autumn; male constantly employed, no female labour; tenure at will, subtenant, 1 pound 5s yearly rent per acre; 1 spring well.

Farmer no.18, family: 2/0 males, 0/4 females; occasional labour: 2 males for 12 days in autumn; 1 female for 12 days in spring, 2 females for 15 days in autumn; males constantly employed, no female labour; tenure at will, 1 pound 2s yearly rent per acre; 1 spring well.

Farmer no.19, family: 1/0 males, 1s/3 females, 1 male house servant; family labour: 1 female for 18 days in spring, for 12 days in summer, for 18 days in autumn; males constantly employed, female cooks, spins; tenure at will, 1 pound 4s yearly rent per acre.

Farmer no.20, family: 1/1 males, 0/2 females, 1 male house servant; occasional labour: 2 males for 18 days in spring, 3 males for 18 days in autumn; 1 female for 15 days in spring, 3 females for 15 days in summer, for 15 days in autumn; male constantly employed, no female labour; tenure 21 years and 1 life, 1 pound 5s yearly rent per acre.

Farmer no.21, family: 2/1,1w males, 0/2 females; occasional labour: 2 females for 10 days in spring, 3 females for 12 days in autumn; family labour: males constantly employed, no female labour; tenure 21 years and 1 life, 1 pound 5s yearly rent per acre.

Farmer no.22, family: 1t,3/2 males, 0/2 females; occasional labour: 2 males for 12 days in autumn; 2 females for 10 days in spring, 3 females for 12 days in autumn; family labour: 1t male for 18 days in spring, 1 male for 18 days in summer, for 30 days in autumn; 1 male occasionally working as carpenter, 3 males constantly employed, no female labour; tenure 21 years and 1 life, 1 pound 3s 11d yearly rent per acre; 1 spring well.

Farmer no.23, family: 3/2 males, 0/2 females, 2 male house servants, 1 female house servant; occasional labour: 3 males for 20 days in spring, for 30 days in autumn; 3 females for 20 days in spring, for 20 days in summer, 4 females for 25 days in autumn; males constantly employed, no female labour; tenure 21 years and 1 life, 1 pound 4s yearly rent per acre; 2 spring wells.

Farmer no.24, family: 1,1w/1 males, 2/2 females; family labour: 1w/1 males for 12/20 days in spring, 1/1 males for 12/18 days in summer, for 12/18 days in autumn; 2 females for 10 days in spring, for 10 days in summer, for 12 days in autumn; 1 male most of time weaving and working in Urbal, 1 male rest of time working in Urbal making turf, females work in Urbal, spin, attend weavers etc.; tenure at will, 10s yearly rent per acre.

Farm no.25, not let.

Farm no.26, not let.

Field observer's signature: Archibald Thompson, date 2nd to 4th June 1840.

Drumconway: Manures

Estimate of a lime-kiln containing 40 barrels of 4 bushels per barrel, each weighing 228 lbs: 10 tons of raw stones at 6d per ton, 5s; 3 days of 1 horse drawing stones at 2s 6d per day, 7s 6d; 1 man 3 days filling kiln and breaking stones at 10d per day, 2s 6d; 40 gauges <guages> of turf at 2d ha'penny per gauge, 8s 4d; 1 man 2 days burning kiln at 1s per day, 2s; emptying kiln, 1 man for 1 day at 10d per day, 10d; [total] 1 pound 6s 2d.

NB The raw stones are gotten in the townland of Ballydawley, parish of Artrea. [Insert footnote: gauge of turf is a cubic yard of turf].

[Form 5] Farmer no.4, dung: 28/14 tons per acre, 1s 10d per ton, 6 cwt per load, 4/2 days employed; lime: cost per barrel see [above], 912 lbs per load; clay: 6 cwt per load, 5 days employed; compost loads: 6 lime, 150 clay; 6 cwt load of compost from the heap to the field, 3 days employed, made in the field.

Farmer no.8, dung: 30/10 tons per acre, 1s 10d per ton, 6 cwt per load, 4/1 and one-third days employed; bog: 6 cwt per load, 4 days employed; lime: 11d per barrel, 912 lbs per load, carried 1 Irish mile, 1 day employed; clay: 6 cwt per load, 3 days employed; compost loads: 100 bog, 6 lime, 105 clay; 6 cwt load of compost from heap to field, 5 days employed, made in the field.

Farmer no.14, dung: 28/9 tons per acre, 1s 10d per ton, 6 cwt per load, 4/1 and one-third days employed; bog: 6 cwt per load, 4 days employed; lime: see [above], 912 lbs per load; clay: 6 cwt, 3 days employed; compost loads: 100 bog, 6 lime, 90 clay; 6 cwt load of compost from heap to the field, 5 days employed, made in the field.

Farmer no.22, dung: 28/14 tons per acre, 1s 10d per ton, 6 cwt per load, 4/2 days employed; bog: 6 cwt per load, 4 days employed; lime: see [above], 912 lbs per load; clay: 6 cwt per load, 2 days employed; compost loads: 120 bog, 6 lime, 60 clay; 6 cwt load of compost from heap to the field, 6 days employed, made at the house.

No.11, dung used alone and in top dressing, compost of sand and clay; lime and clay used in compost only.

No.8, dung used alone and in top dressing, compost: bog, lime and clay used in compost only.

No.14, dung used alone and in top dressing, compost: bog, lime and clay used in compost only.

No.22, dung used alone and in top dressing, compost: bog, lime and clay used in compost only.

Description of acres referred to: Cunningham.

Lime: number of bushels per barrel 4, weight per barrel 228 lbs.

Dung townland, bog townland, lime Ruskey Lower, limestone Ballydawley, parish Artrea, clay townland.

Drumconway: Seed and Produce

[Form 6]

Farmer no.4, wheat: 13 stones seed, 144 produce; oats: 18 stones seed, 140 produce; potatoes: 24 bushels seed, 250 produce; flax: 5 bushels seed, 6 cwt produce; clay and loam, well laboured.

Farmer no.8, wheat: 14 stones seed, 144 produce; oats: 18 stones seed, 130 produce; potatoes: 25 bushels seed, 260 produce; flax: 3 bushels seed, 6 and one-third cwt produce; turnips: 3 lbs seed, 20 tons produce; 3 bushels hay seed, 8 lbs clover seed, 2 and a quarter tons produce; clay, loam and bog, well laboured.

Parish of Tamlaght

Farmer no.14, wheat: 13 stones seed, 160 produce; oats: 18 stones seed, 140 produce; potatoes: 25 bushels seed, 300 produce; flax: 3 bushels seed, 6 cwt produce; 3 bushels hay seed, 8 lbs clover seed, 2 tons produce; clover: 1 bushel hay seed, 16 lbs clover seed, 13 tons produce; clay, loam and bog, well laboured.

Farmer no.22, wheat: 14 stones seed, 120 produce; oats: 18 stones seed, 130 produce; potatoes: 24 bushels seed, 260 produce; clover: 1 bushel hay seed, 16 lbs clover seed, 12 tons produce; clay, loam and bog, well laboured.

Kind of acre: Cunningham.

Value of seed and measure, wheat: 1s 5d per stone, value of produce 1s 2d per stone; time of sowing 1st November to 1st December, time of harvest 1st September to 25th September.

Oats: value of seed 1s 1d per stone, value of produce 11d ha'penny per stone; time of sowing 1st March to 29th April, time of harvest 1st September to 8th October.

Potatoes: value of seed 3d ha'penny per bushel, value of produce 3d ha'penny per bushel; time of sowing 25th April to 31st May, time of harvest 20th October to 20th November.

Flax: value of seed 13s per bushel, value of produce 48s per cwt; time of sowing 25th April to 8th May, time of harvest 1st August to 15th August.

Turnips: value of seed 1s 8d per lb, value of produce 10d per cwt; time of sowing 25th May to 12th June, time of harvest 1st November to 1st December.

Hay: value of seed 2s 6d per bushel, value of produce 2s 8d per cwt; time of sowing 10th March to 8th May, time of harvest 24th June to 1st July.

Clover: value of seed 10d per lb, value of produce 5d per cwt; time of sowing 10th March to 8th May, time of harvest 1st June to 1st October.

Field observer's signature: Archibald Thompson, date 2nd to 4th June 1840.

Drumconway: Table of Trades

[Form 7]

James Ford, weaver, journeyman.
Hugh Wates, weaver, master.
Thomas Bell, weaver, master.
Robert Bell, weaver, journeyman.
Patrick Devlin, weaver, journeyman.
William Hunter Junior, weaver, journeyman.
Andrew Bell, carpenter, master, wages 2s 6d per day.
Alexander Mackreed [Mackree ?], grocer, master.
Robert Henderson, weaver, master.
William Bridget, weaver, master.

Field observer's signature: Archibald Thompson, date 2nd to 4th June 1840.

Drumconway: Condition of Cottiers

[Form 8. All houses have 2 apartments, none are whitewashed, all stone and lime, with straw roofs and clay floors, and all have one-eighth of a acre garden. *All have the same furniture, which is recorded by abbreviations without a key: d = dresser, t = table, c = chair, s = settle bed, [?] earth = [earthenware ?]*.

No.1, brick and lime chimney, 4 glazed windows, good beds, good clothes.
No.2, brick and lime chimney, 3 glazed windows, good beds, good clothes.
No.3, brick and lime chimney, 4 glazed windows, good beds, good clothes.
No.4, brick and lime chimney, 4 glazed windows, bad beds, bad clothes.
No.5, clay chimney, 3 glazed windows, bad beds, bad clothes.
No.6, brick and lime chimney, 4 glazed windows, good beds, good clothes.
No.7, brick and lime chimney, 4 glazed windows, good beds, good clothes.
No.8, brick and lime chimney, 4 glazed windows, good beds, good clothes.

Field observer's signature: Archibald Thompson, date 2nd to 4th June 1840.

Drumconway: Summary of Economy

[Form 9]

Surface: smooth, rising into a small hill, ridge-like, nearly running north and south.

Soils, kind: clay, loam and bog; depth: from 4 to 14 inches.

Subsoil, kind: clay and sandy gravel; depth: unknown.

Exposure: west, east and south.

Springs: 9 spring wells.

Drainage: 1,850 perches of covered drains.

Irrigation: not practised.

Implements: iron and wooden ploughs, wooden harrows, scythed hooks, teethed hooks, spades 16 by 6 inches, shovels hosed.

Acres reclaimed since 1830: 197 and a half acres.

Mills, corn: none; flax: none; fulling: none.

Quarries, kind of: 1 common whinstone quarry worked by 2 men for 10 weeks or 60 days, at 10d each per day. Stones used for making and mending roads and building.

Communications: the leading road from Coagh

to the port called the Battery at Coagh or to Portadown <Portydown> by Maghery ferry, in good order. By-roads in good order.

Markets: Cookstown, Stewartstown, Magherafelt, Coagh and Moneymore.

Breed of horses: Irish; breed of cattle: Irish and English; breed of sheep: Irish; breed of hogs: Irish and Dutch.

Woods or plantations: quarter of an acre plantation [written above: 9 [years ?], 1 and a half acres orchard. Kind: fir and apple trees. When first planted: 1800, 1826, 1830, 1832 and 1836. Present return: none cut or sold, fruit used by farmers, none sold.

Lime-kilns: none trading.

Manufactures: none.

Kind of crops cultivated, oats: Poland, Angus, potato and Blantyre; wheat: red; potatoes: cups, farmers, Downs, Cork reds and lumpers; flax: Riga, Dutch and New York; hay: perennial; clover: red and white; turnips: white globe and yellow Aberdeen.

Field observer's signature: Archibald Thompson, residence William Vance's, Coagh, date 2nd to 4th June 1840.

[Insert addition: Farmer's names and acreages, where got: from farmers individually. Natural meadow: quantity per acre 2 and a half tons; time of harvest August 12th to September 1st; price per ton 2 pounds 7s 6d. Kind of acre: Cunningham. Fences, kind of: soil and thorn, good. Turf, where got: townland. Rent per acre, rough or waste land: from 10s to 42s per acre; arable land [blank] on an average. Rough or waste land, kind of: bog, commons and shrubby pasture].

Statistical Information for Mullaghtironey, May and June 1840

Mullaghtironey: Farmers, Acreages and Crops

[Form 1. Informant the farmer unless indicated].

Farmer no.1, Eccles Hamilton, farmer; 8 and a quarter acres, 4 and three-quarters tillage, 2 and three-eighths pasture, 1 waste, bank: 3 and a half oats, 1 potatoes, a quarter acre flax; rotation: 1 potatoes, 2 oats or flax, 3 oats, 4 grass, 5 grass, 6 grass.

Farmer no.2, Thomas Ferguson, farmer; 2 acres, 1 and seven-eighths tillage: 1 oats, half an acre flax, three-eighth acres clover; rotation: 1 oats, 2 potatoes, 3 oats or flax with clover sown, 4 clover cut, 5 grass.

Farmer no.3, John Ferguson, farmer; 10 acres, 5 and three-eighths tillage, 3 pasture, half an acre meadow, half an acre waste, bank: three-quarter acres wheat, three and a half oats, 1 potatoes, half an acre flax, one-eighth acre vetches; rotation: 1 oats, 2 potatoes, 3 wheat, oats or flax, 4 oats with clover sown for grazing, 5 grass, 6 grass, 7 grass.

Farmer no.4, Andrew Ferguson, farmer; not working, 10 and a quarter acres, 3 and five-eighths tillage, 5 pasture, 1 meadow, half an acre waste, bank: 2 oats, 1 and a half potatoes, one-eighth acre flax; rotation: 1 potatoes, 2 oats or flax, 3 oats, 4 grass, 5 grass.

Farmer no.5, vacant, 40 acres, 20 and three-eighths tillage, 15 and a half pasture, 2 meadow, 1 waste, scrog: 2 wheat, half an acre barley, 13 oats, 3 and a half potatoes, 1 flax, one-eighth acre vetches, a quarter acre clover; rotation: 1 oats, 2 potatoes, 3 wheat or barley with flax, 4 oats or vetches with clover sown, 5 grass with clover cut, 6 grass; drainage: [diagram of drainage system, 40 by 24, 10 13/400].

Farmer no.6, Alexander Campbell, farmer; 10 acres, 8 and five-eighths tillage, three-quarter acres pasture, half an acre meadow: 6 oats, 2 potatoes, half an acre flax, one-eighth acre vetches; rotation: 1 oats, 2 potatoes, 3 oats or flax, 4 oats or vetches, 5 grass, 6 grass; acres under orchard: a quarter acre, 12 years planted.

Farmer no.7, Robert Campbell, farmer; 10 acres, 5 and seven-eighths tillage, 4 pasture: 3 and five-eighths oats, 1 potatoes, 1 and a quarter flax; rotation: 1 oats, 2 potatoes, 3 oats or potatoes, 4 oats with clover sown for grazing, 5 grass, 6 grass.

Farmer no.8, Mathew George, farmer; 16 acres, 11 and three eighths tillage, 2 and three-quarters pasture, 1 and a half meadow: 7 oats, 2 and a half potatoes, a quarter acre flax, one-sixteenth acre vetches, one-sixteenth acre turnips, 1 and a half clover; rotation: 1 potatoes or turnips, 2 oats, flax or vetches, 3 oats with clover sown, 4 clover cut, 5 grass.

Farmer no.9, Thomas Wilson, farmer; 7 and a half acres, 5 tillage, 2 and a quarter pasture: 3 oats, 1 and a half potatoes, half an acre flax; rotation: 1 potatoes, 2 oats or flax, 3 oats, 4 grass, 5 grass.

Farmer no.10, James Mayknow, farmer; 5 acres, 2 and three-quarters tillage, 2 and one-eighth pasture: 1 and a half oats, 1 potatoes, one-eighth acre flax, one-eighth acre clover; rotation: 1 potatoes, 2 oats or flax, 3 oats with clover sown, 4 clover cut, 5 grass, 6 grass.

Farmer no.11, John Shaw, 12 acres, 6 and a half tillage, 3 and a quarter pasture, 2 meadow: 4 oats, 2 potatoes, a quarter acre flax, a quarter acre clover; rotation: 1 potatoes, 2 oats or flax, 3 oats with clover sown, 4 clover cut, 5 grass.

Statistical table for Mullaghtironey

Farmer no. 12, William [Junk or Tunk ?], farmer; 25 acres, 13 and five-eighths tillage, 9 pasture, 1 meadow, 1 and one-eighth waste, scrog: 10 oats, 3 potatoes, five-eighth acres flax; rotation: 1 potatoes, 2 oats or flax with clover sown for cutting next year, 3 oats, 4 grass, 5 grass, 6 grass; acres under orchard: three-quarter acres, 15 years planted.

Farmer no. 13, Kenedy McCullagh, farmer; 12 acres, 5 and a quarter tillage, 5 and a half pasture, 1 meadow: three-quarter acres wheat, 2 oats, 2 potatoes, a quarter acre flax, a quarter acre clover; rotation: 1 potatoes, 2 wheat, oats or flax, 3 oats with clover sown, 4 grass, 5 grass; acres under orchard: one-eighth acre, 10 years planted.

Farmer no. 14, Henry Kane, farmer; 4 and a half acres, 2 and seven-eighths tillage, 1 and a half pasture: half an acre wheat, 1 oats, 1 potatoes, a quarter acre flax, one-eighth acre clover; rotation: 1 potatoes, 2 wheat, oats or flax, 3 oats with clover sown, 5 grass, 6 grass.

Farmer no. 15, Thomas Duff, farmer; 12 acres, 9 and a half tillage, 1 pasture, 1 and a half meadow: 4 oats, 1 and a half potatoes, 2 flax, 2 clover; rotation: 1 oats, 2 potatoes, 3 oats or flax with clover sown, 4 clover cut, 5 grass, 6 grass; acres under orchard: [?] one-eighth acre, 16 years planted.

Farmer no. 16, Widow Gilmore, farmer; 4 acres, 1 tillage, 2 pasture, 1 meadow: 1 potatoes; rotation: 1 oats, 2 potatoes, 3 wheat, 4 oats with clover sown, 5 clover cut, 6 grass, 7 grass.

Farmer no. 17, William Lenox Conyngham Esq., gentleman; 2 acres, plantation; acres under orchard: 2 acres, 16 years planted.

[Totals]: 245.745 [rounded to] 246 statute acres; size of farms 190 and a half Cunningham acres, 108 and seven-eighth acres tillage, 60 pasture, 12 meadow, 4 and one-eighth waste: 4 wheat, half an acre barley, 65 and one-eighth oats, 25 and a half potatoes, 8 and three-eighths flax, seven-sixteenth acres vetches, one-sixteenth acre turnips, 4 and seven-eighths clover.

No. 6 stubbled a quarter acre of orchard.

The waste ground marked "bank" in the column is a sloping bank on the boundary of the townland which cannot be cultivated, it being so steep. It answers for perpetual pasture.

The farm of no. 5 is at present vacant by the death of its late occupier. The crop was auctioned a few days previous to my visiting it. I got the information from his executors and the servant man who had attended to the cultivation of the farm during the season.

I consider that the road which runs through the townland and part of the river which bounds it on the north west side will fully account for the deficiency in the acreage, [initialled] JH.

Field observer's signature: John Hanna, date 26th to 28th May 1840.

Mullaghtironey: Farmers' Stock and Implements

[Prices added to printed form no.2: Agricultural horses 7 pounds to 10 pounds; cattle, old, 4 pounds to 6 pounds, young, 10s to 2 pounds; sheep, old, 1 pound, young, 5s; goats 6d ha'penny; hogs 30s to 4 pounds; geese, old, 2s to 2s 2d; ducks, old, 7d to 9d; hens, old, 5d to 7d; wooden ploughs 1 pound to 35s, iron ploughs 2 pounds; breaks 10s to 14s; drill hoes 30s, carts 3 pounds 10s to 5 pounds; wheel cars 38s; corn fans 2 pounds; spinning wheels 7s 6d to 11s, employed linen looms 2 pounds, unemployed linen looms 2 pounds; box barrows 9s to 14s; turf barrows 2s 4d to 2s 6d; agricultural spades 2s to 2s 4d [insert addition: turf spades given as denominator to agricultural, prices 2s to 2s 4d]; agricultural shovels 1s 6d to 1s 8d; scythe hooks 6d to 10d; teethed hooks 5d to 8d].

Farmer no.1, 1/1 cattle, 1/0 goats, 4/0 hens, 2 spinning wheels, 2 box barrows, 1 turf barrow, 3/1 agricultural spades, 2 agricultural shovels, 3 scythe hooks, 0 teethed hooks.

Farmer no.2, lives in Urbal contiguous, 1/0 hogs.

Farmer no.3, 1/0 agricultural horses, cattle: lets his grass, 1 cart, 1/0 agricultural spades, 1 agricultural shovel, 1 teethed hook.

Farmer no.4, 1 agricultural horse, 3/0 cattle, 3/0 hens, 1 wooden plough, 1 break, 1 cart, 1 box barrow, 1 turf barrow, 1/0 agricultural spades, 1 agricultural shovel, 2 teethed hooks.

Farmer no.5, 2/1 agricultural horses, 3/0 cattle, 1/2 sheep, 4/15 geese, 9/0 ducks, 3/0 hens.

Farmer no.6, 1/0 agricultural horses, 1/0 goats, 1/7 geese, 1/0 hens, 1 wooden plough, 1 break, 1 cart, 3 spinning wheels, 1 employed linen loom, 1 unemployed linen loom, 1 box barrow, 2/0 agricultural spades, 1 agricultural shovel, 1 scythe hook, 3 teethed hooks.

Farmer no.7, lives in Aghaveagh <Aghavey>, cattle grazed on this farm occasionally.

Farmer no.8, 2/0 agricultural horses, 2/0 cattle, 2/0 hogs, 1/13 geese, 2/0 ducks, 6/0 hens, 1 wooden and improved plough, 1 break, 1 drill hoe, 1 cart, 1 spinning wheel, 1 box barrow, 2 turf barrows, 2/1 agricultural spades, 1 agricultural shovel, 1 scythe hook; irrigation by drains.

Farmer no.9, 1/0 agricultural horses, 1/0 cattle, 1/0 hogs, 4/0 ducks, 2/0 hens, 1 wooden plough, 1 break, 1 cart, 3 spinning wheels, 2/0 agricultural spades, 1 agricultural shovel, 3 teethed hooks.

Farmer no.10, 1/1 cattle, 2/0 hogs, 1/4 geese, 4/0 hens, 4 spinning wheels, 1 unemployed linen loom, 1 box barrow, 1 turf barrow, 2/0 agricultural spades, 1 agricultural shovel, 2 teethed hooks.

Farmer no.11, 1/0 agricultural horses, 2/1 cattle, 1/0 hogs, 4/6 ducks, 2/10 hens, 1 wooden plough, 1 break, 1 cart, 2 spinning wheels, 1 box barrow, 1 turf barrow, 2/1 agricultural spades, 1 agricultural shovel, 1 scythe hook, 2 teethed hooks.

Farmer no.12, 2/0 agricultural horses, 3/0 cattle, 2/0 hogs, 3/13 geese, 6/10 ducks, 4/6 hens, 1 wooden plough, 1 break, 1 cart, 1 wheel car, 1 corn fan, 2 spinning wheels, 1 unemployed linen loom, 1 box barrow, 2/0 agricultural spades, 1 agricultural shovel, 4 teethed hooks; inundated.

Farmer no.13, 1/0 agricultural horses, 2/0 cattle, 2/0 hogs, 5/0 geese, 3/0 ducks, 1 wooden plough, 1 break, 1 cart, 2 spinning wheels, 1 unemployed linen loom, 1 box barrow, 2/0 agricultural spades, 1 agricultural shovel, 3 teethed hooks; irrigation: no supply.

Farmer no.14, 1/0 cattle, 2/0 hogs, 2/6 hens, 1 employed linen loom, 1 box barrow, 2/0 agricultural spades, 1 agricultural shovel, 1 scythe hook, 1 teethed hook.

Farmer no.15, lives in Urbal, cattle grazed occasionally on this farm.

Farmer no.16, lives in Aghaveagh, cattle grazed occasionally on this farm.

Farmer no.17, [blank].

No.5, vacant farm: the cattle were on the ground when I visited this farm but were, in a few hours after, disposed of by auction together with all other stock, implements. I enquired from the auctioneer's clerk to what district they were removed. He informed me that none of the livestock were purchased in the townland but that many of the implements were sold to persons of the townland. By this you can judge whether to let the livestock remain against the townland or not. I entered them herein as they were unsold when I visited the farm [initialled] JH.

Field observer's signature: John Hanna, date 26th to 28th May 1840.

Mullaghtironey: Cottiers' Stock and Implements

[Form 3]

Cottier no.1, farmer no.5, William Beatty,

Parish of Tamlaght

labourer; 2/0 hogs, 1 teethed hook; 2 pounds rent per annum.

Cottier no.2, Robert Devlin, labourer; 1 spinning wheel, 1 teethed hook; 2 pounds 10s rent per annum.

Cottier no.3, farmer no.6, James Foster, spinner; [crossed out: 1 beehive], 1 spinning wheel; 15s rent per annum.

Cottier no.4, farmer no.15, Robert Coulter, weaver and waterkeeper; 1/0 hogs, 1/0 hens, 1 spinning wheel, 1 employed linen loom, 1/0 turf barrows, 1/0 agricultural spades, 1 agricultural shovel, 2 teethed hooks; 4 pounds 4s rent per annum.

Field observer's signature: John Hanna, date 26th to 28th May 1840.

Mullaghtironey: Labour and Proprietors

[Form 4. *Additional abbreviation used for occupations in family: p = publican.* Head landlord and immediate landlord is William Lenox <Seymour> Conyngham, all are direct tenants].

Farmer no.1, family: 2/0 males, 2/0 females; family labour: 2 females for 10 days in spring, [blank] for 6 days in summer, [blank] for 14 days in autumn; domestic concerns and spinning; tenure 1 life, 1 pound 5s yearly rent per acre; 1 w well.

Farmer no.2, lives in Urbal, occasional labour: 2 males for 4 days in spring, 1 male for 2 days in summer, 2 males for 10 days in autumn; family employed on the farm in Urbal; tenure at will, 1 pound 1s yearly rent per acre.

Farmer no.3, family: 1/0 males; occasional labour: 2 males for 26 days in spring, 1 male for 10 days in summer, 3 males for 10 days in autumn; 2 females for 10 days in autum; tenure at will, 1 pound 5s yearly rent per acre.

Farmer no.4, family: [crossed out: 1] old male, 1 male house servant, 1 female house servant; occasional labour: 3 males for 10 days in spring, 1 male for 6 days in summer, 4 males for 11 days in autumn; 1 female for 6 days in spring, 1 female for 10 days in autumn; no family labour; tenure at will, tenant, 1 pound 5s yearly rent per acre.

Farmer no.5, 2 constant male labourers; occasional labour: 6 males for 10 days in spring, 2 males for 10 days in summer, 4 males for 9 days in autumn; 2 females for 10 days in spring, for 8 days in autumn; tenure at will, 1 pound 5s yearly rent per acre; 1 spring well.

Farmer no.6, family: 2,1w/3n males, 0/3n females; 2 males farm constantly, 1 male weaves constantly; tenure at will, 11s yearly rent per acre, 1 spring well.

Farmer no.7, lives in Aghaveagh; family labour: 3 males for 10 days in spring, 2 males for 4 days in summer, 3 males for 14 days in autumn; 2 females for 16 days in autumn; employed the remainder of the year on farm in Aghaveagh; tenure 1 life, 10s yearly rent per acre.

Farmer no.8, family: 1/0 males, 1/0 females, 1 male house servant; occasional labour: 4 males for 28 days in spring, 2 males for 6 days in summer, 7 males for 10 days in autumn; 2 females for 14 days in autumn; female attends to domestic concerns constantly; tenure 1 life, 1 pound 6s yearly rent per acre, 1 spring well.

Farmer no.9, family: 2/0 males, 2/2n females; occasional labour: 1 male for 10 days in spring, for 10 days in autumn; family labour: 2 females for 14 days in spring, [blank] for 10 days in summer, [blank] for 16 days in autumn; females at domestic duties and spinning; tenure at will, 1 pound 7s 3d yearly rent per acre.

Farmer no.10, family: 1/1 males, 2/1n,1s females; family labour: 2 females for 6 days in spring, [blank] for 4 days in summer, [blank] for 10 days in autumn; females at domestic duties and spinning; tenure 2 lives, 13s yearly rent per acre.

Farmer no.11, 1/1n males, 1/1n females, 1 male house servant; occasional labour: 4 males for 6 days in spring, 1 male for 8 days in summer, 2 males for 8 days in autumn; 1 female for 6 days in spring, 2 females for 10 days in autumn; 1 female at domestic duties and spinning; holds a farm in Ballydawly; tenure 2 lives, 13s yearly rent per acre.

Farmer no.12, family: 2/2 males, 2/0 females; occasional labour: 6 males for 4 days in spring, 5 males for 6 days in autumn; 2 females for 4 days in autumn; family labour: 2 females for 4 days in spring, [blank] for 4 days in summer, [blank] for 10 days in autumn; females at domestic duties and spinning; holds a farm in Ballynacregan, parish Arboe; tenure at will, 1 pound 3s 6d yearly rent per acre; 1 spring well.

Farmer no.13, family: 2/0 males, 2/2 females; family labour: 2 females for 14 days in spring, [blank] for 6 days in summer, [blank] for 20 days in autumn; females at domestic duties and spinning; tenure at will, 1 pound 4s yearly rent per acre.

Farmer no.14, family: 2,1w/0 males, 1/0 females; family labour: 1 male for 10 days in spring, for 16 days in autumn; 1 female for 10 days in spring, [blank] for 4 days in summer, [blank] for 10 days in autumn; females constantly at domestic duties and spinning, 1 male weaves the remainder; tenure at will, 1 pound 1s yearly rent per acre; 1 spring well.

Farmer no.15, lives in Urbal; occasional labour: 4 males for 11 days in spring, 2 males for 4 days in summer, 4 males for 15 days in autumn; 2 females for 10 days in autumn; tenure at will, 1 pound 1s yearly rent per acre.

Farmer no.16, lives in Aghaveagh; occasional labour: 2 males for 10 days in spring, 1 male for 4 days in summer, 2 males for 10 days in autumn; 1 female for 10 days in autumn; tenure 1 life, 1 pound yearly rent per acre.

[Insert note: No.5: the owner of this farm died about 3 weeks ago and all his stock etc. were auctioned, there being none of his children to enjoy it. The farm is now in the landlord's hands and not yet let to any person. The crops will also remain in the ground until it be ripe. I have herein returned the servant men as they are still on the ground. The occasional labour is taken from them and the executors [initialled] JH].

Field observer's signature: John Hanna, date 26th to 28th May 1840.

Mullaghtironey: Manures

Estimate of 1 lime-kiln containing 25 barrels of 4 bushels, each bushel 57 pounds, valued at 1s per barrel: 6 tons of raw stones at 10d each, 5s; 1 horse, 1d farthing a day, carting stones for Ballydawley, parish of Artrea at 3s per day, 3s 9d; 1 man breaking stones 1 and a half days, 1s 3d; 1 man 1 day filling kiln, 10d; 8 cuts of turf at 1s 8d each, 13s 4d; 1 man attending whilst burning, 2 days and 1 night, 3s; 1 man half day emptying, 5d; [total] 1 pound 8s 1d; no.8 informant [initialled] JH.

[Form 5] Farmer no.3, dung: 24 tons per acre, 2s 6d per ton, 6 and a half cwt per load, carried from townland, 1 person employed for 4 days; lime: 12d per barrel, 10 cwt per load, carried 2 Irish miles, 1 person employed for 2 days; clay: 2d per ton, 7 cwt per load, carried from townland, 1 person employed for 5 days; compost loads: 40 dung, 18 barrels lime, 200 clay; 7 loads of compost from heap to the field, 1 person employed for 12 days, made at the house.

Farmer no.8, dung: 35 tons per acre, 2s 4d per ton, 8 cwt per load, carried from farmyard, 2 people employed for 12 days; bog: 2d per ton, 8 cwt per load, carried 1 Irish mile, 1 person employed for 5 days; lime: 12d per barrel, 8 cwt per load, carried 2 Irish miles, [insert note: see estimate for lime]; clay: 2d per ton, 7 cwt per load, carried from townland, 1 person employed for 4 days; compost loads: 50 dung, 100 bog, 30 barrels of lime, 100 clay; 1 lime-kiln, 100 barrels of lime burned per annum, 8 loads of compost from heap to field, 2 people employed for 5 days, made at the house.

Farmer no.12, dung: 22 tons per acre, 2s 2d per ton, 8 cwt per load, carried from farmyard, 1 person employed for 4 days; bog: 3d per ton, 8 cwt per load, carried 1 Irish mile, 1 person employed for 4 days; lime: 12d per barrel, 10 cwt per load, carried 2 Irish miles; clay: 2d per ton, 8 cwt per load, carried from townland, 1 person employed for 2 days; compost loads: 36 dung, 60 bog, 18 barrels of lime, 120 clay; 8 loads of compost from heap to the field, 1 person employed for 11 days, made at the field.

No.3: dung used alone and in compost, no bog used, lime and clay used in compost.

No.8: dung used alone and in compost, bog used in compost, limestone burned on the land and used in compost, clay used in compost.

No.12: dung used alone and in compost, bog used in compost, lime and clay used in compost.

Nos 8 and 12 purchase the lime in a burned state at the kiln.

Description of acre referred to: Cunningham.

Lime: number of bushels per barrel 4, weight per barrel 228 [lbs].

Dung got in farmyard, bog in townland of Drumconway, lime Ballydawley, parish Artrea, clay in townland.

Mullaghtironey: Seed and Produce

[Form 6]

Farmer no.3, wheat: 14 stones seed, 150 produce; oats: 16 stones seed, 160 produce; potatoes: 26 bushels seed, 260 produce; flax: 3 and a half bushels seed, 6 cwt produce; vetches 3 bushels seed, 12 tons produce; general observations: south east aspect, heavy red clay, well cultivated.

Farmer no.8, wheat: 14 stones seed, 154 produce; oats: 16 stones seed, 154 produce; potatoes: 25 bushels seed, 300 produce; flax: 3 and a half bushels seed, 6 and a half cwt produce; vetches: 3 bushels seed, 14 tons produce; turnips: 2 lbs seed, 25 tons produce; clover: 4 bushels hay seed, 10 lbs clover seed, 12 tons produce; general observations: south west aspect, heavy red clay, well cultivated.

Farmer no.12, barley: 12 stones seed, 120 produce; oats: 18 stones seed, 140 produce; potatoes: 28 bushels seed, 250 produce; flax: 3 and a half bushels seed, 7 cwt produce; general observations: north aspect, red clay, well cultivated.

I have taken information from no.12 for barley, he being accustomed to put in that crop although he has none this year.

Kind of acre: Cunningham.

Parish of Tamlaght

[Informant] no.12. Wheat: value of seed 1s 7d to 1s 4d per stone, value of produce 1s 6d to 1s 2d per stone; time of sowing 10th November to 12th December, time of harvest 1st September to 1st October.

Barley: value of seed 12d to 14d per stone, value of produce 10d to 14d per stone; time of sowing 1st April to 20th April, time of harvest 25th August to 20th September.

Oats: value of seed 12d to 14d per stone, value of produce 9d to 14d per stone; time of sowing 17th March to 10th April, time of harvest 10th September to 10th October.

Potatoes: value of seed 2d ha'penny to 3d ha'penny per stone, value of produce 2d ha'penny to 3d ha'penny per stone; time of sowing 17th April to 17th May, time of harvest 10th October to 10th December.

Flax: value of seed 12s to 14s per bushel, value of produce 40s to 50s per cwt; time of sowing 20th April to 10th May, time of harvest 28th July to 12th August.

Vetches: value of seed 6s 6d to 8s per bushel, value of produce 6d to 8d per cwt; time of sowing 1st March to 1st May, time of harvest 1st August to 1st September.

Turnips: value of seed 14d to 18d per lb, value of produce 5d ha'penny to 7d per cwt; time of sowing 17th May to 12th June, time of harvest 1st November to 1st December.

Mangle-wurzle: none.

Hay: value of seed 2s 6d per bushel; clover: value of seed 11d to 13d per lb, value of produce 8d to 8d ha'penny per cwt; time of sowing 1st April to 17th April, time of harvest 12th June to 1st September.

Field observer's signature: John Hanna, date 26th to 28th May 1840.

Mullaghtironey: Table of Trades

[Form 7]

Robert Coulter, waterkeeper, 4 guineas per annum.

By a waterkeeper, is here meant a person authorised to prevent fishing in the river during the season of salmon being in the river.

Field observer's signature: John Hanna, date 26th to 28th May 1840.

Mullaghtironey: Condition of Cottiers

[Form 8. All houses have brick chimneys, clay dry floors, good beds, good clothes. *All have the same furniture, which is recorded by abbreviations without a key: t = table, s = = settle bed,* e = *earthenware, c = chair, d = dresser, tc = [ticking clock ?].*

No.1, 2 apartments, whitewashed, house stone and lime, straw roof, 3 sash windows, one-eighth acre garden.

No.2, 2 apartments, whitewashed, house stone and lime, straw roof, a quarter acre garden.

No. 3, 1 apartment, not whitewashed, house stone and lime, straw roof, 1 lead window.

No.4, 3 apartments, whitewashed, brick house, slate roof, 5 sash windows, half an acre garden.

Field observer's signature: John Hanna, date 26th to 28th May 1840.

Mullaghtironey: Summary of Economy

[Form 9]

Surface: it is smooth, sloping down to all points of the boundary from an elevated centre.

Soils, kind: heavy, dark red clay; light, red gravelly clay and a little boggy clay, in various parts of the townland; depth: from 6 to 13 inches.

Subsoil, kind: red gravel, heavy red clay and blue clay in various parts of the townland; depth: in parts 12 feet and part unknown.

Exposure: to all winds.

Springs: 6 good spring wells.

Drainage: the only farm drained is no.5, which stands in the elevated part of the townland.

Irrigation: it is a little practised by turning off water from a small rivulet and conveying it to the same source again in the spring.

Implements: wooden improved and wooden ploughs, scythe and teethed reaping hooks, spades 16 by 6 inches, hosed shovels.

Acres reclaimed since 1830: none.

Mills, corn: none; flax: none; fulling: none.

Quarries, kind of: none, application of: none.

Communications: the leading road from Coagh to Stewartstown and Tullyhoge passes through this townland and in very good repair.

Markets: in Stewartstown, Cookstown, Coagh and Moneymore.

Breed of horses: Irish; breed of cattle: Irish and half bred from Irish and Durham; breed of sheep: large lowland; breed of hogs: Irish and half bred from Irish and Dutch called belties.

Woods and plantations: 2 acres planting; kind: fir, ash and alder; when first planted: 1824, present return: none cut. One acre orchards, kind: apple, pear and cherry; when first planted: 15, 15 and 16 years ago; present return: all for farmers' own use.

Lime-kilns: 1, for farmers' own use.

Manufactures: none.

Kind of crops cultivated, oats: blanter, Poland

and potatoe; wheat: red and white and a little golden drop; barley: four-rowed; potatoes: cups, lumpers, copper downs, red and white downs; flax: Riga and Dutch; vetch: spring vetch; turnips: yellow and white Norfolk and large globe.

Field observer's signature: John Hanna, residence William Vance's, Coagh, date 26th to 28th May 1840.

[Insert addition: Farmers' names and acres, where got: from the farmers individually. Natural meadow: quantity per acre 3 tons to 2 and a half tons; it is very good; time of harvest from 25th August to 12th September; price per ton 2 pounds. Kind of acre: Cunningham. Fences, kind of: soil and subsoil planted with whitethorn and faced with stone, good. Turf, where got: in townland Drumconway. Rent per acre: rough or waste land, arable land: from 11s to 27s per acre, no difference of arable or rough. Rough or waste land, kind of: sloping banks on the boundary, too steep for cultivation, and some scrog].

Statistical Information for Urbal, May and June 1840

Urbal: Farmers, Acreages and Crops

[Form 1. Information from the farmers unless indicated].

Farmer no.1, James Ekin, grocer, not working; 17 and a half acres, 4 tillage, 13 and a half pasture: 3 oats, half an acre potatoes, half an acre flax; potatoes belong to cottiers, generally owner, this farm more grazed than tilled; rotation: 1 oats, 2 potatoes, 3 oats, flax, 4 oats with hay sown for grazing, 5 grass, 6 grass, 7 grass.

Farmer no.2, John Pherson, publican and farmer; 8 acres, 4 and a half tillage, 3 and a quarter pasture, a quarter acre waste: three-quarter acres wheat, 2 and a quarter oats, 1 and a half potatoes; rotation: 1 potatoes, 2 wheat or oats, 3 oats, 4 oats with hay sown for grazing, 5 grass, 6 grass, 7 grass.

Farmer no.3, Walter Duff [2 written above], head innkeeper; 2 and three-quarter acres, tillage: 1 oats, 1 potatoes, three-quarter acres flax; rotation: 1 oats, 2 potatoes, 3 flax, 4 oats, 5 potatoes.

Farmer no.4, Patrick McGilland, farmer; 5 and a quarter acres, 4 and a quarter tillage, half an acre pasture, a quarter acre meadow, a quarter acre waste: 2 and a quarter oats, 1 and a quarter potatoes, a quarter acre flax, half an acre clover; rotation: 1 potatoes, 2 oats or flax with clover sown, 3 oats with clover cut twice and hay sown for grazing, 4 grass, 5 grass.

Farmer no.5, Mrs Alicia Newton, farmer, not working; 5 and three-quarter acres, 5 and a quarter pasture, half an acre waste; rotation: 1 grass, 2 grass, grazing for 10 years; acres under orchard: 1 acre, plantation, 2 years old.

Farmer no.6, Michael Donnelly, farmer and carter; three-quarters of an acre, tillage, flax; rotation: 1 potatoes, 2 flax, 3 potatoes.

Farmer no.7, James McComb, farmer and carter; three-quarters of an acre, tillage: three-eighth acres oats, a quarter acre potatoes, one-eighth acre flax; rotation: 1 potatoes, 2 oats, flax, 3 oats, 4 potatoes.

Farmer no.8, Thomas Glendinning <Clendining> [9 written above], shoemaker and farmer; three-quarters of an acre, tillage: three-eighth acres oats, three-eighth acres potatoes; rotation: 1 potatoes, 2 oats, 3 oats.

Farmer no.9, Robert Malaverer, farmer; three-quarters of an acre, tillage: three-eighth acres oats, three-eighth acres potatoes; rotation: 1 potatoes, 2 oats.

Farmer no.10, John Cowdan, shoemaker and farmer; 1 and a quarter acres, tillage: half an acre oats, five-eighth acres potatoes, one-eighth acre flax; rotation: 1 potatoes, 2 oats or flax.

Farmer no.11, William Kilpatrick [10 written above], farmer and thatcher; 1 and a quarter acres, tillage: half an acre oats, three-quarter acres potatoes; rotation: 1 potatoes, 2 oats.

Farmer no.12, Edward Henderson, farmer; 1 and a half acres, tillage: three-quarter acres oats, three-quarter acres potatoes; rotation: 1 potatoes, 2 oats.

Farmer no.13, Thomas Robinson, baker; 1 acre, tillage: half an acre oats, half an acre potatoes; rotation: 1 potatoes, 2 oats.

Farmer no.14, Eliza Rooney, spinner; [crossed out: one-eighth of an acre, tillage, potatoes]; rotation: 1 potatoes.

Farmer no.15, John Speere, [16 written above], process server; [crossed out: one-eighth of an acre, tillage, potatoes]; rotation: 1 potatoes.

Farmer no.16, Joseph Young, sawyer and farmer; [crossed out: one-eighth of an acre, tillage, pasture]; rotation: 1 potatoes.

Farmer no.17, James Latimer and B. Smith [16 written above], farmer; [crossed out: one-eighth of an acre, tillage, potatoes]; rotation: 1 potatoes.

Farmer no.18, Peter McLaughlin, nailer and farmer; [crossed out: a quarter of an acre, tillage, potatoes]; rotation: 1 potatoes, 2 potatoes.

Farmer no.19, [?] Philip [McGovery or McGarvey ?], labourer; a quarter of an acre, tillage, flax; rotation: 1 potatoes, 2 flax, 3 potatoes.

Parish of Tamlaght

Farmer no.20, Sarah Hamilton, spinner; [crossed out: one-eighth of an acre, tillage, potatoes]; rotation: 1 potatoes.

Farmer no.21, John O'Neil, hackler and farmer; [crossed out: one-eighth of an acre, tillage, potatoes]; rotation: 1 potatoes.

Farmer no.22, Alexander Cowdan [21 written above], shoemaker and farmer; [crossed out: one-eighth of an acre, tillage, potatoes]; rotation: 1 potatoes.

Farmer no.23, John Menow, pensioner and farmer; [crossed out: one-eighth of an acre, tillage, potatoes]; rotation: 1 potatoes.

Farmer no.24, James Hamilton, nailer and farmer; [crossed out: half an acre, tillage, potatoes]; rotation: 1 potatoes.

Farmer no.25, Richard Hamilton, nailer and farmer; [crossed out: a quarter of an acre, tillage, potatoes]; rotation: 1 potatoes.

Farmer no.26, Thomas Ferguson, farmer; 10 and a quarter acres, 6 and three-quarters tillage, 1 pasture, 1 meadow, 1 and a half waste: half an acre wheat, 4 oats, 2 potatoes, a quarter acre turnips; rotation: 1 oats, 2 potatoes, turnips, 3 wheat or oats with clover sown, 4 clover cut twice, 5 grass; acres under orchard: three-eighth acres, plantation, 50 [or 30] years old; three-quarters of an acre reclaimed since 1830; drainage: [diagram of drainage system, 40, 5/300].

Farmer no.27, John Morris, farmer; 2 acres, 1 and a half tillage, half an acre pasture: three-quarter acres potatoes, three-quarter acres flax; rotation: 1 potatoes, 2 oats, 3 potatoes, 4 oats with clover sown for grazing, 5 grass.

Farmer no.28, James McKee, farmer; 3 acres, 2 pasture, 1 meadow: half an acre potatoes, 1 flax, half an acre vetches; rotation: 1 potatoes, 2 oats or flax with clover sown, 3 clover cut twice, 4 grass.

Farmer no.29, William Ferguson, farmer; [crossed out: half an acre, tillage, flax]; rotation: 1 potatoes, 2 potatoes.

Farmer no.30, Thomas Hunter, farmer, not working; 1 and three-quarter acres, half an acre tillage, three-quarter acres pasture, half an acre waste: half an acre flax; rotation: 1 potatoes, 2 oats with hay sown for grazing, 3 grass; 1 acre reclaimed since 1830.

Farmer no.31, Matthew Flack, farmer; 20 and three-quarter acres, 8 acres tillage, 11 and a quarter pasture, 1 meadow, half an acre waste: half an acre wheat, 5 potatoes, 2 and a half flax; rotation: 1 potatoes, 2 wheat, oats, 3 oats with hay sown for grazing, 4 grass; 1 acre reclaimed since 1830; drainage: [diagram of drainage system, 36, 3/180].

Farmer no.32, Joseph Young, farmer; 16 and three-quarter acres, 7 and three-quarters tillage, 5 and a quarter pasture, 2 meadow, 1 and three-quarters waste: three-quarter acres wheat, 4 and a half oats, 2 and a half potatoes; rotation: 1 oats, 2 potatoes, 3 wheat or oats, 4 oats with hay sown for grazing, 5 grass, 6 grass; acres under orchard: half an acre, plantation, 30 years old; one-eighth acre orchard, 80 years planted.

Farmer no.33, Robert Young, farmer, not working; 12 acres, 7 and a quarter tillage, 3 and three-quarters pasture, three-quarters of an acre meadow, a quarter of an acre waste: 1 wheat, 3 oats, 2 potatoes, a quarter acre flax, 1 clover; rotation: 1 oats, 2 potatoes, 3 wheat, oats or flax with clover sown, 4 oats with clover cut twice and hay sown for grazing, 5 grass; half an acre reclaimed since 1830.

Farmer no.34, Mr John Cowan, farmer, not working; 40 and three-quarter acres, 27 and three-quarters tillage, 7 and a half pasture, 2 and a half meadow, 3 waste: 3 wheat, 1 barley, 13 oats, 6 potatoes, three-quarter acres flax, 2 hay, 2 clover; rotation: 1 oats, 2 oats, 3 potatoes, 4 wheat, barley, oats or flax with clover sown and hay sown, 5 oats with clover cut twice and hay sown for grazing, 6 grass, 7 grass; acres under orchard: a quarter of an acre, plantation, 8 years old; drainage: [diagram of drainage system, 40, 8/900].

Farmer no.35, James Duff, farmer; 5 and three-quarter acres, 1 and a half tillage, 3 and three-quarters pasture, half an acre waste: half an acre wheat, half an acre oats, half an acre potatoes; rotation: 1 oats, 2 potatoes, 3 wheat, 4 clover sown, 5 clover cut twice, 6 grass, 7 grass.

Farmer no.36, William John Howard, publican and farmer, not working; 7 and a half acres, tillage: 4 and three-quarters oats, 2 potatoes, three-quarter acres clover; rotation: 1 potatoes, 2 oats with clover sown, 3 oats with clover cut twice and hay sown for grazing, 4 grass.

Farmer no.37, James Skiffington, farmer; 2 and three-quarter acres, 1 and seven-eighths tillage, seven-eighth acres pasture: 1 and a quarter oats, five-eighth acres potatoes; rotation: 1 potatoes, 2 oats, 3 oats with hay sown for grazing, 4 grass, 5 grass.

Farmer no.38, Robert Cowan, [37 written above], grocer and farmer, not working; 1 acre, pasture; rotation: 1 grass, 2 grass.

Farmer no.39, James Dogherty, farmer; [crossed out: a quarter of an acre, tillage, potatoes]; rotation: 1 potatoes, 2 potatoes.

Farmer no.40, Mary Coulter, farmer; 2 acres, 1 and a half tillage, a quarter acre pasture, a quarter acre waste: 1 acre oats, half an acre potatoes; rotation: 1 potatoes, 2 oats, 3 oats, 4 grass, 5 grass.

Farmer no.41, Samuel Ferguson, farmer; [crossed out: one-eighth of an acre, tillage, potatoes]; rotation: 1 potatoes, 2 potatoes.

Farmer no.42, James [?] Girvan, farmer; [crossed out: one-eighth of an acre, tillage, potatoes]; rotation: 1 potatoes, 2 potatoes.

Farmer no.43, Joseph Eldertin, farmer and weaver; [crossed out: one-eighth of an acre, tillage, potatoes]; rotation: 1 potatoes, 2 potatoes.

Farm no.44, undivided bog, 4 and a half acres, waste; informant: cess book.

Farm no.45, roads and waters, 4 acres, waste; informant: cess book.

Farm no.46, meeting house ground, 1 acre, waste; informant: cess book.

[Totals]: 240 and a quarter statute acres equals 186 and three-eighth Cunningham acres; farms: 97 and five-eighth acres tillage, 59 and one-eighth acres pasture, 7 and a half acres meadow, 18 and three-quarter acres waste: 7 acres wheat, 1 acre barley, 50 and one-eighth oats, 28 and three-quarters potatoes, 4 and a quarter flax, a quarter acre turnips, 2 hay, 4 and a quarter clover; cabins: 3 and a half acres, tillage, potatoes.

[Insert addition: o.m. 240 and a quarter statute acres].

Urbal: Farmers' Stock and Implements

[Prices added to printed form no.2: horses for agriculture 9 pounds to 10 pounds, horses for transport 9 pounds; cattle 5 pounds 10s to 8 pounds 10s, [insert addition: cattle 7s 6d to 2 pounds], sheep 1 pound 5s [insert addition: 4s], hogs 2 pounds to 4 pounds [insert addition: 12s to 1 pound 10s], geese 2s, ducks 8d, turkeys 2s 6d, hens 8d; iron ploughs 4 pounds 4s, wooden ploughs 1 pound 10s; breaks 18s, rollers 15s, drill hoes 1 pound 5s, carts 5 pounds to 6 pounds 10s, wheel cars 3 pounds, corn fans 3 pounds, spinning wheels 9s; linen looms employed 2 pounds 10s, unemployed 1 pound 15s; box barrows 10s, turf barrows 4s, agricultural spades 2s 3d, turf spades 2s 9d; agricultural shovels 1s 7d, scythe hooks 6d, teethed hooks 5d].

Farmer no.1, lives in Coagh.

Farmer no.2, 1/0 agricultural horses, 1/1 cattle, 2/0 hogs, 4 ducks, 5 hens, 1 wooden plough, 1 break, 1 cart, 1 spinning wheel, 1 box barrow, 2/0 agricultural spades, 1 agricultural shovel, 2 scythe hooks.

Farmer no.3, lives in Coagh.

Farmer no.4, 1/0 agricultural horses, 1/0 cattle, 0/2 hogs, 5 ducks, 7 hens, 1 break, 1 cart, 3 spinning wheels, 1 box barrow, 2/0 agricultural spades, 2 agricultural shovels, 1 scythe hook, 3 teethed hooks.

Farmer no.5, lives in Coagh.

Farmer no.6, 1/0 agricultural horses, 1/0 transport horses, 0/1 hogs, 3 hens, 1 spinning wheel, 1 box barrow, 1/0 agricultural spades, 1 agricultural shovel.

Farmer no.7, 1/0 transport horses, 0/1 hogs, 4 hens, 2 spinning wheels, 1/0 agricultural spades, 1 agricultural shovel, 1 scythe hook.

Farmer no.8, 1 spinning wheel, 1/0 agricultural spades, 1 agricultural shovel, 1 teethed hook.

Farmer no.9, 3 hens, 2 spinning wheels, 1/0 agricultural spades, 1 agricultural shovel, 1 scythe hook.

Farmer no.10, 2 hens, 1 spinning wheel, 1 box barrow, 1/0 agricultural spades, 1 agricultural shovel, 1 scythe hook.

Farmer no.11, 2/0 cattle, 3 ducks, 4 hens, 2 spinning wheels, 1 employed linen loom, 1/0 agricultural spades, 1 shovel, 1 scythe hook.

Farmer no.12, 1/0 cattle, 0/1 hogs, 4 ducks, 2 hens, 2 spinning wheels, 1/0 agricultural spades, 1 agricultural shovel, 1 scythe hook, 1 teethed hook.

Farmer no.13, 1/0 agricultural spades, 1 agricultural shovel.

Farmer no.14, 3 ducks, 4 hens, 1 spinning wheel.

Farmer no.15, 3 hens, 1 spinning wheel, 1/0 agricultural spades.

Farmer no.16, 0/1 hogs, 2 hens, 3 spinning wheels, 1/0 agricultural spades, 1 agricultural shovel.

Farmer no.17, 1/0 agricultural spades.

Farmer no.18, lives in Coagh.

Farmer no.19, lives in Coagh.

Farmer no.20, lives in Coagh.

Farmer no.21, lives in Coagh.

Farmer no.22, lives in Coagh.

Farmer no.23, lives in Coagh.

Farmer no.24, lives in Coagh.

Farmer no.25, lives in Coagh.

Farmer no.26, 2/0 agricultural horses, 2/2 cattle, 0/2 hogs, 8/14 geese, 12 ducks, 10 hens, 1 wooden plough, 1 break, 1 roller, 2 carts, 1 corn fan, 2 spinning wheels, 1 box barrow, 2 turf barrows, 3/1 agricultural spades, 2 agricultural shovels, 3 scythe hooks, 1 teethed hook; irrigation: yes.

Farmer no.27, 1/0 cattle, 0/1 geese, 5 ducks, 6 hens, 1 spinning wheel, 1/0 agricultural spades, 1 agricultural shovel, 1 scythe hook.

Parish of Tamlaght

Farmer no.28, 2/0 cattle, 4 ducks, 5 hens, 1 spinning wheel, 1/0 agricultural spades, 1 agricultural shovel, 2 teethed hooks.

Farmer no.29, 0/1 hogs, 3 ducks, 4 hens, 2 spinning wheels, 2 employed linen looms, 1/0 agricultural spades, 1 agricultural shovel.

Farmer no.30, lives in Drumconway.

Farmer no.31, 1/0 agricultural horses, 2/3 cattle, 2/3 sheep, 0/3 hogs, 5/13 geese, 12 ducks, 10 hens, 1 wooden plough, 1 break, 1 cart, 2 spinning wheels, 1 box barrow, 3 turf barrows, 3/2 agricultural spades, 2 agricultural shovels, 3 scythe hooks, 3 teethed hooks.

Farmer no.32, 2/0 agricultural horses, 2/2 cattle, 0/2 geese, 7 ducks, 8 hens, 1 wooden plough, 1 break, 1 cart, 1 wheel car, 1 spinning wheel, 1 box barrow, 2 turf barrows, 3/1 agricultural spades, 2 agricultural shovels, 2 scythe hooks, 2 teethed hooks.

Farmer no.33, 1/1 agricultural horses, 3/2 cattle, 0/3 hogs, 4/12 geese, 8 ducks, 12 hens, 1 wooden plough, 1 break, 1 roller, 1 cart, 2 spinning wheels, 1 box barrow, 2 turf barrows, 2/1 agricultural spades, 2 agricultural shovels, 2 scythe hooks, 3 teethed hooks.

Farmer no.34, 4/0 agricultural horses, 5/7 cattle, 3/3 sheep, 2/2 hogs, 6/18 geese, 14 ducks, 4/12 turkeys, 0/14 hens, 1 iron plough, 1 wooden plough, 2 breaks, 1 roller, 1 drill hoe, 3 carts, 1 corn fan, 1 spinning wheel, 2 box barrows, 4 turf barrows, 5/2 agricultural spades, 4 agricultural shovels, 5 scythe hooks, 7 teethed hooks.

Farmer no.35, 2/0 agricultural horses, 2/2 cattle, 1/3 hogs, 3/12 geese, 10 ducks, 3/12 turkeys, 10 hens, 1 iron plough, 1 break, 1 cart, 1 wheel car, 1 spinning wheel, 1 box barrow, 2 turf barrows, 3/1 agricultural spades, 2 agricultural shovels, 2 scythe hooks, 2 teethed hooks.

Farmer no.36, lives in Coagh.

Farmer no.37, 1/0 cattle, 0/1 hogs, 5 ducks, 8 hens, 1 spinning wheel, 1 box barrow, 1/0 agricultural spades, 1 agricultural shovel, 1 scythe hook, 1 teethed hook.

Farmer no.38, lives in Coagh.

Farmer no.39, 4 ducks, 6 hens, 2 spinning wheels, 1/0 agricultural spades, 1 agricultural shovel, 1 scythe hook.

Farmer no.40, 1/0 cattle, 0/1 hogs, 6 ducks, 7 hens, 2 spinning wheels, 1/0 agricultural spades, 1 agricultural shovel, 1 teethed hook.

Farmer no.41, 3 ducks, 2 hens, 1 spinning wheel, 1/0 agricultual spades, 1 agricultural shovel.

Farmer no.42, 0/1 hogs, 2 ducks, 3 hens, 1 spinning wheel, 1/0 agricultural spades.

Farmer no.43, 4 ducks, 2 hens, 2 spinning wheels, 1 employed linen loom, 1/0 agricultural spades, 1 agricultural shovel.

Urbal: Cottiers' Stock and Implements

[Form 3]

Cottier no.1, farmer no.1, William Rankin, weaver; 3 ducks, 3 hens, 2 spinning wheels, 1 employed linen loom, 1/0 agricultural spades, 1 agricultural shovel, 1 scythe hook; yearly rent 3 pounds.

Cottier no.2, Thomas Wilkinson, weaver; 5 hens, 1 spinning wheel, 1 employed linen loom, 1/0 agricultural spades, 1 agricultural shovel; yearly rent 3 pounds.

Cottier no.3, farmer no.31, Michael McIlhone, labourer; 0/1 hogs, 2 ducks, 4 hens, 1 spinning wheel, 1/0 agricultural spades, 1 agricultural shovel, 1 teethed hook; yearly rent 1 pound 10s.

Cottier no.4, Michael McIlhone Junior, labourer; 3 hens, 1 spinning wheel, 1/0 agricultural spades, 1 teethed hook; yearly rent 1 pound 6s.

Cottier no.5, farmer no.35, Robert Crooks, scutcher; 3 hens, 1 spinning wheel, 1/0 agricultural spades; yearly rent 2 pounds 10s.

Cottier no.6, John Cairns, scutcher; 5 hens, 2 spinning wheels, 1/0 agricultural spades; yearly rent 2 pounds 10s.

Cottier no.7, James Wilkinson, scutcher; 4 hens, 1 spinning wheel, 1 agricultural shovel, 1 teethed hook; yearly rent 2 pounds 10s.

Cottier no.8, Thomas McAlister, shoemaker; 3 ducks, 4 hens, 1 spinning wheel, 1/0 agricultural spades; yearly rent 2 pounds 10s.

Cottier no.9, farmer no.38, William Rollin, labourer; 4 ducks, 5 hens, 2 spinning wheels, 1/0 agricultural spades, 1 agricultural shovel, 1 scythe hook; yearly rent 2 pounds.

Cottier no.10, farmer no.34, Thomas Cowden, labourer; 0/1 hogs, 5 hens, 1 spinning wheel, 1/0 agricultural spades, 1 agricultural shovel, 1 teethed hook; yearly rent 3 pounds.

Cottier no.11, Charles Campbell, labourer; 4 ducks, 4 hens, 1 spinning wheel, 1/0 agricultural spades, 1 teethed hook; yearly rent 2 pounds 10s.

Urbal: Labour and Proprietors

[Form 4. Head landlord in all cases William Lenox Cunningham. *Additional abbreviations for occupations in family: c = carter, t = thatcher*].

Farmer no.1, lives in Coagh; occasional labour: 3 males for 7 days in spring, 2 for 5 days in summer, 4 for 7 days in autumn; 1 female for 8 days in spring, 2 for 6 days in summer, 3 for 7 days in autumn; immediate landlord William Lenox

Conyngham, tenure 21 years and 1 life, direct tenant, 1 pound 4s 4d yearly rent per acre.

Farmer no.2, family: 1/0 males, 0/1 females, 1 female house servant; occasional labour: 2 males for 12 days in spring, 1 for 10 days in summer, 3 for 8 days in autumn; 1 female for 12 days in spring, 2 for 10 days in summer, 3 for 8 days in autumn; family labour: 1 male for 25 days in spring, for 20 days in summer, for 25 days in autumn; no female family labour, rest of time employed in house; immediate landlord William Lenox Conyngham, tenure at will, direct tenant, 1 pound 15s yearly rent per acre.

Farmer no.3, lives in Coagh; occasional labour: 3 males for 12 days in spring, 2 for 12 days in summer, 2 for 12 days in autumn; 1 female for 12 days in spring, 2 for 10 days in summer, 3 for 7 days in autumn; immediate landlord William Lenox Conyngham, tenure 21 years and 1 life, direct tenant, 1 pound 10s yearly rent per acre.

Farmer no.4, family: 1/0 males, 3s/2 females; family labour: 3 females for 12 days in spring, for 12 days in summer, for 15 days in autumn; male constantly employed, females spin, wash; immediate landlord William Lenox Conyngham, tenure at will, direct tenant, 1 pound 5s yearly rent per acre.

Farmer no.5, lives in Coagh; immediate landlord William Lenox Conyngham, direct tenant.

Farmer no.6, family: 1c/2 males, 1s/4 females; family labour: 1 male for 14 days in spring, for 12 days in summer, for 12 days in autumn; 1 female for 10 days in spring, for 8 days in summer, for 12 days in autumn; male rest of time carting, female spins, cooks; immediate landlord James Brown, tenure at will, subtenant, 6 pounds 10s yearly rent per acre.

Farmer no.7, family: 1c/1 males, 2s/0 females; family labour: 1 male for 10 days in spring, for 8 days in summer, for 8 days in autumn; 2 females for 5 days in spring, for 4 days in summer, for 6 days in autumn; male rest of time carting, female spins, cooks; immediate landlord James Brown, tenure at will, subtenant, 6 pounds 10s yearly rent per acre.

Farmer no.8, family: 2t/4 males, 1/1 females; occasional labour: 1 male for 6 days in spring, for 6 days in summer; family labour: 2 males for 6 days in spring, for 4 days in summer, for 6 days in autumn; 1 female for 6 days in spring, for 6 days in summer, for 6 days in autumn; males rest of time making shoes, female cooks, binding shoes etc.; immediate landlord James Brown, tenure at will, subtenant, 6 pounds 10s yearly rent per acre.

Farmer no.9, family: 1/0 males, 2s/1 females; family labour: 1 male for 12 days in spring, for 8 days in summer, for 12 days in spring; 2 females for 4 days in spring, for 4 days in summer, for 4 days in autumn; male rest of time labouring for others, female spins; immediate landlord James Brown, tenure at will, subtenant, 6 pounds 10s yearly rent per acre.

Farmer no.10, family: 1t/4 males, 1/2 females; occasional labour: 1 male for 9 days in spring, for 8 days in summer, for 5 days in autumn; family labour: 1 male for 10 days in spring, for 8 days in summer, for 8 days in autumn; 1 female for 9 days in spring, for 8 days in summer, for 10 days in autumn; male rest of time making shoes, female cooks, binds shoes; immediate landlord James Brown, tenure at will, subtenant, 5 pounds yearly rent per acre.

Farmer no.11, family: 1t/1w males, 1/2 females; occasional labour: 1 male for 8 days in autumn; family labour: 1 male for 14 days in spring, for 12 days in summer, for 12 days in autumn; 1 female for 10 days in spring, for 8 days in summer, for 10 days in autumn; rest of time scutching, idle, female cooks, attends weaver; immediate landlord James Brown, tenure at will, subtenant, 5 pounds yearly rent per acre.

Farmer no.12, family: 1/3t males, 2/1 females; family labour: 1 male for 14 days in spring, for 14 days in summer, for 14 days in autumn; 2 females for 8 days in spring, for 6 days in summer, for 8 days in autumn; male rest of time idle, females attend shoemakers; immediate landlord James Brown, tenure at will, subtenant, 3 pounds 10s yearly rent per acre.

Farmer no.13, family: 0/1 males, 0/3 females; occasional labour: 2 males for 6 days in spring, 1 for 7 days in summer, 2 for 5 days in autumn; 1 female for 6 days in spring, for 5 days in summer, 2 for 5 days in autumn; immediate landlord James Brown, tenure at will, subtenant, 3 pounds 10s yearly rent per acre.

Farmer no.14, family: 0/1 males, 1s/0 females; occasional labour: 1 male for 3 days in spring; family labour: 1 female for 5 days in spring, for 5 days in summer, for 5 days in autumn; female spins rest of time; immediate landlord James Brown, tenure at will, subtenant, 6 pounds yearly rent per acre.

Farmer no.15, family: 1/1 males, 1/1 females; family labour: 1 male for 3 days in spring, for 2 days in summer, for 2 days in autumn; 1 female for 2 days in spring, for 1 day in summer, for 2 days in autumn; male rest of time serving processes, attending sessions and idle, female cooks;

Parish of Tamlaght

immediate landlord James Brown, tenure at will, subtenant, 6 pounds yearly rent per acre.

Farmer no.16, family: 1t/2 males, 3s/1 females; family labour: 1 male for 3 days in spring, for 2 days in summer, for 2 days in autumn; 3 females for 1 day in spring, for 1 day in summer, for 1 day in autumn; male rest of time employed at his trade, females spin; immediate landlord James Brown, tenure at will, subtenant, 6 pounds yearly rent per acre.

Farmer no.17, family: 1t/2 males, 1/2 females; family labour: 1 male for 2 days in spring, for 2 days in summer, for 2 days in autumn; 1 female for 3 days in spring, for 3 days in summer, for 2 days in autumn; male rest of time at his trade, female cooking; immediate landlord James Brown, tenure at will, subtenant, 6 pounds yearly rent per acre.

Farmer no.18, lives in Coagh; family labour: 1 male for 5 days in spring, for 4 days in summer, for 4 days in autumn; 1 female for 3 days in spring, for 4 days in summer, for 4 days in autumn; male rest of time at his trade, female cooking; immediate landlord James Brown, tenure at will, subtenant, 6 pounds yearly rent per acre.

Farmer no.19, lives in Coagh; family labour: 1 male for 3 days in spring, for 3 days in autumn; 1 female for 2 days in spring, for 4 days in summer, for 8 days in autumn; male works for others, female spins; immediate landlord James Brown, tenure at will, subtenant, 6 pounds yearly rent per acre.

Farmer no.20, lives in Coagh; family labour: 1 male for 3 days in spring, for 2 days in summer, for 2 days in autumn; 1 female for 2 days in spring, for 2 days in summer, for 2 days in autumn; male rest of time weaving, female attends weaver, spins; immediate landlord James Brown, tenure at will, subtenant, 6 pounds yearly rent per acre.

Farmer no.21, lives in Coagh; family labour: 1 male for 2 days in spring, for 2 days in summer, for 2 days in autumn; 1 female for 2 days in spring, for 2 days in summer, for 2 days in autumn; male rest of time hackling, female attends hackling; immediate landlord James Brown, tenure at will, subtenant, 6 pounds yearly rent per acre.

Farmer no.22, lives in Coagh; family labour: 1 male for 3 days in spring, for 2 days in summer, for 2 days in autumn; 1 female for 2 days in spring, for 2 days in summer, for 2 days in autumn; male rest of time making shoes, females attend shoemaking; immediate landlord James Brown, tenure at will, subtenant, 6 pounds yearly rent per acre.

Farmer no.23, lives in Coagh; family labour: 1 male for 3 days in spring, for 3 days in summer, for 3 days in autumn; 1 female for 2 days in spring, for 2 days in summer, for 2 days in autumn; male rest of time idle, female spins; immediate landlord James Brown, tenure at will, subtenant, 6 pounds yearly rent per acre.

Farmer no.24, lives in Coagh; family labour: 1 male for 9 days in spring, for 7 days in summer, for 8 days in autumn; 1 female for 5 days in spring, for 6 days in summer, for 8 days in autumn; male rest of time at his trade, female washes, cooks; immediate landlord Mrs Mary Ekin in perpetuity, tenure at will, subtenant, 3 pounds yearly rent per acre.

Farmer no.25, lives in Coagh; family labour: 1 male for 5 days in spring, for 3 days in summer, for 4 days in autumn; 1 female for 3 days in spring, for 3 days in summer, for 4 days in autumn; male rest of time at his trade, female cooks and washes; immediate landlord Mr Samuel Magill, tenure at will, subtenant, 2 pounds yearly rent per acre.

Farmer no.26, family: 2/0 males, 1/1 females; 1 male house servant, 1 female house servant; occasional labour: 2 males for 15 days in autumn; 2 females for 15 days in autumn; family labour: 2 males for 30 days in spring, for 20 days in summer, for 30 days in autumn; 1 female for 15 days in spring, for 12 days in summer, for 15 days in autumn; males rest of time in market, females spins, cooks; immediate landlord William Lenox Conyngham, tenure at will, tenant, 1 pound 8s yearly rent per acre.

Farmer no.27, family: 1/1 males, 0/1 females; occasional labour: 1 female for 8 days in spring, for 8 days in summer, for 6 days in autumn; family labour: 1 male for 18 days in spring, for 15 days in summer, for 18 days in autumn; male rest of time labouring for others, female labours none; immediate landlord John Cowan, tenure at will, subtenant, 3 pounds yearly rent per acre; 1 spring well.

Farmer no.28, family: 1/3 males, 1s/1 females; family labour: 1 male for 35 days in spring, for 25 days in summer, for 30 days in autumn; 1 female for 12 days in spring, for 12 days in summer, for 16 days in autumn; rest of time in markets, fairs, working for others, female spins; immediate landlord John Cowan, tenure at will, subtenant, 2 pounds 10s yearly rent per acre; 1 spring well.

Farmer no.29, family: 1/2n males, 1s/3 females; family labour: 1 male for 10 days in spring, for 8 days in summer, for 10 days in autumn; 1 female for 6 days in spring, for 6 days in summer, for 10 days in autumn; male rest of time attending weavers, female spins, other females attend weaver; immediate landlord John Cowan, tenure at will, subtenant, 3 pounds yearly rent per acre.

Farmer no.30, lives in Drumconway; family labour: 2 males for 5 days in spring, for 4 days in summer, for 5 days in autumn; 2 females for 3 days in spring, for 3 days in summer, for 5 days in autumn; 1 male weaves, other employed on farm in Drumconway, females spin; immediate landlord William Lenox Conyngham, tenure at will, direct tenant, 10s yearly rent per acre.

Farmer no.31, family: 3/2 males, 2s/1 females; family labour: 2 females for 18 days in spring, for 15 days in summer, for 18 days in autumn; males constantly employed, females spin, wash; immediate landlord William Lenox Conyngham, tenure 21 years and 1 life, direct tenant, 1 pound 3s yearly rent per acre; 1 spring well.

Farmer no.32, family: 3/0 males, 0/1 females; 1 female house servant; occasional labour: 1 male for 12 days in autumn; 1 female for 12 days in spring, 2 for 8 days in summer, 2 for 12 days in autumn; males constantly employed, no female family labour; immediate landlord William Lenox Conyngham, tenure 21 years and 2 lives, direct tenant, 1 pound 2s yearly rent per acre.

Farmer no.33, family: 1/1,1t males, 0/2 females; occasional labour: 2 males for 12 days in spring, 4 for 12 days in autumn; 2 females for 12 days in spring, for 12 days in summer, for 15 days in autumn; males constantly employed, no female family labour; immediate landlord William Lenox Conyngham, tenure 21 years, direct tenant, 1 pound 2s yearly rent per acre; 1 water pump, [value] 3 pounds 1s.

Farmer no.34, family: 0/2 males, 0/3 females, 2 male and 1 female house servant, 2 male constant labourers; occasional labour: 4 males for 30 days in spring, 2 for 30 days in summer, 6 for 30 days in autumn; 3 females for 35 days in spring, for 40 days in summer, 4 for 30 days in autumn; immediate landlord William Lenox Conyngham, tenure 21 years and 2 lives, direct tenant, 1 pound 2s yearly rent per acre; 1 spring well, 1 water pump, [value] 5 pounds.

Farmer no.35, family: 2/4 males, 0/1 females, 1 male and 1 female house servant; family labour: 2 males for 12 days in spring, for 8 days in summer, for 12 days in autumn; rest of time working in Mullaghtironey, farmer attending flax mills and markets, no female labour; immediate landlord William Lenox Conyngham, tenure 61 years, direct tenant, 1 pound yearly rent per acre; 1 spring well.

Farmer no.36, lives in Coagh; occasional labour: 3 males for 17 days in spring, 2 for 12 days in summer, 4 for 18 days in autumn; 2 females for 10 days in spring, 3 for 10 days in summer, 3 for 18 days in autumn; immediate landlord William Lenox Conyngham, tenure at will, direct tenant, 1 pound yearly rent per acre.

Farmer no.37, family: 1/1 males, 1/2 females; family labour: 1 male for 20 days in spring, for 15 days in summer, for 18 days in autumn; 1 female for 10 days in spring, for 8 days in summer, for 10 days in autumn; rest of time working for others, female cooks, washes; immediate landlord Mrs Mary Ekin, in perpetuity, tenure at will, subtenant, 2 pounds 10s yearly rent per acre.

Farmer no.38, lives in Coagh; no family or other labour, land in pasture; immediate landlord Mrs Mary Ekin, tenure at will, subtenant, 2 pounds 10s yearly rent per acre.

Farmer no.39, family: 1/3 males, 2s/1 females; family labour: 1 male for 4 days in spring, for 4 days in summer, for 4 days in autumn; 2 females for 2 days in spring, for 1 day in summer, for 2 days in autumn; male labours for other persons, females spin; immediate landlord Mrs Alicia Newton, in perpetuity, tenure at will, subtenant, 4 pounds yearly rent per acre.

Farmer no.40, family: 0/1 males, 2s/0 females; occasional labour: 1 male for 8 days in spring, for 8 days in autumn; family labour: 2 females for 15 days in spring, for 12 days in summer, for 15 days in autumn; no male (family) labour, females spin, cook, wash; immediate landlord Mrs Alicia Newton, tenure at will, subtenant, 3 pounds yearly rent per acre.

Farmer no.41, family: 1/3 males, 1s/2 females; family labour: 1 male for 4 days in spring, for 2 days in summer, for 3 days in autumn; 1 female for 2 days in spring, for 2 days in summer, for 3 days in autumn; male rest of time working for others, female spins; immediate landlord Mr Samuel Magill, tenure at will, subtenant, 4 pounds yearly rent per acre.

Farmer no.42, family: 1/1 males, 1s/2 females; family labour: 1 male for 4 days in spring, for 2 days in summer, for 3 days in autumn; 1 female for 2 days in spring, for 2 days in summer, for 3 days in autumn; male rest of time working for others, female spins; immediate landlord Mr Samuel Magill, tenure at will, subtenant, 4 pounds yearly rent per acre.

Farmer no.43, family: 1w/0 males, 2s/1 females; family labour: 1w male for 4 days in spring, for 2 days in summer, for 3 days in autumn; 2 females for 1 day in spring, for 1 day in summer, for 2 days in autumn; master weaves rest of time, females spin and attend weaver; immediate landlord Mr Samuel Magill, tenure at will, subtenant, 4 pounds yearly rent per acre.

Parish of Tamlaght   135

Farmer no.44, immediate landlord William Lenox Conyngham, not let.

Farmer no.45, immediate landlord William Lenox Conyngham, not let.

Farmer no.46, immediate landlord William Lenox Conyngham, tenure for ever, 1s yearly rent per acre.

Urbal: Manures

[Form 5. *Fractions may indicate alternative amounts in different years*].

Farmer no.2, dung: 28/0 tons per acre, 2s per ton, 7 cwt per load, 4 people employed for [blank] days.

Farmer no.31, dung: 26/0 tons per acre, 2s per ton, 6 cwt per load, 4 people employed for [blank] days; bog: 6 cwt per load, 7 days employed; clay: 6 cwt per load, 4 days employed; compost loads: 40 dung, 105 bog, 100 clay; 7 cwt load of compost from heap to field, 7 days employed, made up at the house.

Farmer no.32, dung: 28/0 tons per acre, 1s 10d per ton, 6 cwt per load, 4 people employed for [blank] days; bog: 6 cwt per load, 6 days employed; clay: 6 cwt per load, 4 days employed; compost loads: 40 dung, 84 bog, 120 clay; 7 cwt of compost from heap to field, 7 days employed, made up at the house.

Farmer no.33, dung: 27/12 tons per acre, 1s 10d per ton, 6 cwt per load, 3 people employed for 1 and a half days; bog: 8 cwt per load, 6 days employed, lime: 11d per barrel, 912 lbs per load, carried 1 English mile, 1 day employed; clay: 6 cwt per load, 3 days employed; compost loads: 72 bog, 6 lime, 90 clay; 6 cwt of compost from heap to field, 5 days employed, made up at the house.

Farmer no.34, dung: 28/9 tons per acre, 2s per ton, 6 cwt per load, 4/1 and one-third days employed; bog: 10 cwt per load, 10 days employed; lime: 8d per barrel, 1,150 lbs per load, carried 5 English miles, 2 and a half days employed; clay: 6 cwt per load, 4 days employed; compost loads: 80 bog, 5 lime, 120 clay; 1 limekiln; 7 cwt of compost from heap to field, 5 days employed, made up at the field.

No.2: dung used alone, no compost.

No.31: dung used alone and in compost, bog and clay used in compost only.

No.32: dung used alone and in compost, bog and clay used in compost only.

No.33: dung used alone and in top dressing compost, bog, lime and clay used in compost only.

No.34: dung used alone and in top dressing compost, bog, lime and clay used in compost only.

Kind of acre referred to: Cunningham.

Lime: number of bushels per barrel 4; weight per barrel: 230 lbs Tamnalannan, 228 lbs Ruskey Lower.

Dung: townland and Coagh; bog: townland; lime: Ruskey Lower, Tamnalannan, parish of Donaghhenry; clay: townland.

Urbal: Seed and Produce

[Form 6]

Farmer no.2, wheat: 13 stones seed, 128 produce; oats: 18 stones seed, 110 produce; potatoes: 25 bushels seed, 220 produce; general observations: clay land, well laboured.

Farmer no.31, wheat: 13 stones seed, 120 produce; oats: 20 stones seed, 120 produce; potatoes: 25 bushels seed, 230 produce; general observations: clay, loam and bog, well laboured.

Farmer no.32, wheat: 13 stones seed, 120 produce; oats: 20 stones seed, 112 produce; potatoes: 24 bushels seed, 200 produce; general observations: clay, loam and bog, well laboured.

Farmer no.33, wheat: 13 stones seed, 128 produce; oats: 19 stones seed, 110 produce; potatoes: 24 bushels seed, 230 produce; flax: 3 bushels seed, 6 cwt produce; clover: 1 bushel hay seed, 12 lbs clover seed, 12 tons produce; general observations: clay and loam, well laboured.

Farmer no.34, wheat: 13 stones seed, 136 produce; barley: 12 stones seed, 160 produce; oats: 18 stones seed, 120 produce; potatoes: 24 bushels seed, 250 produce; flax: 3 and a quarter bushels seed, 6 and three-quarters produce; turnips: 3 lbs seed, 20 tons produce; hay: 3 bushels hay seed, 7 lbs clover seed, 2 tons produce; clover: 1 and a half bushels hay seed, 12 lbs clover seed, 12 tons produce; general observations: clay and loam, well laboured.

Kind of acre: Cunningham.

Wheat: value of seed 1s 6d per stone, value of produce 1s 2d per stone; time of sowing 1st of April to 30th November, time of harvest 2nd August to 18th September.

Barley: value of seed 1s 5d per stone, value of produce 1s 1d ha'penny per stone; time of sowing 6th April to 28th April, time of harvest 25th August to 12th September.

Oats: value of seed 1s 1d per stone, value of produce 11d ha'penny per stone; time of sowing 10th March to 20th April, time of harvest 1st September to 8th October.

Potatoes: value of seed 3d ha'penny per stone, value of produce 3d ha'penny per lb; time of sowing 20th April to 3rd May, time of harvest 20th October to 20th November.

Flax: value of seed 12s per bushel, value of produce 48s per bushel; time of sowing 25th April to 7th May, time of harvest 1st August to 18th August.

Turnips: value of seed 1s 8d per lb, value of produce 10d per cwt; time of sowing 25th May to 10th June, time of harvest 1st November to 1st December.

Hay: value of seed 2s per bushel, value of produce 2s 8d per cwt; time of sowing 10th March to 7th May, time of harvest 21st June to 1st July.

Clover: value of seed 10d per lb, value of produce 5d per cwt; time of sowing 10th March to 7th May, time of harvest 1st June to 1st October.

Field observer's signature: Archibald Thompson, date 27th to 30th May, 1st June 1840.

Urbal: Table of Trades

[Form 7]

William Ranken, weaver, master.
Thomas Wilkinson, weaver, master.
Harry Bell, weaver, master.
Thomas Ferguson, weaver, journeyman.
Samuel Ferguson, weaver, journeyman.
Joseph Elderton, weaver, master.
John Pherson, publican, master.
Thomas Glendinning, shoemaker, master, 1s 6d per day.
Robert Young, carpenter, master.
James Young, carpenter, journeyman, 1s 6d per day.
Michael Donnelly, carter, master.
John McCombs, carter, master.
John Cowdan, shoemaker, master, 1s 3d per day.
William Kilpatrick, scutcher, master, 1s 8d per day.
Thomas Robinson, baker, master.
[?] John Speare, process server, master.
Joseph Young, sawyer, master, 2s per day.
James Latimer, blacksmith, master, 2s 6d per day.
Robert Crooks, scutcher, master, 1s 6d per day.
John Cairns, scutcher, master, 1s 6d per day.
James Wilkinson, scutcher, master, 1s 6d per day.
Thomas McAlister, shoemaker, master, 1s 2d per day.
John Henderson, shoemaker, master, 1s 3d per day.
Joseph Henderson, shoemaker, apprentice, 1s 3d per day.
Edward Henderson Junior, shoemaker, apprentice, 1s 3d per day.

Field observer's signature: Archibald Thompson, date 27th to 30th May, 1st June 1840.

Urbal: Condition of Cottiers

[Form 8. No houses whitewashed, all with brick and lime chimneys, glazed windows, clay floors and one-eighth of an acre garden. *Furniture is recorded by abbreviations without a key: d = dresser, t = table, c = chair, s = settle bed, ew = earthenware, tn = tinware*].

No.1, 2 apartments, stone and lime house, straw roof, 4 windows, good beds, furniture: d, t, c, s, ew, tn, good clothes.

No.2, 2 apartments, stone and lime house, straw roof, 4 windows, good beds, furniture: d, t, c, s, ew, tn, good clothes.

No.3, 1 apartment, stone and lime house, straw roof, 1 window, bad beds, furniture: t, c, s, ew, tn, bad clothes.

No.4, 1 apartment, stone and lime house, straw roof, 1 window, bad beds, furniture: t, c, s, ew, tn, bad clothes.

No.5, 2 apartments, brick and lime house, slated roof, 4 windows, good beds, furniture: d, t, c, s, ew, tn, good clothes.

No.6, 2 apartments, brick and lime house, slated roof, 4 windows, good beds, furniture: d, t, c, s, ew, tn, good clothes.

No.7, 2 apartments, stone and lime house, straw roof, 4 windows, good beds, furniture: d, t, c, s, ew, tn, good clothes.

No.8, 2 apartments, stone and lime house, straw roof, 4 windows, good beds, furniture: d, t, c, s, ew, tn, good clothes.

No.9, 2 apartments, stone and lime house, straw roof, 4 windows, good beds, furniture: d, t, c, s, ew, tn, good clothes.

No.10, 2 apartments, stone and lime house, straw roof, 4 windows, good beds, furniture: d, t, c, s, ew, tn, good clothes.

No.11, 2 apartments, stone and lime house, straw roof, 4 windows, good beds, furniture: d, t, c, s, ew, tn, good clothes.

Field observer's signature: Archibald Thompson, date 27th to 30th May 1840.

Urbal: Summary of Economy

[Form 9]

Surface: smooth, undulating.
Soils, kind: clay loam and bog; depth: from 5 to 15 inches.
Subsoil, kind: clay and gravel; depth: unknown.
Exposure: to all winds.
Springs: 5 spring wells and 2 pumps.

Parish of Tamlaght

Drainage: 1,380 perches of covered drains, no drains permanently open.

Irrigation: practised by farmer no.26 on 1 acre of meadow from November to April.

Implements: iron and wooden ploughs, wooden harrows, scythe and teethed hooks, spades 16 by 6 inches, shovels, hosed.

Acres reclaimed since 1830: 3 and a quarter acres.

Corn mills: none; flax mills: 1; fulling mills: none.

Quarries: none.

Communications: the leading road from Coagh to Stewartstown passes through the townland, in good order; by-roads in good order.

Markets: Cookstown, Stewartstown, Magherafelt, Moneymore, Coagh.

Breed of horses: Irish; breed of cattle: Irish and English; breed of sheep: Irish; breed of hogs: Irish and Dutch.

Woods or plantations: 1 and five-eighth acres plantation, one-eighth acre of orchard; kind: fir, ash, sycamore and alder and apple trees; when first planted: 1810, 1815, 1832, 1835, 1828; present return: none cut or sold, fruit used by farmers.

Lime-kilns: none trading.

Manufactures: none.

Kind of crops cultivated, oats: potato, Poland, Angus and Blantyre; barley: common four-rowed; wheat: red; potatoes: cup, farmers, lumpers and downs; flax: Riga, Dutch and New York; hay: perennial and white grass seed; clover: red and white; turnips: white globe and yellow Aberdeens.

Field observer's signature: Archibald Thompson, residence William Vance's, Coagh, date 11th June 1840.

[Insert addition: Farmers' names and where got: from cess applotter. Nature of meadow: quantity per acre 2 and a half tons; time of harvest August 12th to September 1st; price per ton 2 pounds 10s. Kind of acre: Cunningham. Kind of fences: soil and thorn, good. Turf, where got: townland and Drumconvis. Rent per acre: rough or waste land from 10s to 35s for tenants, arable land from 50s to 120s for subtenants, on an average. Rough or waste land, kind of: plantations, commons, roads and bog].

Office Copy of Draft Memoir

NATURAL FEATURES

Hills

The ground lies high, forming part of the limestone ridge extending from Moneymore brae to Coagh. The north eastern portion is a basaltic formation of black whinstone.

Rivers

The Coagh river flows east along the southern boundary, dividing the counties of Londonderry and Tyrone. It is not navigable, abounds with trout of a large kind and a few salmon which run up from Lough Neagh.

MODERN TOPOGRAPHY

Public Buildings

A small neat church is situated in the townland of Tamlaght.

Communications

The principal roads are those leading from Coagh to Moneymore, The Loup <Loop> and Little bridge. They are repaired with broken stone and kept in good order.

There is no communication by public conveyance: the nearest places at which jaunting cars can be hired are Moneymore and Cookstown.

Parish of Tullyniskan, County Tyrone

Statistical Report by Lieutenant G. Dalton, July 1834, with insertions from Office Copy

NATURAL STATE

Name

The following authorities give different modes of spelling the name of this parish: McCrea and Knox, county map, Tullyniskal; Beaufort's Map of Ireland, Tullaniskin; *Carlisle's Topographical dictionary*, Tullaniskin; *Irish ecclesiastical register*, 1824, Tullaniskin; House of Commons' *Report on the population of Ireland*, Tullaghniskin; *McEvoy's Statistical survey*, Tullyniskin, Tullyniskal.

Locality

It is in the county Tyrone and western portion of the barony of Dungannon, is bounded on the north by Desertcreat parish, east by Donaghenry, west by Donaghmore and Drumglass, and south by Killyman parish. Its mean length is 4 and a half miles by 2 broad and contains 4,461 acres, of which 4,183 are cultivated, 236 uncultivated and 42 water. It is valued at 260 pounds per annum to the county cess.

NATURAL FEATURES

Hills

There is no very high ground in this parish, though the surface is very uneven. The principal hills are in the townland of Edendork in the south and in those of Bloomhill and Glencon in the north. The former is nearly 400 feet above the sea and the latter is little inferior in height.

[Insert addition: The surface, though varied, does not present any remarkable eminence. The highest points are Edenork, 386 feet, Mineveigh, 342, Bloomhill, 364. On the eastern side the level of the country is not more than 90 feet above that of the sea].

Lakes

There is 1 small lake in this parish, dividing the townland of Cullian with that of Corgorin, Drumglass parish; and another, a larger one, divides the townlands Farlough, Ballymenagh and Cullian, and is generally called after the first of them. The height of the former above the sea is about 270 feet. There are also 2 mill-ponds.

[Insert addition: Farlough, situated on the western side of the road from Stewartstown to Dungannon, extends over 20 acres 2 roods 28 perches. There is [a] second lake, situated on the western boundary, the extent of which is equal to 8 acres 3 roods 5 perches].

Rivers

The parish is traversed north west to south east by a small river commonly called the Farlough river, though in the southern part of the parish and through Killyman parish it is named the Torrent river. It comes from Pomeroy parish, through Donaghmore, Tullyniskan <Tullaniskin> and the north of Killyman parish, where it falls into the Blackwater river. It feeds several mills and also a canal, but is shallow and not of great depth or breadth.

[Insert addition: A considerable stream traverses the parish from north west to south east. During its course through the southern part of Tullyniskan it is termed the Farlough river, but for the remainder it is known as the River Torrent. The source is a small lake situate on the western side of Pomeroy parish, at an elevation of 800 feet above the level of the sea].

Bogs

The only bogs belonging to this parish are in the northern portion of it, and are with slight exceptions only the edges of extensive bogs belonging to Desertcreat, Pomeroy and Donaghenry parishes.

[Insert addition: There are about 300 acres of bog in the north of the parish].

NATURAL HISTORY

Zoology

The lakes contain small pike, perch and eels, and the river small par or mountain trout and eels.

MODERN TOPOGRAPHY

Public Buildings

[Insert addition: The church, situate in Doras townland, the Presbyterian meeting house in Gortnaglush, the Roman Catholic chapel in Cullian].

Parish of Tullyniskan

Gentlemen's Seats

In the north of the parish is Bloomhill, the seat of James Scott Esquire. It is a large and good family house and was built by James Richardson Esquire about the year 1783. He then gave it the name it now bears, as it was before a portion of Hughan townland. It is built on churchland held under the primate.

In the townland of Farlough is Lisdhu, the seat of the Honourable Andrew Stuart. It is a large and excellent family house, having offices and gardens of a very superior description and some ornamental planting. It stands on very high ground facing the east and commands a beautiful and extensive view of country bounded by Lough Neagh and the Antrim hills. It was built about the year 1782 by a gentleman of the name of William Pike, and has at subsequent periods had large additions made both to it and to the offices.

[Insert addition: Lisdhu, the seat of the Honourable Andrew Stuart, is situated towards the centre of the parish and about 250 yards from the western side of the road communicating between Stewartstown and Cookstown].

Bleach Greens

There are 3 bleach greens in this parish, 2 of which are in active use for the bleaching of coarse linens. They are both situated in the townland of Farlough and in the centre of the parish, being also close to roads leading from Cookstown to Dungannon. [Insert footnote: That belonging to Mr Pike is the most extensive in this part of the country].

Spade Manufactories

There are also 2 spade manufactories, one in Drumreagh-Otra belonging to Mr Geraghty and the other in Darry townland, belonging to Mr Lackey of Coalisland. These manufactories supply all the neighbouring markets and occasionally send a cargo of spades and shovels and plough irons to America.

Potteries

In Darry townland is a tile manufactory and in Greenagh and Gortjonis are several [insert addition: in Gortgonis are 4 small potteries]. In these potteries 7 persons are employed at 1 spinning

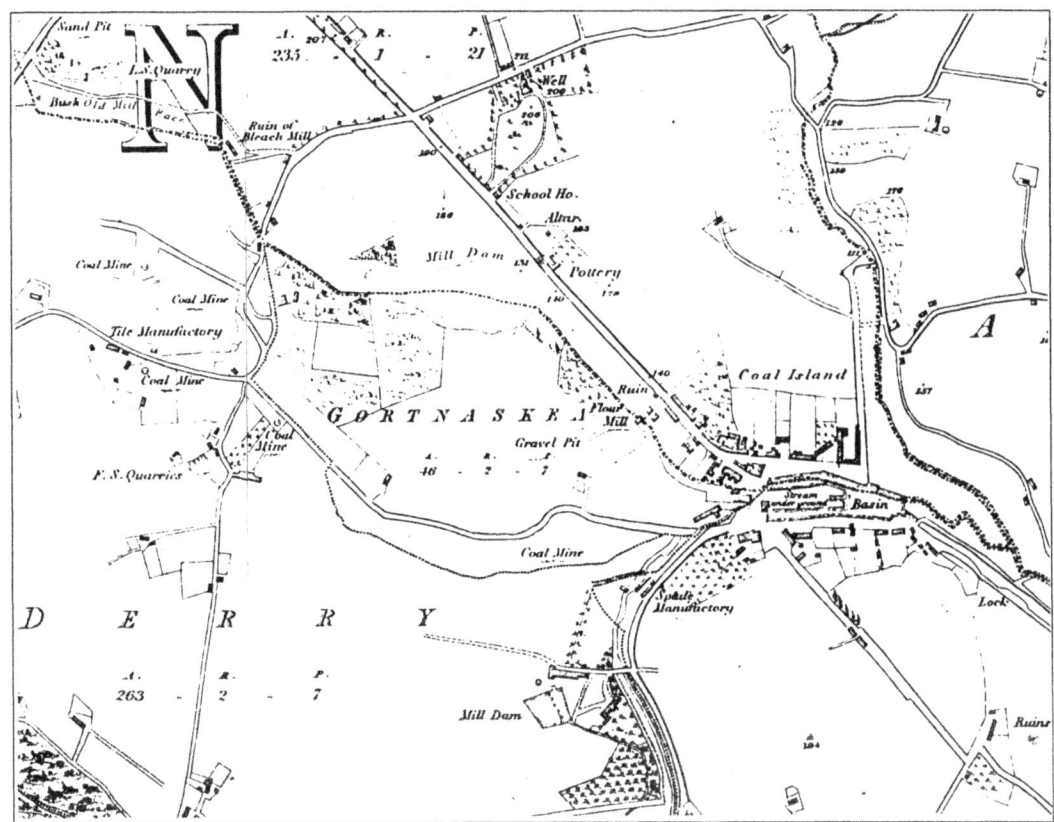

Map of Coalisland from the first 6" O.S. maps, 1830s

wheel, the spinner at 2s 3d per diem and the labourers at about 10d. 60 half pieces are sold for about 30s or 35s according to the season. Red clay is generally found in the potter's own land, white clay is purchased at 4s 2d per ton. For the lead ore used in glazing they send to Belfast or Dublin.

Linen

Linen weaving of a coarse description is carried on to a great extent throughout the parish.

Flour Mill

In Gortin townland is an extensive flour mill.

Communications

The high road from Cookstown to Dungannon and also from Stewartstown to Dungannon (the latter a mail coach road) traverse the parish from north to south. There are also several by-roads, the principal of which is one from Dungannon to Coalisland. The average breadth of the high roads is 36 feet and their length throughout the parish is 9 miles. They are not kept in very good order and are not judiciously laid out.

In the north east portion of the parish is a canal, commencing at the village of Coalisland and running to the Blackwater river, by which it communicates with Lough Neagh. For its description, see report on Clonoe parish.

General Appearance and Scenery

The north of the parish is a wild bleak country, bare and unplanted, consisting of large bogs and bad land of a light gravelly description. The south is richer and more highly cultivated and is in parts planted, particularly in the neighbourhood of Lisdhu and of Mr Pike's, where there are several rising and beautiful plantations.

SOCIAL ECONOMY

Local Government

The magistrates residing in this parish are the Honourable A. Stuart of Lisdhu, who is also deputy lieutenant of the county, James Richardson Esquire of Coalisland and John Murray Esquire. There is no police force in it.

Schools

There are 3, 1 in connection with the Association for Discountenancing Vice, 1 with the Education Society and 1 built by charity, the master being paid solely by the scholars.

Religion

The people are Catholics, Protestants, Presbyterians and Quakers. The numbers of the two former are nearly equal, the Presbyterians are numerous, and there are several families of Quakers.

Habits of the People

In the northern portion of this parish, where the land is of bad quality, the people seem very poor and the houses, which are built of stone or mud, seem very uncomfortable and bad. The same may be said of the south end of the parish, whilst in the centre, which is rich and good land chiefly occupied by Presbyterians and Quakers, the houses are of a much better description, as is the general appearance of the people. The custom of Beal Tinne is kept up.

Emigration

Emigration to America prevails, but not to a great extent, as does the custom of going to England and Scotland to assist in the harvest, but more among single men than families.

PRODUCTIVE ECONOMY

Linen

The linen manufacture is general, almost the entire population being weavers and spinners.

Coal

In the townland of Darry is a coalfield which supplies the immediate neighbourhood and from which quantities of coal are sent by water to Newry and Belfast, being shipped in lighters from Coalisland. The mine is worked by a gin turned by horses, the depth of the shaft being 70 yards. The coal is sold at the same rate as at the Drumglass collieries, and is considered equally good. The seam is 3 and a half feet in thickness.

Fairs and Markets

A corn market is held weekly in the village of Coalisland, part of which is in this parish. The corn when purchased is shipped on the canal and sent by water to Newry or Belfast. This market is said to be on the decline; the inhabitants attend the fairs and markets of Dungannon and Stewartstown.

Rural Economy

The principal proprietors are the Earl of Castlestewart and James Richardson Esquire, and

Parish of Tullyniskan

there is also much churchland, chiefly held by James Scott Esquire of Bloomhill under the primate. The southern portions of the parish contain the best soil. In the north it is of a very poor description, the hills being of a light gravelly nature and the bottoms reclaimed or only partly reclaimed from bog. The farms, the average size of which may be taken at 8 acres, and at 18s per acre, are too small to admit of any regular course of crops. Oats may be considered the principal one grown, with a little wheat and flax, but no barley. Flax is reckoned profitable to those who have it manufactured by their own children.

The best and principal farmer in the north of this parish is James Scott Esquire of Bloomhill, who has spent much time and labour <labor> in the improvement of a large tract of poor and bad land held by him under the primate. Great improvements have also of late years been made in the southern portions of the parish, particularly in the townlands of Farlough, Drumreagh-Etra and the Glebe, in all which hay of a superior description is grown.

Lime

Lime is obtained from quarries in Drumreagh-Etra townland, and in the northern parts of the parish it is obtained from quarries in Donaghenry parish. Mixed up with bog earth it is useful in reclaiming boggy land. Paring and burning the surface of poor land to obtain manure is also practised.

There is a limestone quarry in the townland of Drumreagh-Etra and freestone quarries in Darry, Edendork, Curran and Quinton, all which are worked.

Cattle

The common Irish breed of cattle is that most commonly seen in this parish, some of the better farmers and resident gentry having also Ayrshire and Devon cows. Few horses are bred in this part of the country, and those are generally speaking of an inferior description. The fairs of Moy and Moneymore are those most frequented for horses, to which may be added Dungannon, Cookstown, Stewartstown, Castlecaulfield and Donaghmore for cattle, pigs and poultry. The farmers are apt to overstock their land and there are twice the number of pigs kept that ought to be. The poor carry poultry for sale to the neighbouring towns and gentlemen's houses. They are of a good description but are generally too poor for killing when first purchased.

Uses made of the Bogs

Some of the bogs are sufficiently hard to graze young cattle during the summer, and their edges are annually cut for fuel for the neighbouring farms. In the south of the parish where coal is abundant it is not in such great request as in many other parts of the country.

General Remarks

This small parish is, with the exception of its bogs, cultivated throughout, but a great proportion of it consists of poor and bad land divided into very small farms and held by tenants too poor to do much towards improvement. Through the centre is a vein of better soil, where the farms are larger and the tenants more wealthy, and this part of it is in a high state of cultivation, producing excellent crops which find a ready sale in the neighbouring markets; but the low price of all agricultural produce, added to the want of money and to high rents, render it difficult for the farmer to make much by his land and prevent him from speculating and laying out much in its improvement. As in Drumglass parish, abundance of good and cheap coal and the vicinity of water carriage afford facility for manufacturing industry.

SOCIAL ECONOMY

Table of Schools

[Table contains the following headings: townland, number of pupils subdivided by religion and sex, how supported, when established].

Cullian: Protestants 10, Catholics 34, males 27, females 17, total 44. This school is supported by the parishioners by whom it was built. The master is paid from 6d to 1s per month by each pupil; established 1824.

Sessia: Protestants 81, Catholics 31, males 72, females 40, total 112. This school was built by the Reverend Robert Kingsmore and is supported by him. The master receives 30 guineas per annum from the Association for Discountenancing Vice, 8 pounds of which is expended annually for a dinner given by the committee to such pupils as are able to pay 1d per week; established 1821.

Creenagh: Protestants 21, Catholics 19, males 24, females 16, total 40. The school is principally supported by the parishioners. It was built by John Hilland, a tenant of Lord Castlestewart's. The master is paid 1d per week by each pupil. Reverend Robert Kingsmore subscribes 10s and Lord Castlestewart 2 pounds per annum; established 1820.

Ecclesiastical Summary

[Table] Name Tullyniskan, diocese Armagh, province Armagh; rectory, is not a union but was formerly with Drumglass parish; patron the Archbishop of Armagh, incumbent the Reverend R. Kingsmore; extent of glebe 245 acres. The tithes belong to the rector and are compounded for under the act for that purpose for 200 pounds sterling. [Signed] George Dalton, Lieutenant Royal Engineers, 25th July 1834.